Julia Programming Projects

Learn Julia 1.x by building apps for data analysis,
visualization, machine learning, and the web

Adrian Salceanu

BIRMINGHAM - MUMBAI

Julia Programming Projects

Commissioning Editor: Aaron Lazar
Acquisition Editor: Sandeep Mishra
Content Development Editor: Tiksha Sarang
Technical Editor: Riddesh Dawne
Copy Editor: Safis Editing
Project Coordinator: Prajakta Naik
Proofreader: Safis Editing
Indexer: Tejal Daruwale Soni
Graphics: Jisha Chirayil
Production Coordinator: Aparna Bhagat

First published: December 2018

Production reference: 1241218

Published by Packt Publishing Ltd.
Livery Place
35 Livery Street
Birmingham
B3 2PB, UK.

ISBN 978-1-78829-274-0

www.packtpub.com

To my wonderful daughter, Mira: know that with hard work, patience,
and determination, anything can be achieved, my love.
To my beloved wife, Felicia, for her endless love and care – we'd be lost without you.

– Adrian Salceanu

`mapt.io`

Mapt is an online digital library that gives you full access to over 5,000 books and videos, as well as industry leading tools to help you plan your personal development and advance your career. For more information, please visit our website.

Why subscribe?

- Spend less time learning and more time coding with practical eBooks and Videos from over 4,000 industry professionals

- Improve your learning with Skill Plans built especially for you

- Get a free eBook or video every month

- Mapt is fully searchable

- Copy and paste, print, and bookmark content

Packt.com

Did you know that Packt offers eBook versions of every book published, with PDF and ePub files available? You can upgrade to the eBook version at `www.packt.com` and as a print book customer, you are entitled to a discount on the eBook copy. Get in touch with us at `customercare@packtpub.com` for more details.

At `www.packt.com`, you can also read a collection of free technical articles, sign up for a range of free newsletters, and receive exclusive discounts and offers on Packt books and eBooks.

Contributors

About the author

Adrian Salceanu has been a professional software developer for over 15 years. For the last 10, he's been leading agile teams in developing real-time, data-intensive web and mobile products. Adrian is a public speaker and an enthusiastic contributor to the open source community, focusing on high-performance web development. He's the organizer of the Barcelona Julia Users group and the creator of Genie, a high-performance, highly productive Julia web framework. Adrian has a Master's degree in computing and a postgraduate degree in advanced computer science.

> *To my family, for their understanding and support during the long weekends I spent writing.*
>
> *To Antony and Richard, for creating a work environment that encourages personal and professional growth. It is a privilege to be a part of the OLBG team.*
>
> *To the Julia community, for their amazing work and their continuous efforts in growing Julia, and for being so helpful and welcoming.*
>
> *To the creators of the open source software used in the book; your work is priceless.*
>
> *To the Julia contributors, for their support and patience in helping me throughout my journey.*

About the reviewers

David Buchaca Prats is a mathematician who focuses his passion toward building more efficient artificial neural networks. The difficulty of implementing efficient models led him to love the Julia programming language, which allows scientists to write concise code for doing so quickly.

Zhuo Qingliang (also known as KDr2 online) is presently working at paodingai.com, a start-up fintech company in China that is dedicated to improving the financial industry by using artificial intelligence technologies. He has over 10 years of experience in Linux, C, C++, Java, Python, and Perl development. He is interested in programming, consulting work, and contributing to the open source community (including, of course, the Julia community).

He maintains a personal website at `http://kdr2.com`; you can find out more about him there.

Packt is searching for authors like you

If you're interested in becoming an author for Packt, please visit `authors.packtpub.com` and apply today. We have worked with thousands of developers and tech professionals, just like you, to help them share their insight with the global tech community. You can make a general application, apply for a specific hot topic that we are recruiting an author for, or submit your own idea.

Table of Contents

Preface

Julia is a new programming language offering a unique combination of performance and productivity that promises to change scientific computing, and programming in general.

Julia picks the best parts of existing programming languages, providing out-of-the-box features such as a powerful REPL, an expressive syntax, Lisp-style metaprogramming capabilities, powerful numeric and scientific programming libraries, a built-in package manager, efficient Unicode support, and easily called C and Python functions.

It has C-like execution speed with excellent applications in multi-core, GPU, and cloud-based computing. *Julia Programming Projects* explains all this with the support of Julia v1.0.

After six years in development as an open source project, Julia is now ready to take the stage with the release of v1.0.

Who this book is for

Data scientists, statisticians, business analysts, and developers who are interested in learning how to use Julia to crunch numbers, analyze data, and build apps will find this book useful. A basic knowledge of programming is assumed.

What this book covers

Chapter 1, *Getting Started with Julia Programming*, introduces you to the Julia language, covering what it is and what its strengths are. Then, the chapter guides you through setting up a working Julia environment, looking at the various options for running Julia, locally and online. We'll cover installation, REPL, and IDE options, as well as the basics for extending the language through the integrated package manager.

Chapter 2, *Creating Our First Julia App*, will show you how to perform data analysis against the Iris dataset with Julia. We take a look at RDatasets, a package that provides access to 700 learning datasets distributed with the R language. We'll load the Iris dataset and we'll manipulate it using standard data analysis functions. We also look more closely at the data by employing common visualization techniques using Gadfly. In the process, we cover strings and regular expressions, numbers, tuples, ranges, and arrays. Finally, we'll see how to persist and (re)load our data with CSV, Feather, and MongoDB.

Chapter 3, *Setting Up the Wiki Game*, introduces our first fully featured Julia project, a Wikipedia web crawler disguised as a popular game. In the first iteration, we will build a program that gets a random web page from Wikipedia. Then we'll learn about parsing the HTML response using CSS selectors. We'll use this to introduce key concepts such as functions, pairs, dictionaries, exceptions, and conditional evaluation.

Chapter 4, *Building the Wiki Game Web Crawler*, will build upon the foundations set in the previous chapter, and we'll build a Wikipedia web scraper that implements the requirements of the wiki game.

Chapter 5, *Adding a Web UI for the Wiki Game*, will see us finish the Wiki Game by adding a web UI. We'll build a simple web app that will allow the player to start a new game, render the Wikipedia articles picked by the game engine, and navigate between linked Wikipedia articles. The UI will also keep track of and display current game progress and determine a session as a win or a loss.

Chapter 6, *Implementing Recommender Systems with Julia*, will have you take on a more challenging example project and build a few basic recommender systems. We'll set up a supervised machine learning system powered by Julia and we will develop some simple movie recommenders.

Chapter 7, *Machine Learning for Recommender Systems*, will show you how to implement a more powerful recommender system using the Recommender.jl package. We will use a sample dataset to train our system and generate book recommendations as we'll learn about model-based recommenders.

Chapter 8, *Leveraging Unsupervised Learning Techniques*, will teach you how to perform unsupervised machine learning, namely clustering, using Julia. We will practice by using the San Francisco businesses registry. We'll use the powerful DataFrames package in combination with Query.jl to slice and dice the dataset, and we'll get more insight using visualizations. In the process, we will learn about metaprogramming and Clustering.jl.

Chapter 9, *Working with Dates, Time, and Time Series*, is the first of two chapters about dates, time, and time series. Here we introduce you to the basics of working with dates, time zones, and time series. We'll use the TimeSeries.jl package and Plots.jl to analyze time series data, and we'll learn about the TimeArray data structure.

Chapter 10, *Time Series Forecasting*, is where we will perform analysis on the EU unemployment data and forecast unemployment numbers. You will learn how to develop a forecasting model, train it, and generate predictions.

`Chapter 11`, *Creating Julia Packages*, is the final chapter and walks you through developing a fully featured Julia package. We'll discuss more advanced package management features, unit testing, benchmarking, and performance tips, adding and generating documentation for Julia software, and package publishing and registration.

To get the most out of this book

Familiarity with another programming language is assumed, as the book focuses on Julia specifics without introducing general programming and computer science concepts.

You'll need a computer with an internet connection running Windows, macOS, or a popular Linux flavor, as well as the ability to install and start programs (a command shell, an **integrated development environment** (**IDE**), an editor, and so on).

Download the example code files

You can download the example code files for this book from your account at `www.packt.com`. If you purchased this book elsewhere, you can visit `www.packt.com/support` and register to have the files emailed directly to you.

You can download the code files by following these steps:

1. Log in or register at `www.packt.com`.
2. Select the **SUPPORT** tab.
3. Click on **Code Downloads & Errata**.
4. Enter the name of the book in the **Search** box and follow the onscreen instructions.

Once the file is downloaded, please make sure that you unzip or extract the folder using the latest version of:

- WinRAR/7-Zip for Windows
- Zipeg/iZip/UnRarX for Mac
- 7-Zip/PeaZip for Linux

The code bundle for the book is also hosted on GitHub at `https://github.com/PacktPublishing/Julia-Programming-Projects`. In case there's an update to the code, it will be updated on the existing GitHub repository.

We also have other code bundles from our rich catalog of books and videos available at `https://github.com/PacktPublishing/`. Check them out!

Download the color images

We also provide a PDF file that has color images of the screenshots/diagrams used in this book. You can download it here: `https://www.packtpub.com/sites/default/files/downloads/9781788292740_ColorImages.pdf`.

Conventions used

There are a number of text conventions used throughout this book.

`CodeInText`: Indicates code words in text, database table names, folder names, filenames, file extensions, pathnames, dummy URLs, user input, and Twitter handles. Here is an example: "The difficulty levels are already defined in the `Gameplay` module, so don't forget to declare that we're `using Gameplay`."

A block of code is set as follows:

```
function articleinfo(content)
  dom = articledom(content)
  (extractcontent(dom.root), extractlinks(dom.root),
extracttitle(dom.root), extractimage(dom.root))
end
```

When we wish to draw your attention to a particular part of a code block, the relevant lines or items are set in bold:

```
@from i in df begin
    @where i.Parking_Tax == true
    @select i
    @collect DataFrame
end
```

Any command-line input or output is written as follows:

```
pkg> add PackageName@vX.Y.Z
pkg> add IJulia@v1.14.1
```

Bold: Indicates a new term, an important word, or words that you see onscreen. For example, words in menus or dialog boxes appear in the text like this. Here is an example: "But **versicolor** and **virginica**? Not so much."

Warnings or important notes appear like this.

 Tips and tricks appear like this.

Get in touch

Feedback from our readers is always welcome.

General feedback: If you have questions about any aspect of this book, mention the book title in the subject of your message and email us at customercare@packtpub.com.

Errata: Although we have taken every care to ensure the accuracy of our content, mistakes do happen. If you have found a mistake in this book, we would be grateful if you would report this to us. Please visit www.packt.com/submit-errata, selecting your book, clicking on the Errata Submission Form link, and entering the details.

Piracy: If you come across any illegal copies of our works in any form on the Internet, we would be grateful if you would provide us with the location address or website name. Please contact us at copyright@packt.com with a link to the material.

If you are interested in becoming an author: If there is a topic that you have expertise in and you are interested in either writing or contributing to a book, please visit authors.packtpub.com.

Reviews

Please leave a review. Once you have read and used this book, why not leave a review on the site that you purchased it from? Potential readers can then see and use your unbiased opinion to make purchase decisions, we at Packt can understand what you think about our products, and our authors can see your feedback on their book. Thank you!

For more information about Packt, please visit packt.com.

1
Getting Started with Julia Programming

Julia is a high-level, high-performance dynamic programming language, focusing on numerical computing and general programming. It is relatively new—the four creators, Jeff Bezanson, Stefan Karpinski, Viral Shah, and Alan Edelman, set out to create it in 2009, with the first public reference to the language in 2012, when they published a blog post explaining their vision and their goals. 2012 is considered the official birth year of Julia, making it only six years old. Since its initial public release, Julia has received code contributions from hundreds of scientists, programmers, and engineers across the world. It is developed in the open, with the source code available on GitHub, and is one of the most popular repositories with almost 20,000 stars (at the time of writing, and counting). Julia v1.0, the much anticipated first stable release, came in August 2018 during the Julia conference in London, as the brilliant outcome of the collaboration between over 700 open source contributors and thousands of package creators and early users. By that time, the language had been downloaded over two million times already!

Julia came out as a fresh alternative to traditional scientific computing languages, which were either productive *or* fast, but not both. This is known as the **two language problem**, where the initial prototyping code is written in a dynamic, highly productive language (such as R or Python), which allows exploratory coding and quick iterations, skipping taxing build and compile times. But later on, the developers would be forced to rewrite their programs (or at least the performance critical parts of their programs), using a compiled language that would satisfy the high-performance requirements of scientific computing.

The creators of Julia thought that software development technology has evolved enough that it can support a language that combines both high productivity and high performance. This was their manifesto, underlying their goals for Julia:

> *"We want a language that's open source, with a liberal license. We want the speed of C with the dynamism of Ruby. We want a language that's homoiconic, with true macros like Lisp, but with obvious, familiar mathematical notation like MATLAB. We want something as usable for general programming as Python, as easy for statistics as R, as natural for string processing as Perl, as powerful for linear algebra as MATLAB, as good at gluing programs together as the shell. Something that is dirt simple to learn, yet keeps the most serious hackers happy. We want it interactive and we want it compiled."*

> *"(Did we mention it should be as fast as C?)"*

As incredible as it may seem, Julia has managed to satisfy all these demands, making for a unique language that is easy to learn, intuitive, friendly, productive, and fast. Let's take a closer look at all these features.

The topics we will cover in this chapter are:

- A quick look at Julia—what is it, the main features and strengths, and why it could be the best choice for your next project
- How to set up and interact with the Julia language on your local machine
- The best IDEs and editors for productive Julia development
- Getting starting with Julia by learning about its powerful REPL
- How to use the built-in package manager, `Pkg`, to extend the language with third-party libraries

Technical requirements

The Julia package ecosystem is under continuous development and new package versions are released on a daily basis. Most of the times this is great news, as new releases bring new features and bug fixes. However, since many of the packages are still in beta (version 0.x), any new release can introduce breaking changes. As a result, the code presented in the book can stop working. In order to ensure that your code will produce the same results as described in the book, it is recommended to use the same package versions. Here are the external packages used in this chapter and their specific versions:

```
IJulia@v1.14.1
OhMyREPL@v0.4.1
Revise@v0.7.14
```

In order to install a specific version of a package you need to run:

```
pkg> add PackageName@vX.Y.Z
```

For example:

```
pkg> add IJulia@v1.14.1
```

Alternatively you can install all the used packages by downloading the `Project.toml` file provided with the chapter and using `pkg>` instantiate as follows:

```
julia>
download("https://raw.githubusercontent.com/PacktPublishing/Julia-Programmi
ng-Projects/master/Chapter01/Project.toml", "Project.toml")
pkg> activate .
pkg> instantiate
```

Why Julia?

In a nutshell, Julia truly is a new breed of programming language that successfully manages to combine the high performance of compiled languages with the agility of the dynamic ones, through a friendly syntax that feels natural and intuitive right from the start. Julia is *fast* (programs are compiled at runtime to efficient native code for multiple platforms), *general* (the standard library supports, out of the box, powerful programming tasks including asynchronous I/O, process control, parallel, and distributed computing, logging, profiling, package management, and more), *dynamic and optionally typed* (it is dynamically-typed with optional type declarations and comes with a powerful **read-eval-print loop** (REPL) for interactive and exploratory coding). It is also *technical* (excelling at numerical computing) and *composable* (thanks to its rich ecosystem of packages that are designed to work together seamlessly and with high performance).

Although initially it focused on addressing the needs of high-performance numerical analysis and computational science, recent releases have positioned the language in the area of general computing, with many classes of specialized functions being moved out of the core into dedicated modules. As such, it is also a great fit for client and server-side programming, due to its powerful capabilities for concurrent, parallel, and distributed computing.

Julia implements a type system based on parametric polymorphism and multiple dispatch, it is garbage-collected, uses eager evaluation, packs a powerful regular expression engine, and can call C and Fortran functions without glue code.

Let's take a look at the most important features of the language, the parts that make Julia stand out. If you're considering Julia for your next project, you can use this as a quick checklist against your requirements.

Good performance

The key to Julia's performance is the combination between the LLVM-based **just-in-time (JIT)** compiler and a series of strategic design decisions that allow the compiler to generate code that approaches, and most of the times matches, the performance of C.

To give you an idea of where Julia stands in this regard, the official website provides a series of micro-benchmarks against other mainstream languages (including C, Python, R, Java, JavaScript, Fortran, Go, Rust, MATLAB, and Octave) implementing some algorithms for computing the Fibonacci sequence, the Mandelbrot set, a `quicksort` and a few others. They are designed to evaluate compiler performance against common code patterns such as function calls, string parsing, sorting, iterations, recursion, and more. There is a plot of the benchmarks, available at `https://julialang.org/benchmarks/`, which illustrates Julia's consistent top performance across all of the tests. The following plot depicts this:

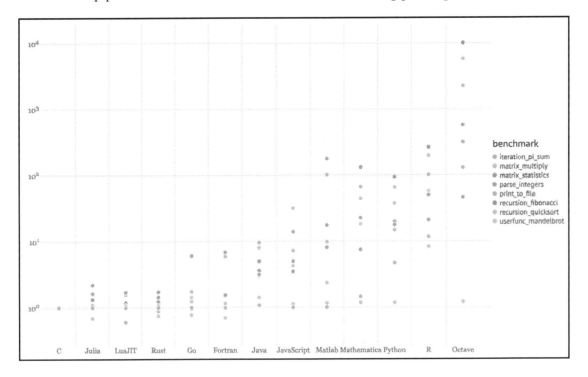

For more details about the testing methodology, you can visit `https://julialang.org/benchmarks/`.

Concise, readable, and intuitive syntax

The creators of Julia have carefully picked the most successful elements of syntax from other languages, with the goal of producing expressive, concise, and readable code. Julia provides powerful and expressive language constructs for high-level numerical computing, in the same way as languages such as R, MATLAB, and Python do. It builds upon the experience brought by existing mathematical programming languages but also borrows much from popular dynamic ones, such as Lisp, Perl, Python, Lua, and Ruby.

To give you a quick taste of idiomatic Julia, here's how to open a file, read it, output it, and then have the file automatically closed by Julia:

```
open(".viminfo") do io
    read(io, String) |> println
end
```

In the preceding snippet, we open the `.viminfo` file for reading passing `io`, an `IOStream` instance, into the underlying code block. The stream is then read into a `String` that is finally displayed onto the console by piping it into the `println` function. The code is very readable and easy to understand if you have some coding experience, even if this is your first time looking at Julia code.

This so-called `do` syntax (named after the `do` part following the `open` function) is inspired by Ruby's blocks—and it is, in fact, syntactic sugar for passing anonymous functions as method arguments. It is efficiently used in the preceding example to succinctly express a powerful design pattern for safely handling files, guaranteeing that the resources are not accidentally left open.

This goes to show the amount of attention that was put by the designers of the language to make Julia safe, beginner-friendly, expressive, concise, readable, and intuitive.

Powerful and productive dynamic type system

Julia's type system is a key feature of the language and one that has a major impact on both its performance and productivity. The type system is dynamic and optional, meaning that the developer can, but is not required to, provide type information to the compiler. If not provided, Julia will perform type inference, which is the process of deducing the types of later values from the types of input values. This is a very powerful technique, as it frees the programmers from having to worry about types, allowing them to focus on the application logic and making for a gentler learning curve. This is especially useful for prototyping and exploratory programming, when the complete set of constraints and requirements is not known beforehand.

However, understanding and correctly using the type system offers important performance benefits. Julia allows optionally adding type information, making it possible to indicate that a certain value must be of a specific kind. This is one of the cornerstones of the language, allowing performant method dispatching and facilitating the automatic generation of efficient, specialized code for different argument types. The type system allows the definition of rich type hierarchies, with user-defined types as fast and compact as the built-in ones.

Designed for parallelism and distributed computation

If the languages of the 70s and 80s were designed under the strict requirements imposed by the limited CPU and RAM resources, the ones in the 90s and the 2000s had the optimistic outlook that these resources are forever expanding. However, the last decade had seen something of a stagnation in this regard, with a shift toward multi-CPU, multi-core, and distributed computing. In this regard, Julia's inception only 6 years ago gave it an edge compared to older languages, putting parallel and distributed computing at its center as one of its most important features.

Efficient intercommunication with other languages

One of the most serious barriers in the adoption of a new language is that it takes time for the ecosystem to catch up—and in the beginning, it cannot offer libraries of the quality and richness of the already established languages. This is less of an issue now, when Julia benefits from a large, enthusiastic and continuously growing developer community. But being able to seamlessly communicate with other languages is a very efficient way to enrich existing functionality and to effortlessly supplement any missing features.

Julia has the ability to directly call C and Fortran functions (that is, without glue code)—especially important for scientific computing, where these languages have a strong presence and a long history.

Optional packages extend this capability by adding support for calling functions written in other languages, most notably Python, via `PyCall`. And there are others, supporting interaction with Java, C++, MATLAB, Rust, and more.

Powerful REPL and shell-like capabilities

The REPL represents a language shell, an interactive computer programming environment at the command line. Julia has an excellent REPL, supporting sophisticated code inputting and evaluation. It includes powerful editing features such as searchable history, tab-completion, and syntax highlighting, to name just a few.

It also comes with three special modes—*shell*, which allows executing commands as if at the OS Terminal; *help*, which provides access to documentation without leaving the REPL; and pkg, used for installing and managing application dependencies.

And more...

Julia comes with its own powerful package manager that resolves dependencies and handles the adding and removal of extra packages. Like most modern languages, Julia has full support for Unicode. And finally, it is distributed under the liberal MIT license—it is free and open source.

Installing Julia

If the previous section convinced you to use Julia for your next project, or at least made you curious to learn more, then it's time to set up your Julia development environment.

Julia has superb cross-platform support, running on all major operating systems. The install process is straightforward—the language can be set up on your local machine, in a **virtual machine** (**VM**), in a Docker container, or on a server somewhere in the cloud.

Let's start by looking at local installation options for the *big three* operating systems (Windows, Linux, and macOS). Feel free to skip directly to the right one for you.

Windows

Windows has come a long way as a development platform and there are a few good alternatives for getting Julia up and running.

Official Windows installer

The simplest option is to download the Windows installer corresponding to your platform (32 or 64-bit), from `https://julialang.org/downloads/`. Get the `.exe` and run it. Follow the standard installation procedure and in the end, you will have Julia installed as a program. Double-clicking `julia.exe` opens a command prompt with the Julia REPL, just like the one illustrated here:

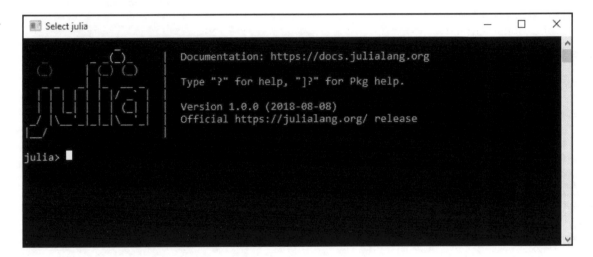

Using Chocolatey

Chocolatey is a package manager for Windows, similar to `apt` or `yum` on Linux, or `brew` on Mac. If you don't have it, get it by following the instructions at `https://chocolatey.org`.

Chocolatey has the latest version of Julia, as can be confirmed with a search, as follows:

```
$ choco search julia
Chocolatey v0.10.11
Julia 1.0.0 [Approved]
1 packages found.
```

Installing is as simple as this:

```
$ choco install julia
Chocolatey v0.10.11
Installing the following packages:
julia
By installing you accept licenses for the packages.
Progress: Downloading Julia 1.0.0... 100%
Julia v1.0.0 [Approved]
Chocolatey installed 1/1 packages.
```

Windows Subsystem for Linux

One of the recent additions to Windows 10 is the Subsystem for Linux. This allows setting up a Linux development environment, including most command-line tools, utilities, and applications—directly on Windows, unmodified, and without the overhead of running a VM.

In order to be able to use the Linux Subsystem your PC must be running the 64-bit version of Windows 10 Anniversary Update or later (build 1607+). It also needs to be enabled first—so open a PowerShell as an administrator and run the following:

```
$ Enable-WindowsOptionalFeature -Online -FeatureName Microsoft-Windows-
Subsystem-Linux
```

Once the subsystem is enabled (computer restart might be required) you can choose one of the Linux versions available, directly from the Windows Store. At the time of writing, five versions were available—Ubuntu, openSUSE , SLES, Debian, and Kali.

Ubuntu is the default option for Windows 10 and has the best user ratings in the Windows Store, so let's go with that. It can be installed from `https://www.microsoft.com/en-us/store/p/ubuntu/9nblggh4msv6`. Alternatively, you can just open a command prompt and type `$ bash`. This will trigger the installation of the Ubuntu Linux Subsystem.

Once you find yourself at the shell prompt of your Linux subsystem, you can proceed and issue the commands for installing Julia. For Ubuntu you need to run the following:

```
$ sudo apt-get install julia
```

Make sure to confirm the required selections—then after a couple of minutes you should have Julia up and running.

macOS

Installing Julia on macOS is straightforward. There are two main options, depending on whether you prefer a visual installer or are more at home in front of the Terminal prompt.

Official image

Visit `https://julialang.org/downloads/` and look for the macOS package (`.dmg`). Once it's downloaded, double-click the `.dmg` file and drag and drop the Julia app into the `/Applications` folder. Now you can simply open the Julia app—which in turn will launch a new Terminal session, loading the Julia environment, as follows:

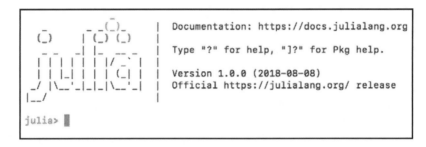

Homebrew

`Homebrew` is a well-known package manager for macOS in the line of `apt` and `yum` on Linux. It's not really necessary for installing Julia, but it's worth setting it up as it can be very useful during development since it can seamlessly install database servers, libraries, and other components for your projects.

As per the instructions at `https://brew.sh`, it can be installed by running the following command in a Terminal window:

```
$ /usr/bin/ruby -e "$(curl -fsSL
https://raw.githubusercontent.com/Homebrew/install/master/install)"
```

It might take a while but once `Homebrew` is installed, a new command-line utility, `brew`, will become available.

Finally, `$ brew cask install julia` will download and install the latest version of Julia. In the process, it will also link the `julia` binary to `/usr/local/bin/julia` so you can interact with the language from the command line by simply typing `$ julia`.

As soon as you get the confirmation that the installation was successful you can run $
julia to start a new REPL session:

```
==> Installing Cask julia
==> Moving App 'Julia-1.0.app' to '/Applications/Julia-1.0.app'.
==> Linking Binary 'julia' to '/usr/local/bin/julia'.
🍺  julia was successfully installed!
~  julia

               _
   _       _ _(_)_     |  Documentation: https://docs.julialang.org
  (_)     | (_) (_)    |
   _ _   _| |_  __ _   |  Type "?" for help, "]?" for Pkg help.
  | | | | | | |/ _` |  |
  | | |_| | | | (_| |  |  Version 1.0.0 (2018-08-08)
 _/ |\__'_|_|_|\__'_|  |  Official https://julialang.org/ release
|__/                   |

julia> █
```

Linux and FreeBSD

Julia is already available in the software repositories of the major Linux distributions, but unfortunately, these are not up to date. For example, at the time of writing, Ubuntu was providing v0.4.5 and Debian v0.4.7. The best approach is to use the generic Linux binaries provided on Julia's download page, at https://julialang.org/downloads/.

Please follow the instructions corresponding to your Linux distribution, as indicated at https://julialang.org/downloads/platform.html#generic-binaries.

Docker

Docker is a software technology that provides an additional layer of abstraction of operating-system-level virtualization. In plain English, Docker sets up *containers* that behave like VMs, but without the added overhead of starting and maintaining VMs. You can run Docker on all the major operating systems.

Docker is widely used as a development and deployment strategy, so many technologies are readily available in the form of Docker images, and Julia is no exception.

Start by installing Docker for your platform. The official Julia container can be found in the Docker store at `https://store.docker.com/images/julia`. Go get it.

If you need help setting up Docker or installing containers, follow the instructions at `https://www.docker.com`.

At the command prompt, type `$ docker pull julia`. Once the Julia image is configured by Docker, run it with `$ docker exec -it --rm julia`. This will start the container and load a new Julia REPL:

```
~     docker run -it --rm julia

               _
      _       _ _(_)_            |  Documentation: https://docs.julialang.org
     (_)     | (_) (_)           |
      _ _   _| |_  __ _          |  Type "?" for help, "]?" for Pkg help.
     | | | | | | |/ _` |         |
     | | |_| | | | (_| |         |  Version 1.0.0 (2018-08-08)
    _/ |\__'_|_|_|\__'_|         |  Official https://julialang.org/ release
   |__/                          |

julia>
```

JuliaPro

Julia Computing, the company behind the Julia programming language, offers a *batteries included* distribution. It's called **JuliaPro** and it's arguably the easiest way to get started with Julia straight away. It includes the compiler, a profiler, the Juno IDE, and over 160 top quality curated packages for plotting, data visualization, machine learning, databases, and more.

JuliaPro can be downloaded for free at `https://shop.juliacomputing.com/Products/` (registration required). Once you get it, follow the install process specific to your platform. When done you'll have everything needed to begin using Julia productively.

A paid enterprise version is also available, offering a few extra features, such as Excel integration and support with SLA.

JuliaBox

Finally, there's also JuliaBox (`https://www.juliabox.com`), another free offering from Julia Computing. JuliaBox allows running a Julia Docker container on the fly, in their cloud. It provides access to IJulia Jupyter notebooks (`https://github.com/JuliaLang/IJulia.jl`), file sync with Google Drive, importing GitHub repositories, and many other features.

 If you are not familiar with Jupyter notebooks, you can learn more about them by visiting `http://jupyter.org`.

Choosing an IDE

An IDE is very important when working with a programming language. A powerful source code editor, code completion, and a good linter and debugger can significantly influence the learning curve and the productivity of using a language. You will be happy to learn that there are some very good IDE and editor options for Julia—and chances are you'll find your favorite one among these.

The IDE choices reflect the pragmatism of the language as a whole. From choosing LLVM as the compiler to providing efficient ways for calling functions from other languages, to using `git` and GitHub to power the package manager, the Julia core team takes a *don't reinvent the wheel* approach. Following the same line of thinking, the Julia community has built powerful IDEs upon existing industry established editors, such as Atom and Visual Studio Code.

Juno (Atom)

Juno (`http://junolab.org`) is the most advanced Julia IDE and the de facto editor of choice for Julia professionals. It is based on the Atom editor and it can be considered the official development tool, being also distributed with the previously mentioned JuliaPro distribution.

To get it, either download and install JuliaPro from `https://juliacomputing.com/products/juliapro.html` or do a manual install of Atom and the required plugins.

If you choose the manual install, first you need to download Atom from `https://atom.io`. Once it's up and running, go to the **Settings** pane (you can use the shortcut *Ctrl/cmd* and ,) and then go to the **Install** panel. Type `uber-juno` into the search box and press *Enter*. Next, click the **install** button on the package with the same name. Atom will pick it up from here, installing all the required Atom and Julia packages.

Once configured, the IDE options will be available in Atom's menu, under **Packages** > **Julia**. Various panes can also be enabled from here, to list variables, visualize plots, or search the documentation.

For further information, check out `http://junolab.org` and `https://github.com/JunoLab/uber-juno/blob/master/setup.md`.

Visual Studio Code

Visual Studio Code is a cross-platform extendable editor from Microsoft. It is available for all the *big three* platforms at `https://code.visualstudio.com`. Once installed, run it and from the menu click **View** > **Extensions** or use the shortcut *Shift* and *Ctrl/cmd* and *X*. Search for `julia` and install the Julia extension from *julialang*.

The Julia support in Visual Studio Code is not (yet) as powerful as Juno, but if you prefer it, it makes for a great coding experience, providing syntax highlighting, code completion, hover help, evaluation of Julia code, linting, code navigation, and more. Visual Studio Code is also snappier and uses fewer resources than Atom, which makes it an appealing option when running on a less powerful workstation (although Atom has greatly improved in this regard with recent versions).

The extension might need a bit of help figuring out where it can find the Julia binary. If that is the case, you'll get an informative error message, asking you to set the `julia.executablePath` configuration option. This should point to the julia binary, and depends on your operating system and the way you installed Julia (see the previous section for details on the installation).

To set the configuration, go to **Preferences** > **Settings** (*Ctrl/cmd* and ,) and in the right pane, the one used to overwrite the defaults, add the following:

```
"julia.executablePath": "/path/to/your/julia/folder/bin/julia"
```

IJulia (JuliaBox)

We already mentioned JuliaBox (https://www.juliabox.com) in the previous section—it allows creating, editing, and running IJulia Jupyter notebooks in the cloud. IJulia can also be installed on the local development machine.

IJulia is a Julia language backend for the Jupyter interactive environment (also used by IPython). It allows us to interact with the Julia language using Jupyter/IPython's powerful graphical notebook, which combines code, formatted text, math, and multimedia in a single document.

Although IJulia/Jupyter is not really an IDE, nor a classical editor, it is a powerful environment for editing and executing Julia scripts, and it's especially popular for data science and scientific computing. Let's take a few moments to set it up.

Start a new Julia REPL and execute the following:

```
julia> using Pkg
julia> Pkg.add("IJulia")
```

This will install the IJulia package, while also adding a required minimal Python and Jupyter distribution called **Miniconda**. This Python distribution is private to Julia (not in your PATH). Once finished, continue by executing the following:

```
julia> using IJulia
julia> notebook()
```

This will open the home page of your local Jupyter install in your default browser, at http://localhost:8888/tree. From the toolbar choose New > Julia 1.0.0 (or whatever version you are currently running) to create a new notebook. You can now create rich documents using embedded executable Julia code.

> There's another way of running IJulia as a desktop app, through Interact. You can download it and give it a try at https://nteract.io/desktop.

If you're new to Jupyter, it's worth learning more about it. Go check it out at http://jupyter.org.

You can also find IJulia notebooks for each chapter in this book in the chapter's support file repository. The notebooks will allow you to go through the code we're writing, step by step. For instance, you can find the code for this chapter at `https://github.com/PacktPublishing/Julia-Programming-Projects/blob/master/Chapter01/Chapter%201.ipynb`. You can download it on your computer and open it with the local IJulia installation, or upload it to JuliaBox through their Google Drive integration.

Other options

The preceding choices are the most common IDE and editor options for Julia. But there are a few more out there.

For the `vim` enthusiasts, there's also `julia-vim` (`https://github.com/JuliaEditorSupport/julia-vim`).

If you prefer Emacs, you'll be pleased to know that Julia supports it as well `https://github.com/JuliaEditorSupport/julia-emacs`.

If you'd rater go with one of the IDEs provided by JetBrains (like IntelliJ IDEA), you'll be happy to hear that a plugin is available, at `https://plugins.jetbrains.com/plugin/10413-julia`

Finally, there is also support for Sublime Text, available at `https://github.com/JuliaEditorSupport/Julia-sublime`. The plugin provides a good Julia editing experience, supporting syntax highlighting, code completion, and jumping to definition, among other things.

Getting started with Julia

If you followed through the first part of the chapter, by now you should have a fully functional local Julia installation, the knowledge to start a Julia REPL session, and have your preferred IDE ready for coding. If that is not the case, please refer to the previous sections. From this point on we're getting down to business—it's time to write some Julia code!

The Julia REPL

The first thing we need to understand is how to use the powerful REPL. As a Julia developer, you'll spend a significant amount of time doing exploratory programming, interacting with the shell and the filesystem, and managing packages. The REPL will be your trusted sidekick. It's worth getting to know it well, it will save you a lot of time down the line.

The acronym REPL stands for read-eval-print loop. Simply put, it's a language-specific shell, an interactive coding environment that allows inputting expressions, evaluates them, and outputs the result.

REPLs are very useful as they provide a simple way to interact with the language, to try out ideas and prototype, facilitating exploratory programming and debugging. It is especially powerful in the context of data analysis, where one can quickly connect to a data source, load a data sample and then slice and dice, rapidly testing different hypothesis.

Julia provides an excellent REPL experience, with rich functionality that covers quick evaluation of Julia statements, searchable history, tab-completion, syntax highlighting, dedicated help and shell modes, to name just a few.

If you do not have a working Julia installation, please see the *Installing Julia* section.

Interacting with the REPL

Depending on your OS and your preferences, the REPL can be started by simply invoking $ julia with no arguments, or by double-clicking the julia executable.

You will be greeted with a screen like this one (the Julia version might be different than mine):

Now Julia is waiting for us to input our code, evaluating it line by line. You can confirm that by checking the Terminal prompt, which says `julia>`. This is called the **julian mode**. Let's take it for a spin.

You can follow through the IJulia Jupyter notebook provided with this chapter's support files. If you are not familiar with Jupyter and don't know how to run it locally, you can use Juliabox (`juliabox.com`). All you have to do is create an account, log in, and then load the notebook from `https://github.com/PacktPublishing/Julia-Programming-Projects/` `blob/master/Chapter01/Chapter%201.ipynb`.

Input the following lines, pressing *Enter* after each one:

```
julia> 2+2
julia> 2^3
```

So we can use Julia like a simple calculator. Not very useful, but this is only the beginning and illustrates how powerful this rapid input and feedback cycle can be when we deal with complex computations.

`println` is a very useful function that prints whatever value it receives, appending a new line afterward. Type the following code:

```
julia> println("Welcome to Julia")
```

Under each line, you should see the output generated by each expression. Your window should now look like this.

```
julia> 2+2
4
julia> 2^3
8
julia> println("Welcome to Julia")
Welcome to Julia
```

Let's try some more. The REPL interprets one line at a time, but everything is evaluated in a common scope. This means that we can define variables and refer to them later on, as follows:

```
julia> greeting = "Hello"
"Hello"
```

This looks great! Let's use the `greeting` variable with `println`:

```
julia> println(greeting)
ERROR: UndefVarError: greting not defined
```

Oops! A little typo there, and the REPL promptly returned an error. It's not `greting`, it's `greeting`. This also tells us that Julia does not allow using variables without properly initializing them. It just looked for the `greting` variable, unsuccessfully—and it threw an undefined variable error. Let's try that again, this time more carefully:

```
julia> println(greeting)
Hello
```

OK, that's much better! We can see the output: the `Hello` value we stored in the `greeting` variable.

The ans variable

The REPL provides a few helping features, specific to this interactive environment (they won't be available when executing a Julia script). One of these is the `ans` variable, automatically set up and updated by Julia.

If you type `julia> 2^3`—unsurprisingly, you'll get `8`. Now input `julia> ans`—you'll get `8` again! What's up with that? `ans` is a special variable that exists only in the REPL and that automatically stores the last returned value. It can prove very useful when working with the REPL, but more importantly, you need to be aware of its existence so that you don't accidentally declare a variable with the same name. Otherwise, you'll run into some very hard to understand bugs with your variable's value constantly overwritten.

Prompt pasting

The REPL comes with a very powerful feature called **prompt pasting**. This allows us to copy-paste-execute Julia code and snippets that include both the `julia>` prompt and the output of the expression. It activates when pasting text that starts with `julia>`. In that case, only expressions starting with `julia>` are parsed, and all the others are ignored. This makes it possible to paste a chunk of code that has been copied from another REPL session or from the documentation, without having to scrub away prompts and outputs.

 Prompt pasting does not work in IJulia Jupyter notebooks.

To see this in action, copy and paste the following snippet, as is:

```
julia> using Dates

julia> Dates.now()
```

```
2018-09-02T21:13:03.122
julia> ans
2018-09-02T21:13:03.122
```

If all goes well, both expressions should output your current time, and not the one from the snippet, effectively replacing the results in the snippet with the results in your Julia session.

 This feature does not work with the default Windows command prompt due to its limitations.

Tab completion

In both the Julian, pkg, and help modes you can press the *Tab* key after entering the first few characters of a function to get a list of all the matches:

```
julia> pri[TAB]
primitive type    print                 print_shortest    print_with_color
println           printstyled
```

It can also be used to substitute LaTeX math symbols with their Unicode equivalents. To do this, type a backslash as the first character, then the first few characters of the symbol, then *Tab*. This will complete the name of the symbol or will display a list of options if there's more than one matching name. Pressing *Tab* again on the complete name of the symbol will perform the replacement:

```
julia> \pi[TAB]
julia> π
π = 3.1415926535897...

julia> \om[TAB] \omega \ominus
julia> \ome[TAB]
julia> \omega[TAB]
julia> ω
```

Cleaning the REPL scope

Julia does not have the concept of null so you can't really deallocate a variable from memory. If, however, you need to free an expensive resource referenced by a variable, you can replace its value with something like 0 and the previous value will be automatically garbage collected. You can even invoke the garbage collector yourself straight away by calling gc().

Additional REPL modes

The Julia REPL comes with four operational modes—and additional ones can be defined as needed. The currently active mode is indicated by its prompt. In the previous examples we've used the *julian* mode `julia>`, which evaluates the inputted expression. The other three available modes are *help*, `help?>`, *shell*, `shell>`, and package management, `pkg>`.

The active mode can be switched by typing a specific character right at the beginning of the line. The prompt will change in response, to indicate the current mode. The mode will stay active until the current line is evaluated, automatically switching back to julian (with the exception of the `pkg>` mode which is *sticky*—that is, it stays active until explicitly exited by typing backspace at the beginning of the line). The alternative modes can be exited without evaluating the expression by deleting everything on the line until the prompt changes back to `julia>`, or by pressing *Ctrl + C*.

Accessing the documentation with the help mode

The help mode provides access to documentation without having to get out of the REPL. To access it, simply type `?` at the beginning of the line. You should see the `help?>` prompt. Now you can input text, and Julia will search the documentation for matching entries, as follows:

```
julia> ?
help?> println
search: println printstyled print_with_color print print_shortest sprint
isprint

  println([io::IO], xs...)

  Print (using print) xs followed by a newline. If io is not supplied,
prints to stdout.

  Examples
  =========

  julia> println("Hello, world")
  Hello, world

  julia> io = IOBuffer();

  julia> println(io, "Hello, world")

  julia> String(take!(io))
  "Hello, world\n"
```

In IJulia, the additional modes are activated by prefixing the input with the desired mode activator. For instance, to access the help for the previous `println` function, we need to input `?println`.

The output supports rich formatting, via Markdown:

```
julia> using Profile
help?> Profile.print
```

Resulting a rich output as in the following screenshot:

```
help?> Profile.print
WARNING: Base.Profile is deprecated, run `using Profile` instead
 in module Main
WARNING: Base.Profile is deprecated, run `using Profile` instead
 in module Main
  print([io::IO = stdout,] [data::Vector]; kwargs... )

  Prints profiling results to io (by default, stdout). If you do not supply a data vector, the internal buffer of
  accumulated backtraces will be used.

  The keyword arguments can be any combination of:

    •    format – Determines whether backtraces are printed with (default, :tree) or without (:flat) indentation
         indicating tree structure.

    •    C – If true, backtraces from C and Fortran code are shown (normally they are excluded).

    •    combine – If true (default), instruction pointers are merged that correspond to the same line of code.

    •    maxdepth – Limits the depth higher than maxdepth in the :tree format.

    •    sortedby – Controls the order in :flat format. :filefuncline (default) sorts by the source line, whereas
         :count sorts in order of number of collected samples.

    •    noisefloor – Limits frames that exceed the heuristic noise floor of the sample (only applies to format
         :tree). A suggested value to try for this is 2.0 (the default is 0). This parameter hides samples for
         which n ≤ noisefloor * √N, where n is the number of samples on this line, and N is the number of
         samples for the callee.

    •    mincount – Limits the printout to only those lines with at least mincount occurrences.


  print([io::IO = stdout,] data::Vector, lidict::LineInfoDict; kwargs... )

  Prints profiling results to io. This variant is used to examine results exported by a previous call to retrieve.
  Supply the vector data of backtraces and a dictionary lidict of line information.

  See Profile.print([io], data) for an explanation of the valid keyword arguments.
```

More complex expressions can be queried, including macros, types, and variables.

For example, `help?> @time`:

```
@time

A macro to execute an expression, printing the time it took to execute, the number of allocations, and the total
number of bytes its execution caused to be allocated, before returning the value of the expression.

See also @timev, @timed, @elapsed, and @allocated.

julia> @time rand(10^6);
  0.001525 seconds (7 allocations: 7.630 MiB)

julia> @time begin
          sleep(0.3)
          1+1
       end
  0.301395 seconds (8 allocations: 336 bytes)
2
```

Or `help?> IO`:

```
search: IO IOStream IOBuffer IOContext fdio Union union union! UnionAll options Rational RadioMenu rationalize

  No documentation found.

  Summary
  ≡≡≡≡≡≡≡≡≡

  abstract type IO <: Any

  Subtypes
  ≡≡≡≡≡≡≡≡≡≡

  Base.AbstractPipe
  Base.DevNullStream
  Base.Filesystem.AbstractFile
  Base.GenericIOBuffer
  Base.LibuvStream
  Base.SecretBuffer
  Base64.Base64DecodePipe
  Base64.Base64EncodePipe
  Core.CoreSTDERR
  Core.CoreSTDOUT
  IOStream
  Mmap.Anonymous
```

Shell mode

The shell mode is used to switch to a command-line interface similar to the system shell, for directly executing OS commands. To enter it, input a semicolon ; at the very beginning of the julian prompt:

```
julia> ;
```

Upon typing ; the prompt changes (in place) to shell>:

 To enter shell mode in IJulia and execute a shell command, prefix the command with ;, for example ; ls.

Now we can execute system-wide commands directly, without the need to wrap them in Julia code. This will list the last ten lines of your repl_history.jl file. This file is used by Julia to keep a history of the commands executed in the REPL, so your output will be different from mine:

```
julia> using REPL
shell> tail -n 10 ~/.julia/logs/repl_history.jl
IO
# time: 2018-09-02 21:56:47 CEST
# mode: julia
REPL.find_hist_file()
# time: 2018-09-02 21:58:47 CEST
# mode: shell
tail -n 10 ~/.julia/logs/repl_history.jl
```

While in REPL mode we can access Julia's API, making this a very powerful combo. For example, in order to programmatically get the path to the REPL history file, we can use the REPL.find_hist_file() function, as follows:

```
julia> REPL.find_hist_file()
"/Users/adrian/.julia/logs/repl_history.jl"
```

The path to the file will be different for you.

We can use this in the shell mode by wrapping the command in $():

```
shell> tail -n 10 $(REPL.find_hist_file())
    REPL.find_hist_file()
# time: 2018-09-02 21:58:47 CEST
# mode: shell
    tail -n 10 ~/.julia/logs/repl_history.jl
# time: 2018-09-02 22:00:03 CEST
```

```
# mode: shell
    tail -n 10 $(REPL.find_hist_file())
```

Similarly to the help mode, the shell mode can be exited without executing any command by pressing backspace at the beginning of the line or typing *Ctrl + C*.

In IJulia, the command can be executed by prefixing the input with `;`, like this:

```
;tail -n 10 ~/.julia/logs/repl_history.jl
```

Search modes

Besides the help and the shell modes, there are two search modes. These are not necessarily Julia specific, being common to many *nix style editing apps.

Press the *Ctrl* key and the *R* key at the same time in order to initiate a reverse incremental search. The prompt will change to `(reverse-i-search)`. Start typing your query and the most recent result will show. To find older results, type *Ctrl + R* again.

The counterpart of *Ctrl + R* is *Ctrl + S*, initiating an incremental search. The two may be used in conjunction to move through the previous or next matching results, respectively.

The startup.jl file

If you want to automatically execute some code every time you run Julia, you can add it to a special file called `startup.jl`. This file is not automatically created, so you'll have to add it yourself to your Julia configuration directory. Any code you add to it will be run by Julia each time it starts up. Let's have some fun and do this using Julia—and practice a bit of what we've learned so far.

First, go into shell mode and run these three commands:

```
shell> mkdir $(dirname(REPL.find_hist_file()))/../config

shell> cd $(dirname(REPL.find_hist_file()))/../config
/Users/adrian/.julia/config

shell> touch startup.jl
```

Then, in julian mode, execute the following:

```
julia> write("startup.jl", "println(\"Welcome to Julia!\")")
28
```

What did we just do? In shell mode, we created a new directory, called `config`, just one folder up from where our history file was. Then we `cd` into the newly created folder, where we created a new file called `startup.jl`. Finally, we asked Julia to add the line `"println(\"Welcome to Julia!\")"` to the `startup.jl` file. Next time we start the Julia REPL we'll be greeted by this welcome message. Check this out:

REPL hooks

It is also possible to define a function that will be automatically called before starting a REPL session. To achieve this, you need to use the `atreplinit(f)` function, which registers a one-argument function `f` to be called before the REPL interface is initialized in interactive sessions. This function should be called from within the `startup.jl` file.

Let's say that we edit our `startup.jl` file so that it now looks like this:

```
println("Welcome to Julia!")

atreplinit() do (f)
  println("And welcome to you too!")
end
```

Our REPL will now greet us twice:

```
Welcome to Julia!

                _
    _       _ _(_)_      |  Documentation: https://docs.julialang.org
   (_)     | (_) (_)     |
    _ _   _| |_  __ _     |  Type "?" for help, "]?" for Pkg help.
   | | | | | | |/ _` |    |
   | | |_| | | | (_| |    |  Version 1.0.0 (2018-08-08)
  _/ |\__'_|_|_|\__'_|    |  Official https://julialang.org/ release
 |__/                     |

And welcome to you too!
julia>
```

The `atreplinit` function can be used in tandem with `isinteractive`, which returns a `Boolean true` or `false` value that tells us whether or not Julia is running an interactive session.

Exiting the REPL

In order to exit the REPL, you can type ^ D (*Ctrl* + *D*). However, that will only work if you're at the beginning of the line (when the text buffer is empty). Otherwise just type ^C (*Ctrl* + *C*) to first interrupt (or *c*ancel) and clear the line. You can also run `exit()`, which will stop the execution of the current Julia process.

> For the complete list of key bindings at the REPL and how to customise them, you can read the official documentation at `https://docs.julialang.org/en/v1.0/stdlib/REPL/#Key-bindings-1`.

The package system

Your Julia installation comes with a powerful package manager called `Pkg`. This handles all the expected operations, such as adding and removing packages, resolving dependencies and keeping installed packages up to date, running tests, and even assisting with publishing our own packages.

Packages play a pivotal role by providing a wide range of functionality, seamlessly extending the core language. Let's take a look at the most important package management functions.

Adding a package

In order to be known to `Pkg`, the packages must be added to a registry that is available to Julia. `Pkg` supports working with multiple registries simultaneously—including private ones hosted behind corporate firewalls. By default, `Pkg` is configured to use Julia's General registry, a repository of free and open sources packages maintained by the Julia community.

`Pkg` is quite a powerful beast and we'll use it extensively throughout the book. Package management is a common task when developing with Julia so we'll have multiple opportunities to progressively dive deeper. We'll take our first steps now as we'll learn how to add packages—and we'll do this by stacking a few powerful new features to our Julia setup.

OhMyREPL

One of my favourite packages is called `OhMyREPL`. It implements a few super productive features for the Julia REPL, most notably syntax highlighting and brackets pairing. It's a great addition that makes the interactive coding experience even more pleasant and efficient.

Julia's `Pkg` is centered around GitHub. The creators distribute the packages as git repos, hosted on GitHub—and even the General registry is a GitHub repository itself. `OhMyREPL` is no exception. If you want to learn more about it before installing it—always a good idea when using code from third parties — you can check it out at `https://github.com/KristofferC/OhMyREPL.jl`

Keep in mind that even if it's part of the General registry, the packages come with no guarantees and they're not necessarily checked, validated or endorsed by the Julia community. However, there are a few common sense indicators which provide insight into the quality of the package, most notably the number of stars, the status of the tests as well as the support for the most recent Julia versions.

The first thing we need to do in order to add a package is to enter the `Pkg` REPL-mode. We do this by typing] at the beginning of the line:

```
julia>]
```

The cursor will change to reflect that we're now ready to manage packages:

```
(v1.0) pkg>
```

IJulia does not (yet) support the `pkg>` mode, but we can execute `Pkg` commands by wrapping them in `pkg"..."` as in `pkg"add OhMyREPL"`.

`Pkg` uses the concept of *environments*, allowing us to define distinct and independent sets of packages on a per-project basis. This is a very powerful and useful feature, as it eliminates dependency conflicts caused by projects that rely on different versions of the same package (the so-called **dependency hell**).

Given that we haven't created any project yet, `Pkg` will just use the default project, `v1.0`, indicated by the value between the parenthesis. This represents the Julia version that you're running on—and it's possible that you'll get a different default project depending on your very own version of Julia.

Now we can just go ahead and `add OhMyREPL`:

```
(v1.0) pkg> add OhMyREPL
  Updating registry at `~/.julia/registries/General`
  Updating git-repo `https://github.com/JuliaRegistries/General.git`
 Resolving package versions...
  Updating `~/.julia/environments/v1.0/Project.toml`
  [5fb14364] + OhMyREPL v0.3.0
  Updating `~/.julia/environments/v1.0/Manifest.toml`
  [a8cc5b0e] + Crayons v1.0.0
  [5fb14364] + OhMyREPL v0.3.0
  [0796e94c] + Tokenize v0.5.2
  [2a0f44e3] + Base64
  [ade2ca70] + Dates
  [8ba89e20] + Distributed
  [b77e0a4c] + InteractiveUtils
  [76f85450] + LibGit2
  [8f399da3] + Libdl
  [37e2e46d] + LinearAlgebra
  [56ddb016] + Logging
  [d6f4376e] + Markdown
  [44cfe95a] + Pkg
  [de0858da] + Printf
  [3fa0cd96] + REPL
  [9a3f8284] + Random
  [ea8e919c] + SHA
  [9e88b42a] + Serialization
  [6462fe0b] + Sockets
  [8dfed614] + Test
  [cf7118a7] + UUIDs
  [4ec0a83e] + Unicode
```

The IJulia equivalent of the previous command is `pkg"add OhMyREPL"`.

When running `pkg> add` on a fresh Julia installation, `Pkg` will clone Julia's General registry and use it to look up the names of the package we requested. Although we only explicitly asked for `OhMyREPL`, most Julia packages have external dependencies that also need to be installed. As we can see, our package has quite a few—but they were promptly installed by `Pkg`.

Custom package installation

Sometimes we might want to use packages that are not added to the general registry. This is usually the case with packages that are under (early) development—or private packages. For such situations, we can pass `pkg> add` the URL of the repository, instead of the package's name:

```
(v1.0) pkg> add https://github.com/JuliaLang/Example.jl.git
   Cloning git-repo `https://github.com/JuliaLang/Example.jl.git`
  Updating git-repo `https://github.com/JuliaLang/Example.jl.git`
 Resolving package versions...
  Updating `~/.julia/environments/v1.0/Project.toml`
  [7876af07] + Example v0.5.1+ #master
(https://github.com/JuliaLang/Example.jl.git)
  Updating `~/.julia/environments/v1.0/Manifest.toml`
  [7876af07] + Example v0.5.1+ #master
(https://github.com/JuliaLang/Example.jl.git)
```

Another common scenario is when we want to install a certain branch of a package's repository. This can be easily achieved by appending `#name_of_the_branch` at the end of the package's name or URL:

```
(v1.0) pkg> add OhMyREPL#master
   Cloning git-repo `https://github.com/KristofferC/OhMyREPL.jl.git`
  Updating git-repo `https://github.com/KristofferC/OhMyREPL.jl.git`
 Resolving package versions...
 Installed Crayons — v0.5.1
  Updating `~/.julia/environments/v1.0/Project.toml`
  [5fb14364] ~ OhMyREPL v0.3.0 ⇒ v0.3.0 #master
(https://github.com/KristofferC/OhMyREPL.jl.git)
  Updating `~/.julia/environments/v1.0/Manifest.toml`
```

```
    [a8cc5b0e] ↓ Crayons v1.0.0 ⇒ v0.5.1
    [5fb14364] ~ OhMyREPL v0.3.0 ⇒ v0.3.0 #master (https://github.com/
KristofferC/OhMyREPL.jl.git)
```

Or, for unregistered packages, use the following:

```
(v1.0) pkg> add https://github.com/JuliaLang/Example.jl.git#master
```

If we want to get back to using the published branch, we need to `free` the package:

```
(v1.0) pkg> free OhMyREPL
 Resolving package versions...
   Updating `~/.julia/environments/v1.0/Project.toml`
   [5fb14364] ~ OhMyREPL v0.3.0 #master
(https://github.com/KristofferC/OhMyREPL.jl.git) ⇒ v0.3.0
   Updating `~/.julia/environments/v1.0/Manifest.toml`
   [a8cc5b0e] ↑ Crayons v0.5.1 ⇒ v1.0.0
   [5fb14364] ~ OhMyREPL v0.3.0 #master
(https://github.com/KristofferC/OhMyREPL.jl.git) ⇒ v0.3.0
```

Revise

That was easy, but practice makes perfect. Let's add one more! This time we'll install `Revise`, another must-have package that enables a streamlined development workflow by monitoring and detecting changes in your Julia files and automatically reloading the code when needed. Before `Revise` it was notoriously difficult to load changes in the current Julia process, developers usually being forced to restart the REPL—a time-consuming and inefficient process. `Revise` can eliminate the overhead of restarting, loading packages, and waiting for code to compile.

> You can learn more about Revise by reading its docs at
> `https://timholy.github.io/Revise.jl/latest/`.

Unsurprisingly, we only have to invoke `add` one more time, this time passing in `Revise` for the package name:

```
(v1.0) pkg> add Revise
Resolving package versions...
 Installed Revise — v0.7.5
   Updating `~/.julia/environments/v1.0/Project.toml`
   [295af30f] + Revise v0.7.5
   Updating `~/.julia/environments/v1.0/Manifest.toml`
   [bac558e1] + OrderedCollections v0.1.0
```

```
[295af30f] + Revise v0.7.5
[7b1f6079] + FileWatching
```

The add command also accepts multiple packages at once. We added them one by one now, for learning purposes, but otherwise, we could've just executed (v1.0) pkg> add OhMyREPL Revise.

Checking the package status

We can confirm that the operations were successful by checking our project's status, using the aptly named status command:

```
(v1.0) pkg> status
    Status `~/.julia/environments/v1.0/Project.toml`
  [7876af07] Example v0.5.1+ #master
(https://github.com/JuliaLang/Example.jl.git)
  [5fb14364] OhMyREPL v0.3.0
  [295af30f] Revise v0.7.5
```

The status command displays all the installed packages, including, from left to right, the short version of the package's id (called the **UUID**), the name of the package and the version number. Where appropriate, it will also indicate the branch that we're tracking, as in the case of Example, where we're on the master branch.

Pkg also supports a series of shortcuts, if you want to save a few keystrokes. In this case, st can be used instead of status.

Using packages

Once a package has been added, in order to access its functionality we have to bring into scope. That's how we tell Julia that we intend to use it, asking the compiler to make it available for us. For that, first, we need to exit pkg mode. Once we're at the julian prompt, in order to use OhMyREPL, all we need to do is execute:

```
julia> using OhMyREPL
[ Info: Precompiling OhMyREPL [5fb14364-9ced-5910-84b2-373655c76a03]
```

That's all it takes—OhMyREPL is now automatically enhancing the current REPL session. To see it in action, here is what the *regular* REPL looks like:

```
julia> fun(x) = 2 + 3x * (3 / 2)
fun (generic function with 1 method)
```

And here is the same code, enhanced by OhMyREPL:

```
julia> fun(x) = 2 + 3x * (3 / 2)
fun (generic function with 1 method)
```

Syntax highlighting and bracket matching make the code more readable, reducing syntax errors. Looks pretty awesome, doesn't it?

OhMyREPL has a few more cool features up its sleeve—you can learn about them by checking the official documentation at
https://kristofferc.github.io/OhMyREPL.jl/latest/index.html.

One more step

OhMyREPL and Revise are excellent development tools and it's very useful to have them loaded automatically in all the Julia sessions. This is exactly why the startup.jl file exists—and now we have the opportunity to put it to good use (not that our heartfelt and welcoming greetings were not impressive enough!).

Here's a neat trick, to get us started—Julia provides an edit function that will open a file in the configured editor. Let's use it to open the startup.jl file:

```
julia> edit("~/.julia/config/startup.jl")
```

This will open the file in the default editor. If you haven't yet deleted our previously added welcome messages, feel free to do it now (unless you really like them and in that case, by all means, you can keep them). Now, Revise needs to be used before any other module that we want to track—so we'll want to have it at the top of the file. As for OhMyREPL, it can go next. Your startup.jl file should look like this:

```
using Revise
using OhMyREPL
```

Save it and close the editor. Next time you start Julia, both `Revise` and `OhMyREPL` will be already loaded.

Updating packages

Julia boosts a thriving ecosystem and packages get updated at a rapid pace. It's a good practice to regularly check for updates with `pkg> update`:

```
(v1.0) pkg> update
```

When this command is issued, Julia will first retrieve the latest version of the general repository, where it will check if any of the packages need to be updated.

Beware that issuing the `update` command will update all the available packages. As we discussed earlier, when mentioning *dependency hell*, this might not be the best thing. In the upcoming chapters, we will see how to work with individual projects and manage dependencies per individual application. Until then though, it's important to know that you can cherry pick the packages that you want to update by passing in their names:

```
(v1.0) pkg> update OhMyREPL Revise
```

`Pkg` also exposes a preview mode, which will show what will happen when running a certain command without actually making any of the changes:

```
(v1.0) pkg> preview update OhMyREPL
(v1.0) pkg> preview add HTTP
```

The shortcut for `pkg> update` is `pkg> up`.

Pinning packages

Sometimes though we might want to ensure that certain packages will not be updated. That's when we `pin` them:

```
(v1.0) pkg> pin OhMyREPL
 Resolving package versions...
  Updating `~/.julia/environments/v1.0/Project.toml`
  [5fb14364] ~ OhMyREPL v0.3.0 ⇒ v0.3.0
  Updating `~/.julia/environments/v1.0/Manifest.toml`
  [5fb14364] ~ OhMyREPL v0.3.0 ⇒ v0.3.0
```

Pinned packages are marked with the ⚲ symbol—also present now when checking the status:

```
(v1.0) pkg> st
    Status `~/.julia/environments/v1.0/Project.toml`
  [5fb14364] OhMyREPL v0.3.0
  [295af30f] Revise v0.7.5
```

If we want to unpin a package, we can use `pkg> free`:

```
(v1.0) pkg> free OhMyREPL
  Updating `~/.julia/environments/v1.0/Project.toml`
  [5fb14364] ~ OhMyREPL v0.3.0 ⇒ v0.3.0
  Updating `~/.julia/environments/v1.0/Manifest.toml`
  [5fb14364] ~ OhMyREPL v0.3.0 ⇒ v0.3.0

(v1.0) pkg> st
    Status `~/.julia/environments/v1.0/Project.toml`
  [5fb14364] OhMyREPL v0.3.0
  [295af30f] Revise v0.7.5
```

Removing packages

If you no longer plan on using some packages you can delete (or remove them), with the (you guessed it) `pkg> remove` command. For instance, let's say that we have the following configuration:

```
(v1.0) pkg> st
    Status `~/.julia/environments/v1.0/Project.toml`
  [7876af07] Example v0.5.1+ #master
(https://github.com/JuliaLang/Example.jl.git)
  [5fb14364] OhMyREPL v0.3.0
  [295af30f] Revise v0.7.5
```

We can remove the `Example` package with the following code:

```
(v1.0) pkg> remove Example
  Updating `~/.julia/environments/v1.0/Project.toml`
  [7876af07] – Example v0.5.1+ #master
(https://github.com/JuliaLang/Example.jl.git)
  Updating `~/.julia/environments/v1.0/Manifest.toml`
  [7876af07] – Example v0.5.1+ #master (https://github.com/JuliaLang/
Example.jl.git)
```

Sure enough, it's now gone:

```
(v1.0) pkg> st
    Status `~/.julia/environments/v1.0/Project.toml`
  [5fb14364] OhMyREPL v0.3.0
  [295af30f] Revise v0.7.5
```

The shortcut for `pkg> remove` is `pkg> rm`.

Besides the explicit removal of undesired packages, `Pkg` also has a built-in auto-cleanup function. As package versions evolve and package dependencies change, some of the installed packages will become obsolete and will no longer be used in any existing project. `Pkg` keeps a log of all the projects used so it can go through the log and see exactly which projects are still needing which packages—and thus identify the ones that are no longer necessary. These can be deleted in one swoop with the `pkg> gc` command:

```
(v1.0) pkg> gc Active manifests at:
`/Users/adrian/.julia/environments/v1.0/Manifest.toml`
`/Users/adrian/.julia/environments/v0.7/Manifest.toml` Deleted
/Users/adrian/.julia/packages/Acorn/exWWb: 40.852 KiB Deleted
/Users/adrian/.julia/packages/BufferedStreams/hCA7W: 102.235 KiB Deleted
/Users/adrian/.julia/packages/Crayons/e1SsX: 49.133 KiB Deleted
/Users/adrian/.julia/packages/Example/1jaU2: 4.625 KiB Deleted
/Users/adrian/.julia/packages/Genie/XOia2: 2.031 MiB Deleted
/Users/adrian/.julia/packages/HTTPClient/ZQR55: 37.669 KiB Deleted
/Users/adrian/.julia/packages/Homebrew/18kUw: 277.296 MiB Deleted
/Users/adrian/.julia/packages/LibCURL/Qs5og: 11.599 MiB Deleted
/Users/adrian/.julia/packages/LibExpat/6jLDP: 127.247 KiB Deleted
/Users/adrian/.julia/packages/LibPQ/N71DU: 134.734 KiB Deleted
/Users/adrian/.julia/packages/Libz/zMAun: 80.744 KiB Deleted
/Users/adrian/.julia/packages/Nettle/LMDZh: 50.371 KiB
```

```
Deleted /Users/adrian/.julia/packages/OhMyREPL/limOC: 448.493 KiB
Deleted /Users/adrian/.julia/packages/WinRPM/rDDZz: 24.925 KiB
Deleted 14 package installations : 292.001 MiB
```

Besides the dedicated `Pkg` REPL mode, Julia also provides a powerful API for programmatically managing packages. We won't cover it, but if you want to learn about it, you can check the official documentation at https://docs.julialang.org/en/latest/stdlib/Pkg/#References-1.

Discovering packages

Package discovery is not yet as simple as it could be, but there are a few good options. I recommend starting with this list of curated Julia packages: `https://github.com/svaksha/Julia.jl`. It groups a large collection of packages by domain, covering topics such as AI, Biology, Chemistry, Databases, Graphics, Data Science, Physics, Statistics, Super-Computing and more.

If that is not enough, you can always go to `https://discourse.julialang.org` where the Julia community discusses a multitude of topics related to the language. You can search and browse the existing threads, especially the package announcements section, hosted at `https://discourse.julialang.org/c/community/packages`.

Of course you can always ask the community for help—Julians are very friendly and welcoming, and a lot of effort is put towards moderation, in order to keep the discussion civilized and constructive. A free Discourse account is required in order to create new topics and post replies.

Finally, `https://juliaobserver.com/packages` is a third party website that provides a more polished way to look for packages—and it also performs a GitHub search, thus including unregistered packages too.

Registered versus unregistered

Although I already touched upon the topic in the previous paragraphs, I want to close the discussion about `Pkg` with a word of caution. The fact that a package is registered does not necessarily mean that it has been vetted in terms of functionality or security. It simply means that the package has been submitted by the creator and that it met certain technical requirements to be added to the general registry. The package sources are available on GitHub, and like with any open source software, make sure that you understand what it does, how it should be used, and that you accept the licensing terms.

This concludes our initial discussion about package management. But as this is one of the most common tasks, we'll come back to it again and again in future chapters, where we'll also see a few scenarios for more advanced usage.

Summary

Julia is a new programming language that takes advantage of recent innovations in compiler technology to offer the functionality, ease-of-use, and intuitive syntax of dynamic programming languages at the speed of C. One if its goals is to eliminate the so-called **two language problem**—when the users code in a high-level language, such as R and Python, but performance-critical parts have to be rewritten in C or C++. Julia feels like a dynamic language and offers all the productivity features associated with these. But at the same time, it eliminates the performance trade-offs, proving to be productive enough for prototyping and exploratory coding, and efficient enough for performance-critical applications.

Its built-in package manager provides access to over 2,000 third-party libraries that seamlessly extend the language with powerful new features—and we've learned how to take advantage of these. And if that is not enough, Julia has the ability to call functions written in other languages, such as C, Fortran, Python, or Java, to name just a few.

Julia is free and open source (MIT licensed) and can be deployed on all the major operating systems, including Windows, the main Linux distributions, and macOS. It also comes with some very good IDE and editor options.

Now that we have successfully set up our development environment, it's time to dive deeper into Julia's syntax. In the next chapter, we'll take a look at some of the basic building blocks of the language—defining variables and constants, manipulating and using `Strings` and numeric types, and working with `Arrays`. As a testament to Julia's productivity, that's all we'll need (together with some extra packages that we'll add) in order to perform powerful exploratory data analysis on the Iris flowers dataset. Meet you in the next chapter!

2
Creating Our First Julia App

Now that you have a working Julia installation and your IDE of choice is ready to run, it's time to put them to some good use. In this chapter, you'll learn how to apply Julia for data analysis—a domain that is central to the language, so expect to be impressed!

We will learn to perform exploratory data analysis with Julia. In the process, we'll take a look at `RDatasets`, a package that provides access to over 700 learning datasets. We'll load one of them, the Iris flowers dataset, and we'll manipulate it using standard data analysis functions. Then we'll look more closely at the data by employing common visualization techniques. And finally, we'll see how to persist and (re)load our data.

But, in order to do that, first we need to take a look at some of the language's most important building blocks.

We will cover the following topics in this chapter:

- Declaring variables (and constants)
- Working with `Strings` of characters and `regular expressions`
- Numbers and numeric types
- Our first Julia data structures—`Tuple`, `Range`, and `Array`
- * Exploratory data analysis using the Iris flower dataset—`RDatasets` and core `Statistics`
- Quick data visualization with `Gadfly`
- * Saving and loading tabular data with `CSV` and `Feather`
- Interacting with MongoDB databases

Technical requirements

The Julia package ecosystem is under continuous development and new package versions are released on a daily basis. Most of the times this is great news, as new releases bring new features and bug fixes. However, since many of the packages are still in beta (version 0.x), any new release can introduce breaking changes. As a result, the code presented in the book can stop working. In order to ensure that your code will produce the same results as described in the book, it is recommended to use the same package versions. Here are the external packages used in this chapter and their specific versions:

```
CSV@v0.4.3
DataFrames@v0.15.2
Feather@v0.5.1
Gadfly@v1.0.1
IJulia@v1.14.1
JSON@v0.20.0
RDatasets@v0.6.1
```

In order to install a specific version of a package you need to run:

```
pkg> add PackageName@vX.Y.Z
```

For example:

```
pkg> add IJulia@v1.14.1
```

Alternatively you can install all the used packages by downloading the `Project.toml` file provided with the chapter and using `pkg>` instantiate as follows:

```
julia>
download("https://raw.githubusercontent.com/PacktPublishing/Julia-Programmi
ng-Projects/master/Chapter02/Project.toml", "Project.toml")
pkg> activate .
pkg> instantiate
```

Defining variables

We have seen in the previous chapter how to use the REPL in order to execute computations and have the result displayed back to us. Julia even lends a helping hand by setting up the `ans` variable, which automatically holds the last computed value.

But, if we want to write anything but the most trivial programs, we need to learn how to define variables ourselves. In Julia, a variable is simply a name associated to a value. There are very few restrictions for naming variables, and the names themselves have no semantic meaning (the language will not treat variables differently based on their names, unlike say Ruby, where a name that is all caps is treated as a constant).

Let's see some examples:

```
julia> book = "Julia v1.0 By Example"
julia> pi = 3.14
julia> ANSWER = 42
julia> my_first_name = "Adrian"
```

 You can follow along through the examples in the chapter by loading the accompanying Jupyter/IJulia notebook provided with this chapter's support files.

The variables, names are case-sensitive, meaning that ANSWER and answer (and Answer and aNsWeR) are completely different things:

```
julia> answer
ERROR: UndefVarError: answer not defined
```

Unicode names (UTF-8-encoded) are also accepted as variables names:

```
julia> δ = 130
```

Remember that you can type many Unicode math symbols by typing backslash (\) then the name of the symbol and then the *Tab* key. For example, \pi[*Tab*] will output π.

Emojis also work, if your terminal supports them:

```
julia> 🚀 = "apollo 11"
```

The only explicitly disallowed names for variables are the names of built-in Julia statements (do, end, try, catch, if, and else, plus a few more):

```
julia> do = 3
ERROR: syntax: invalid "do" syntax
julia> end = "Paris"
ERROR: syntax: unexpected end
```

Attempting to access a variable that hasn't been defined will result in an error:

```
julia> MysteryVar
ERROR: UndefVarError: MysteryVar not defined
```

It's true that the language does not impose many restrictions, but a set of code style conventions is always useful—and even more so for an open source language. The Julia community has distilled a set of best practices for writing code. In regard to naming variables, the names should be lowercase and in just one word; word separation can be done with underscores (_), but only if the name would be difficult to read without them. For example, `myvar` versus `total_length_horizontal`.

 Given that the degree of difficulty in reading a name is a subjective thing, I'm a bit split about this naming style. I normally prefer the crystal-clear clarity of separating at word boundaries. But nevertheless, it is better to follow the recommendation, given that function names in the Julia API adhere to it. By adhering to the same conventions, your code will be consistent throughout.

Constants

Constants are variables that, once declared, can't be changed. They are declared by prefixing them with the `const` keyword:

```
julia> const firstmonth = "January"
```

Very importantly in Julia, constants are not concerned with their value, but rather with their *type*. It is a bit too early to discuss types in Julia, so for now it suffices to say that a type represents what kind of a value we're dealing with. For instance, `"abc"` (within double quotes) is of type `String`, `'a'` (within single quotes) is of type `Char`, and `1000` is of type `Int` (because it's an integer). Thus, in Julia, unlike most other languages, we can change the value assigned to a constant as long as the `type` remains the same. For instance, we can at first decide that eggs and milk are acceptable meal choices and go `vegetarian`:

```
julia> const mealoption = "vegetarian"
```

And we can change our mind later on, if we decide to go `vegan`. Julia will let it slide with just a warning:

```
julia> mealoption = "vegan"
WARNING: redefining constant mealoption
"vegan"
```

However, attempting to say that `mealoption` = 2 will result in an error:

```
julia> mealoption = 2
ERROR: invalid redefinition of constant mealoption
```

This makes sense, right? Who's ever heard of that kind of diet?

However, the nuances can be more subtle than that, most notably when working with numbers:

```
julia> const amount = 10.25
10.25
julia> amount = 10
ERROR: invalid redefinition of constant amount
```

Julia doesn't allow it because internally `10` and `10.00`, despite having the same arithmetical value, are values of different types (`10` is an integer, while `10.00` is a `float`). We'll take a closer look at numeric types in just a moment, so it will all become clearer:

```
julia> amount = 10.00
WARNING: redefining constant amount
10.0
```

Thus, we need to pass the new value as `10.00`—a `float`, in order to obey the same type requirement.

Why are constants important?

It's mostly about performance. Constants can be especially useful as global values. Because global variables are long-lived and can be modified at any time and from any location in your code, the compiler is having a hard time optimizing them. If we tell the compiler that the value is constant and thus that the type of the value won't change, the performance problem can be optimized away.

Of course, just because constants alleviate some critical performance problems brought about by global variables, it doesn't mean that we are encouraged to use them. Global values in Julia, like in other languages, must be avoided whenever possible. Besides performance issues, they can create subtle bugs that are hard to catch and understand. Also, keep in mind that, since Julia allows changing the value of a constant, accidental modification becomes possible.

Comments

Common programming wisdom says the following:

"Code is read much more often than it is written, so plan accordingly."

Code comments are a powerful tool that make the programs easier to understand later on. In Julia, comments are marked with the # sign. Single-line comments are denoted by a # and everything that follows this, until the end of the line, is ignored by the compiler. Multiline comments are enclosed between #= ... =#. Everything within the opening and the closing comment tags is also ignored by the compiler. Here is an example:

```julia
julia> #=
          Our company charges a fixed
          $10 fee per transaction.
       =#
const flatfee = 10 # flat fee, per transaction
```

In the previous snippet, we can see both multiline and single-line comments in action. A single-line comment can also be placed at the beginning of the line.

Strings

A string represents a sequence of characters. We can create a string by enclosing the corresponding sequence of characters between double quotes, as shown in the following:

```julia
julia> "Measuring programming progress by lines of code is like measuring
aircraft building progress by weight."
```

If the string also includes quotes, we can escape these by prefixing them with a backslash \:

```julia
julia> "Beta is Latin for \"still doesn't work\"."
```

Triple-quoted strings

However, escaping can get messy, so there's a much better way of dealing with this—by using triple quotes """...""".

```julia
julia> """Beta is Latin for "still doesn't work"."""
```

Within triple quotes, it is no longer necessary to escape the single quotes. However, make sure that the single quotes and the triple quotes are separated—or else the compiler will get confused:

```
julia> """Beta is Latin for "still doesn't work""""
syntax: cannot juxtapose string literal
```

The triple quotes come with some extra special powers when used with multiline text. First, if the opening `"""` is followed by a newline, this newline is stripped from the string. Also, whitespace is preserved but the string is dedented to the level of the least-indented line:

```
julia> """
                Hello
        Look
    Here"""


julia> print(ans)
Hello
Look
Here
```

The previous snippet illustrates how the first line is stripped and the whitespace is preserved—but the indentation starts with the least indented line (the space in front of `Here` was removed).

Here is how it looks in Jupyter/IJulia:

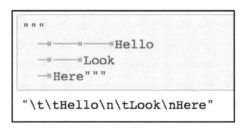

The longer arrow stands for a *Tab* (represented by a `\t` in the output), while the shorter arrow is a space. Note that each line had a space as the first character—but it was removed. The least indented line, the last one, was shifted to the left, removing all its whitespace and beginning with **Here**, while the remaining whitespace on the other lines was preserved (now beginning with a *Tab*).

Concatenating strings

Two or more strings can be joined together (concatenated) to form a single string by using the star * operator:

```
julia> "Hello " * "world!" "Hello world!"
```

Alternatively, we can invoke the string function, passing in all the words we want to concatenate:

```
julia> string("Itsy", " ", "Bitsy", " ", "Spider")
"Itsy Bitsy Spider"
```

Concatenation works great with variables too:

```
julia> username = "Adrian"
julia> greeting = "Good morning"
julia> greeting * ", " * username
"Good morning, Adrian"
```

However, again, we need to be careful when dealing with types (types are central to Julia, so this will be a recurring topic). Concatenation only works for strings:

```
julia> username = 9543794
julia> greeting = "Good morning"
julia> greeting * ", " * username
MethodError: no method matching *(::String, ::Int64)
```

Performing the concatenation by invoking the string function does work even if not all the arguments are strings:

```
julia> string(greeting, ", ", username)
  "Good morning, 9543794"
```

Thus, string has the added advantage that it automatically converts its parameters to strings. The following example works too:

```
julia> string(2, " and ", 3)
"2 and 3"
```

But this does not:

```
julia> 2 * " and " * 3
ERROR: MethodError: no method matching *(::Int64, ::String)
```

 There is also a `String` method (with capital S). Remember that in Julia names are case-sensitive, so `string` and `String` are two different things. For most purposes we'll need the lowercase function, `string`. You can use Julia's help system to access the documentation for `String`, if you want to learn about it.

Interpolating strings

When creating longer, more complex strings, concatenation can be noisy and error-prone. For such cases, we're better off using the $ symbol to perform variable interpolation into strings:

```
julia> username = "Adrian"
julia> greeting = "Good morning"
julia> "$greeting, $username"
"Good morning, Adrian"
```

More complex expressions can be interpolated by wrapping them into $(...):

```
julia> "$(uppercase(greeting)), $(reverse(username))"
"GOOD MORNING, nairdA"
```

Here we invoke the `uppercase` function which changes all the letters of the string into their uppercase counterparts—and the `reverse` function which reverses the order of the letters in the word. Their output is then interpolated in a string. Between the $(...) boundaries, we can use any Julia code we want.

Just like the `string` function, interpolation takes care of converting the values to strings:

```
julia> "The sum of 1 and 2 is $(1 + 2)"
"The sum of 1 and 2 is 3"
```

Manipulating strings

Strings can be treated as a list of characters, so we can index into them—that is, access the character at a certain position in the word:

```
julia> str = "Nice to see you"
julia> str[1]
'N': ASCII/Unicode U+004e (category Lu: Letter, uppercase)
```

The first character of the string Nice to see you is N.

Indexing in Julia is 1-based, which means that the first element of a list is found at index 1. This can be surprising if you've programmed before, given that most programming languages use 0-based indexing. However, I assure you that 1-based indexing makes for a very pleasant and straightforward coding experience.

 Julia has support for arrays with arbitrary indices, allowing, for example, to start numbering at 0. However, arbitrary indexing is a more advanced feature that we won't cover here. If you are curious, you can check the official documentation at https://docs.julialang.org/en/v1/devdocs/offset-arrays/.

We can also extract a part of the string (a substring) by indexing with a range, providing the starting and the ending positions:

```
julia> str[9:11]
"see"
```

It is important to notice that indexing via a singular value returns a Char , while indexing via a range returns a String (remember, for Julia these are two completely different things):

```
julia> str[1:1]
"N"
```

N is a String of just one letter, as indicated by its double quotes:

```
julia> str[1]
'N': ASCII/Unicode U+004e (category Lu: Letter, uppercase)
```

N is a `Char`, as shown by the single quotes:

```
julia> str[1:1] == str[1]
false
```

They are not equal.

Unicode and UTF-8

In Julia, string literals are encoded using UTF-8. UTF-8 is a variable-width encoding, meaning that not all characters are represented using the same number of bytes. For example, ASCII characters are encoded using a single byte—but other characters can use up to four bytes. This means that not every byte index into a UTF-8 string is necessarily a valid index for a corresponding character. If you index into a string at such an invalid byte index, an error will be thrown. Here is what I mean:

```
julia> str = "Søren Kierkegaard was a Danish Philosopher"
julia> str[1]
'S': ASCII/Unicode U+0053 (category Lu: Letter, uppercase)
```

We can correctly retrieve the character at index 1:

```
julia> str[2]
'ø': Unicode U+00f8 (category Ll: Letter, lowercase)
```

And at index 2, we successfully get the ø character:

```
julia> str[3]
StringIndexError("Søren Kierkegaard was a Danish Philosopher", 3)
```

However, ø has two bytes, so index 3 is used by ø as well and we cannot access the string at this position:

```
julia> str[4]
'r': ASCII/Unicode U+0072 (category Ll: Letter, lowercase)
```

The third letter, r, is found at position 4.

Thus ø is a two-byte character that occupies the locations 2 and 3—so the index 3 is invalid, matching the second byte of ø. The next valid index can be computed using `nextind(str, 2)`—but the recommended way is to use iteration over the characters (we'll discuss `for` loops a bit later in this chapter):

```
julia> for s in str
           println(s)
       end
S
ø
r
e
n

K
... output truncated...
```

Because of variable-length encodings, the number of characters in a string is not necessarily the same as the last index (as you have seen, the third letter, r, was at index 4):

```
julia> length(str) 42
julia> str[42] 'e': ASCII/Unicode U+0065 (category Ll: Letter, lowercase)
```

For such cases, Julia provides the `end` keyword, which can be used as a shorthand for the last index. You can perform arithmetic and other operations with `end`, just like a normal value:

```
julia> str[end]
'r': ASCII/Unicode U+0072 (category Ll: Letter, lowercase)
julia> str[end-10:end]
"Philosopher"
```

The `end` value can be computed programmatically using the `endof(str)` function. Attempting to index outside the bounds of a string will result in a `BoundsError`:

```
julia> str[end+1]
ERROR: BoundsError: attempt to access "Søren Kierkegaard was a Danish
Philosopher"
  at index [44]
```

Regular expressions

Regular expressions are used for powerful pattern-matching of substrings within strings. They can be used to search for a substring in a string, based on patterns—and then to extract or replace the matches. Julia provides support for Perl-compatible regular expressions.

The most common way to input regular expressions is by using the so-called **nonstandard string literals**. These look like regular double-quoted strings, but carry a special prefix. In the case of regular expressions, this prefix is "r". The prefix provides for a different behavior, compared to a normal string literal.

For example, in order to define a regular string that matches all the letters, we can use `r"[a-zA-Z]*"`.

Julia provides quite a few nonstandard string literals—and we can even define our own if we want to. The most widely used are for regular expressions (`r"..."`), byte array literals (`b"..."`), version number literals (`v"..."`), and package management commands (`pkg"..."`).

Here is how we build a regular expression in Julia—it matches numbers between 0 and 9:

```
julia> reg = r"[0-9]+"
r"[0-9]+"
julia> match(reg, "It was 1970")
RegexMatch("1970")
```

Our regular expression matches the substring `1970`.

We can confirm that the nonstandard string literal `reg` is in fact a `Regex` and not a regular `String` by checking its `type` with the `typeof` function:

```
julia> typeof(reg)
Regex
```

This gives away the fact that there's also a `Regex` constructor available:

```
julia> Regex("[0-9]+")
r"[0-9]+"
```

The two constructs are similar:

```
julia> Regex("[0-9]+") == reg
true
```

Using the constructor can come in handy when we need to create regular expressions using more complex strings that might include interpolation or concatenation. But in general, the `r"..."` format is more used.

The behavior of the regular expression can be affected by using some combination of the flags i, m, s, and x. These modifiers must be placed right after the closing double quote mark:

```julia
julia> match(r"it was", "It was 1970") # case-sensitive no match
julia> match(r"it was"i, "It was 1970") # case-insensitive match
RegexMatch("It was")
```

As you might expect, i performs a case-insensitive pattern match. Without the i modifier, match returns nothing—a special value that does not print anything at the interactive prompt—to indicate that the regex does not match the given string.

These are the available modifiers:

- i—case-insensitive pattern matching.
- m—treats string as multiple lines.
- s—treats string as single line.
- x—tells the regular expression parser to ignore most whitespace that is neither backslashed nor within a character class. You can use this to break up your regular expression into (slightly) more readable parts. The # character is also treated as a metacharacter introducing a comment, just as in ordinary code.

The occursin function is more concise if all we need is to check if a regex or a substring is contained in a string—if we don't want to extract or replace the matches:

```julia
julia> occursin(r"hello", "It was 1970")
false
julia> occursin(r"19", "It was 1970")
true
```

When a regular expression does match, it returns a RegexMatch object. These objects encapsulate how the expression matches, including the substring that the pattern matches and any captured substrings:

```julia
julia> alice_in_wonderland = "Why, sometimes I've believed as many as six
impossible things before breakfast."

julia> m = match(r"(\w+)+", alice_in_wonderland)
RegexMatch("Why", 1="Why")
```

The \w regex will match a *word*, so in this snippet we captured the first word, Why.

We also have the option to specify the index at which to start the search:

```
m = match(r"(\w+)+", alice_in_wonderland, 6)
RegexMatch("sometimes", 1="sometimes")
```

Let's try something a bit more complex:

```
julia> m = match(r"((\w+)(\s+|\W+))", alice_in_wonderland)
RegexMatch("Why, ", 1="Why, ", 2="Why", 3=", ")
```

The resultant RegexMatch object m exposes the following properties (or fields, in Julia's lingo):

- m.match (Why,) contains the entire substring that matched.
- m.captures (an array of strings containing Why, Why, and ,) represents the captured substrings.
- m.offset, the offset at which the whole match begins (in our case 1).
- m.offsets, the offsets of the captured substrings as an array of integers (for our example being [1, 1, 4]).

Julia does not provide a g modifier, for a *greedy* or *global* match. If you need all the matches, you can iterate over them using eachmatch(), with a construct like the following:

```
julia> for m in eachmatch(r"((\w+)(\s+|\W+))", alice_in_wonderland)
           println(m)
end
```

Or, alternatively, we can put all the matches in a list using collect():

```
julia> collect(eachmatch(r"((\w+)(\s+|\W+))", alice_in_wonderland))
13-element Array{RegexMatch,1}:
RegexMatch("Why, ", 1="Why, ", 2="Why", 3=", ")
RegexMatch("sometimes ", 1="sometimes ", 2="sometimes", 3=" ")
RegexMatch("I'", 1="I'", 2="I", 3="'")
RegexMatch("ve ", 1="ve ", 2="ve", 3=" ")
RegexMatch("believed ", 1="believed ", 2="believed", 3=" ")
RegexMatch("as ", 1="as ", 2="as", 3=" ")
RegexMatch("many ", 1="many ", 2="many", 3=" ")
RegexMatch("as ", 1="as ", 2="as", 3=" ")
RegexMatch("six ", 1="six ", 2="six", 3=" ")
RegexMatch("impossible ", 1="impossible ", 2="impossible", 3=" ")
RegexMatch("things ", 1="things ", 2="things", 3=" ")
RegexMatch("before ", 1="before ", 2="before", 3=" ")
RegexMatch("breakfast.", 1="breakfast.", 2="breakfast", 3=".")
```

For more info about regular expressions, check the official documentation at https://docs.julialang.org/en/stable/manual/strings/#Regular-Expressions-1.

Raw string literals

If you need to define a string that does not perform interpolation or escaping, for example to represent code from another language that might contain $ and \ which can interfere with the Julia parser, you can use raw strings. They are constructed with `raw"..."` and create ordinary `String` objects that contain the enclosed characters exactly as entered, with no interpolation or escaping:

```julia
julia> "This $will error out"
ERROR: UndefVarError: will not defined
```

Putting a $ inside the string will cause Julia to perform interpolation and look for a variable called `will`:

```julia
julia> raw"This $will work"
"This \$will work"
```

But by using a raw string, the $ symbol will be ignored (or rather, automatically escaped, as you can see in the output).

Numbers

Julia provides a broad range of primitive numeric types, together with the full range of arithmetic and bitwise operators and standard mathematical functions. We have at our disposal a rich hierarchy of numeric types, with the most generic being `Number`—which defines two subtypes, `Complex` and `Real`. Conversely, `Real` has four subtypes—`AbstractFloat`, `Integer`, `Irrational`, and `Rational`. Finally, `Integer` branches into four other subtypes—`BigInt`, `Bool`, `Signed`, and `Unsigned`.

Let's take a look at the most important categories of numbers.

Integers

Literal integers are represented simply as follows:

```
julia> 42
```

The default Integer type, called `Int`, depends on the architecture of the system upon which the code is executed. It can be either `Int32` or `Int64`. On my 64-bit system, I get it as follows:

```
julia> typeof(42)
Int64
```

The `Int` type will reflect that, as it's just an alias to either `Int32` or `Int64`:

```
julia> @show Int
Int = Int64
```

Overflow behavior

The minimum and maximum values are given by the `typemin()` and `typemax()` functions:

```
julia> typemin(Int), typemax(Int)
(-9223372036854775808, 9223372036854775807)
```

Attempting to use values that go beyond the boundaries defined by the minimum and the maximum values will not throw an error (or even a warning), resulting instead in a wraparound behavior (meaning that it will jump over at the other end):

```
julia> typemin(Int) - 1
9223372036854775807
julia> typemin(Int) - 1 == typemax(Int)
true
```

Substracting 1 from the minimum value will return the maximum value instead:

```
julia> typemax(Int) + 1 == typemin(Int)
true
```

The reverse is also `true`—adding 1 to the maximum value will return the minimum value.

For working with values outside these ranges, we'll use the `BigInt` type:

```
julia> BigInt(typemax(Int)) + 1
9223372036854775808
```

No wraparound here; the result is what we expected.

Floating-point numbers

Floating-point numbers are represented by numerical values separated by a dot:

```
julia> 3.14
3.14
julia> -1.0
-1.0
julia> 0.25
0.25
julia> .5
0.5
```

By default they are `Float64` values, but they can be converted to `Float32`:

```
julia> typeof(1.)
Float64
julia> f32 = Float32(1.)
1.0f0
julia> typeof(f32)
Float32
```

To improve readability, the underscore (_) separator can be used with both integers and floats:

```
julia> 1_000_000, 0.000_000_005
(1000000, 5.0e-9)
```

Rational numbers

Julia also provides a Rational number type. This allows us to work with exact ratios, instead of having to deal with the precision loss inherent in floats. Rational numbers are represented as their numerator and denominator values, separated by two forward slashes `//`:

```
julia> 3//2
3//2
```

Rational numbers can be converted to other types, if there is no data loss:

```
julia> 1//2 + 2//4
1//1

julia> Int(1//1)
1

julia> float(1//3)
0.3333333333333333

julia> Int(1//3)
ERROR: InexactError: Int64(Int64, 1//3)

julia> float(1//3) == 1/3
true
```

> Julia also includes support for Complex numbers. We won't discuss, them but you can read about the topic in the official documentation at `https://docs.julialang.org/en/v1/manual/complex-and-rational-numbers/#Complex-Numbers-1`.

Numerical operators

Julia supports the full range of arithmetic operators for its numeric types:

- +—(unary and binary plus)
- -—(unary and binary minus)
- *—(times)

- / —(divide)
- \ —(inverse divide)
- ^ —(power)
- % —(remainder)

The language also supports handy update operators for each of these (+=,−=,*=,/=,\=,÷=,%=,and ^=). Here they are in the wild:

```
julia> a = 2
2
julia> a *= 3 # equivalent of a = a * 3
6
julia> a ^= 2 # equivalent of a = a ^ 2
36
julia> a += 4 # equivalent of a = a + 4
40
```

Numerical comparisons can be performed with the following set of operators:

- == —(equality)
- != or ≠ —(inequality)
- < —(less than)
- <= or ≤ —(less than or equal to)
- > —(greater than)
- >= or ≥ —(greater than or equal to)

In Julia, the comparisons can also be chained:

```
julia> 10 > 5 < 6 == 6 >= 3 != 2
true
```

Vectorized dot operators

Julia defines corresponding *dot* operations for every binary operator. These are designed to work element-wise with collections of values (called **vectorized**). That is, the operator that is *dotted* is applied for each element of the collection.

In the following example, we'll square each element of the `first_five_fib` collection:

```
julia> first_five_fib = [1, 1, 2, 3, 5]
5-element Array{Int64,1}:
 1
 1
 2
 3
 5
julia> first_five_fib .^ 2
5-element Array{Int64,1}:
  1
  1
  4
  9
 25
```

In the previous example, `first_five_fib` was not touched and the resultant collection was returned, but *dotted* updating operators are also available, updating the values in place. They match the previously discussed update operators (with the added *dot*). For example, to update `first_five_fib` in place, we'd use the following:

```
julia> first_five_fib .^= 2
```

Vectorized code is an important part of the language due to its readability and conciseness, but also because it provides important performance optimizations. For more details, check https://docs.julialang.org/en/ stable/manual/functions/#man-vectorized-1.

There's more to it

This section barely scratches the surface. For a deeper dive into Julia's numeric types, read the official documentation at
https://docs.julialang.org/en/stable/manual/mathematical-operations/.

Tuples

Tuples are one of the simplest data types and data structures in Julia. They can have any length and can contain any kind of value—but they are immutable. Once created, a tuple cannot be modified. A tuple can be created using the literal tuple notation, by wrapping the comma-separated values within brackets (. . .):

```
(1, 2, 3)
```

```
julia> ("a", 4, 12.5)
("a", 4, 12.5)
```

In order to define a one-element tuple, we must not forget the trailing comma:

```
julia> (1,)
(1,)
```

But it's OK to leave off the parenthesis:

```
julia> 'e', 2
('e', 2)
```

```
julia> 1,
(1,)
```

We can index into tuples to access their elements:

```
julia> lang = ("Julia", v"1.0")
("Julia", v"1.0.0")
```

```
julia> lang[2]
v"1.0.0"
```

Vectorized *dot* operations also work with tuples:

```
julia> (3,4) .+ (1,1) (4, 5)
```

Named tuples

A named tuple represents a tuple with labeled items. We can access the individual components by label or by index:

```
julia> skills = (language = "Julia", version = v"1.0")
(language = "Julia", version = v"1.0.0")

julia> skills.language
"Julia"


julia> skills[1]
"Julia"
```

Named tuples can be very powerful as they are similar to full-blown objects, but with the limitation that they are immutable.

Ranges

We've seen ranges a bit earlier, when learning to index into `strings`. They can be as simple as the following:

```
julia> r = 1:20
1:20
```

As with previous collections, we can index into ranges:

```
julia> abc = 'a':'z'
'a':1:'z'

julia> abc[10]
'j': ASCII/Unicode U+006a (category Ll: Letter, lowercase)

julia> abc[end]
'z': ASCII/Unicode U+007a (category Ll: Letter, lowercase)
```

A range can be expanded into its corresponding values by using the splat operator, "`...`". For example, we can splat it into a tuple:

```
julia> (1:20...,)
(1, 2, 3, 4, 5, 6, 7, 8, 9, 10, 11, 12, 13, 14, 15, 16, 17, 18, 19, 20)
```

We can also splat it into a list:

```
julia> [1:20...]
20-element Array{Int64,1}
```

> The same is true for Tuples, which can also be splatted into lists, among other things: `[(1,2,3)...]`.

We can see that the range steps in increments of one, by default. We can change that by passing it an optional step parameter. Here is an example of a range between 0 and 20 with a step of five:

```
julia> (0:5:20...,)
(0, 5, 10, 15, 20)
```

Now our values go from 5 to 5.

This opens the possibility to also go in descending order, by using a negative step:

```
julia> (20:-5:-20...,)
(20, 15, 10, 5, 0, -5, -10, -15, -20)
```

Ranges are not limited to integers—you've seen earlier a range of `chars`; and these are ranges of `floats`:

```
julia> (0.5:10)
0.5:1.0:9.5
julia> (0.5:10...,)
(0.5, 1.5, 2.5, 3.5, 4.5, 5.5, 6.5, 7.5, 8.5, 9.5)
```

We can also use the `collect` function to expand the range into a list (an array):

```
julia> collect(0.5:0.5:10)
20-element Array{Float64,1}
```

Arrays

An array is a data structure (and the corresponding *type*) that represents an ordered collection of elements. More specifically, in Julia, an array is a collection of objects stored in a multi-dimensional grid.

Arrays can have any number of dimensions and are defined by their type and number of dimensions—`Array{Type, Dimensions}`.

A one-dimensional array, also called a **vector**, can be easily defined using the array literal notation, the square brackets `[...]`:

```
julia> [1, 2, 3]
3-element Array{Int64,1}:
 1
 2
 3
```

You can also constrain the type of the elements:

```
julia> Float32[1, 2, 3, 4]
4-element Array{Float32,1}:
 1.0
 2.0
 3.0
 4.0
```

A two D array (also called a **matrix**) can be initialized using the same array literal notation, but this time without the commas:

```
julia> [1 2 3 4]
1×4 Array{Int64,2}:
 1  2  3  4
```

We can add more rows using semicolons:

```
julia> [1 2 3; 4 5 6; 7 8 9]
3×3 Array{Int64,2}:
 1  2  3
 4  5  6
 7  8  9
```

Julia comes with a multitude of functions that can construct and initialize arrays with different values, such as `zeroes`, `ones`, `trues`, `falses`, `similar`, `rand`, `fill`, and more. Here are a few of these in action:

```
julia> zeros(Int, 2)
2-element Array{Int64,1}:
 0
 0


julia> zeros(Float64, 3)
3-element Array{Float64,1}:
```

```
 0.0
 0.0
 0.0

julia> ones(2)
2-element Array{Float64,1}:
 1.0
 1.0

julia> ones(Int, 2)
2-element Array{Int64,1}:
 1
 1

julia> ones(Int, 3, 4)
3×4 Array{Int64,2}:
 1  1  1  1
 1  1  1  1
 1  1  1  1

julia> trues(2)
2-element BitArray{1}:
 true
 true

julia> rand(Int, 4, 2)
4×2 Array{Int64,2}:
  9141724849782088627   6682031028895615978
 -3827856130755187476  -1731760524632072533
 -3369983903467340663  -7550830795386270701
 -3159829068325670125   1153092130078644307

julia> rand(Char, 3, 2)
3×2 Array{Char,2}:
 '\U63e7a'   '\Ub8723'
                    '林'
 '\Uda56f'
 '\U7b7fd'   '\U5f749'

julia> fill(42, 2, 3)
2×3 Array{Int64,2}:
 42  42  42
 42  42  42
```

`Array` elements can be accessed by their index, passing in a value for each dimension:

```
julia> arr1d = rand(5) 5-element Array{Float64,1}: 0.845359 0.0758361
0.379544 0.382333 0.240184
julia> arr1d[5]
 0.240184
julia> arr2d = rand(5,2)
5×2 Array{Float64,2}:
 0.838952  0.312295
 0.800917  0.253152
 0.480604  0.49218
 0.716717  0.889667
 0.703998  0.773618

julia> arr2d[4, 1]
0.7167165812985592
```

We can also pass a colon (:) to select all indices within the entire dimension—or a range to define subselections:

```
julia> arr2d = rand(5,5)
5×5 Array{Float64,2}:
 0.618041  0.887638   0.633995  0.868588  0.19461
 0.400213  0.699705   0.719709  0.328922  0.326825
 0.322572  0.807488   0.866489  0.960801  0.476889
 0.716221  0.504356   0.206264  0.600758  0.843445
 0.705491  0.0334613  0.240025  0.235351  0.740302
```

This is how we select rows 1 to 3 and columns 3 to 5:

```
julia> arr2d[1:3, 3:5]
3×3 Array{Float64,2}:
 0.633995  0.868588  0.19461
 0.719709  0.328922  0.326825
 0.866489  0.960801  0.476889
```

The solitary colon : stands for all—so here we pick all the rows and columns 3 to 5:

```
julia> arr2d[:, 3:5]
5×3 Array{Float64,2}:
 0.633995  0.868588  0.19461
 0.719709  0.328922  0.326825
 0.866489  0.960801  0.476889
 0.206264  0.600758  0.843445
 0.240025  0.235351  0.740302
```

Another option is an `Array` of Booleans to select elements at its `true` indices. Here we select the rows corresponding to the `true` values and the columns 3 to 5:

```julia
julia> arr2d[[true, false, true, true, false], 3:5]
3x3 Array{Float64,2}:
 0.633995  0.868588  0.19461
 0.866489  0.960801  0.476889
 0.206264  0.600758  0.843445
```

In a similar way to indexing into an array, we can also assign values to the selected items:

```julia
julia> arr2d[1, 1] = 0.0
```

```julia
julia> arr2d[[true, false, true, true, false], 3:5] = ones(3, 3)
julia> arr2d
5x5 Array{Float64,2}:
 0.0       0.641646  1.0       1.0        1.0
 0.750895  0.842909  0.818378  0.484694   0.661247
 0.938833  0.193142  1.0       1.0        1.0
 0.195541  0.338319  1.0       1.0        1.0
 0.546298  0.920886  0.720724  0.0529883  0.238986
```

Iteration

The simplest way to iterate over an array is with the `for` construct:

```julia
for element in yourarray
    # do something with element
end
```

Here's an example:

```julia
julia> for person in ["Alison", "James", "Cohen"]
           println("Hello $person")
       end

Hello Alison
Hello James
Hello Cohen
```

If you also need the index while iterating, Julia exposes the `eachindex(yourarray)` iterator:

```julia
julia> people = ["Alison", "James", "Cohen"]
3-element Array{String,1}:
 "Alison"
```

```
    "James"
    "Cohen"

julia> for i in eachindex(people)
           println("$i. $(people[i])")
       end


1. Alison
2. James
3. Cohen
```

Mutating arrays

We can add more elements to the end of a collection by using the push! function:

```
julia> arr = [1, 2, 3]
3-element Array{Int64,1}:
  1
  2
  3


julia> push!(arr, 4)
4-element Array{Int64,1}:
  1
  2
  3
  4

julia> push!(arr, 5, 6, 7)
7-element Array{Int64,1}:
  1
  2
  3
  4
  5
  6
  7
```

Note the ending exclamation mark ! for the push! function. This is a perfectly legal function name in Julia. It is a convention to warn that the function is *mutating*—that is, it will modify the data passed as argument to it, instead of returning a new value.

We can remove elements from the end of an `array` using `pop!`:

```
julia> pop!(arr)
7

julia> arr
6-element Array{Int64,1}:
 1
 2
 3
 4
 5
 6
```

The call to the `pop!` function has removed the last element of `arr` and returned it.

If we want to remove an element other than the last, we can use the `deleteat!` function, indicating the index that we want to be removed:

```
julia> deleteat!(arr, 3)
5-element Array{Int64,1}:
 1
 2
 4
 5
 6
```

Finally, a word of warning when mutating arrays. In Julia, the arrays are passed to functions by reference. This means that the original array is being sent as the argument to the various mutating functions, and not its copy. Beware not to accidentally make unwanted modifications. Similarly, when assigning an array to a variable, a new reference is created, but the data is not copied. So for instance:

```
julia> arr = [1,2,3]
3-element Array{Int64,1}:
 1
 2
 3

julia> arr2 = arr
3-element Array{Int64,1}:
 1
 2
 3
```

Now we pop an element off arr2:

```
julia> pop!(arr2)
3
```

So, arr2 looks like this:

```
julia> arr2
2-element Array{Int64,1}:
  1
  2
```

But our original array was modified, too:

```
julia> arr
2-element Array{Int64,1}:
  1
  2
```

Assigning arr to arr2 does not copy the values of arr into arr2 , it only creates a new binding (a new name) that points to the original arr array. To create a separate array with the same values, we need to use the copy function:

```
julia> arr
2-element Array{Int64,1}:
  1
  2

julia> arr2 = copy(arr)
2-element Array{Int64,1}:
  1
  2
```

Now, if we pop an element off the copied array:

```
julia> pop!(arr2)
2
```

Our original array is untouched:

```
julia> arr
2-element Array{Int64,1}:
  1
  2
```

Only the copy was modified:

```
julia> arr2
1-element Array{Int64,1}:
 1
```

Comprehensions

Array comprehensions provide a very powerful way to construct arrays. It is similar to the previously discussed array literal notation, but instead of passing in the actual values, we use a computation over an iterable object.

An example will make it clear:

```
julia> [x += 1 for x = 1:5]
10-element Array{Int64,1}:
 2
 3
 4
 5
 6
```

This can be read as—*for each element* x *within the range* 1 *to* 5, *compute* x+1 *and put the resultant value in the array.*

Just like with the *plain* array literals, we can constrain the type:

```
julia> Float64[x+=1 for x = 1:5]
5-element Array{Float64,1}:
 2.0
 3.0
 4.0
 5.0
 6.0
```

Similarly, we can create multi-dimensional arrays:

```
julia> [x += y for x = 1:5, y = 11:15]
5x5 Array{Int64,2}:
 12  13  14  15  16
 13  14  15  16  17
 14  15  16  17  18
 15  16  17  18  19
 16  17  18  19  20
```

Comprehensions can be filtered using the `if` keyword:

```julia
julia> [x += 1 for x = 1:10 if x/2 > 3]
4-element Array{Int64,1}:
  8
  9
 10
 11
```

In this case, we only kept the values where `x/2` was greater than `3`.

Generators

But the superpower of the comprehensions is activated when they are used for creating generators. Generators can be iterated to produce values on demand, instead of allocating an array and storing all the values in advance. You'll see what that means in a second.

Generators are defined just like array comprehensions, but without the square brackets:

```julia
julia> (x+=1 for x = 1:10)
Base.Generator{UnitRange{Int64},##41#42}(#41, 1:10)
```

They allow us to work with potentially infinite collections. Check the following example, where we want to print the numbers from one to one million with a cube less than or equal to `1_000`:

```julia
julia> for i in [x^3 for x=1:1_000_000]
           i >= 1_000 && break
           println(i)
       end
1
8
27
64
125
216
343
512
729
```

This computation uses significant resources because the comprehension creates the full array of 1 million items, despite the fact that we only iterate over its first nine elements.

We can see that by benchmarking the code using the handy `@time` construct:

```
@time for i in [x^3 for x=1:1_000_000]
    i >= 1_000 && break
    println(i)
end


0.035739 seconds (58.46 k allocations: 10.493 MiB)
```

Over 10 MB of memory and almost 60,000 allocations. Compare this with using a generator:

```
@time for i in (x^3 for x=1:1_000_000)
    i >= 1_000 && break
    println(i)
end



0.019681 seconds (16.63 k allocations: 898.414 KiB)
```

Less than 1 MB and a quarter of the number of allocations. The difference will be even more dramatic if we increase from 1 million to 1 billion:

```
julia> @time for i in [x^3 for x=1:1_000_000_000]
           i >= 1_000 && break
           println(i)
       end
1
8
27
64
125
216
343
512
729



10.405833 seconds (58.48 k allocations: 7.453 GiB, 3.41% gc time)
```

Over 10 seconds and 7 GB of memory used!

On the other hand, the generator runs practically in constant time:

```
julia> @time for i in (x^3 for x=1:1_000_000_000)
           i >= 1_000 && break
           println(i)
       end
1
```

```
8
27
64
125
216
343
512
729
```

```
    0.020068 seconds (16.63 k allocations: 897.945 KiB
```

Exploratory data analysis with Julia

Now that you have a good understanding of Julia's basics, we can apply this knowledge to our first project. We'll start by applying **exploratory data analysis** (**EDA**) to the Iris flower dataset.

If you already have experience with data analysis, you might've used the Iris dataset before. If so, that's great! You'll be familiar with the data and the way things are done in your (previous) language of choice, and can now focus on the Julia way.

On the contrary, if this is the first time you've heard about the Iris flower dataset, no need to worry. This dataset is considered the `Hello World` of data science—and we'll take a good look at it using Julia's powerful toolbox. Enjoy!

The Iris flower dataset

Also called **Fisher's Iris dataset**, it was first introduced in 1936 by British statistician and biologist Ronald Fisher. The dataset consists of 50 samples from each of three species of Iris flower (Iris setosa, Iris virginica, and Iris versicolor). It is sometimes called **Anderson's Iris dataset** because Edgar Anderson collected the data. Four features were measured—the length and the width of the sepals and petals (in centimeters).

Using the RDatasets package

Finding good-quality data for learning, teaching, and statistical software development can be challenging. That's why the industry practically standardized the use of over 10,00 high-quality datasets. These were originally distributed with the statistical software environment R. Hence, they've been aptly named the `RDatasets`.

The Iris flower dataset is part of this collection. There are many ways to download it, but the most convenient is through the RDatasets package. This package provides an easy way for Julia users to experiment with most of the standard datasets available in R or included with R's most popular packages. Sounds great; let's add it.

First, switch to package management mode:

```
julia> ]
pkg> add RDatasets
```

Once the package is added, let's tell Julia that we want to use it:

```
julia> using RDatasets
```

We can peek at the included datasets by calling RDatasets.datasets(). It returns a list of all the 700+ datasets available with RDatasets. It includes details about the data package, the name of the dataset, its title (or info), number of rows, and number of columns. These are the first 20 rows:

```
julia> RDatasets.datasets()
```

The output is as follows:

Row	Package	Dataset	Title	Rows	Columns
1	COUNT	affairs	affairs	601	18
2	COUNT	azdrg112	azdrg112	1798	4
3	COUNT	azpro	azpro	3589	6
4	COUNT	badhealth	badhealth	1127	3
5	COUNT	fasttrakg	fasttrakg	15	9
6	COUNT	lbw	lbw	189	10
7	COUNT	lbwgrp	lbwgrp	6	7
8	COUNT	loomis	loomis	410	11
9	COUNT	mdvis	mdvis	2227	13
10	COUNT	medpar	medpar	1495	10
11	COUNT	rwm	rwm	27326	4
12	COUNT	rwm5yr	rwm5yr	19609	17
13	COUNT	ships	ships	40	7
14	COUNT	titanic	titanic	1316	4
15	COUNT	titanicgrp	titanicgrp	12	5
16	Ecdat	Accident	Ship Accidents	40	5
17	Ecdat	Airline	Cost for U.S. Airlines	90	6
18	Ecdat	Airq	Air Quality for Californian Metropolitan Areas	30	6
19	Ecdat	Benefits	Unemployement of Blue Collar Workers	4877	18
20	Ecdat	Bids	Bids Received By U.S. Firms	126	12

You can see that the datasets are part of a Package—we can use that to filter by it. The Iris flower dataset is part of the *datasets* package.

All we have to do now is load the data:

```julia
julia> iris = dataset("datasets", "iris")
```

The output is as follows:

```
150×5 DataFrame
 Row   SepalLength   SepalWidth   PetalLength   PetalWidth   Species

  1    5.1           3.5          1.4           0.2          setosa
  2    4.9           3.0          1.4           0.2          setosa
  3    4.7           3.2          1.3           0.2          setosa
  4    4.6           3.1          1.5           0.2          setosa
  5    5.0           3.6          1.4           0.2          setosa
  6    5.4           3.9          1.7           0.4          setosa
  7    4.6           3.4          1.4           0.3          setosa
  8    5.0           3.4          1.5           0.2          setosa
  9    4.4           2.9          1.4           0.2          setosa
 10    4.9           3.1          1.5           0.1          setosa
```

The returned value is a `DataFrame` object with 150 rows and five columns—SepalLength, SepalWidth, PetalLength, PetalWidth, and Species, plus an automatically added id column called Row.

Dataframes are the *de facto* standard for working with tabular data in Julia. They are a key part of Julia's data analysis toolset and we'll discuss them in detail in the next chapters. For now, it suffices to say that, as you can see in the previous examples, it represents a data structure that looks very much like a table or a spreadsheet.

You can programmatically retrieve the names of the columns using the following:

```julia
julia> names(iris)
5-element Array{Symbol,1}:
 :SepalLength
 :SepalWidth
 :PetalLength
 :PetalWidth
 :Species
```

To check the size, use the following:

```julia
julia> size(iris)
(150, 5)
```

The result is a tuple that matches the number of rows and columns—(rows, cols). Yep, as already established, 150 rows over 5 columns.

Let's take a look at the data:

```julia
julia> head(iris)
```

The output is as follows:

```
6×5 DataFrame
 Row │ SepalLength │ SepalWidth │ PetalLength │ PetalWidth │ Species
─────┼────────────┼────────────┼─────────────┼────────────┼─────────
 1   │ 5.1        │ 3.5        │ 1.4         │ 0.2        │ setosa
 2   │ 4.9        │ 3.0        │ 1.4         │ 0.2        │ setosa
 3   │ 4.7        │ 3.2        │ 1.3         │ 0.2        │ setosa
 4   │ 4.6        │ 3.1        │ 1.5         │ 0.2        │ setosa
 5   │ 5.0        │ 3.6        │ 1.4         │ 0.2        │ setosa
 6   │ 5.4        │ 3.9        │ 1.7         │ 0.4        │ setosa
```

The head function shows the top six rows. Optionally, it takes a second parameter to indicate the number of rows: head(iris, 10). There's also its twin, tail(), which will display the bottom rows of the DataFrame:

```julia
julia> tail(iris, 10)
```

The output is as follows:

```
10×5 DataFrame
 Row │ SepalLength │ SepalWidth │ PetalLength │ PetalWidth │ Species
─────┼────────────┼────────────┼─────────────┼────────────┼──────────
 1   │ 6.7        │ 3.1        │ 5.6         │ 2.4        │ virginica
 2   │ 6.9        │ 3.1        │ 5.1         │ 2.3        │ virginica
 3   │ 5.8        │ 2.7        │ 5.1         │ 1.9        │ virginica
 4   │ 6.8        │ 3.2        │ 5.9         │ 2.3        │ virginica
 5   │ 6.7        │ 3.3        │ 5.7         │ 2.5        │ virginica
 6   │ 6.7        │ 3.0        │ 5.2         │ 2.3        │ virginica
 7   │ 6.3        │ 2.5        │ 5.0         │ 1.9        │ virginica
 8   │ 6.5        │ 3.0        │ 5.2         │ 2.0        │ virginica
 9   │ 6.2        │ 3.4        │ 5.4         │ 2.3        │ virginica
 10  │ 5.9        │ 3.0        │ 5.1         │ 1.8        │ virginica
```

In regard to the species present in the dataset, we see *setosa* in the head rows and *virginica* at the bottom. We should have three species, though, according to the description of the data. Let's ask for a row count grouped by Species:

```julia
julia> by(iris, :Species, nrow)
```

The output is as follows:

```
3×2 DataFrame
 Row │ Species    │ x1
─────┼────────────┼────
  1  │ setosa     │ 50
  2  │ versicolor │ 50
  3  │ virginica  │ 50
```

The `by` function takes three parameters—the dataset, the name of the column, and a grouping function—in this case, `nrow`, which computes the number of rows. We can see that the third species is *versicolor*, and for each of the species we have `50` records.

 I'm sure you're wondering why, in the preceding example, the name of the column is prefixed by a colon `":"`. It is a `Symbol`. We'll discuss more about symbols when we learn about metaprogramming. For now, you can just think of symbols as identifiers or labels.

Using simple statistics to better understand our data

Now that it's clear how the data is structured and what is contained in the collection, we can get a better understanding by looking at some basic stats.

To get us started, let's invoke the `describe` function:

```julia
julia> describe(iris)
```

The output is as follows:

```
5×8 DataFrame
 Row │ variable     mean      min      median   max        nunique   nmissing   eltype
─────┼───────────────────────────────────────────────────────────────────────────────────────────
  1  │ SepalLength  5.84333   4.3      5.8      7.9                              Float64
  2  │ SepalWidth   3.05733   2.0      3.0      4.4                              Float64
  3  │ PetalLength  3.758     1.0      4.35     6.9                              Float64
  4  │ PetalWidth   1.19933   0.1      1.3      2.5                              Float64
  5  │ Species                setosa            virginica  3                     CategoricalString{UInt8}
```

This function summarizes the columns of the `iris` `DataFrame`. If the columns contain numerical data (such as `SepalLength`), it will compute the minimum, median, mean, and maximum. The number of missing and unique values is also included. The last column reports the type of data stored in the row.

A few other stats are available, including the 25th and the 75th percentile, and the first and the last values. We can ask for them by passing an extra `stats` argument, in the form of an array of symbols:

```julia
julia> describe(iris, stats=[:q25, :q75, :first, :last])
```

The output is as follows:

```
5×5 DataFrame
 Row │ variable      q25   q75   first    last
─────┼───────────────────────────────────────────
  1  │ SepalLength   5.1   6.4   5.1      5.9
  2  │ SepalWidth    2.8   3.3   3.5      3.0
  3  │ PetalLength   1.6   5.1   1.4      5.1
  4  │ PetalWidth    0.3   1.8   0.2      1.8
  5  │ Species                   setosa   virginica
```

Any combination of stats labels is accepted. These are all the options—`:mean`, `:std`, `:min`, `:q25`, `:median`, `:q75`, `:max`, `:eltype`, `:nunique`, `:first`, `:last`, and `:nmissing`.

In order to get all the stats, the special `:all` value is accepted:

```julia
julia> describe(iris, stats=:all)
```

The output is as follows:

```
5×13 DataFrame
 Row │ variable      mean      std        min      q25   median   q75   max        nunique   nmissing   first    last       eltype
─────┼────────────────────────────────────────────────────────────────────────────────────────────────────────────────────────────────────
  1  │ SepalLength   5.84333   0.828066   4.3      5.1   5.8      6.4   7.9                              5.1      5.9        Float64
  2  │ SepalWidth    3.05733   0.435866   2.0      2.8   3.0      3.3   4.4                              3.5      3.0        Float64
  3  │ PetalLength   3.758     1.7653     1.0      1.6   4.35     5.1   6.9                              1.4      5.1        Float64
  4  │ PetalWidth    1.19933   0.762238   0.1      0.3   1.3      1.8   2.5                              0.2      1.8        Float64
  5  │ Species                            setosa                       virginica   3                    setosa   virginica  CategoricalString{UInt8}
```

We can also compute these individually by using Julia's `Statistics` package. For example, to calculate the mean of the `SepalLength` column, we'll execute the following:

```julia
julia> using Statistics
julia> mean(iris[:SepalLength])
5.843333333333334
```

In this example, we use `iris[:SepalLength]` to select the whole column. The result, not at all surprisingly, is the same as that returned by the corresponding `describe()` value.

In a similar way we can compute the `median()`:

```julia
julia> median(iris[:SepalLength])
5.8
```

And there's (a lot) more, such as, for instance, the standard deviation `std()`:

```julia
julia> std(iris[:SepalLength])
0.828066127977863
```

Or, we can use another function from the `Statistics` package, `cor()`, in a simple script to help us understand how the values are correlated:

```julia
julia> for x in names(iris)[1:end-1]
          for y in names(iris)[1:end-1]
            println("$x \t $y \t $(cor(iris[x], iris[y]))")
          end
          println("-------------------------------------------")
       end
```

Executing this snippet will produce the following output:

```
SepalLength     SepalLength     1.0
SepalLength     SepalWidth      -0.11756978413300191
SepalLength     PetalLength     0.8717537758865831
SepalLength     PetalWidth      0.8179411262715759
-------------------------------------------------------
SepalWidth      SepalLength     -0.11756978413300191
SepalWidth      SepalWidth      1.0
SepalWidth      PetalLength     -0.42844010433053953
SepalWidth      PetalWidth      -0.3661259325364388
-------------------------------------------------------
PetalLength     SepalLength     0.8717537758865831
PetalLength     SepalWidth      -0.42844010433053953
PetalLength     PetalLength     1.0
PetalLength     PetalWidth      0.9628654314027963
-------------------------------------------------------
PetalWidth      SepalLength     0.8179411262715759
PetalWidth      SepalWidth      -0.3661259325364388
PetalWidth      PetalLength     0.9628654314027963
PetalWidth      PetalWidth      1.0
-------------------------------------------------------
```

The script iterates over each column of the dataset with the exception of `Species` (the last column, which is not numeric), and generates a basic correlation table. The table shows strong positive correlations between `SepalLength` and `PetalLength` (87.17%), `SepalLength` and `PetalWidth` (81.79%), and `PetalLength` and `PetalWidth` (96.28%). There is no strong correlation between `SepalLength` and `SepalWidth`.

We can use the same script, but this time employ the `cov()` function to compute the covariance of the values in the dataset:

```
julia> for x in names(iris)[1:end-1]
         for y in names(iris)[1:end-1]
           println("$x \t $y \t $(cov(iris[x], iris[y]))")
         end
         println("--------------------------------------------")
       end
```

This code will generate the following output:

```
SepalLength    SepalLength    0.6856935123042507
SepalLength    SepalWidth     -0.04243400447427293
SepalLength    PetalLength    1.2743154362416105
SepalLength    PetalWidth     0.5162706935123043
-------------------------------------------------
SepalWidth     SepalLength    -0.04243400447427293
SepalWidth     SepalWidth     0.189979418344519
SepalWidth     PetalLength    -0.3296563758389262
SepalWidth     PetalWidth     -0.12163937360178968
-------------------------------------------------
PetalLength    SepalLength    1.2743154362416105
PetalLength    SepalWidth     -0.3296563758389262
PetalLength    PetalLength    3.1162778523489933
PetalLength    PetalWidth     1.2956093959731543
-------------------------------------------------
PetalWidth     SepalLength    0.5162706935123043
PetalWidth     SepalWidth     -0.12163937360178968
PetalWidth     PetalLength    1.2956093959731543
PetalWidth     PetalWidth     0.5810062639821031
-------------------------------------------------
```

The output illustrates that `SepalLength` is positively related to `PetalLength` and `PetalWidth`, while being negatively related to `SepalWidth`. `SepalWidth` is negatively related to all the other values.

Moving on, if we want a random data sample, we can ask for it like this:

```
julia> rand(iris[:SepalLength])
7.4
```

Optionally, we can pass in the number of values to be sampled:

```
julia> rand(iris[:SepalLength], 5)
5-element Array{Float64,1}:
 6.9
 5.8
 6.7
 5.0
 5.6
```

We can convert one of the columns to an array using the following:

```
julia> sepallength = Array(iris[:SepalLength])
150-element Array{Float64,1}:
 5.1
 4.9
 4.7
 4.6
 5.0
# ... output truncated ...
```

Or we can convert the whole DataFrame to a matrix:

```
julia> irisarr = convert(Array, iris[:,:])
150×5 Array{Any,2}:
 5.1  3.5  1.4  0.2  CategoricalString{UInt8} "setosa"
 4.9  3.0  1.4  0.2  CategoricalString{UInt8} "setosa"
 4.7  3.2  1.3  0.2  CategoricalString{UInt8} "setosa"
 4.6  3.1  1.5  0.2  CategoricalString{UInt8} "setosa"
 5.0  3.6  1.4  0.2  CategoricalString{UInt8} "setosa"
# ... output truncated ...
```

Visualizing the Iris flowers data

Visualization is a powerful tool in exploratory data analysis, helping us to identify patterns that would otherwise be hard to spot just by looking at the numbers. Julia provides access to some excellent plotting packages that are very easy to set up and use.

We'll illustrate with some plots created with Gadfly.

We'll start by adding Gadfly with pkg> add "Gadfly"and we'll continue with julia> using Gadfly. This will bring into scope Gadfly's plot()method. Now, let's find some interesting data to visualize.

In the previous section, we have identified that there is a strong covariant relation between `SepalLength` and `PetalLength`. Let's plot the data:

```julia
julia> plot(iris, x=:SepalLength, y=:PetalLength, color=:Species)
```

 At the time of writing, Gadfly support for Julia v1 was still incomplete. If that is still the case, the unstable yet working version of Gadfly can be installed using—`pkg> add Compose#master, Gadfly#master, Hexagon`.

Executing the `plot()` function will generate the following graph:

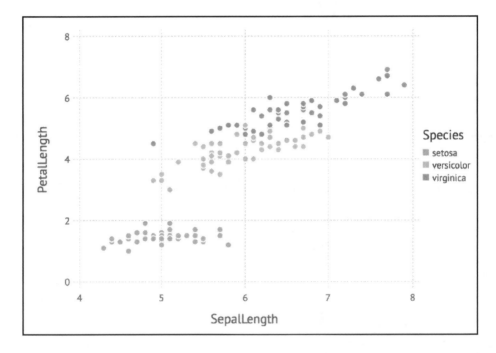

Sure enough, the plot will indicate that `SepalLength` and `PetalLength` vary together for both Iris versicolor and Iris virginica. For Iris setosa, it's not that obvious, with `PetalLength` staying pretty much unchanged while the sepal length grows.

A box plot will confirm the same; the sepal length of Iris setosa has little variation:

```
julia> plot(iris, x=:Species, y=:PetalLength, Geom.boxplot)
```

Plotting our values looks like this:

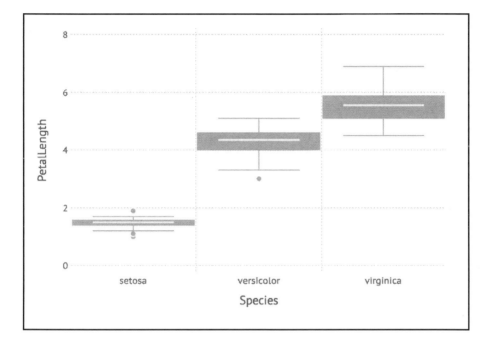

I have a feeling that a histogram would be even better for illustrating the distribution of the `PetalLength`:

```julia
julia> plot(iris, x=:PetalLength, color=:Species, Geom.histogram)
```

Generating a histogram using the `PetalLength` produces the following:

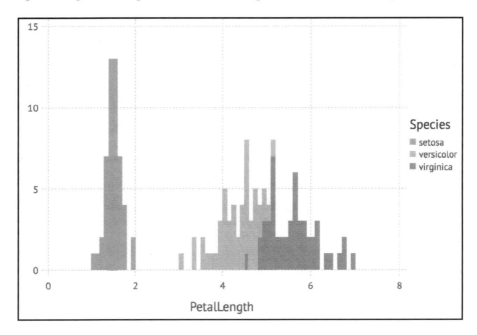

If we visualize the `PetalWidth` values as a histogram, we'll notice a similar pattern:

```julia
julia> plot(iris, x=:PetalWidth, color=:Species, Geom.histogram)
```

The output is as follows:

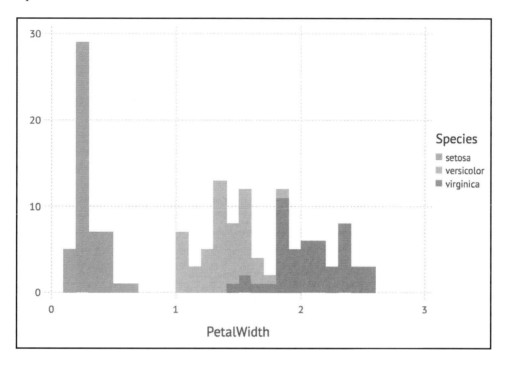

Plotting the petal width and height for the three species should now provide a strong indication that, for example, we can successfully classify Iris setosa based on the two values:

```
julia> plot(iris, x=:PetalWidth, y=:PetalLength, color=:Species)
```

The output is as follows:

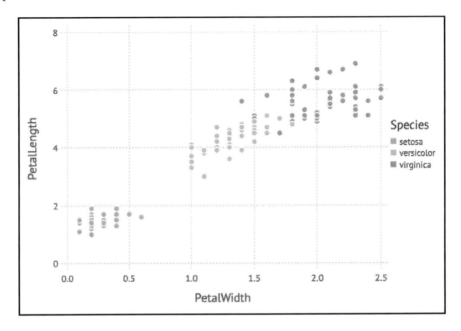

Loading and saving our data

Julia comes with excellent facilities for reading and storing data out of the box. Given its focus on data science and scientific computing, support for tabular-file formats (CSV, TSV) is first class.

Let's extract some data from our initial dataset and use it to practice persistence and retrieval from various backends.

We can reference a section of a DataFrame by defining its bounds through the corresponding columns and rows. For example, we can define a new DataFrame composed only of the PetalLength and PetalWidth columns and the first three rows:

```
julia> iris[1:3, [:PetalLength, :PetalWidth]]
3×2 DataFrames.DataFrame
| Row | PetalLength | PetalWidth |
|-----+-------------+------------|
|  1  |    1.4      |    0.2     |
|  2  |    1.4      |    0.2     |
|  3  |    1.3      |    0.2     |
```

The generic indexing notation is `dataframe[rows, cols]`, where `rows` can be a number, a range, or an `Array` of `boolean` values where `true` indicates that the row should be included:

```
julia> iris[trues(150), [:PetalLength, :PetalWidth]]
```

This snippet will select all the `150` rows since `trues(150)` constructs an `array` of `150` elements that are all initialized as `true`. The same logic applies to `cols`, with the added benefit that they can also be accessed by name.

Armed with this knowledge, let's take a sample from our original dataset. It will include some 10% of the initial data and only the `PetalLength`, `PetalWidth`, and `Species` columns:

```
julia> test_data = iris[rand(150) .<= 0.1, [:PetalLength, :PetalWidth,
:Species]]
10x3 DataFrames.DataFrame
```

Row	PetalLength	PetalWidth	Species
1	1.1	0.1	"setosa"
2	1.9	0.4	"setosa"
3	4.6	1.3	"versicolor"
4	5.0	1.7	"versicolor"
5	3.7	1.0	"versicolor"
6	4.7	1.5	"versicolor"
7	4.6	1.4	"versicolor"
8	6.1	2.5	"virginica"
9	6.9	2.3	"virginica"
10	6.7	2.0	"virginica"

What just happened here? The secret in this piece of code is `rand(150) .<= 0.1`. It does a lot—first, it generates an array of random `Float` values between 0 and 1; then, it compares the array, element-wise, against 0.1 (which represents 10% of 1); and finally, the resultant `Boolean` array is used to filter out the corresponding rows from the dataset. It's really impressive how powerful and succinct Julia can be!

In my case, the result is a `DataFrame` with the preceding 10 rows, but your data will be different since we're picking random rows (and it's quite possible you won't have exactly 10 rows either).

Saving and loading using tabular file formats

We can easily save this data to a file in a tabular file format (one of CSV, TSV, and others) using the CSV package. We'll have to add it first and then call the write method:

```
pkg> add CSV
julia> using CSV
julia> CSV.write("test_data.csv", test_data)
```

And, just as easily, we can read back the data from tabular file formats, with the corresponding CSV.read function:

```
julia> td = CSV.read("test_data.csv")
10×3 DataFrames.DataFrame
 | Row | PetalLength | PetalWidth | Species      |
 |-----+-------------+------------+--------------+
 |-----|
 | 1   | 1.1         | 0.1        | "setosa"     |
 | 2   | 1.9         | 0.4        | "setosa"     |
 | 3   | 4.6         | 1.3        | "versicolor" |
 | 4   | 5.0         | 1.7        | "versicolor" |
 | 5   | 3.7         | 1.0        | "versicolor" |
 | 6   | 4.7         | 1.5        | "versicolor" |
 | 7   | 4.6         | 1.4        | "versicolor" |
 | 8   | 6.1         | 2.5        | "virginica"  |
 | 9   | 6.9         | 2.3        | "virginica"  |
 | 10  | 6.7         | 2.0        | "virginica"  |
```

Just specifying the file extension is enough for Julia to understand how to handle the document (CSV, TSV), both when writing and reading.

Working with Feather files

Feather is a binary file format that was specially designed for storing data frames. It is fast, lightweight, and language-agnostic. The project was initially started in order to make it possible to exchange data frames between R and Python. Soon, other languages added support for it, including Julia.

Support for Feather files does not come out of the box, but is made available through the homonymous package. Let's go ahead and add it and then bring it into scope:

```
pkg> add Feather
julia> using Feather
```

Now, saving our `DataFrame` is just a matter of calling `Feather.write`:

```julia
julia> Feather.write("test_data.feather", test_data)
```

Next, let's try the reverse operation and load back our Feather file. We'll use the counterpart `read` function:

```julia
julia> Feather.read("test_data.feather")
10×3 DataFrames.DataFrame
| Row | PetalLength | PetalWidth | Species      |
|-----|-------------|------------|--------------|
| 1   | 1.1         | 0.1        | "setosa"     |
| 2   | 1.9         | 0.4        | "setosa"     |
| 3   | 4.6         | 1.3        | "versicolor" |
| 4   | 5.0         | 1.7        | "versicolor" |
| 5   | 3.7         | 1.0        | "versicolor" |
| 6   | 4.7         | 1.5        | "versicolor" |
| 7   | 4.6         | 1.4        | "versicolor" |
| 8   | 6.1         | 2.5        | "virginica"  |
| 9   | 6.9         | 2.3        | "virginica"  |
| 10  | 6.7         | 2.0        | "virginica"  |
```

Yeah, that's our sample data all right!

In order to provide compatibility with other languages, the Feather format imposes some restrictions on the data types of the columns. You can read more about Feather in the package's official documentation at `https://juliadata.github.io/Feather.jl/latest/index.html`.

Saving and loading with MongoDB

Before closing this chapter, let's take a look at using a NoSQL backend for persisting and retrieving our data. Don't worry, we'll extensively cover interaction with relational databases in the upcoming chapters too.

In order to follow through this chapter, you'll need a working MongoDB installation. You can download and install the correct version for your operating system from the official website, at `https://www.mongodb.com/download-center?jmp=nav#community`. I will use a Docker image which I installed and started up through Docker's Kitematic (available for download at `https://github.com/docker/kitematic/releases`).

Next, we need to make sure to add the `Mongo` package. The package also has a dependency on `LibBSON`, which is automatically added. `LibBSON` is used for handling `BSON`, which stands for *Binary JSON*, a binary-encoded serialization of JSON-like documents. While we're at it, let's add the `JSON` package as well; we will need it. I'm sure you know how to do that by now—if not, here is a reminder:

```
pkg> add Mongo, JSON
```

 At the time of writing, Mongo.jl support for Julia v1 was still a work in progress. This code was tested using Julia v0.6.

Easy! Let's let Julia know that we'll be using all these packages:

```
julia> using Mongo, LibBSON, JSON
```

We're now ready to connect to MongoDB:

```
julia> client = MongoClient()
```

Once successfully connected, we can reference a `dataframes` collection in the `db` database:

```
julia> storage = MongoCollection(client, "db", "dataframes")
```

Julia's MongoDB interface uses dictionaries (a data structure called `Dict` in Julia) to communicate with the server. We'll look at `dicts` in more detail in the next chapter. For now, all we need to do is to convert our `DataFrame` to such a `Dict`. The simplest way to do it is to sequentially serialize and then deserialize the `DataFrame` by using the `JSON` package. It generates a nice structure that we can later use to rebuild our `DataFrame`:

```
julia> datadict = JSON.parse(JSON.json(test_data))
```

Thinking ahead, to make any future data retrieval simpler, let's add an identifier to our dictionary:

```
julia> datadict["id"] = "iris_test_data"
```

Now we can insert it into Mongo:

```
julia> insert(storage, datadict)
```

In order to retrieve it, all we have to do is query the Mongo database using the "id" field we've previously configured:

```
Julia> data_from_mongo = first(find(storage, query("id" =>
"iris_test_data")))
```

We get a BSONObject, which we need to convert back to a DataFrame. Don't worry, it's straightforward. First, we create an empty DataFrame:

```
julia> df_from_mongo = DataFrame()
0×0 DataFrames.DataFrame
```

Then we populate it using the data we retrieved from Mongo:

```
for i in 1:length(data_from_mongo["columns"])
  df_from_mongo[Symbol(data_from_mongo["colindex"]["names"][i])] =
Array(data_from_mongo["columns"][i])
end
julia> df_from_mongo
10×3 DataFrames.DataFrame
| Row | PetalLength | PetalWidth | Species      |
|     |             |            |              |
| 1   | 1.1         | 0.1        | "setosa"     |
| 2   | 1.9         | 0.4        | "setosa"     |
| 3   | 4.6         | 1.3        | "versicolor" |
| 4   | 5.0         | 1.7        | "versicolor" |
| 5   | 3.7         | 1.0        | "versicolor" |
| 6   | 4.7         | 1.5        | "versicolor" |
| 7   | 4.6         | 1.4        | "versicolor" |
| 8   | 6.1         | 2.5        | "virginica"  |
| 9   | 6.9         | 2.3        | "virginica"  |
| 10  | 6.7         | 2.0        | "virginica"  |
```

And that's it! Our data has been loaded back into a DataFrame.

Summary

Julia's intuitive syntax makes for a lean learning curve. The optional typing and the wealth of shorthand constructors result in readable, noise-free code, while the large collection of third-party packages makes accessing, manipulating, visualizing, plotting, and saving data a breeze.

Just by learning Julia's basic data structures and a few related functions, coupled with its powerful data manipulation toolset, we were able to implement an efficient data analysis workflow and extract valuable insight from the Iris flowers dataset. That was all we needed in order to perform efficient exploratory data analysis with Julia.

In the next chapter, we'll continue our journey by learning how to build a web crawler. Web mining, the process of extracting information from the web, is an important part of data mining and a key component of data acquisition in general. Julia is a great choice when building web mining software, given not only its built-in performance and its rapid prototyping features, but also the availability of powerful libraries that cover everything, from HTTP clients, to DOM parsing, to text analysis.

Setting Up the Wiki Game

3

I hope you're excited about Julia by now. The friendly, expressive, and intuitive syntax, the powerful **read-eval-print loop** (**REPL**), the great performance, and the richness of both built-in and third-party libraries are a game-changing combination for data science in particular—and programming in general. The fact that in just two introductory chapters we were able to grasp the basics of the language and configure a data science setup powerful enough to analyze the Iris dataset is quite amazing—congratulations, we've done a great job!

But we are literally just starting. The foundation we've laid is now strong enough to allow us to develop pretty much any kind of program using Julia. Hard to believe? Well, here's the proof—in the next three chapters, we'll develop a web-based game with Julia!

It will follow the narrative of the internet-famous *Six Degrees of Wikipedia*. If you've never heard of it, the idea is that any two articles on Wikipedia can be connected, using only the links on the pages, in six clicks or fewer. It is also called **six degrees of separation**.

In case you're wondering what this has to do with Julia, it is a playful excuse to learn about data mining and web scraping and to learn more about the language and apply our newly acquired knowledge to build a web app.

In this chapter, we will lay the foundations of the web scraper. We'll take a look at how requests are made over the web in a client-server architecture and how to use the `HTTP` package to fetch web pages. We'll learn about HTML documents, HTML and CSS selectors, and `Gumbo`, a HTML parser for Julia. In the process, we'll experiment with more code in the REPL and we'll learn about other key features of the language, such as dictionaries, error handling, functions, and conditional statements. We'll also get to set up our first Julia project.

The topics we will cover in this chapter include the following:

- What web scraping is and how it is used for data harvesting
- How to use Julia to make requests and fetch web pages
- Understanding the `Pair` type
- Learning about the dictionary, one of Julia's more versatile data structures
- Exception handling, to help us capture errors in our code
- Functions, the basic building blocks and one of the most important code units in Julia—we'll learn how to define and use them to create reusable, modular code
- A handful of useful Julia tricks, such as the pipe operator and short-circuit evaluation
- Setting up a Julia project using `Pkg`

Technical requirements

The Julia package ecosystem is under continuous development and new package versions are released on a daily basis. Most of the times this is great news, as new releases bring new features and bug fixes. However, since many of the packages are still in beta (version 0.x), any new release can introduce breaking changes. As a result, the code presented in the book can stop working. In order to ensure that your code will produce the same results as described in the book, it is recommended to use the same package versions. Here are the external packages used in this chapter and their specific versions:

```
Gumbo@v0.5.1
HTTP@v0.7.1
IJulia@v1.14.1
OrderedCollections@v1.0.2
```

In order to install a specific version of a package you need to run:

```
pkg> add PackageName@vX.Y.Z
```

For example:

```
pkg> add IJulia@v1.14.1
```

Alternatively you can install all the used packages by downloading the `Project.toml` file provided with the chapter and using `pkg>` instantiate as follows:

```
julia>
download("https://raw.githubusercontent.com/PacktPublishing/Julia-Programmi
ng-Projects/master/Chapter03/Project.toml", "Project.toml")
pkg> activate .
pkg> instantiate
```

Data harvesting through web scraping

The technique for extracting data from web pages using software is called **web scraping**. It is an important component of data harvesting, typically implemented through programs called **web crawlers**. Data harvesting or data mining is a useful technique, often used in data science workflows to collect information from the internet, usually from websites (as opposed to APIs), and then to process that data for different purposes using various algorithms.

At a very high level, the process involves making a request for a web page, fetching its content, parsing its structure, and then extracting the desired information. This can be images, paragraphs of text, or tabular data containing stock information and prices, for example—pretty much anything that is present on a web page. If the content is spread across multiple web pages, the crawler will also extract the links and will automatically follow them to pull the rest of the pages, repeatedly applying the same crawling process.

The most common use of web scrapers is for web indexing, as done by search engines such as Google or Bing. Online price monitoring and price comparison, personal data mining (or contact scraping), and online reputation systems, as well as product review platforms, represent other common use cases for web scrapers.

How the web works – a crash course

The internet has become an integral part of our lives over the last decade. Most of us use it extensively to access a wealth of information, day in and day out. Googling things like rambunctious (noisy and lacking in restraint or discipline), catching up with friends on social networks, checking out the latest gourmet restaurants on Instagram, watching a blockbuster on Netflix, or reading the Wikipedia entry about Attitogon (a place in Togo where they practice voodoo)—they're all just a click away. All these, although different in nature, function in pretty much the same way.

An internet-connected device, be it a computer using Wi-Fi or a smartphone connected to a mobile data network, together with an app for accessing the web (generally a web browser such as Chrome or Firefox, but also a dedicated one such as Facebook or Netflix's mobile apps), represent *the client*. At the other end we have *the server*—a computer that stores the information, be it in the form of web pages, videos, or entire web apps.

When a client wants to access the information available on the server, it initiates a *request*. If the server determines that the client has the permission to access the resource, a copy of the information is downloaded from the server onto the client, to be displayed.

Making HTTP requests

The **Hypertext Transfer Protocol (HTTP)** is a communication protocol for transmitting documents over a network. It was designed for communication between web browsers and web servers. HTTP implements the standard client-server model, where a client opens a connection and makes a request, then waits for a response.

Learning about HTTP methods

HTTP defines a set of request methods to indicate the action to be performed for a given resource. The most common method is GET, which is meant to retrieve data from the server. It is used when navigating the internet using links. The POST method requests the server to accept an enclosed data payload, most commonly the result of submitting a web form. There are a few more methods, including HEAD, PUT, DELETE, PATCH, and others—but they are less used and less supported by clients and web servers. As we won't need them for our web crawler, they won't be covered.

 If you're interested, you can read about them at
https://developer.mozilla.org/en-US/docs/Web/HTTP/Methods.

Understanding HTTPS

HTTP Secure (HTTPS) is basically HTTP over an encrypted connection. It started as an alternative protocol used primarily for processing payments over the web and transferring sensitive corporate information. But in recent years, it has begun to see widespread usage, with a push from major companies to replace plain HTTP connections on the internet. For the purpose of our discussion, HTTP and HTTPS can be used interchangeably.

Understanding HTML documents

In order to extract data from the fetched web pages, we need to isolate and manipulate the structural elements that contain the desired information. That's why a basic understanding of the generic structure of the web pages is helpful when performing web scraping. If you've done web scraping before, maybe using a different programming language, or if you just know enough about HTML documents, feel free to skip this section. On the other hand, if you're new to this or just need a quick refresher, please read on.

Hypertext Markup Language (**HTML**) is the gold standard for creating web pages and web applications. HTML goes hand in hand with HTTP, the protocol for transmitting HTML documents over the internet.

The building blocks of HTML pages are the *HTML elements*. They provide both the content and the structure of a web page. They can be nested to define complex relationships with each other (such as parents, children, siblings, ancestors, and so on). HTML elements are denoted by *tags*, written between angle brackets (`<tag>...</tag>`). The official W3C specification defines a wealth of such tags, representing everything from headings and paragraphs, to lists, forms, links, images, quotes, and much more.

To give you an idea, here's how the main heading is represented in HTML on Julia's Wikipedia page at `https://en.wikipedia.org/wiki/Julia_(programming_language)`:

```
<h1>Julia (programming language)</h1>
```

This HTML code renders in a modern browser, like this:

Julia (programming language)

A more elaborate example can present a nested structure such as the following:

```
<div>
    <h2>Language features</h2>
    <p>According to the official website, the main features of the language
are:</p>
    <ul>
        <li>Multiple dispatch</li>
        <li>Dynamic type sytem</li>
        <li>Good performance</li>
    </ul>
</div>
```

The snippet renders a secondary heading (`<h2>`), a paragraph of text (`<p>`), and an unordered list (`<ul>`), with three list items (`<li>`), all within a page section (`<div>`):

> ## Language features
>
> According to the official website, the main features of the language are:
>
> - Multiple dispatch
> - Dynamic type
> - Good performance

HTML selectors

HTML's purpose is to provide content and structure. That's all we need in order to convey any kind of information, no matter how complex. However, as computers and web browsers became more powerful and the use of web pages more widespread, users and developers wanted more. They asked for ways to extend HTML to also include beautiful formatting (design) and rich behavior (interactivity).

That is why **Cascading Style Sheets** (**CSS**) was created—a style language that defines the design of HTML documents. Additionally, JavaScript emerged as the programming language of choice for the client side, adding interactivity to web pages.

The style rules and the interactive features provided by CSS and JavaScript are associated with well-defined HTML elements. That is, styling and interactivity have to explicitly target elements from the associated HTML document. For example, a CSS rule can target the main heading of the page—or a JavaScript validation rule can target text input in the login form. If you think of a web page as a structured collection of HTML elements, this targeting is achieved by *selecting* (sub-collections of) elements.

Selecting elements can be done, in its simplest form, by identifying the HTML tags by type and structure (hierarchy). In the previous example, where we looked at representing a list of Julia's features, we can select all the list items (the `<li>` elements) by indicating a hierarchy like `div > ul > li`, representing all the `li` items, nested within a `ul` element, nested within a `div`. These are called **HTML selectors**.

However, this approach has limitations. On the one hand, when dealing with large, complex, and deeply nested HTML documents, we have to handle equally complex hierarchies, a tedious and error-prone task. On the other hand, such an approach might not provide enough specificity to allow us to select the element we want to target. For example, on the same Julia Wikipedia page, how would we differentiate the list of features from the list of external links? They both have similar structures.

The list of **External links** on Julia's Wikipedia page looks like this:

External links [edit]

- Official website &
- The Julia manual &
- Julia Package Listing & – a searchable listing of all (currently over 1500 with combined over 30,000 & GitHub stars) *registered* packages

---

The **Language features** section has a similar structure:

Language features [edit]

According to the official website, the main features of the language are:

- Multiple dispatch: providing ability to define function behavior across many combinations of argument types
- Dynamic type system: types for documentation, optimization, and dispatch
- Good performance, approaching that of statically-typed languages like C

The fact that the two HTML elements are structurally identical makes it difficult to select the list items for the language features alone.

Learning about the HTML attributes

This is where HTML attributes come into play. These are key-value pairs that enhance HTML tags, providing extra information. For example, in order to define a link, we're going to use the `<a>` tag—`<a>This is a link</a>`.

But clearly, this is not enough. If this is a link, what does it link to? As developers, we need to provide extra information about the linked location. This is done by adding the `href` attribute with its corresponding value:

```
<a href="https://julialang.org/">This is a link to Julia's home page</a>
```

Ah yes, now we're talking! A super handy link to Julia's home page.

In general, all the attributes can be used when selecting HTML elements. But not all of them are equally useful. The most important one is arguably the `id` attribute. It allows us to assign a unique identifier to an element and then reference it in a very efficient way. Another important attribute is the `class`, extensively used for CSS styling rules.

This is what our previous example would look like with extra attributes:

```
<a href="https://julialang.org/" id="julia_link" class="external_link">This
is a link to Julia's home page</a>
```

Learning about CSS and JavaScript selectors

Historically, JavaScript started off using selectors based on the `id` attribute and the names of the HTML elements (the tags). Later on, the CSS specification came with a more powerful set of selectors, employing not only the `class`, the `id`, and the tags, but also the presence of attributes and their values, states of the elements (such as `focused` or `disabled`), and more specific element hierarchies that take into account relationships.

Here are a few examples of CSS selectors that can be used to target the previously discussed `<a>` tag:

- `#julia_link` is the selector for the `id` attribute (the #)
- `.external_link` is the selector for the `class` attribute (the .)
- `a` is the selector for the `<a>` tag
- `a[href*="julialang.org"]` will select all the `<a>` tags with a `href` attribute that contains `"julialang.org"`

You can read more about CSS selectors at `https://developer.mozilla.org/en-US/docs/Web/CSS/CSS_Selectors`. It's worth keeping this resource close as web scraping relies heavily on CSS selectors, as we'll see in the next chapter.

Understanding the structure of a link

Links, in technical lingo called **Uniform Resource Locators** (**URLs**), are strings of characters that uniquely identify a resource on the internet. They are informally known as **web addresses**. Sometimes you might see them called **Uniform Resource Identifiers** (**URIs**).

In our previous example, Julia's Wikipedia web page was accessible at the URL `https://en.wikipedia.org/wiki/Julia_(programming_language)`. This URL refers to the resource `/wiki/Julia_(programming_language)` whose representation, as a HTML document, can be requested via the HTTPS protocol (`https:`) from a network host whose domain name is `wikipedia.org`. (Wow, that's a mouthful, but now you can understand how complex the process of requesting a web page on the internet is).

Thus, a common URL can be broken down into the following parts—`scheme://host/path?query#fragment`.

For example, if we take a look at `https://en.wikipedia.org/wiki/Julia_(programming_language)?uselang=en#Interaction`, we have `https` as the `scheme`, `en.wikipedia.org` as the `host`, `/wiki/Julia_(programming_language)` as the `path`, `?uselang=en` as the `query`, and, finally, `#Interaction` as the `fragment`.

Accessing the internet from Julia

Now that you have a good understanding of how web pages are accessed on the internet through client-server interactions, let's see how we can do this with Julia.

The most common web clients are the web browsers—apps such as Chrome or Firefox. However, these are meant to be used by human users, rendering web pages with fancy styled UIs and sophisticated interactions. Web scraping can be done manually through a web browser, it's true, but the most efficient and scalable way is through a fully automated, software-driven process. Although web browsers can be automated (with something like Selenium from `https://www.seleniumhq.org`), it's a more difficult, error-prone, and resource-intensive task. For most use cases, the preferred approach is to use a dedicated HTTP client.

Making requests with the HTTP package

`Pkg`, Julia's built-in package manager, provides access to the excellent `HTTP` package. It exposes a powerful functionality for building web clients and servers—and we'll use it extensively.

As you're already accustomed to, extra functionality is only two commands away—`pkg> add HTTP` and `julia> using HTTP`.

Recall our discussion about HTTP methods from the previous section; the most important ones were `GET`, used to ask for a resource from the server, and `POST`, which sends a data payload to the server and accepts the response. The `HTTP` package exposes a matching set of functions—we get access to `HTTP.get`, `HTTP.post`, `HTTP.delete`, `HTTP.put`, and so on.

```
julia>
HTTP.get("https://en.wikipedia.org/wiki/Julia_(programming_language)")
```

The result will be a `Response` object that represents Julia's Wikipedia page in all its glory. The REPL displays the headers and the first lines of the response body, truncating the rest:

```
julia> HTTP.get("https://en.wikipedia.org/wiki/Julia_(programming_language)")
HTTP.Messages.Response:
"""
HTTP/1.1 200 OK
Date: Mon, 17 Sep 2018 10:35:38 GMT
Content-Type: text/html; charset=UTF-8
Content-Length: 193324
Connection: keep-alive
Server: mw2174.codfw.wmnet
Vary: Accept-Encoding,Cookie,Authorization
X-Content-Type-Options: nosniff
P3P: CP="This is not a P3P policy! See https://en.wikipedia.org/wiki/Special:CentralAutoLogin/P3P for more info."
X-Powered-By: HHVM/3.18.6-dev
Content-language: en
Last-Modified: Sun, 16 Sep 2018 06:23:32 GMT
Backend-Timing: D=94531 t=1537079074050651
X-Varnish: 343909603 326005351, 885580661 879616280, 1013404048 653558799
Via: 1.1 varnish (Varnish/5.1), 1.1 varnish (Varnish/5.1), 1.1 varnish (Varnish/5.1)
Age: 18448
X-Cache: cp2016 hit/5, cp3030 hit/2, cp3042 hit/26
X-Cache-Status: hit-front
Strict-Transport-Security: max-age=106384710; includeSubDomains; preload
Set-Cookie: WMF-Last-Access=17-Sep-2018;Path=/;HttpOnly;secure;Expires=Fri, 19 Oct 2018 00:00:00 GMT
Set-Cookie: WMF-Last-Access-Global=17-Sep-2018;Path=/;Domain=.wikipedia.org;HttpOnly;secure;Expires=Fri, 19 Oct 2018 0
0:00:00 GMT
X-Analytics: ns=0;page_id=38455554;https=1;nocookies=1
X-Client-IP: 83.51.206.212
Cache-Control: private, s-maxage=0, max-age=0, must-revalidate
Set-Cookie: GeoIP=ES:CT:Sitges:41.24:1.81:v4; Path=/; secure; Domain=.wikipedia.org
Accept-Ranges: bytes

<!DOCTYPE html>
<html class="client-nojs" lang="en" dir="ltr">
<head>
<meta charset="UTF-8"/>
<title>Julia (programming language) - Wikipedia</title>
<script>document.documentElement.className = document.documentElement.className.replace( /(^|\s)client-nojs(\s|$)/, "$
1client-js$2" );</script>
<script>(window.RLQ=window.RLQ||[]).push(function(){mw.config.set({"wgCanonicalNamespace":"","wgCanonicalSpecialPageNa
me":false,"wgNamespaceNumber":0,"wgPageName":"Julia_(programming_language)","wgTitle":"Julia (programming language)","
wgCurRevisionId":859773913,"wgRevisionId":859773913,"wgArticleId":38455554,"wgIsArticle":true,"wgIsRedirect":false,"wg
Action":"view","wgUserName":null,"wgUserGroups":["*"],"wgCategories":["CS1 maint: Multiple names: authors list","Use d
my dates from October 2015","Official website different in Wikidata and Wikipedia","2012 software","Array programming
languages","Computational notebook","Data mining and machine learning software","Data-centric programming languages"
⋮
193324-byte body
"""
```

The screenshot shows the details of the `HTTP.Messages.Response` object we received—the list of HTTP headers and the first part of the response body. Let's make sure we keep it in a variable so we can reference it later. Remember that Julia provisionally stores the result of the last computation in the `ans` REPL variable, so let's pick it up from there:

```
julia> resp = ans
```

Handling HTTP responses

After receiving and processing a request, the server sends back a HTTP response message. These messages have a standardized structure. They contain a wealth of information, with the most important pieces being the status code, the headers, and the body.

HTTP status codes

The status code is a three-digit integer where the first digit represents the category, while the next two digits are used to define the subcategory. They are as follows:

- **1XX - Informational**: Request was received. This indicates a provisional response.
- **2XX - Success**: This is the most important response status, acknowledging that the request was successfully received, understood, and accepted. It's what we're looking for in our web-mining scripts.
- **3XX - Redirection**: This class of status codes indicates that the client must take additional action. It usually means that additional requests must be made in order to get to the resource, so our scripts will have to handle this scenario. We also need to actively prevent cyclical redirects. We won't deal with such complex scenarios in our project, but in real-life applications, 3XX status codes will require specialized handling based on the subcategory.

Wikipedia provides a good description of the various 3XX status codes and instructions for what to do in each case: `https://en.wikipedia.org/wiki/List_of_HTTP_status_codes#3xx_Redi rection`.

- **4XX - Client Error**: This means that we've probably made a mistake when sending our request. Maybe the URL is wrong and the resource cannot be found (404) or maybe we're not allowed to access the page (401 and 403 status codes). There's a long list of 4XX response codes and, similar to 3XX ones, our program should handle the various scenarios to ensure that the requests are eventually successful.

- **5XX - Server Error**: Congratulations, you found or caused a problem on the server! Depending on the actual status code, this may or may not be actionable. 503 (service unavailable) or 504 (gateway timeout) are relevant as they indicate that we should try again later.

Learning about HTTP headers

HTTP headers allow the client and the server to pass additional information. We won't go into the details of header transmission since Julia's HTTP library saves us from having to deal with raw headers. However, a few are worth mentioning, as they are important for web scraping:

- `Age`, `Cache-Control`, and `Expires` represent the validity of the page and can be used to set data refresh times

- `Last-Modified`, `Etag`, and `If-Modified-Since` can be used for content versioning, to check if the page has changed since it was last retrieved

- `Cookie` and `Set-Cookie` have to be used in order to read and write cookies that are required for correct communication with the server

- The `Content-*` family of headers, such as `Content-Disposition`, `Content-Length`, `Content-Type`, `Content-Encoding`, and so on, help when handling and validating the response message

 Check https://developer.mozilla.org/en-US/docs/Web/HTTP/Headers and https://en.wikipedia.org/wiki/List_of_HTTP_header_fields for a complete discussion on the HTTP header fields.

The HTTP message body

The message body, the most important part and the reason for web scraping (the content of the web page itself), is actually an optional part of the response. The presence of the body, its properties, and its size are specified by the `Content-*` family of headers.

Understanding HTTP responses

The result of the HTTP.get invocation is an object that closely mirrors a raw HTTP response. The package makes our lives easier by extracting the raw HTTP data and neatly setting it up in a data structure, which makes manipulating it a breeze.

Let's take a look at its properties (or *fields* in Julia's lingo):

```
julia> fieldnames(typeof(resp))
(:version, :status, :headers, :body, :request)
```

The fieldnames function accepts a type as its argument and returns a tuple containing the names of the fields (or properties) of the argument. In order to get the type of a value, we can use the typeof function, like in the previous example.

Right! The status, headers, and body fields should by now sound familiar. The version field represents the version of the HTTP protocol (the HTTP/1.1 part in the first line of the response). Most web servers on the internet today use version 1.1 of the protocol, but a new major version, 2.0, is almost ready for wide deployment. Finally, the request field holds a reference to the HTTP.Messages.Request object that triggered the current response.

The status code

Let's take a closer look at the status code:

```
julia> resp.status 200
```

Sure enough, we got back a valid response, hereby confirmed by the 200 status code.

The headers

What about the headers? As already mentioned, they contain critical information indicating whether a message body is present. Let's check them out:

```
julia> resp.headers
```

The output is as follows:

```
25-element Array{Pair{SubString{String},SubString{String}},1}:
                       "Date" ⟹ "Mon, 17 Sep 2018 11:02:39 GMT"
               "Content-Type" ⟹ "text/html; charset=UTF-8"
             "Content-Length" ⟹ "193324"
                 "Connection" ⟹ "keep-alive"
                     "Server" ⟹ "mw2174.codfw.wmnet"
                       "Vary" ⟹ "Accept-Encoding,Cookie,Authorization"
      "X-Content-Type-Options" ⟹ "nosniff"
                        "P3P" ⟹ "CP=\"This is not a P3P policy! See https://en.wikipedia.org/wiki/Special:Central.
                "X-Powered-By" ⟹ "HHVM/3.18.6-dev"
           "Content-language" ⟹ "en"
              "Last-Modified" ⟹ "Sun, 16 Sep 2018 06:23:32 GMT"
              "Backend-Timing" ⟹ "D=94531 t=1537079074050651"
                  "X-Varnish" ⟹ "343909603 326005351, 885580661 879616280, 2790139 653558799"
                        "Via" ⟹ "1.1 varnish (Varnish/5.1), 1.1 varnish (Varnish/5.1), 1.1 varnish (Varnish/5.1)"
                        "Age" ⟹ "20069"
                    "X-Cache" ⟹ "cp2016 hit/5, cp3030 hit/2, cp3042 hit/29"
             "X-Cache-Status" ⟹ "hit-front"
  "Strict-Transport-Security" ⟹ "max-age=106384710; includeSubDomains; preload"
                 "Set-Cookie" ⟹ "WMF-Last-Access=17-Sep-2018;Path=/;HttpOnly;secure;Expires=Fri, 19 Oct 2018 00:0
                 "Set-Cookie" ⟹ "WMF-Last-Access-Global=17-Sep-2018;Path=/;Domain=.wikipedia.org;HttpOnly;secure;
                "X-Analytics" ⟹ "ns=0;page_id=38455554;https=1;nocookies=1"
                "X-Client-IP" ⟹ "83.51.206.212"
              "Cache-Control" ⟹ "private, s-maxage=0, max-age=0, must-revalidate"
                 "Set-Cookie" ⟹ "GeoIP=ES:CT:Sitges:41.24:1.81:v4; Path=/; secure; Domain=.wikipedia.org"
              "Accept-Ranges" ⟹ "bytes"
```

Your output will be different in regard to some of the values, but it should be easy to spot the key HTTP headers we mentioned before. `Content-Length` confirms the presence of a response body. The `Content-Type` provides information about how to interpret the encoding of the message body (it's a HTML document using UTF-8 character encoding). And we can use the `Last-Modified` value to optimize the caching and the update frequency of our web crawler.

The message body

Since we just confirmed that we have a response body, let's see it:

```
julia> resp.body
193324-element Array{UInt8,1}:
 0x3c
 0x21
 0x44
# ... output truncated ...
```

Oops, that doesn't look like the web page we were expecting. No worries though, these are the bytes of the raw response—which we can easily convert to a human-readable HTML string. Remember that I mentioned the `String` method when learning about strings? Well, this is where it comes in handy:

```julia
julia> resp_body = String(resp.body)
```

Your REPL should now be outputting a long HTML string that represents Julia's Wikipedia page.

If we take a look at the first `500` characters, we'll start to see familiar patterns:

```julia
julia> resp_body[1:500]
```

The output is as follows:

```
"<!DOCTYPE html>\n<html class=\"client-nojs\" lang=\"en\" dir=\"ltr\">\n<head>\n<meta charset=\"UTF-8\"/>\n<
title>Julia (programming language) - Wikipedia</title>\n<script>document.documentElement.className = documen
t.documentElement.className.replace( /(^|\\s)client-nojs(\\s|\$)/, \"\$1client-js\$2\" );</script>\n<script>
(window.RLQ=window.RLQ||[]).push(function(){mw.config.set({\"wgCanonicalNamespace\":\"\",\"wgCanonicalSpecia
lPageName\":false,\"wgNamespaceNumber\":0,\"wgPageName\":\"Julia_(programming_language)\",\"wgTitle\":\"J"
```

Sure enough, using Chrome's view page source will reveal the same HTML:

```
1  <!DOCTYPE html>
2  <html class="client-nojs" lang="en" dir="ltr">
3  <head>
4  <meta charset="UTF-8"/>
5  <title>Julia (programming language) - Wikipedia</title>
6  <script>document.documentElement.className =
   document.documentElement.className.replace( /(^|\s)client-nojs(\s|$)/,
   "$1client-js$2" );</script>
7  <script>(window.RLQ=window.RLQ||[]).push(function()
   {mw.config.set({"wgCanonicalNamespace":"","wgCanonicalSpecialPageName":false
   ,"wgNamespaceNumber":0,"wgPageName":"Julia_(programming_language)","wgTitle"
   :"Julia (programming
```

It's confirmed—we just took our first successful step toward building our web crawler!

Learning about pairs

While looking at the response header, you might've noticed that its type is an `Array` of `Pair` objects:

```julia
julia> resp.headers
25-element Array{Pair{SubString{String},SubString{String}},1}
```

A `Pair` represents a Julia data structure—and the corresponding type. The `Pair` contains a couple of values that are generally used to reference key-value relationships. The types of the two elements determine the concrete type of the `Pair`.

For example, we can construct a `Pair` with the following:

```julia
julia> Pair(:foo, "bar")
:foo => "bar"
```

If we check its type we'll see that it's a `Pair` of `Symbol` and `String`:

```julia
julia> typeof(Pair(:foo, "bar"))
Pair{Symbol,String}
```

We can also create `Pairs` by using the `x => y` literal notation:

```julia
julia> 3 => 'C'
3 => 'C'

julia> typeof(3 => 'C')
Pair{Int64,Char}
```

The `=>` double arrow should look familiar. It's what we saw in the response header, for example:

```julia
"Content-Type" => "text/html; charset=UTF-8"
```

Obviously, once created, it is possible to access the values stored in a `Pair`. One way to do it is by indexing into it:

```julia
julia> p = "one" => 1
"one" => 1

julia> p[1]
"one"

julia> p[2]
1
```

We can also access the `first` and `second` fields in order to get to the `first` and `second` values, respectively:

```
julia> p.first
"one"

julia> p.second
1
```

Just like the tuples, the `Pairs` are immutable, so this won't work:

```
julia> p.first = "two"
ERROR: type Pair is immutable

julia> p[1] = "two"
ERROR: MethodError: no method matching setindex!(::Pair{String,Int64}
```

`Pairs` are one of the building blocks of Julia and can be used, among other things, for creating dictionaries, one of the most important types and data structures.

Dictionaries

The dictionary, called `Dict`, is one of Julia's most powerful and versatile data structures. It's an associative collection—it *associates* keys with values. You can think of a `Dict` as a look-up table implementation—given a single piece of information, the key, it will return the corresponding value.

Constructing dictionaries

Creating an empty instance of a `Dict` is as simple as the following:

```
julia> d = Dict()
Dict{Any,Any} with 0 entries
```

The information between the curly brackets, `{Any,Any}`, represents the types of keys and values of the `Dict`. Thus, the concrete type of a `Dict` itself is defined by the type of its keys and values. The compiler will do its best to infer the type of the collection from the types of its parts. In this case, since the dictionary was empty, no information could be inferred, so Julia defaulted to `Any` and `Any`.

An {Any,Any} type of Dict allows us to add any kind of data, indiscriminately. We can use the setindex! method to add a new key-value pair to the collection:

```
julia> setindex!(d, "World", "Hello")
Dict{Any,Any} with 1 entry:
  "Hello" => "World"
```

However, adding values to a Dict is routinely done using the square bracket notation (which is similar to indexing into it, while also performing an assignment):

```
julia> d["Hola"] = "Mundo"
"Mundo"
```

Till now, we've only added Strings—but like I said, because our Dict accepts any kind of keys and value, there aren't any constraints:

```
julia> d[:speed] = 6.4
6.4
```

Here is our Dict now:

```
julia> d
Dict{Any,Any} with 3 entries:
  "Hello" => "World"
  :speed  => 6.4
  "Hola"  => "Mundo"
```

Note that the key => value pairs are not in the order in which we added them. Dicts are not ordered collections in Julia. We'll talk more about this in a few paragraphs.

If the key already exists, the corresponding value will be updated, returning the new value:

```
julia> d["Hello"] = "Earth" "Earth"
```

Here's our updated Dict. Note that "Hello" now points to "Earth" and not "World":

```
julia> d
Dict{Any,Any} with 3 entries:
  "Hello" => "Earth"
  :speed  => 6.4
  "Hola"  => "Mundo"
```

If we provide some initial data when instantiating the `Dict`, the compiler will be able to do better at identifying the types:

```
julia> dt = Dict("age" => 12)
Dict{String,Int64} with 1 entry:
  "age" => 12
```

We can see that the type of the `Dict` is now constraining the keys to be `String`, and the values to be `Int`—which are the types of the `Pair` we used to instantiate the `Dict`. Now, if a different type is passed for a key or a value, Julia will attempt to convert it—if that fails, an error will occur:

```
julia> dt[:price] = 9.99
MethodError: Cannot `convert` an object of type Symbol to an object of type
String
```

In some instances, the automatic conversion works:

```
julia> dx = Dict(1 => 11)
Dict{Int64,Int64} with 1 entry:
  1 => 11
julia> dx[2.0] = 12
12
```

Julia has silently converted `2.0` to the corresponding `Int` value:

```
julia> dx
Dict{Int64,Int64} with 2 entries:
  2 => 12
  1 => 11
```

But that won't always work:

```
julia> dx[2.4] = 12
InexactError: Int64(Int64, 2.4)
```

We can store randomly complex data in a `Dict` and its type will be correctly inferred by Julia:

```
julia> clients_purchases = Dict(
        "John Roche" => ["soap", "wine", "apples", "bread"],
        "Merry Lou"  => ["bottled water", "apples", "cereals", "milk"]
        )
Dict{String,Array{String,1}} with 2 entries:
  "John Roche" => ["soap", "wine", "apples", "bread"]
  "Merry Lou"  => ["bottled water", "apples", "cereals", "milk"]
```

You can also specify and constrain the type of `Dict` upon constructing it, instead of leaving it up to Julia:

```
julia> dd = Dict{String, Int}("" => 2.0)
Dict{String, Int64} with 1 entry:
  "x" => 2
```

Here, we can see how the type definition overruled the type of the `2.0` value, which is a `Float64` (of course, as in the previous example, Julia has converted `2.0` to its integer counterpart).

We can also use `Pairs` to create a `Dict`:

```
julia> p1 = "a" => 1
"a"=>1
julia> p2 = Pair("b", 2)
"b"=>2
julia> Dict(p1, p2)
Dict{String, Int64} with 2 entries:
  "b" => 2
  "a" => 1
```

We can also use an `Array` of `Pair`:

```
julia> Dict([p1, p2])
Dict{String, Int64} with 2 entries:
  "b" => 2
  "a" => 1
```

We can do the same with arrays of tuples:

```
julia> Dict([("a", 5), ("b", 10)])
Dict{String, Int64} with 2 entries:
  "b" => 10
  "a" => 5
```

Finally, a `Dict` can be constructed using comprehensions:

```
julia> using Dates
julia> Dict([x => Dates.dayname(x) for x = (1:7)])
Dict{Int64, String} with 7 entries:
  7 => "Sunday"
  4 => "Thursday"
  2 => "Tuesday"
  3 => "Wednesday"
  5 => "Friday"
  6 => "Saturday"
  1 => "Monday"
```

Your output will be different as it's likely that the keys won't be ordered from 1 to 7. That's a very important point—as already mentioned, in Julia, the `Dict` is not ordered.

Ordered dictionaries

If you ever need your dictionaries to stay ordered, you can use the `OrderedCollections` package (https://github.com/JuliaCollections/OrderedCollections.jl), specifically the `OrderedDict`:

```
pkg> add OrderedCollections
julia> using OrderedCollections, Dates
julia> OrderedDict(x => Dates.monthname(x) for x = (1:12))
DataStructures.OrderedDict{Any,Any} with 12 entries:
  1  => "January"
  2  => "February"
  3  => "March"
  4  => "April"
  5  => "May"
  6  => "June"
  7  => "July"
  8  => "August"
  9  => "September"
  10 => "October"
  11 => "November"
  12 => "December"
```

Now the elements are stored in the order in which they are added to the collection (from 1 to 12).

Working with dictionaries

As we've already seen, we can index into a `Dict` using the square bracket notation:

```
julia> d = Dict(:foo => 1, :bar => 2)
Dict{Symbol,Int64} with 2 entries:
  :bar => 2
  :foo => 1

julia> d[:bar]
2
```

Attempting to access a key that has not been defined will result in a `KeyError`, as follows:

```
julia> d[:baz]
ERROR: KeyError: key :baz not found
```

To avoid such situations, we can check if the key exists in the first place:

```julia
julia> haskey(d, :baz)
false
```

As an alternative, if we want to also get a default value when the key does not exist, we can use the following:

```julia
julia> get(d, :baz, 0)
0
```

The `get` function has a more powerful twin, `get!`, which also stores the searched key into the `Dict`, using the default value:

```julia
julia> d
Dict{Symbol,Int64} with 2 entries:
  :bar => 2
  :foo => 1

julia> get!(d, :baz, 100)
100

julia> d
Dict{Symbol,Int64} with 3 entries:
  :baz => 100
  :bar => 2
  :foo => 1

julia> haskey(d, :baz)
true
```

In case you're wondering, the exclamation mark at the end of the function name is valid—and denotes an important Julia naming convention. It should be taken as a warning that using the function will modify its arguments' data. In this case, the `get!` function will add the `:baz = 100` Pair to the `d` Dict.

Removing a key-value `Pair` is just a matter of invoking `delete!` (note the presence of the exclamation mark here too):

```julia
julia> delete!(d, :baz)
Dict{Symbol,Int64} with 2 entries:
  :bar => 2
  :foo => 1

julia> haskey(d, :baz)
false
```

As requested, the `:baz` key and its corresponding value have vanished.

We can ask for the collections of keys and values using the aptly named functions `keys` and `values`. They will return iterators over their underlying collections:

```
julia> keys(d)
Base.KeySet for a Dict{Symbol,Int64} with 2 entries. Keys:
  :bar
  :foo

julia> values(d)
Base.ValueIterator for a Dict{Symbol,Int64} with 2 entries. Values:
  2
  1
```

Use `collect` to retrieve the corresponding arrays:

```
julia> collect(keys(d))
2-element Array{Symbol,1}:
  :bar
  :foo

julia> collect(values(d))
2-element Array{Int64,1}:
  2
  1
```

We can combine a `Dict` with another `Dict`:

```
julia> d2 = Dict(:baz => 3)
Dict{Symbol,Int64} with 1 entry:
  :baz => 3

julia> d3 = merge(d, d2)
Dict{Symbol,Int64} with 3 entries:
  :baz => 3
  :bar => 2
  :foo => 1
```

If some of the keys are present in multiple dictionaries, the values from the last collection will be preserved:

```
julia> merge(d3, Dict(:baz => 10))
Dict{Symbol,Int64} with 3 entries:
  :baz => 10
  :bar => 2
  :foo => 1
```

Using the HTTP response

Armed with a good understanding of Julia's dictionary data structure, we can now take a closer look at the `headers` property of `resp`, our `HTTP` response object.

To make it easier to access the various headers, first let's convert the array of `Pair` to a `Dict`:

```
julia> headers = Dict(resp.headers)
Dict{SubString{String},SubString{String}} with 23 entries:
"Connection"     => "keep-alive"
  "Via"          => "1.1 varnish (Varnish/5.1), 1.1 varnish (Varni...
  "X-Analytics"  => "ns=0;page_id=38455554;https=1;nocookies=1"
#... output truncated... #
```

We can check the `Content-Length` value to determine whether or not we have a response body. If it's larger than `0`, that means we got back a HTML message:

```
julia> headers["Content-Length"]
"193324"
```

It's important to remember that all the values in the `headers` dictionary are strings, so we can't go comparing them straight away:

```
julia> headers["Content-Length"] > 0
ERROR: MethodError: no method matching isless(::Int64, ::String)
```

We'll need to parse it into an integer first:

```
julia> parse(Int, headers["Content-Length"]) > 0
true
```

Manipulating the response body

Earlier, we read the response body into a `String` and stored it into the `resp_body` variable. It's a long HTML string and, in theory, we could use `Regex` and other string-processing functions to find and extract the data that we need. However, such an approach would be extremely complicated and error-prone. The best way to search for content in a HTML document is via HTML and CSS selectors. The only problem is that these selectors don't operate on strings—they only work against a **Document Object Model (DOM)**.

Building a DOM representation of the page

The DOM represents an in-memory structure of an HTML document. It is a data structure that allows us to programmatically manipulate the underlying HTML elements. The DOM represents a document as a logical tree, and we can use selectors to traverse and query this hierarchy.

Parsing HTML with Gumbo

Julia's `Pkg` ecosystem provides access to `Gumbo`, a HTML parser library. Provided with a HTML string, `Gumbo` will parse it into a document and its corresponding DOM. This package is an important tool for web scraping with Julia, so let's add it.

As usual, install using the following:

```
pkg> add Gumbo
julia> using Gumbo
```

We're now ready to parse the HTML string into a DOM as follows:

```
julia> dom = parsehtml(resp_body)
 HTML Document
```

The `dom` variable now references a `Gumbo.HTMLDocument`, an in-memory Julia representation of the web page. It's a simple object that has only two fields:

```
julia> fieldnames(typeof(dom))
(:doctype, :root)
```

The `doctype` represents the HTML `<!DOCTYPE html>` element, which is what the Wikipedia page uses:

```
julia> dom.doctype
"html"
```

Now, let's focus on the `root` property. This is effectively the outermost element of the HTML page—the `<html>` tag containing the rest of the elements. It provides us with an entry point into the DOM. We can ask `Gumbo` about its attributes:

```
julia> dom.root.attributes
Dict{AbstractString,AbstractString} with 3 entries:
  "class" => "client-nojs"
  "lang"  => "en"
  "dir"   => "ltr"
```

It's a `Dict`, the keys representing HTML attributes and the values—the attributes' values. And sure enough, they match the page's HTML:

```
1 <!DOCTYPE html>
2 <html class="client-nojs" lang="en" dir="ltr">
```

There's also a similar `attrs` method, which serves the same purpose:

```
julia> attrs(dom.root)
Dict{AbstractString,AbstractString} with 3 entries:
  "class" => "client-nojs"
  "lang"  => "en"
  "dir"   => "ltr"
```

When in doubt, we can just ask about the name of an element using the `tag` method:

```
julia> tag(dom.root)
:HTML
```

`Gumbo` exposes a `children` method which returns an array containing all the nested `HTMLElement`. If you just go ahead and execute `julia> children(dom.root)`, the REPL output will be hard to follow. The REPL representation of an `HTMLElement` is its HTML code, which, for top-level elements with many children, will fill up many Terminal screens. Let's use a `for` loop to iterate over the children and show just their tags:

```
julia> for c in children(dom.root)
           @show tag(c)
       end
tag(c) = :head
tag(c) = :body
```

Much better!

Since the children are part of a collection, we can index into them:

```
julia> body = children(dom.root)[2];
```

Please note the closing semicolon (;). When used in the REPL at the end of an expression, it will suppress the output (so we won't see the very long HTML code of the `<body>` that would otherwise be output). The `body` variable will now reference an instance of `HTMLElement{:body}`:

```
HTMLElement{:body}:
<body class="mediawiki ltr sitedir-ltr mw-hide-empty-elt ns-0 ns-subject
page-Julia_programming_language rootpage-Julia_programming_language skin-
vector action-view">
# ... output truncated ...
```

The last method that we'll need is `getattr`, which returns the value of an attribute name. If the attribute is not defined for the element, it raises a `KeyError`:

```
julia> getattr(dom.root, "class")
"client-nojs"

julia> getattr(dom.root, "href") # oops!
ERROR: KeyError: key "href" not found
```

Asking about the `href` attribute of a `<html>` tag doesn't make any sense. And sure enough, we promptly got a `KeyError`, since `href` was not an attribute of this `HTMLElement`.

Coding defensively

An error like the previous one, when part of a larger script, has the potential to completely alter a program's execution, leading to undesired and potentially costly results. In general, when something unexpected occurs during the execution of a program, it may leave the software in an erroneous state, making it impossible to return a correct value. In such cases, rather than pushing on and potentially propagating the problem throughout the whole execution stack, it's preferable to explicitly notify the calling code about the situation by throwing an `Exception`.

Many functions, both in Julia's core and within third-party packages, make good use of the error-throwing mechanism. It's good practice to check the docs for the functions you use and to see what kinds of errors they throw. An error is called an exception in programming lingo.

As in the case of `getattr`, the author of the `Gumbo` package warned us that attempting to read an attribute that was not defined would result in a `KeyError` exception. We'll learn soon how to handle exceptions by capturing them in our code, getting info about the problem, and stopping or allowing the exception to propagate further up the call stack. Sometimes it's the best approach, but it's not a technique we want to abuse since handling errors this way can be resource-intensive. Dealing with exceptions is considerably slower than performing simple data integrity checks and branching.

For our project, the first line of defense is to simply check if the attribute is in fact defined in the element. We can do this by retrieving the keys of the attributes `Dict` and checking if the one we want is part of the collection. It's a one-liner:

```
julia> in("href", collect(keys(attrs(dom.root))))
false
```

Clearly, `href` is not an attribute of the `<html>` tag.

Using this approach, we can easily write logic to check for the existence of an attribute before we attempt to look up its value.

The pipe operator

Reading multiple nested functions can be taxing on the brain. The previous example, `collect(keys(attrs(dom.root)))`, can be rewritten to improve readability using Julia's pipe operator, `|>`.

For example, the following snippet nests three function calls, each inner function becoming the argument of the outermost one:

```
julia> collect(keys(attrs(dom.root)))
3-element Array{AbstractString,1}:
 "class"
 "lang"
 "dir"
```

This can be rewritten for improved readability as a chain of functions using the pipe operator. This code produces the exact same result:

```
julia> dom.root |> attrs |> keys |> collect
3-element Array{AbstractString,1}:
 "class"
 "lang"
 "dir"
```

What the `|>` operator does is that it takes the output of the first value and *pipes* it as the argument of the next function. So `dom.root |> attrs` is identical to `attrs(dom.root)`. Unfortunately, the pipe operator works only for one-argument functions. But it's still very useful for decluttering code, massively improving readability.

> For more advanced piping functionality you can check out the `Lazy` package, specifically `@>` and `@>>` at
> `https://github.com/MikeInnes/Lazy.jl#macros`.

Handling errors like a pro

Sometimes, coding defensively won't be the solution. Maybe a key part of your program requires reading a file on the network or accessing a database. If the resource can't be accessed due to a temporary network failure, there's really not much you can do in the absence of the data.

The try...catch statements

If you identify parts of your code where you think the execution can go off the rails due to conditions that are out of your control (that is, *exceptional* conditions—hence the name *exception*), you can use Julia's `try...catch` statements. This is exactly what it sounds like—you instruct the compiler to *try* a piece of code and if, as a result of a problem, an exception is *thrown*, to *catch* it. The fact that an exception is *caught* implies that it won't propagate throughout the whole application.

Let's see it in action:

```
julia> try
    getattr(dom.root, "href")
catch
    println("The $(tag(dom.root)) tag doesn't have a 'href' attribute.")
end
The HTML tag doesn't have a 'href' attribute.
```

In this example, once an error is encountered, the execution of the code in the `try` branch is stopped exactly at that point, and the execution flow continues right away, in the `catch` branch.

It becomes clearer if we modify the snippet as follows:

```julia
julia> try
    getattr(dom.root, "href")
    println("I'm here too")
catch
    println("The $(tag(dom.root)) tag doesn't have a 'href' attribute.")
end
The HTML tag doesn't have a 'href' attribute.
```

The newly added line, `println("I'm here too")`, is not executed, as demonstrated by the fact that the message is not output.

Of course, things change if no exception is thrown:

```julia
julia> try
getattr(dom.root, "class")
    println("I'm here too")
catch
    println("The $(tag(dom.root)) tag doesn't have a 'href' attribute.")
end
I'm here too
```

The `catch` construct takes an optional argument, the `Exception` object that's been thrown by the `try` block. This allows us to inspect the exception and branch our code depending on its properties.

In our example, the `KeyError` exception is built into Julia. It is thrown when we attempt to access or delete a non-existent element (such as a key in a `Dict` or an attribute of a `HTMLElement`). All instances of `KeyError` have a key property, which provides information about the missing data. Thus, we can make our code more generic:

```julia
julia> try
    getattr(dom.root, "href")
catch ex
    if isa(ex, KeyError)
        println("The $(tag(dom.root)) tag doesn't have a '$(ex.key)'
attribute.")
    else
        println("Some other exception has occurred")
    end
end
The HTML tag doesn't have a 'href' attribute.
```

Here, we pass the exception into the `catch` block as the `ex` variable. We then check if we're dealing with a `KeyError` exception—if we are, we use this information to display a custom error by accessing the `ex.key` field to retrieve the missing key. If it's a different type of exception, we show a generic error message:

```julia
julia> try
       error("Oh my!")
catch ex
    if isa(ex, KeyError)
            println("The $(tag(dom.root)) tag doesn't have a '$(ex.key)'
attribute.")
    else
            println("Some exception has occurred")
    end
end
Some exception has occurred
```

The finally clause

In code that performs state changes or uses resources such as files or databases, there is typically some clean-up work (such as closing files or database connections) that needs to be done when the code is finished. This code would normally go into the `try` branch—but what happens if an exception is thrown?

In such cases, the `finally` clause comes into play. This can be added after a `try` or after a `catch` branch. The code within the `finally` block is *guaranteed* to be executed, regardless of whether exceptions are thrown or not:

```julia
julia> try
    getattr(dom.root, "href")
catch ex
    println("The $(tag(dom.root)) tag doesn't have a '$(ex.key)'
attribute.")
finally
    println("I always get called")
end
The HTML tag doesn't have a 'href' attribute.
I always get called
```

It is illegal to have a `try` without a `catch` or a `finally`:

```julia
julia> try getattr(dom.root, "href") end syntax: try without catch or
finally
```

We need to provide either a `catch` or a `finally` block (or both).

The `try`/`catch`/`finally` blocks will return the last expression evaluated, so we can capture it in a variable:

```
julia> result = try
           error("Oh no!")
       catch ex
           "Everything is under control"
       end
"Everything is under control"

julia> result
"Everything is under control"
```

Throwing exceptions on errors

As developers, we too have the option to create and throw exceptions when our code encounters a problem and shouldn't continue. Julia provides a long list of built-in exceptions that cover a multitude of use cases. You can read about them at `https://docs.julialang.org/en/stable/manual/control-flow/#Built-in-Exceptions-1`.

In order to throw an exception, we use the aptly named `throw` function. For example, if we want to replicate the error raised by Gumbo's `getattr` method, all we have to do is call the following:

```
julia> throw(KeyError("href"))
ERROR: KeyError: key "href" not found
```

If the built-in exceptions provided by Julia aren't relevant enough for your situation, the language provides a generic error type, the `ErrorException`. It takes an additional `msg` argument which should offer more details about the nature of the error:

```
julia> ex = ErrorException("To err is human, but to really foul things up
you need a computer.")
ErrorException("To err is human, but to really foul things up you need a
computer.")

julia> throw(ex)
ERROR: To err is human, but to really foul things up you need a computer.

julia> ex.msg
"To err is human, but to really foul things up you need a computer."
```

Julia provides a shortcut for throwing `ErrorException`, the `error` function:

```
julia> error("To err is human - to blame it on a computer is even more
so.")
ERROR: To err is human - to blame it on a computer is even more so.
```

Rethrowing exceptions

But what do we do if we realize that the exception we've caught cannot (or should not) be handled by our code? For example, say we were expecting to catch a possible missing attribute, but it turned out we got a `Gumbo` parsing exception instead. Such an issue would have to be handled higher up the execution stack, maybe by trying to fetch the web page again and reparsing it, or by logging an error message for the admin.

If we `throw` the exception ourselves, the origin (the `stacktrace`) of the initial error would be lost. For such cases, Julia provides the `rethrow` function, which can be used as follows:

```
julia> try
            Dict()[:foo]
        catch ex
            "nothing to see here"
        end
"nothing to see here"
```

If we simply throw the exception ourselves, this is what happens:

```
julia> try
            Dict()[:foo]
        catch ex
            throw(ex)
        end
ERROR: KeyError: key :foo not found
Stacktrace:
 [1] top-level scope at REPL
```

We throw the `KeyError` exception, but the origin of the exception is lost; it appears as if it originates in our code in the `catch` block. Contrast this with the following example, where we use `rethrow`:

```
julia> try
            Dict()[:foo]
        catch ex
            rethrow(ex)
        end
ERROR: KeyError: key :foo not found
```

```
Stacktrace:
 [1] getindex(::Dict{Any,Any}, ::Symbol) at ./dict.jl:474
 [2] top-level scope at REPL[140]
```

The original exception is being rethrown, without changing the stacktrace. Now we can see that the exception originated within the `dict.jl` file.

Learning about functions

Before we get to write our first full-fledged Julia program, the web crawler, we need to take yet another important detour. It's the last one, I promise.

As our code becomes more and more complex, we should start using functions. The REPL is great for exploratory programming due to its quick input-output feedback loop, but for any non-trivial piece of software, using functions is the way to go. Functions are an integral part of Julia, promoting readability, code reuse, and performance.

In Julia, a function is an object that takes a tuple of values as an argument and returns a value:

```
julia> function add(x, y)
           x + y
       end
add (generic function with 1 method)
```

There's also a compact *assignment form* for function declaration:

```
julia> add(x, y) = x + y
add (generic function with 1 method)
```

This second form is great for simple one-line functions.

Invoking a function is simply a matter of calling its name and passing it the required arguments:

```
julia> add(1, 2)
3
```

The return keyword

If you have previous programming experience, you might be surprised to see that invoking the add function correctly returns the expected value, despite the fact that we didn't put any explicit return statement in the function's body. In Julia, a function automatically returns the result of the last expression that was evaluated. This is usually the last expression in the body of the function.

An explicit return keyword is also available. Using it will cause the function to exit immediately, with the value passed to the return statement:

```julia
julia> function add(x, y)
           return "I don't feel like doing math today"
           x + y
       end
add (generic function with 1 method)

julia> add(1, 2)
"I don't feel like doing math today"
```

Returning multiple values

Although Julia does not support returning multiple values, it does offer a neat trick that's very close to the actual thing. Any function can return a tuple. And because constructing and destructing tuples is very flexible, this approach is very powerful and readable:

```julia
julia> function addremove(x, y)
           x+y, x-y
       end
addremove (generic function with 1 method)

julia> a, b = addremove(10, 5)
(15, 5)

julia> a
15

julia> b
5
```

Here we defined a function, addremove, which returns a tuple of two integers. We can extract the values within the tuple by simply assigning a variable corresponding to each of its elements.

Optional arguments

Function arguments can have sensible defaults. For such situations, Julia allows defining default values. When they are provided, the corresponding arguments no longer have to be passed explicitly on every call:

```
julia> function addremove(x=100, y=10)
           x+y, x-y
       end
addremove (generic function with 3 methods)
```

This function has default values for both x and y. We can invoke it without passing any of the arguments:

```
julia> addremove()
(110, 90)
```

This snippet demonstrates how Julia uses the default values when they are not provided upon function invocation.

We can pass the first argument only—and for the second one, the default value will be used:

```
julia> addremove(5)
(15, -5)
```

Finally, we can pass both arguments; all the defaults will be overwritten:

```
julia> addremove(5, 1)
(6, 4)
```

Keyword arguments

The functions that require a long list of arguments can be hard to use, as the programmer has to remember the order and the types of the expected values. For such cases, we can define functions that accept labeled arguments instead. These are called **keyword arguments**.

In order to define functions that accept keyword arguments, we need to add a semicolon after the function's list of unlabeled arguments and follow it with one or more keyword=value pairs. We actually encountered such functions in Chapter 2, *Creating Our First Julia App*, when we used Gadfly to plot the Iris flower dataset:

```
plot(iris, x=:SepalLength, y=:PetalLength, color=:Species)
```

In this example, x, y, and `color` are all keyword arguments.

The definition of a function with keyword arguments looks like this:

```
function thermal_confort(temperature, humidity; scale = :celsius, age = 35)
```

Here, we define a new function, `thermal_confort`, which has two required arguments, `temperature` and `humidity`. The function also accepts two keyword arguments, `scale` and `age`, which have the default values of :celsius and 35, respectively. It is necessary for all the keyword arguments to have default values.

Invoking such a function implies using the positional as well as the keyword arguments:

```
thermal_confort(27, 56, age = 72, scale = :fahrenheit)
```

If the values for the keyword arguments are not supplied, the default values are used.

Keyword argument default values are evaluated left to right, which means that default expressions may refer to prior keyword arguments:

```
function thermal_confort(temperature, humidity; scale = :celsius, age = 35,
health_risk = age/100)
```

Note that we reference the keyword argument `age` in the default value of `health_risk`.

Documenting functions

Julia comes out of the box with powerful code-documenting features. The usage is straightforward—any string appearing at the top level, right before an object, will be interpreted as documentation (it's called a **docstring**). The docstring is interpreted as markdown, so we can use markup for rich formatting.

The documentation for the `thermal_confort` function could be as follow:

```
"""
        thermal_confort(temperature, humidity; <keyword arguments>)
Compute the thermal comfort index based on temperature and humidity. It can
optionally take into account the age of the patient. Works for both Celsius
and Fahrenheit.
# Examples:
```julia-repl
julia> thermal_confort(32, 78)
12
```

Arguments
```

```
    - temperature: the current air temperature
    - humidity: the current air humidity
    - scale: whether :celsius or :fahrenheit, defaults to :celsius
    - age: the age of the patient
    """
    function thermal_confort(temperature, humidity; scale = :celsius, age = 35)
```

Now we can access the documentation of our function by using the REPL's help mode:

```
help?> thermal_confort
```

The output is as follows:

```
help?> thermal_confort
search: thermal_confort

    thermal_confort(temperature, humidity; <keyword arguments>)


  Compute the thermal comfort index based on temperature and humidity. It can optionally take int
o account the age of the patient. Works for both Celsius and
  Fahrenheit.

  Examples:
  ≡≡≡≡≡≡≡≡≡≡

  julia> thermal_confort(32, 78)
  12


  Arguments
  ≡≡≡≡≡≡≡≡≡≡

    •   temperature: the current air temperature

    •   humidity: the current air humidity

    •   scale: whether :celsius or :fahrenheit, defaults to :celsius

    •   age: the age of the patient
```

Pretty useful, isn't it? Docstrings can also be used to generate complete documentation for your Julia projects, with the help of external packages which build full API docs as standalone websites, markdown documents, PDF documents, etcetera. We'll see how to do this in Chapter 11, *Creating Julia Packages*.

Writing a basic web crawler – take one

We're now ready to write our first fully-fledged Julia program—a simple web crawler. This first iteration will make a request for Julia's Wikipedia page, will parse it and extract all the internal URLs, storing them in an `Array`.

Setting up our project

The first thing we need to do is to set up a dedicated project. This is done by using `Pkg`. It is a very important step as it allows us to efficiently manage and version the packages on which our program depends.

For starters, we need a folder for our software. Create one—let's call it `WebCrawler`. I'll use Julia to make it, but you do it however you like:

```julia
julia> mkdir("WebCrawler")
"WebCrawler"

julia> cd("WebCrawler/")
```

Now we can use `Pkg` to add the dependencies. When we start a new project, we need to initialise it. This is achieved with the following:

```
pkg> activate .
```

This tells `Pkg` that we want to manage dependencies in the current project as opposed to doing it globally. You will notice that the cursor has changed, indicating the name of the active project, `WebCrawler`:

```
(WebCrawler) pkg>
```

All the other packages we installed up until this point were in the global environment, which was indicated by the `(v1.0)` cursor:

```
(v1.0) pkg>
```

> `(v1.0)` is the global environment, labeled with the currently installed Julia version. If you try the examples on a different Julia version, you'll get a different label.

If we check the status, we'll see that no packages were installed yet in the project's environment:

```
(WebCrawler) pkg> st
    Status `Project.toml`
```

Our software will have two dependencies—HTTP and Gumbo. It's time to add them:

```
(WebCrawler) pkg> add HTTP
(WebCrawler) pkg> add Gumbo
```

Now we can create a new file to host our code. Let's call it webcrawler.jl. It can be created using Julia:

```
julia> touch("webcrawler.jl")
"webcrawler.jl"
```

Writing a Julia program

Unlike our previous work in the REPL and IJulia notebooks, this will be a standalone program: all the logic will go inside this webcrawler.jl file, and when ready, we'll use the julia binary to execute it.

Julia files are parsed top to bottom, so we need to provide all the necessary instructions in the right order (using statements, variables initialization, function definitions, etcetera). We'll pretty much condense all the steps we took so far in this chapter to build this small program.

To make things simpler, it's best to use a full-fledged Julia editor. Open webcrawler.jl in Atom/Juno or Visual Studio Code (or whatever your favorite editor is).

The first thing we want to do is to inform Julia that we plan on using the HTTP and Gumbo packages. We can write a single using statement and list multiple dependencies, separated by a comma:

```
using HTTP, Gumbo
```

Also, we decided that we wanted to use Julia's Wikipedia page to test our crawler. The link is https://en.wikipedia.org/wiki/Julia_(programming_language). It's good practice to store such configuration-like values in constants, rather than spreading *magic strings* throughout the whole code base:

```
const PAGE_URL =
"https://en.wikipedia.org/wiki/Julia_(programming_language)"
```

We also said that we wanted to store all the links in an `Array`—let's set that up too. Remember that constants in Julia are concerned mostly with types, so there is no problem if we push values into the array after it's declared:

```
const LINKS = String[]
```

Here, we initialize the `LINKS` constant as an empty `Array` of `String`. The notation `String[]` produces the same result as `Array{String,1}()` and `Vector{String}()`. It basically represents the empty `Array` literal `[]` plus the `Type` constraint `String`—creating a `Vector` of `String` values.

The next steps are—fetch the page, look for a successful response (status `200`), and then check the headers to see if we received a message body (`Content-Length` greater than zero). In this first iteration, we only have to do this one time. But thinking ahead, for the final version of our game, we'll have to repeat this process up to six times per game session (because there will be up to Six Degrees of Wikipedia, so we'll have to crawl up to six pages). The best thing we can do is to write a generic function which takes a page URL as its only parameter, fetches the page, performs the necessary checks, and returns the message body if available. Let's call this function `fetchpage`:

```
function fetchpage(url)
    response = HTTP.get(url)
    if response.status == 200 && parse(Int,
Dict(response.headers)["Content-Length"]) > 0
        String(response.body)
    else
        ""
    end
end
```

First, we call `HTTP.get(url)`, storing the `HTTP.Messages.Response` object in the `response` variable. Then we check if the response status is `200` and if the `Content-Length` header is greater than `0`. If they are, we read the message body into a string. If not, we return an empty string, `""`, to represent the empty body. That's a lot of *ifs*—looks like it's time we take a closer look at the conditional `if/else` statements, as they're really important.

Conditional evaluation of if, elseif, and else statements

All, except maybe the most basic, programs must be able to evaluate variables and execute different logical branches depending on their current values. Conditional evaluation allows portions of the code to be executed (or not) depending on the value of a Boolean expression. Julia provides the if, elseif, and else statements for writing conditional expressions. They work like this:

```julia
julia> x = 5
5

julia> if x < 0
           println("x is a negative number")
       elseif x > 0
           println("x is a positive number greater than 0")
       else
           println("x is 0")
       end
x is a positive number greater than 0
```

If the condition x < 0 is true, then its underlying block is evaluated. If not, the expression x > 0 is evaluated, as part of the elseif branch. If it is true, its corresponding block is evaluated. If neither expression is true, the else block is evaluated.

The elseif and else blocks are optional, and we can use as many elseif blocks as we want. The conditions in the if,elseif and else construct are evaluated until the first one returns true. Then the associated block is evaluated and its last computed value is returned, exiting the conditional evaluation. Thus, conditional statements in Julia also return a value—the last executed statement in the branch that was chosen. The following code shows this:

```julia
julia> status = if x < 0
                    "x is a negative number"
                elseif x > 0
                    "x is a positive number greater than 0"
                else
                    "x is 0"
                end
"x is a positive number greater than 0"

julia> status
"x is a positive number greater than 0"
```

Finally, it's very important to keep in mind that `if` blocks do not introduce local scope. That is, variables defined within them will be accessible after the block is exited (of course, provided that the respective branch has been evaluated):

```julia
julia> status = if x < 0
            "x is a negative number"
        elseif x > 0
            y = 20
            "x is a positive number greater than 0"
        else
            "x is 0"
        end
"x is a positive number greater than 0"

julia> y
20
```

We can see here that the `y` variable, initialized within the `elseif` block, is still accessible outside the conditional expression.

This can be avoided if we declare the variable to be `local`:

```julia
julia> status = if x < 0
            "x is a negative number"
        elseif x > 0
            local z = 20
            "x is a positive number greater than 0"
        else
            "x is 0"
        end
"x is a positive number greater than 0"

julia> z
UndefVarError: z not defined
```

When declared `local`, the variable no longer *leaks* outside the `if` block.

The ternary operator

An `if,then` and `else` type of condition can be expressed using the ternary operator ? :. Its syntax is as follows:

```
x ? y : z
```

If x is true, the expression y is evaluated—otherwise, z gets evaluated instead. For instance, consider the following code:

```julia
julia> x = 10
10

julia> x < 0 ? "negative" : "positive"
"positive"
```

Short-circuit evaluation

Julia provides an even more concise type of evaluation—short-circuit evaluation. In a series of Boolean expressions connected by && and || operators, only the minimum number of expressions are evaluated—as many as are necessary in order to determine the final Boolean value of the entire chain. We can exploit this to return certain values, depending on what gets to be evaluated. For instance:

```julia
julia> x = 10
10

julia> x > 5 && "bigger than 5"
"bigger than 5"
```

In an expression A && B, the second expression B is only evaluated if and only if A evaluates to true. In this case, the whole expression has the return value of the sub-expression B, which in the previous example is bigger than 5.

If, on the contrary, A evaluates to false, B does not get evaluated at all. Thus, beware—the whole expression will return a false Boolean (not a string!):

```julia
julia> x > 15 && "bigger than 15"
false
```

The same logic applies to the logical or operator, ||:

```julia
julia> x < 5 || "greater than 5"
"greater than 5"
```

In an expression A || B, the second expression B is only evaluated if A evaluates to false. The same logic applies when the first sub-expression is evaluated to true; true will be the return value of the whole expression:

```julia
julia> x > 5 || "less than 5"
true
```

Beware of operator precedence

Sometimes short-circuit expressions can confuse the compiler, resulting in errors or unexpected results. For example, short-circuit expressions are often used with assignment operations, as follows:

```
julia> x > 15 || message = "That's a lot"
```

This will fail with the `syntax: invalid assignment location "(x > 15) || message"` error because the = assignment operator has higher precedence than logical or and `||`. It can easily be fixed by using brackets to explicitly control the evaluation order:

```
julia> x > 15 || (message = "That's a lot")
"That's a lot"
```

It's something to keep in mind as it's a common source of errors for beginners.

Carrying on with the crawler's implementation

So far, your code should look like this:

```
using HTTP, Gumbo

const PAGE_URL =
"https://en.wikipedia.org/wiki/Julia_(programming_language)"
const LINKS = String[]

function fetchpage(url)
   response = HTTP.get(url)
   if response.status == 200 && parse(Int, Dict(response.headers)["Content-
Length"]) > 0
      String(response.body)
   else
      ""
   end
end
```

It should be now clear that either the response body or an empty string is returned by the `if/else` statement. And since this is the last piece of code evaluated inside the `fetchpage` function, this value also becomes the return value of the whole function.

All good, we can now use the `fetchpage` function to get the HTML content of the Wikipedia page and store it in the `content` variable:

```
content = fetchpage(PAGE_URL)
```

If the fetch operation is successful and the `content` is not an empty string, we can pass the HTML string to `Gumbo` to construct the DOM. Then, we can loop through all the children of this DOM's `root` element and look for links (using the `a` tag selector). For each element, we want to check the `href` attribute and store its value only if it points to another Wikipedia page:

```
if ! isempty(content)
   dom = Gumbo.parsehtml(content)
   extractlinks(dom.root)
end
```

The function for extracting the links is:

```
function extractlinks(elem)
   if   isa(elem, HTMLElement) &&
        tag(elem) == :a && in("href", collect(keys(attrs(elem))))
         url = getattr(elem, "href")
         startswith(url, "/wiki/") && push!(LINKS, url)
   end

   for child in children(elem)
      extractlinks(child)
   end
end
```

Here, we declare an `extractlinks` function which takes a `Gumbo` element, called `elem`, as its only parameter. We then check if `elem` is a `HTMLElement` and, if it is, we check if it corresponds to a link tag (the `:a` Julia `Symbol` which represents an `<a>` HTML tag). Then we check if the element defines a `href` attribute in order to avoid getting a `KeyError`. If all is good, we get the value of the `href` element. And finally, if the value of the `href` is an internal URL—that is, a URL that starts with `/wiki/`—we add it to our `LINKS` Array.

Once we're done checking the element for links, we check if it contains other nested HTML elements. If it does, we want to repeat the same process for each of its children. That's what the final `for` loop does.

The only thing left to do is to display the populated `LINKS` Array, at the very end of our file. Since some of the links might come up in the page more than once, let's make sure we reduce the `Array` to the unique elements only, by using the `unique` function:

```
display(unique(LINKS))
```

Now we can execute this script by opening a terminal in the folder where the file is stored. And then run—`$ julia webcrawler.jl`.

There's plenty of links, so the output will be quite long. Here's the top of the list:

```
$ julia webcrawler.jl
440-element Array{String,1}:
 "/wiki/Programming_paradigm"
 "/wiki/Multi-paradigm_programming_language"
 "/wiki/Multiple_dispatch"
 "/wiki/Object-oriented_programming"
 "/wiki/Procedural_programming"
# ... output truncated ...
```

By looking at the output, we'll notice that in the first optimization some links point to special Wikipedia pages—the ones containing parts such as `/File:`, `/Category:`, `/Help:`, `/Special:`, and so on. So we can just go ahead and skip all the URLs that contain a column, `:`, since these are not articles and are not useful for our game.

To do this, look for the line that reads:

```
startswith(url, "/wiki/") && push!(LINKS, url)
```

Replace the preceding line with the following:

```
startswith(url, "/wiki/") && ! occursin(":", url) && push!(LINKS, url)
```

If you run the program now, you should see a list of all the URLs from Julia's Wikipedia page that link to other Wikipedia articles.

This is the full code:

```
using HTTP, Gumbo

const PAGE_URL =
"https://en.wikipedia.org/wiki/Julia_(programming_language)"
const LINKS = String[]

function fetchpage(url)
  response = HTTP.get(url)
  if response.status == 200 && parse(Int, Dict(response.headers)["Content-
```

```
      Length"]) > 0
          String(response.body)
        else
          ""
        end
      end

      function extractlinks(elem)
        if isa(elem, HTMLElement) && tag(elem) == :a && in("href",
      collect(keys(attrs(elem))))
            url = getattr(elem, "href")
            startswith(url, "/wiki/") && ! occursin(":", url) && push!(LINKS,
      url)
        end

        for child in children(elem)
          extractlinks(child)
        end
      end
      content = fetchpage(PAGE_URL)

      if ! isempty(content)
        dom = Gumbo.parsehtml(content)
        extractlinks(dom.root)
      end

      display(unique(LINKS))
```

Summary

Web scraping is a key component of data mining and Julia provides a powerful toolbox for handling these tasks. In this chapter, we addressed the fundamentals of building a web crawler. We learned how to request web pages with a Julia web client and how to read the responses, how to work with Julia's powerful `Dict` data structure to read HTTP information, how to make our software more resilient by handling errors, how to better organize our code by writing functions and documenting them, and how to use conditional logic to make decisions.

Armed with this knowledge, we built the first version of our web crawler. In the next chapter, we will improve it and will use it to extract the data for our upcoming Wiki game. In the process, we'll dive deeper into the language, learning about types, methods and modules, and how to interact with relational databases.

4
Building the Wiki Game Web Crawler

Wow, Chapter 3, *Setting Up the Wiki Game*, was quite a ride! Laying the foundation of our Wikipedia game took us on a real learning *tour-de-force*. After the quick refresher on how the web and web pages work, we dived deeper into the key parts of the language, studying the dictionary data structure and its corresponding data type, conditional expressions, functions, exception handling, and even the very handy piping operator (|>). In the process, we built a short script that uses a couple of powerful third-party packages, HTTP and Gumbo, to request a web page from Wikipedia, parse it as an HTML DOM, and extract all internal links from within the page. Our script is part of a proper Julia project, which employs Pkg to efficiently manage dependencies.

In this chapter, we'll continue the development of our game, implementing the complete workflow and the gameplay. Even if you are not a seasoned developer, it's easy to imagine that even a simple game like this will end up with multiple logical parts. We could maybe have a module for the Wikipedia page crawler, one for the gameplay itself, and one for the UI (the web app that we'll create in the next chapter). Breaking down a problem into smaller parts always makes for a simpler solution. And, that's especially true when writing code—having small, specialized functions, grouped by responsibility, makes the software easier to reason about, develop, extend, and maintain. In this chapter, we'll learn about Julia's constructs for structuring the code, and we'll discuss a few more key elements of the language: the type system, constructors, methods, and multiple dispatch.

In this chapter, we'll cover the following topics:

- *Six Degrees of Wikipedia*, the gameplay
- Organizing our code using modules and loading code from multiple files (the so-called **mixin behavior**)
- Types and the type system, which are key to Julia's flexibility and performance

- Constructors, special functions which allow us to create new instances of our types
- Methods and multiple dispatch, some of the most important aspects of the language
- Interacting with relational databases (specifically, MySQL)

I hope you are ready to dive in.

Technical requirements

The Julia package ecosystem is under continuous development and new package versions are released on a daily basis. Most of the times this is great news, as new releases bring new features and bug fixes. However, since many of the packages are still in beta (version 0.x), any new release can introduce breaking changes. As a result, the code presented in the book can stop working. In order to ensure that your code will produce the same results as described in the book, it is recommended to use the same package versions. Here are the external packages used in this chapter and their specific versions:

```
Cascadia@v0.4.0
Gumbo@v0.5.1
HTTP@v0.7.1
IJulia@v1.14.1
JSON@v0.20.0
MySQL@v0.7.0
```

In order to install a specific version of a package you need to run:

```
pkg> add PackageName@vX.Y.Z
```

For example:

```
pkg> add IJulia@v1.14.1
```

Alternatively you can install all the used packages by downloading the Project.toml file provided with the chapter and using pkg> instantiate as follows:

```
julia>
download("https://raw.githubusercontent.com/PacktPublishing/Julia-Programmi
ng-Projects/master/Chapter04/Project.toml", "Project.toml")
pkg> activate .
pkg> instantiate
```

Six Degrees of Wikipedia, the gameplay

As we've seen in the previous chapter, the **Six Degrees of Wikipedia game** is a play on the concept of the *six degrees of separation* theory—the idea that all living things (and pretty much everything in the world) are six or fewer steps away from each other. For example, a chain of *a friend of a friend* can be made to connect any two people in a maximum of six steps.

For our own game, the goal of the player is to link any two given Wikipedia articles, passing through six or fewer other Wikipedia pages. In order to make sure that the problem has a solution (the *six degrees of separation* theory has not been demonstrated) and that indeed there is a path from our starting article to the end article, we'll pre-crawl the full path. That is, we'll begin with a random Wikipedia page, which will be our starting point, and we'll link through a number of pages toward our destination, the end article. The algorithm for picking the next linked page will be the simplest—we'll just pick any random internal link.

To make things more interesting, we will also offer a difficulty setting—easy, medium, or hard. This will affect how far apart the start page and the end page will be. For an easy game, they will be two pages away, for medium, four, and for hard, six. Of course, this logic in not super rigorous. Yes, intuitively, we can say that two articles that are further apart will be less related and harder to link. But, it's also possible that the player will find a shorter path. We won't worry about that, though.

The game will also allow the players to go back if they can't find the solution in the maximum number of steps.

Finally, if the player gives up, we'll add an option to show the solution—the path we found from the start article to the destination.

This sounds exciting—let's write some code!

Some additional requirements

In order to follow through this chapter, you will need the following:

- A working Julia installation
- An internet connection
- A text editor

Organizing our code

Up to this point, we've been mostly coding at the REPL. Recently, in the previous chapter, we've started to rely more on the IDE to whip up short Julia files.

But, as our skillset grows and we develop more and more ambitious projects, so will grow the complexity of our programs. This, in turn, will lead to more lines of code, more logic, and more files—and more difficulties in maintaining and understanding all these down the line. As the famous coding axiom goes, the code is read many more times than it is written—so we need to plan accordingly.

Each language comes with its own philosophy and toolset when it comes to code organization. In Julia, we have files, modules, and packages. We'll learn about all of these next.

Using modules to tame our code

Modules group together related functions, variables, and other definitions. But, they are not just organizational units—they are language constructs that can be understood as variable workspaces. They allow us to define variables and functions without worrying about name conflicts. Julia's `Module` is one of the cornerstones of the language—a key structural and logical entity that helps make code easier to develop, understand, and maintain. We'll make good use of modules by architecting our game around them.

A module is defined using the `module <<name>>...end` construct:

```
module MyModule
# code here
end
```

Let's start a new REPL session and look at a few examples.

Say we want to write a function that retrieves a random Wikipedia page—it's one of our game's features. We could call this function `rand`.

As you may suspect, creating random *things* is a pretty common task, so we're not the first ones to think about it. You can see for yourself. Try this at the REPL:

```
julia> rand
rand (generic function with 56 methods)
```

Turns out, 56 `rand` methods are already defined.

This will make it difficult to add our own variant:

```
julia> function rand()
           # code here
       end
error in method definition: function Base.rand must be explicitly imported
to be extended
```

Our attempt to define a new `rand` method raised an error because it was already defined and loaded.

It's easy to see how this can lead to a nightmare scenario when choosing the names of our functions. If all the defined names would live in the same workspace, we'd get into endless name conflicts as we'd run out of relevant names for our functions and variables.

Julia's module allows us to define separate workspaces, providing a level of encapsulation that separates our variables and functions from everybody else's. By using modules, name conflicts are eliminated.

Modules are defined within `module...end` language constructs. Try this example (at the REPL), where we define our `rand` function within a module called `MyModule`:

```
julia> module MyModule

       function rand()
           println("I'll get a random Wikipedia page")
       end

       end
Main.MyModule
```

This snippet defines a module called `MyModule`—and within it, a function called `rand`. Here, `MyModule` effectively encapsulates the `rand` function, which no longer clashes with Julia's `Base.rand`.

As you can see from its full name, `Main.MyModule`, our newly created module, is actually added within another existing module called `Main`. This module, `Main`, is the default module within which code executed at the REPL is evaluated.

In order to access our newly defined function, we need to reference it within `MyModule`, by *dotting in*:

```
julia> MyModule.rand()
I'll get a random wikipedia page
```

Defining modules

Since modules are designed to be used with larger code bases, they're not REPL-friendly. Because once they are defined, we cannot extend them with extra definitions and we're forced to retype and redefine the whole module, and it's best to use a full-fledged editor.

Let's create a new folder to host our code. Within it, we'll want to create a new folder called `modules/`. Then, within the `modules/` folder, add three files—`Letters.jl`, `Numbers.jl`, and `module_name.jl`.

 Files containing Julia code use, by convention, the `.jl` file extension.

Productive REPL sessions with Julia

Why not use Julia's file-wrangling powers to set up this file structure? Let's take a look at how to do this, as it will come in handy in our day-to-day work.

Remember, you can type `;` into the REPL, at the beginning of the line, to trigger the shell mode. Your cursor will change from `julia>` to `shell>` to confirm the change of context. In IJulia/Jupyter, you have to prefix the code in the cell with `;` in order to be executed in shell mode.

Now, we can perform the following:

```
shell> mkdir modules # create a new dir called "modules"
shell> cd modules # switch to the "modules" directory
```

Don't forget that Julia's shell mode calls commands as if they run straight into the OS Terminal—so the invoked binaries must exist on that platform. Both `mkdir` and `cd` are supported on all major operating systems, so we're safe here. But, when it comes to creating the files, we're out of luck—the `touch` command is not available on Windows. No problem though—all we need to do in this case is to invoke the Julia function with the same name. This will create the files programmatically, in a platform-agnostic way:

```
julia> for f in ["Letters.jl", "Numbers.jl", "module_name.jl"]
           touch(f)
       end
```

If you want to make sure that the files were created, use `readdir`:

```
julia> readdir()
3-element Array{String,1}:
 "Letters.jl"
 "Numbers.jl"
 "module_name.jl"
```

Please make sure that you name the files exactly as indicated, respecting the case.

Another handy productivity trick is invoking `edit`, which opens a file or directory in your default Julia editor. The next snippet will open `Letters.jl` in whatever default editor you have configured:

```
julia> edit("Letters.jl")
```

If the default editor is not your favorite Julia IDE, you can change it by setting one of the `JULIA_EDITOR`, `VISUAL`, or `EDITOR` environment variables to point to the editor of your choice. For instance, on my Mac, I can ask for the path to the Atom editor with the following:

```
shell> which atom
/usr/local/bin/atom
```

And then, I can set `JULIA_EDITOR` as follows:

```
julia> ENV["JULIA_EDITOR"] = "/usr/local/bin/atom"
```

The three variables have slightly different purposes, but in this case, setting any of them will have the same effect—changing the default editor for the current Julia session. Keep in mind, though, that they have different *weights*, with JULIA_EDITOR taking precedence over VISUAL, which takes precedence over EDITOR.

Setting up our modules

Let's start by editing Letters.jl to make it look like this:

```
module Letters

using Random

export randstring

const MY_NAME = "Letters"

function rand()
  Random.rand('A':'Z')
end

function randstring()
  [rand() for _ in 1:10] |> join
end

include("module_name.jl")

end
```

Here, we have defined a module called Letters. In it, we added a rand function that uses Julia's Random.rand to return a random letter between A and Z in the form of a Char. Next, we added a function called Letters.randstring, which returns a String of 10 random characters. This string is generated using a Char[] array comprehension (the _ variable name is perfectly legal in Julia and, by convention, it designates a variable whose value is not used) which is piped into the join function to return the string result.

Please note that this is an over complicated way to generate a random string as Julia provides the Random.randstring function. But, at this point, it's important to exploit every opportunity to practice writing code, and I just didn't want to waste the chance of using Julia's comprehension syntax and the pipe operator. Practice makes perfect!

Switching our focus towards the first lines of code, we declared that we'll be `using` `Random`—and we instructed the compiler to make `randstring` public via `export` `randstring`. Finally, we have also declared a constant called `MY_NAME`, which points to the `Letters` string (which is the name of the module itself).

The last line of the module, `include("module_name.jl")`, loads the contents of `module_name.jl` into `Letters`. The `include` function is typically used to load source code interactively, or to combine files in packages that are split into multiple source files—and we'll see how this works soon.

Next, let's edit `Number.jl`. It will have a similar `rand` function that will return a random `Integer` between 1 and 1_000. It exports `halfrand`, a function that gets a value from `rand` and divides it by 2. We pass the result of the division to the `floor` function, which will convert it to the closest less than or equal value. And, just like `Letters`, it also includes `module_name.jl`:

```
module Numbers

using Random

export halfrand

const MY_NAME = "Numbers"

function rand()
  Random.rand(1:1_000)
end
function halfrand()
  floor(rand() / 2)
end

include("module_name.jl")
end
```

Thus, for both modules, we defined a `MY_NAME` constant. We'll reference it by editing the `module_name.jl` file to make it look like this:

```
function myname()
  MY_NAME
end
```

The code returns the corresponding value of the constant, depending on the actual module where we include the `module_name.jl` file. This illustrates Julia's mixin behavior, where included code acts as if it was written directly into the including file. We'll see how this works next.

Referencing modules

Despite the fact that we are only *now* formally discussing modules, we've been using them all along. The `using` statement which we employed so many times takes as its parameter a module name. It's a key language construct that tells the compiler to bring the module's definitions into the current scope. Referencing functions, variables, and types defined in other modules is a routine part of programming in Julia—accessing the functionality provided by a third-party package, for example, revolves around bringing its main module into scope via `using`. But, `using` is not the only tool in Julia's arsenal. We have a few more commands at our disposal, such as `import`, `include`, and `export`.

The `using` directive allows us to reference functions, variables, types, and so on exported by other modules. This tells Julia to make the module's exported definitions available in the current workspace. If the definitions were exported by the module's author, we can invoke them without having to prefix them with the module's name (prefixing the name of the function with the module name represents the fully qualified name). But, be careful though as this is a double-edged sword—if two used modules export functions with the same name, the functions will still have to be accessed using the fully qualified name—otherwise Julia will throw an exception as it won't know which of the functions we refer to.

As for `import`, it is somewhat similar, in that it also brings definitions from another module into scope. But, it differs in two important aspects. First, calling `import MyModule` would still require prefixing the definitions with the module's name, thereby avoiding potential name clashes. Second, if we want to extend functions defined in other modules with new methods, we *have* to use `import`.

On the other hand, `include` is conceptually different. It is used to evaluate the contents of a file into the current context (that is, into the current module's *global* scope). It's a way to reuse code by providing mixin-like behavior, as we have already seen.

The fact that the included file is evaluated in the module's global scope is a very important point. It means that, even if we include a file within a function's body, the contents of the file will not be evaluated within the function's scope, but within the module's scope. To see this in action, let's create a file called `testinclude.jl` in our `modules/` folder. Edit `testinclude.jl` and append this line of code:

```
somevar = 10
```

Now, if you run the following code in the REPL or in IJulia, you'll see what I mean:

```
julia> function testinclude()
           include("testinclude.jl")
           println(somevar)
       end

julia> testinclude()
10
```

Apparently, it all worked fine. The `testinclude.jl` file was included and the `somevar` variable was defined. However, `somevar` was not created within the `testinclude` function, but as a global variable in the `Main` module. We can see that easily, as we can access the `somevar` variable directly:

```
julia> somevar
10
```

Keep this behavior in mind as it can lead to hard-to-understand bugs by exposing variables in the global scope.

Finally, `export` is used by a module's author to expose definitions, much like a public interface. As we've seen, exported functions and variables are brought into scope by the module's users via `using`.

Setting up the LOAD_PATH

Let's look at some examples that illustrate scoping rules when working with modules. Please open a new Julia REPL.

We've seen the `using` statement many times throughout the previous chapters, and now we understand its role—to bring another module and its definitions (variables, functions, types) into scope. Let's try it with our newly created modules:

```
julia> using Letters
ERROR: ArgumentError: Package Letters not found in current path:
- Run `Pkg.add("Letters")` to install the Letters package.
```

Ouch, an exception! Julia informs us that it doesn't know where to find the `Letters` module and advises us to use `Pkg.add("Letters")` to install it. But, since `Pkg.add` only works with registered packages and we haven't published our modules to Julia's registry, that won't help. Turns out we just need to tell Julia where to find our code.

When asked to bring a module into scope via `using`, Julia checks a series of paths to look up the corresponding files. These lookup paths are stored in a `Vector` called the `LOAD_PATH`—and we can append our `modules/` folder to this collection by using the `push!` function:

```
julia> push!(LOAD_PATH, "modules/")
4-element Array{String,1}:
 "@"
 "@v#.#"
 "@stdlib"
 "modules/"
```

Your output might be different, but what matters is that after calling `push!`, the `LOAD_PATH` collection now has an extra element indicating the path to the `modules/` folder.

In order for Julia to match the name of a module with its corresponding file, *the file must have exactly the same name as the module*, plus the `.jl` extension. It's OK for a file to include more than one module, but Julia will not be able to automatically find the extra ones by filename.

In regard to naming the modules themselves, the convention is to use CamelCase. Thus, we'll end up with a module called `Letters` defined in a `Letters.jl` file, or with a `WebSockets` module in a file named `WebSockets.jl`.

Loading modules with using

Now that we've added our folder to the `LOAD_PATH`, we're ready to use our modules:

```
julia> using Letters
```

At this point, two things have happened:

- All the exported definitions are now directly callable in the REPL, in our case, `randstring`
- The definitions that were not exported are accessible by *dotting into* `Letters`—for example, `Letters.rand()`

Let's try it:

```
julia> randstring() # has been exported and is directly accessible
"TCNXFLUOUU"

julia> myname() # has not been exported so it's not available in the
REPLERROR: UndefVarError: myname not defined
```

```
julia> Letters.myname()  # but we can access it under the Letters namespace
"Letters"
```

```
julia> Letters.rand()  # does not conflict with Base.rand
'L': ASCII/Unicode U+004c (category Lu: Letter, uppercase)
```

We can see what a module exports with the `names` function:

```
julia> names(Letters)
2-element Array{Symbol,1}:
 :Letters
 :randstring
```

If we want to get all the definitions of a module, exported or not, `names` takes a second parameter, `all`, a `Boolean`:

```
julia> names(Letters, all = true)
11-element Array{Symbol,1}:
 # output truncated
 :Letters
 :MY_NAME
 :eval
 :myname
 :rand
 :randstring
```

We can easily recognize the variables and functions we defined.

As we can see, for instance, `myname` was not brought directly into scope, since it wasn't exported in `Letters`. But, it turns out that we can still get the exported-like behavior if we explicitly tell Julia to use the function:

```
julia> using Letters: myname
julia> myname()  # we no longer need to "dot into" Letters.myname()
"Letters"
```

If we want to bring multiple definitions from the same module directly into scope, we can pass a comma-separated list of names:

```
julia> using Letters: myname, MY_NAME
```

Loading modules with import

Now, let's look at the effects of the import function, using Numbers:

```
julia> import Numbers
julia> names(Numbers)
2-element Array{Symbol,1}:
 :Numbers
 :halfrand
julia> halfrand()
ERROR: UndefVarError: halfrand not defined
```

We can see here that, unlike using, the import function *does not bring into scope* the exported definitions.

However, explicitly importing a definition itself will bring it directly into scope, disregarding whether it was exported or not:

```
julia> import Numbers.halfrand, Numbers.MY_NAME
```

This snippet is equivalent to the following:

```
julia> import Numbers: halfrand, MY_NAME

julia> halfrand()
271.0
```

Loading modules with include

Manipulating the LOAD_PATH works great when developing standalone apps, like the one we're working on now. However, this approach is not available for a package developer. For such instances—and for all the cases when for one reason or another using the LOAD_PATH is not an option—a common way of loading modules is by including their files.

For example, we can include our Letters module at the REPL, as follows (start a new REPL session):

```
julia> include("modules/Letters.jl")
Main.Letters
```

This will read and evaluate the contents of the `modules/Letters.jl` file in the current scope. And as a result, it will define the `Letters` module within our current module, `Main`. But, this is not enough—at this point, none of the definitions within `Letters` were exported:

```
julia> randstring()
ERROR: UndefVarError: randstring not defined
```

We need to bring them into scope:

```
julia> using Letters
ERROR: ArgumentError: Package Letters not found in current path:
- Run `Pkg.add("Letters")` to install the Letters package.
```

Not again! What just happened? This is an important distinction when using `include` with modules. The `Letters` module, like we just said, is included in the current module, `Main`, so we need to reference it accordingly:

```
julia> using Main.Letters

julia> randstring()
"QUPCDZKSAH"
```

We can also reference this kind of nested module hierarchy by using relative *paths*. For example, a dot, `.`, stands for *current module*. So, the previous `Main.Letters` nesting can be expressed as `.Letters`— it's exactly the same thing:

```
julia> using .Letters
```

Similarly, we could use two dots, `..`, to reference the parent module, three dots for the parent of the parent, and so on.

Nesting modules

As we've just seen, sometimes, the logic of our program will dictate that a module has to be part of another module, effectively nesting them. This is used with predilection when developing our own packages. The best way to organize a package is to expose a top module and include all the other definitions (functions, variables, and other modules) within it (to encapsulate the functionality). An example should help clarify things.

Let's make a change—in the `Letters.jl` file, under the line saying `include("module_name.jl")`, go ahead and add another line—`include("Numbers.jl")`.

With this change, the `Numbers` module will effectively be defined within the `Letters` module. In order to access the functions of the nested module, we *dot into* as deep as necessary:

```
julia> using .Letters

julia> Letters.Numbers.halfrand()
432.5
```

Setting up our game's architecture

Let's create a home for our game—make a new folder called `sixdegrees/`. We'll use it to organize our game's files. Each file will contain a module and each module will package related functionality. We'll make use of Julia's auto-loading features, which means that the filename of each module will be the same as the module's name, plus the `.jl` extension.

The first thing we need to do, though, once we go into the `sixdegrees/` folder, is to initialize our project through `Pkg`—so we can use Julia's dependency management features:

```
julia> mkdir("sixdegrees")
"sixdegrees"

julia> cd("sixdegrees/")

julia> ] # go into pkg mode

(v1.0) pkg> activate .

(sixdegrees) pkg>
```

We'll be using the `HTTP` and the `Gumbo` packages, so it's a good idea to add them, now that we're dealing with dependencies:

```
(sixdegrees) pkg> add HTTP Gumbo
```

The next thing we need is a container for Wikipedia-related code—a module that encapsulates the functionality for requesting an article and extracting the internal URLs. We already have a first iteration of the code in the `webcrawler.jl` file we wrote in Chapter 3, *Setting Up the Wiki Game*. Now, all we need to do is create a `Wikipedia` module and fill it up with the contents of `webcrawler.jl`.

Within the `sixdegrees` folder, create a new file called `Wikipedia.jl`. Set it up with the following code:

```
module Wikipedia
using HTTP, Gumbo

const RANDOM_PAGE_URL = "https://en.m.wikipedia.org/wiki/Special:Random"

export fetchrandom, fetchpage, articlelinks

function fetchpage(url)
  response = HTTP.get(url)
  if response.status == 200 && length(response.body) > 0
    String(response.body)
  else
    ""
  end
end

function extractlinks(elem, links = String[])
  if  isa(elem, HTMLElement) && tag(elem) == :a && in("href",
collect(keys(attrs(elem))))
        url = getattr(elem, "href")
        startswith(url, "/wiki/") && ! occursin(":", url) && push!(links,
url)
  end
  for child in children(elem)
    extractlinks(child, links)
  end
  unique(links)
end

function fetchrandom()
  fetchpage(RANDOM_PAGE_URL)
end

function articlelinks(content)
  if ! isempty(content)
    dom = Gumbo.parsehtml(content)

    links = extractlinks(dom.root)
```

```
    end
  end

end
```

The preceding code should look familiar as it shares much of its logic with `webcrawler.jl`. But, there are some important changes.

First of all, we wrapped everything into a `module` declaration.

 Please note a very important convention: in Julia, we do not indent the code within modules as this would cause the whole file to be indented, which would affect readability.

On the third line, where we used to have the link to Julia's Wikipedia entry, we now define a `String` constant, `RANDOM_PAGE_URL`, which points to a special Wikipedia URL that returns a random article. Also, we switched to the mobile version of the Wikipedia website, as indicated by the `en.m.` subdomains. Using the mobile pages will make our lives easier as they are simpler and have less markup.

In the `fetchpage` function, we're no longer looking for the `Content-Length` header and we're instead checking the `length` of the `response.body` property. We're doing this because requesting the special random Wikipedia page performs a redirect and, in the process, the `Content-Length` header is dropped.

We have also replaced some of the logic at the bottom of the file. Instead of automatically fetching Julia's Wikipedia page and dumping the list of internal links onto the screen, we now define two more functions: `fetchrandom` and `articlelinks`. These functions will be the public interface of the `Wikipedia` module, and they are exposed using the `export` statement. The `fetchrandom` function does exactly what the name says—it calls the `fetchpage` function passing in the `RANDOM_PAGE_URL` const, effectively fetching a random Wikipedia page. `articlelinks` returns an array of strings representing the linked articles.

Finally, we removed the `LINKS` constant—global variables should be avoided. The `extractlinks` function has been refactored accordingly, now accepting a second parameter, `links`, a `Vector` of `String`, which is used to maintain state during recursion.

Checking our code

Let's make sure that, after this refactoring, our code still works as expected. Julia comes out of the box with unit-testing capabilities, and we'll look at these in Chapter 11, *Creating Julia Packages*. For now, we'll do it the old-fashioned way, by manually running the code and inspecting the output.

We'll add a new file inside the sixdegrees/ folder, called six_degrees.jl. Looking at its name, you can guess that it will be a plain Julia file and not a module. We'll use it to orchestrate the loading of our game:

```
using Pkg
pkg"activate ."

include("Wikipedia.jl")
using .Wikipedia

fetchrandom() |> articlelinks |> display
```

The code is straightforward and minimalistic—we use Pkg to activate the current project. Then, we include the Wikipedia.jl file in the current module, and then we ask the compiler to bring the Wikipedia module into scope. Finally, we use the previously discussed fetchrandom and articlelinks to retrieve the list of articles URLs from a random Wikipedia page and display it.

Time to run our code! In the REPL, make sure that you cd into the sixdegrees folder and execute:

```
julia> include("six_degrees.jl")
21-element Array{String,1}:
 "/wiki/Main_Page"
 "/wiki/Arena"
 "/wiki/Saskatoon,_Saskatchewan"
 "/wiki/South_Saskatchewan_River"
 "/wiki/New_York_Rangers"
# ... output omitted ... #
```

Since we're pulling a random Wikipedia article each time we run our code, your output will be different than in this snippet. The important thing is that you get a non-empty Array{String,1} with entries that start with /wiki/.

Alternatively, you can use the run code or run file option in Visual Studio Code and Atom. Here's Atom running the `six_degrees.jl` file:

Building our Wikipedia crawler - take two

Our code runs as expected, refactored and neatly packed into a module. However, there's one more thing I'd like us to refactor before moving on. I'm not especially fond of our `extractlinks` function.

First of all, it naively iterates over all the HTML elements. For example, say that we also want to extract the title of the page—every time we want to process something that's not a link, we'll have to iterate over the whole document again. That's going to be resource-hungry and slow to run.

Secondly, we're reinventing the wheel. In Chapter 3, *Setting Up the Wiki Game*, we said that CSS selectors are the *lingua franca* of DOM parsing. We'd benefit massively from using the concise syntax of CSS selectors with the underlying optimizations provided by specialized libraries.

Fortunately, we don't need to look too far for this kind of functionality. Julia's Pkg system provides access to Cascadia, a native CSS selector library. And, the great thing about it is that it works hand in hand with Gumbo.

In order to use Cascadia, we need to add it to our project's list of dependencies:

```
(sixdegrees) pkg> add Cascadia
```

Next, tell Julia we'll be using it—modify Wikipedia.jl so that the third line reads as follows:

```
using HTTP, Gumbo, Cascadia
```

With the help of Cascadia, we can now refactor the extractlinks function, as follows:

```
function extractlinks(elem)
  map(eachmatch(Selector("a[href^='/wiki/']:not(a[href*=':'])"), elem)) do
e
    e.attributes["href"]
  end |> unique
end
```

Let's take a closer look at all that happens here. The first thing that stands out is the Selector function. This is provided by Cascadia and constructs a new CSS selector object. The string that is passed to it as its only parameter is a CSS selector that reads as—all <a> elements that have a href attribute whose value starts with '/wiki/' and does not contain a column (:).

Cascadia also exports the eachmatch method. More accurately, it *extends* the existing Base.eachmatch method that we've seen previously with regular expressions. This provides a familiar interface—and we'll see how to extend methods later in this chapter, in the *Methods* section. The Cascadia.eachmatch function returns a Vector of elements that match the selector.

Building the Wiki Game Web Crawler

Once we retrieve the collection of matched elements, we pass it to the map function. The map function is one of the most used tools in the functional programming toolbox. It takes as its arguments a function, f, and a collection, c—and it transforms the collection, c, by applying f to each element, returning the modified collection as the result. Its definition is as follows:

```
map(f, c...) -> collection
```

So then, what's with the strange-looking do e ... end part in the previous snippet? That doesn't look like invoking the previous map function, it's true. But it is, in fact, the exact same function invocation, except with a more readable syntax, provided by Julia's blocks.

Using blocks

Because, in Julia, functions are first-class language constructs, they can be referenced and manipulated like any other type of variable. They can be passed as arguments to other functions or can be returned as the result of other function calls. The functions that take another function as their argument or return another function as their result are called **higher-order functions**.

Let's look at a simple example using map. We'll take a Vector of Int, and we'll apply to each element of its collection a function that doubles the value. You can follow along in a new REPL session (or in the accompanying IJulia notebook):

```
julia> double(x) = x*2
double (generic function with 1 method)

julia> map(double, [1, 2, 3, 5, 8, 13])
6-element Array{Int64,1}:
  2
  4
  6
 10
 16
 26
```

In this snippet, you can see how we passed the reference to the double function as the argument of the higher-order function map. As a result, we got back the Vector, which was passed as the second argument, but with all the elements doubled.

That's all good, but having to define a function just to use it as a one-off argument for another function is inconvenient and a bit wasteful. For this reason, the programming languages that support functional features, including Julia, usually support *anonymous functions*. An anonymous function, or a *lambda*, is a function definition that is not bound to an identifier.

We can rewrite the preceding `map` invocation to use an anonymous function, which is defined on the spot by using the arrow `->` syntax:

```
julia> map(x -> x*2, [1, 2, 3, 5, 8, 13])
6-element Array{Int64,1}:
  2
  4
  6
 10
 16
 26
```

In the definition, x `->` x`*`2, the x at the left of the arrow represents the argument that is passed into the function, while x`*`2 represents the body of the function.

Great! We have achieved the same end result without having to separately define `double`. But, what if we need to use a more complex function? For instance, note the following:

```
julia> map(x ->
             if x % 2 == 0
                  x * 2
             elseif x % 3 == 0
                  x * 3
             elseif x % 5 == 0
                  x * 5
             else
                  x
             end,
        [1, 2, 3, 5, 8, 13])
```

That's pretty hard to follow! Because Julia allows us to indent our code, we can enhance the readability of this example to make it more palatable, but the result is still far from great.

Because these situations occur often, Julia provides the block syntax for defining anonymous functions. All the functions that take another function as their *first* argument can be used with the block syntax. Support for this kind of invocation is baked into the language, so you don't need to do anything—your functions will support it as well, out of the box, as long as the function is the first positional argument. In order to use it, we skip passing in the first argument when invoking the higher-order function—and instead, at the end of the arguments list, outside of the arguments tuple, we add a do...end block. Within this block, we define our lambda.

So, we can rewrite the previous example as follows:

```
map([1, 2, 3, 5, 8, 13]) do x
      if x % 2 == 0
            x * 2
      elseif x % 3 == 0
            x * 3
      elseif x % 5 == 0
            x * 5
      else
            x
      end
end
```

Much more readable!

Implementing the gameplay

Our Wikipedia parser is pretty robust now, and the addition of Cascadia greatly simplifies the code. It's time to think about the actual gameplay.

The most important thing, the core of the game, is to create the riddle—asking the player to find a path from the initial article to the end article. We previously decided that in order to be sure that a path between two articles really exists, we will pre-crawl all the pages, from the first to the last. In order to navigate from one page to the next, we'll simply randomly pick one of the internal URLs.

We also mentioned including difficulty settings. We will use the common-sense assumption that the more links there are between the start article and the end article, the less related their subjects will be; and thus, the more difficult to identify the path between them, resulting in a more challenging level.

All right, time to get coding! For starters, create a new file inside the sixdegrees/ folder. Name it Gameplay.jl and copy and paste the following:

```julia
module Gameplay

using ..Wikipedia

export newgame

const DIFFICULTY_EASY = 2
const DIFFICULTY_MEDIUM = 4
const DIFFICULTY_HARD = 6

function newgame(difficulty = DIFFICULTY_HARD)
  articles = []

  for i in 1:difficulty
    article = if i == 1
      fetchrandom()
    else
      rand(articles[i-1][:links]) |> Wikipedia.fetchpage
    end

article_data = Dict(:content => article,
  :links => articlelinks(article))
    push!(articles, article_data)
  end

  articles
end

end
```

Gamplay.jl defines a new module and brings Wikipedia into scope. Here, you can see how we reference the Wikipedia module in the parent scope by using ... It then defines three constants that map the difficulty settings to degrees of separation (named DIFFICULTY_EASY, DIFFICULTY_MEDIUM, and DIFFICULTY_HARD).

It then defines a function, `newgame`, which accepts a difficulty argument, by default set to hard. In the body of the function, we loop for a number of times equal to the difficulty value. On each iteration, we check the current degree of separation—if it's the first article, we call `fetchrandom` to start off the crawling process. If it's not the first article, we pick a random link from the list of links of the previously crawled article (`rand(articles[i-1][:links])`). We then pass this URL to `fetchpage`. When discussing conditionals, we learned that in Julia `if`/`else` statements return the value of the last-evaluated expression. We can see it put to good use here, with the result of the evaluation being stored in the `article` variable.

Once we've fetched the article, we store its content and its links within a `Dict` called `article_data`. And, `article_data` is in turn added to the `articles` array. On its last line, the `newgame` function returns the `articles` vector that now contains all the steps, from first to last. This function is also exported.

That wasn't too hard! But, there's a small glitch. If you try to run the code now, it will fail. The reason is that the article links are *relative*. This means that they are not fully qualified URLs; they look like `/wiki/Some_Article_Title`. When `HTTP.jl` makes a request, it needs the full link, protocol, and domain name included. But don't worry, that's easy to fix in `Wikipedia.jl`. Please switch your editor to the `Wikipedia` module and replace the `const RANDOM_PAGE_URL` line with the following three lines:

```
const PROTOCOL = "https://"
const DOMAIN_NAME = "en.m.wikipedia.org"
const RANDOM_PAGE_URL = PROTOCOL * DOMAIN_NAME * "/wiki/Special:Random"
```

We broke the random page URL into its components—the protocol, the domain name, and the rest of the relative path.

We'll use a similar approach to turn relative URLs into absolute URLs when fetching articles. For this, change the body of `fetchpage` and add this as its first line of code:

```
url = startswith(url, "/") ? PROTOCOL * DOMAIN_NAME * url : url
```

Here, we check the `url` argument—if it starts with `"/"`, it means it's a relative URL so we need to turn it into its absolute counterpart. We used the ternary operator, as you can tell.

Our code should work just fine now, but spreading this `PROTOCOL * DOMAIN_NAME * url` throughout our game is a bit of a code smell. Let's abstract this away into a function:

```
function buildurl(article_url)
    PROTOCOL * DOMAIN_NAME * article_url
end
```

A *code smell* in programming parlance refers to a practice that violates fundamental design principles and negatively impacts quality. It is not a *bug per se,* but indicates weakness in design that may increase the risk of bugs or failures in the future.

The `Wikipedia.jl` file should now look like this:

```
module Wikipedia

using HTTP, Gumbo, Cascadia

const PROTOCOL = "https://"
const DOMAIN_NAME = "en.m.wikipedia.org"
const RANDOM_PAGE_URL = PROTOCOL * DOMAIN_NAME * "/wiki/Special:Random"

export fetchrandom, fetchpage, articlelinks

function fetchpage(url)
  url = startswith(url, "/") ? buildurl(url) : url
  response = HTTP.get(url)

  if response.status == 200 && length(response.body) > 0
    String(response.body)
  else
    ""
  end
end

function extractlinks(elem)
  map(eachmatch(Selector("a[href^='/wiki/']:not(a[href*=':'])"), elem)) do
e
    e.attributes["href"]
  end |> unique
end

function fetchrandom()
  fetchpage(RANDOM_PAGE_URL)
end

function articlelinks(content)
  if ! isempty(content)
    dom = Gumbo.parsehtml(content)
    links = extractlinks(dom.root)
  end
end

function buildurl(article_url)
```

```
        PROTOCOL * DOMAIN_NAME * article_url
    end

    end
```

Finishing touches

Our gameplay evolves nicely. Only a few pieces left. Thinking about our game's UI, we'll want to show the game's progression, indicating the articles the player has navigated through. For this, we'll need the titles of the articles. If we could also include an image, that would make our game much prettier.

Fortunately, we are now using CSS selectors, so extracting the missing data should be a piece of cake. All we need to do is add the following to the `Wikipedia` module:

```
import Cascadia: matchFirst

function extracttitle(elem)
    matchFirst(Selector("#section_0"), elem) |> nodeText
end

function extractimage(elem)
    e = matchFirst(Selector(".content a.image img"), elem)
    isa(e, Void) ? "" : e.attributes["src"]
end
```

The `extracttitle` and `extractimage` functions will retrieve the corresponding content from our article pages. In both cases, since we only want to select a single element, the main page heading and the first image respectively, we use `Cascadia.matchFirst`. The `matchFirst` function is not publicly exposed by `Cascadia`—but since it's quite useful, we `import` it.

The `#section_0` selector identifies the main page heading, a `<h1>` element. And, because we need to extract the text between its `<h1>`...`</h1>` tags, we invoke the `nodeText` method provided by `Cascadia`.

You can see in the following screenshot, which shows the main heading of a Wikipedia page in Safari's inspector, how to identify the desired HTML elements and how to pick their CSS selectors by inspecting the source of the page and the corresponding DOM element. The HTML property, `id="section_0"`, corresponds to the `#section_0` CSS selector:

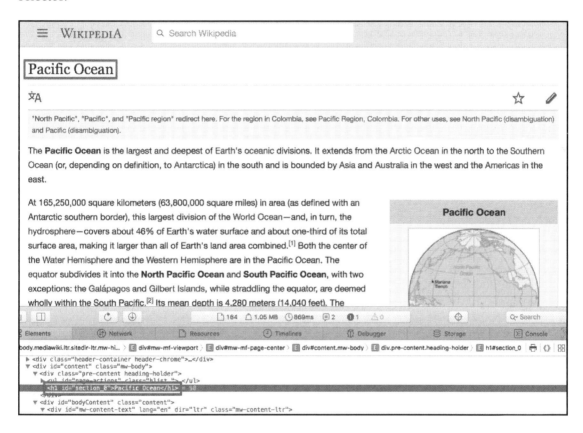

As for `extractimage`, we look for the main article image, represented by the "`.content a.image img`" selector. Since not all the pages have it, we check if we do indeed get a valid element. If the page does not have an image, we'll get an instance of `Nothing`, called `nothing`. This is an important construct—`nothing` is the singleton instance of `Nothing`, indicating the absence of an object, corresponding to `NULL` in other languages. If we do get an `img` element, we extract the value of its `src` attribute, which is the URL of the image.

Here is another Wikipedia screenshot, in which I marked the image element that we're targeting. The flag is the first image on Wikipedia's **Australia** page—a perfect match:

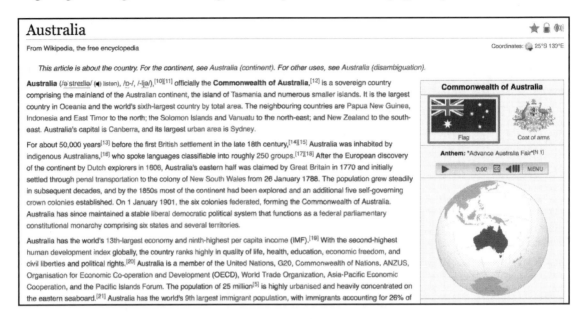

Next, we could extend the `Gameplay.newgame` function, to handle the new functions and values. But by now, this doesn't feel right—too much of the logic of `Wikipedia` would leak into the `Gameplay` module, coupling them; a dangerous anti-pattern. Instead, let's make the extraction of the data and setting up of the article, `Dict`, the full responsibility of `Wikipedia`, completely encapsulating the logic. Make the `Gameplay.newgame` function looks as shown in the following code:

```
function newgame(difficulty = DIFFICULTY_HARD)
    articles = []
    for i in 1:difficulty
      article = if i == 1
                  fetchrandom()
                else
                  rand(articles[i-1][:links]) |> Wikipedia.fetchpage
                end
      push!(articles, articleinfo(article))
    end

    articles
  end
```

Then, update the Wikipedia module to read as follows:

```
module Wikipedia

using HTTP, Gumbo, Cascadia
import Cascadia: matchFirst

const PROTOCOL = "https://"
const DOMAIN_NAME = "en.m.wikipedia.org"
const RANDOM_PAGE_URL = PROTOCOL * DOMAIN_NAME * "/wiki/Special:Random"

export fetchrandom, fetchpage, articleinfo

function fetchpage(url)
  url = startswith(url, "/") ? buildurl(url) : url

  response = HTTP.get(url)

  if response.status == 200 && length(response.body) > 0
    String(response.body)
  else
    ""
  end
end

function extractlinks(elem)
  map(eachmatch(Selector("a[href^='/wiki/']:not(a[href*=':'])"), elem)) do
e
    e.attributes["href"]
  end |> unique
end

function extracttitle(elem)
  matchFirst(Selector("#section_0"), elem) |> nodeText
end

function extractimage(elem)
  e = matchFirst(Selector(".content a.image img"), elem)
  isa(e, Nothing) ? "" : e.attributes["src"]
end

function fetchrandom()
  fetchpage(RANDOM_PAGE_URL)
end

function articledom(content)
  if ! isempty(content)
    return Gumbo.parsehtml(content)
```

```
    end

    error("Article content can not be parsed into DOM")
  end

  function articleinfo(content)
    dom = articledom(content)

    Dict( :content => content,
          :links => extractlinks(dom.root),
          :title => extracttitle(dom.root),
          :image => extractimage(dom.root)
    )
  end

  function buildurl(article_url)
    PROTOCOL * DOMAIN_NAME * article_url
  end

end
```

The file has a few important changes. We've removed the `articlelinks` function and instead added `articleinfo` and `articledom`. The new `articledom` function parses the HTML using Gumbo and generates the DOM, which, very importantly, is only parsed once. We don't want to parse the HTML into a DOM every time we extract a type of element, as would've been the case if we kept the previous `articlelinks` function. As for `articleinfo`, it is responsible for setting up an article, `Dict`, with all the relevant information—content, links, title, and image.

We can do a test run of our code, by modifying the `six_degrees.jl` file, as follows:

```
using Pkg
pkg"activate ."

include("Wikipedia.jl")
include("Gameplay.jl")

using .Wikipedia, .Gameplay

for article in newgame(Gameplay.DIFFICULTY_EASY)
  println(article[:title])
end
```

We start a new game, which goes through two articles (`Gameplay.DIFFICULTY_EASY`) and for each article we display its title. We can see it in action by either running it in a REPL session via `julia> include("six_degrees.jl")`, or by simply running the file in Visual Studio Code or Atom. Here it is in the REPL:

```
julia> include("six_degrees.jl")
Miracle Bell
Indie pop
```

One more thing

Our test run shows that our difficulty settings have a small glitch. We should crawl a certain number of articles *after* the starting point. Our initial article should not count. This is super easy to fix. In `Gameplay.newgame`, we need to replace `for i in 1:difficulty` with `for i in 1:difficulty+1` (note the +1 at the end). Now, if we try again, it works as intended:

```
julia> include("six_degrees.jl")
John O'Brien (Australian politician)
Harlaxton, Queensland
Ballard, Queensland
```

Learning about Julia's type system

Our game works like a charm, but there is one thing we can improve—storing our article info as a `Dict`. Julia's dictionaries are very flexible and powerful, but they are not a good fit in every case. The `Dict` is a generic data structure that is optimized for search, delete, and insert operations. None of these are needed here—our articles have a fixed structure and contain data that doesn't change once created. It's a perfect use case for objects and **object-oriented programming** (OOP). Looks like it's time to learn about types.

Julia's type system is the bread and butter of the language—it is all-pervasive, defining the language's syntax and being the driving force behind Julia's performance and flexibility. Julia's type system is dynamic, meaning that nothing is known about types until runtime, when the actual values manipulated by the program are available. However, we can benefit from the advantages of static typing by using type annotations—indicating that certain values are of specific types. This can greatly improve the performance of the code and also enhance readability and simplify debugging.

It's impossible to talk about Julia and not talk about types. And sure enough, we've seen many primitive types so far—`Integer`, `Float64`, `Boolean`, `Char`, and so on. We've also been exposed to types while learning about the various data structures, such as `Array`, `Dict`, or tuple. These are all built into the language, but it turns out that Julia makes it very easy to create our own.

Defining our own types

Julia supports two categories of type—primitive and composite. A primitive type is a concrete type whose data consists of plain old bits. A composite type is a collection of named fields, an instance of which can be treated as a single value. In many languages, composite types are the only kind of user-definable type, but Julia lets us declare our own primitive types as well, rather than providing only a fixed set of built-in ones.

 We won't talk about defining primitive types here, but you can read more about them in the official documentation at `https://docs.julialang.org/en/v1/manual/types/`.

In order to represent our articles, we're best served by an immutable composite type. Once our article object is created, its data won't change. Immutable composite types are introduced by the `struct` keyword followed by a block of field names:

```
struct Article
    content
    links
    title
    image
end
```

Since we provide no type information for the fields—that is, we don't tell Julia what type we want each field to be—they will default to any, allowing to hold any type of value. But, since we already know what data we want to store, we would greatly benefit from constraining the type of each field. The `::` operator can be used to attach type annotations to expressions and variables. It can be read as *is an instance of*. Thus, we define the `Article` type as follows:

```
struct Article
    content::String
    links::Vector{String}
    title::String
    image::String
end
```

All the fields are of `String` type, with the exception of `links`, which is a one-dimensional `Array` of `String`, also called a `Vector{String}`.

Type annotations can provide important performance benefits—while also eliminating a whole class of type-related bugs.

Constructing types

New objects of `Article` type are created by applying the `Article` type name like a function. The arguments are the values for its fields:

```
julia> julia = Article(
          "Julia is a high-level dynamic programming language",
          ["/wiki/Jeff_Bezanson", "/wiki/Stefan_Karpinski",
           "/wiki/Viral_B._Shah", "/wiki/Alan_Edelman"],
          "Julia (programming language)",
          "/220px-Julia_prog_language.svg.png"
       )
Article("Julia is a high-level dynamic programming language",
["/wiki/Jeff_Bezanson", "/wiki/Stefan_Karpinski", "/wiki/Viral_B._Shah",
"/wiki/Alan_Edelman"], "Julia (programming language)", "/220px-
Julia_prog_language.svg.png")
```

The fields of the newly created object can be accessed using the standard *dot notation*:

```
julia> julia.title
"Julia (programming language)"
```

Because we declared our type to be immutable, the values are read-only, so they can't be changed:

```
julia> julia.title = "The best programming language, period"
ERROR: type Article is immutable
```

Our `Article` type definition won't allow us to change the `julia.title` property. But, immutability should not be dismissed as it does come with considerable advantages, per the official Julia documentation:

- It can be more efficient. Some structs can be packed efficiently into arrays, and in some cases, the compiler is able to avoid allocating immutable objects entirely.
- It is not possible to violate the invariants provided by the type's constructors.
- Code using immutable objects can be easier to reason about.

But, that's not the whole story. An immutable object can have fields that reference mutable objects, such as, for instance, `links`, which points to an `Array{String, 1}`. This array is still mutable:

```
julia> push!(julia.links, "/wiki/Multiple_dispatch")
5-element Array{String,1}:
 "/wiki/Jeff_Bezanson"
 "/wiki/Stefan_Karpinski"
 "/wiki/Viral_B._Shah"
 "/wiki/Alan_Edelman"
 "/wiki/Multiple_dispatch"
```

We can see that there is no error when trying to alter the `links` property, by pushing one more URL to the underlying collection. If a property points to a mutable type, that type can be mutated, as long as its type stays the same:

```
julia> julia.links = [1, 2, 3]
MethodError: Cannot `convert` an object of type Int64 to an object of type
String
```

We are not allowed to change the type of the `links` field—Julia tries to accommodate and attempts to convert the values we provided from `Int` to `String`, but fails.

Mutable composite types

It is also possible (and equally easy) to construct mutable composite types. The only thing we need to do is to use the `mutable struct` statement, instead of just `struct`:

```
julia> mutable struct Player
           username::String
           score::Int
       end
```

Our `Player` object should be mutable, as we'll need to update the `score` property after each game:

```
julia> me = Player("adrian", 0)
Player("adrian", 0)

julia> me.score += 10
10

julia> me
Player("adrian", 10)
```

Type hierarchy and inheritance

Like all programming languages that implement OOP features, Julia allows developers to define rich and expressive type hierarchies. However, unlike most OOP languages, there is a very important difference—*only the final (upper) type in the hierarchy can be instantiated in Julia*. All its parents are just nodes in the type graph, and we can't create instances of them. They are *abstract types* and are defined using the `abstract` type keywords:

```
julia> abstract type Person end
```

We can use the <: operator to indicate that a type is a subtype of an existing *parent*:

```
julia> abstract type Mammal end
julia> abstract type Person <: Mammal end
julia> mutable struct Player <: Person
           username::String
           score::Int
       end
```

Or, in another example, this is Julia's numerical types hierarchy:

```
abstract type Number end
abstract type Real        <: Number end
abstract type AbstractFloat <: Real end
abstract type Integer    <: Real end
abstract type Signed     <: Integer end
abstract type Unsigned <: Integer end
```

The fact that super-types can't be instantiated can seem limiting, but they have a very powerful role. We can define functions that take a super-type as their argument, in effect accepting all its subtypes:

```
julia> struct User <: Person
           username::String
           password::String
       end

julia> sam = User("sam", "password")
User("sam", "password")

julia> function getusername(p::Person)
           p.username
       end

julia> getusername(me)
"adrian"
```

```
julia> getusername(sam)
"sam"

julia> getusername(julia)
ERROR: MethodError: no method matching getusername(::Article)
Closest candidates are:
  getusername(::Person) at REPL[25]:2
```

Here, we can see how we defined a `getusername` function, which accepts an argument of (abstract) type, `Person`. As both `User` and `Player` are subtypes of `Person`, their instances are accepted as arguments.

Type unions

Sometimes, we might want to allow a function to accept a set of types that are not necessarily part of the same type hierarchy. We could, of course, allow the function to accept any type, but depending on the use case, it could be desirable to strictly limit the arguments to a well-defined subset of types. For such cases, Julia provides *type unions*.

A type union is a special abstract type that includes as objects all instances of any of its argument types, constructed using the special `Union` function:

```
julia> GameEntity = Union{Person,Article}
Union{Article, Person}
```

Here, we have defined a new type union, `GameEntity`, which includes two types—`Person` and `Article`. Now, we can define functions that know how to handle `GameEntities`:

```
julia> function entityname(e::GameEntity)
           isa(e, Person) ? e.username : e.title
       end
entityname (generic function with 1 method)

julia> entityname(julia)
"Julia (programming language)"

julia> entityname(me)
"adrian"
```

Using article types

We can refactor our code to eliminate the generic `Dict` data structure and represent our articles with specialized `Article` composite types.

Let's create a new file in our `sixdegrees/` work folder, and name it `Articles.jl`. Edit the file by typing in the corresponding `module` declaration. Then, add the definition of our type and `export` it:

```
module Articles

export Article

struct Article
  content::String
  links::Vector{String}
  title::String
  image::String
end

end
```

We could've added the `Article` type definition to the `Wikipedia.jl` file, but chances are this will grow and it's better to keep them separated instead.

Another thing to note is that both the `module` and the `type` are Julia entities that are loaded in the same scope. For this reason, we can't use the name `Article` for both the `module` and the `type`—we'd end up with a name clash. However, the pluralized name `Articles` is a good name for the module, since it will encapsulate the logic for dealing with *articles* in general, while the `Article` type represents an *article* entity—hence the singular form.

However, since conceptually an `Article` object references a Wikipedia page, it should be part of the `Wikipedia` namespace. That's easy, we just need to include it into the `Wikipedia` module. Add this after the `import Cascadia: matchFirst` line:

```
include("Articles.jl")
using .Articles
```

We're including the `Articles` module file and bringing it into scope.

Next, in the same `Wikipedia.jl` file, we need to modify the `articleinfo` function. Please make sure it reads as follows:

```
function articleinfo(content)
   dom = articledom(content)
   Article(content,
             extractlinks(dom.root),
             extracttitle(dom.root),
             extractimage(dom.root))
end
```

Instead of creating a generic `Dict` object, we're now instantiating an instance of `Article`.

We also need to make a few changes to `Gameplay.jl` to use the `Article` types instead of `Dict`. It should now look like this:

```
module Gameplay

using ..Wikipedia, ..Wikipedia.Articles

export newgame

const DIFFICULTY_EASY = 2
const DIFFICULTY_MEDIUM = 4
const DIFFICULTY_HARD = 6

function newgame(difficulty = DIFFICULTY_HARD)
   articles = Article[]
   for i in 1:difficulty+1
     article = if i == 1
                  fetchrandom()
               else
                  rand(articles[i-1].links) |> fetchpage
               end
     push!(articles, articleinfo(article))
   end

   articles
end

end
```

Note that on the third line we bring `Wikipedia.Articles` into scope. Then, in the `newgame` function, we initiate the `articles` array to be of `Vector{Article}` type. And then, we update the code in the `for` loop to deal with `Article` objects—`rand(articles[i-1].links)`.

The last change is in `six_degrees.jl`. Since `newgame` now returns a vector of `Article` objects instead of a `Dict`, we print the title by accessing the `title` field:

```
using Pkg
pkg"activate ."

include("Wikipedia.jl")
include("Gameplay.jl")

using .Wikipedia, .Gameplay

articles = newgame(Gameplay.DIFFICULTY_EASY)

for article in articles
  println(article.title)
end
```

A new test run should confirm that all works as expected (your output will be different since, remember, we're pulling random articles):

```
julia> include("six_degrees.jl")
Sonpur Bazari
Bengali language
Diacritic
```

Inner constructors

The external constructor (where we invoke the `type` as a function) is a default constructor where we provide the values for all the fields, in the right order—and get back an instance of the corresponding type. But, what if we want to provide additional constructors, that maybe impose certain constraints, perform validations, or are simply more user-friendly? For this purpose, Julia provides *internal constructors*. I've got a good use case for them.

I'm not especially fond of our `Article` constructor—it takes too many arguments that need to be passed in the exact right order. It's hard to remember how to instantiate it. We've learned earlier about keyword arguments—and it would be awesome to provide an alternative constructor that takes keyword arguments. Inner constructors are what we need.

Inner constructors are very much like the outer constructors, but with two major differences:

- They are declared inside the block of a type declaration, rather than outside of it like normal methods.
- They have access to a special locally existent function called `new` that creates objects of the same type.

On the other hand, external constructors have a clear limitation (by design)—we can create as many as we want, but they can only instantiate objects by invoking the existing internal constructors (they do not have access to the `new` function). This way, if we define internal constructors that implement some business logic constraints, *Julia guarantees that the external constructors cannot go around them.*

Our inner constructor with keyword arguments will look like this:

```
Article(; content = "", links = String[], title = "", image = "") =
new(content, links, title, image)
```

Note the use of `;`, which separates the empty list of positional arguments from the list of keyword arguments.

This constructor allows us to instantiate `Article` objects using keyword arguments, which we can provide in any order:

```
julia = Article(
        title = "Julia (programming language)",
        content = "Julia is a high-level dynamic programming language",
        links = ["/wiki/Jeff_Bezanson", "/wiki/Stefan_Karpinski",
                "/wiki/Viral_B._Shah", "/wiki/Alan_Edelman"],
        image = "/220px-Julia_prog_language.svg.png"
        )
```

However, there's a small problem. When we don't provide any internal constructor, Julia provides the default one. But, if any inner constructor is defined, no default constructor method is provided anymore—it is presumed that we have supplied ourselves all the necessary inner constructors. In this case, if we want to get back the default constructor with the positional arguments, we'll have to also define it ourselves as an internal one:

```
Article(content, links, title, image) = new(content, links, title, image)
```

The final version of the `Articles.jl` file should now be the following, with the two internal constructors:

```
module Articles

export Article

struct Article
  content::String
  links::Vector{String}
  title::String
  image::String

  Article(; content = "", links = String[], title = "", image = "") =
new(content, links, title, image)
  Article(content, links, title, image) = new(content, links, title, image)
end

end
```

It is worth pointing out that, in this case, our keyword constructor could've been equally added as an external constructor and defined outside the `struct...end` body. What kind of constructor you use is an architectural decision that has to be taken on a case-by-case basis, taking into account the differences between the internal and the external constructors.

Methods

If you come from an OOP background, you may have noticed a very interesting aspect throughout our discussion of types. Unlike other languages, objects in Julia do not define behavior. That is, Julia's types only define fields (properties) but do not encapsulate functions.

The reason is Julia's implementation of *multiple dispatch,* a distinctive feature of the language.

Multiple dispatch is explained in the official documentation as follows:

> *"The choice of which method to execute when a function is applied is called dispatch. Julia allows the dispatch process to choose which of a function's methods to call based on the number of arguments given, and on the types of all of the function's arguments. This is different than traditional object-oriented languages, where dispatch occurs based only on the first argument [. . .]. Using all of a function's arguments to choose which method should be invoked, rather than just the first, is known as multiple dispatch. Multiple dispatch is particularly useful for mathematical code, where it makes little sense to artificially deem the operations to belong to one argument more than any of the others."*

Julia allows us to define functions that provide specific behavior for certain combinations of argument types. A definition of one possible behavior for a function is called a **method**. The signatures of method definitions can be annotated to indicate the types of arguments, in addition to their number, and more than a single method definition may be provided. An example will help.

Let's say we have our previously defined `Player` type, as follows:

```julia
julia> mutable struct Player
           username::String
           score::Int
       end
```

And here, we see a corresponding `getscore` function:

```julia
julia> function getscore(p)
           p.score
       end
getscore (generic function with 1 method)
```

So far, so good. But, as our game grows incredibly successful, we could end up adding an app store to offer in-app purchases. This will lead us to also define a `Customer` type that could have a homonymous `credit_score` field, which stores their credit score:

```julia
julia> mutable struct Customer
           name::String
           total_purchase_value::Float64
           credit_score::Float64
       end
```

Of course, we'd need a corresponding `getscore` function:

```julia
julia> function getscore(c)
           c.credit_score
       end
getscore (generic function with 1 method)
```

Now, how would Julia know which function to use? It wouldn't. As both functions are defined to accept any type of argument, the last-defined function overwrites the previous one. We need to specialize the two `getscore` declarations on the type of their arguments:

```julia
julia> function getscore(p::Player)
           p.score
       end
getscore (generic function with 1 method)

julia> function getscore(c::Customer)
           c.credit_score
       end
getscore (generic function with 2 methods)
```

If you look closely at the output for each function declaration, you'll see something interesting. After the definition of `getscore(p::Player)`, it says `getscore (generic function with 1 method)`. But, after defining `getscore(c::Customer)`, it shows `getscore (generic function with 2 methods)`. So now, we have defined two methods for the `getscore` function, each specializing on its argument type.

But, what if we add the following?

```julia
julia> function getscore(t::Union{Player,Customer})
           isa(t, Player) ? t.score : t.credit_score
       end
getscore (generic function with 3 methods)
```

Or, alternatively, note the following that we might add:

```julia
julia> function getscore(s)
           if in(:score, fieldnames(typeof(s)))
               s.score
           elseif in(:credit_score, fieldnames(typeof(s)))
               s.credit_score
           else
               error("$(typeof(s)) does not have a score property")
           end
       end
getscore (generic function with 4 methods)
```

Can you guess which methods will be used when invoking `getscore` with a `Player`, a `Customer`, and an `Article` object? I'll give you a hint: when a function is applied to a particular set of arguments, the most specific method applicable to those arguments is invoked.

If we want to see which method is called for a given set of arguments, we can use `@which`:

```julia
julia> me = Player("adrian", 10)
Player("adrian", 10)

julia> @which getscore(me)
getscore(p::Player) in Main at REPL[58]:2
```

The same goes for `Customer` types:

```julia
julia> sam = Customer("Sam", 72.95, 100)
Customer("Sam", 72.95, 100.0)

julia> @which getscore(sam)
getscore(c::Customer) in Main at REPL[59]:2
```

We can see how the most specialized method is invoked—`getscore(t::Union{Player, Customer})`, which is more generic, is actually never used.

However, what about the following?

```julia
julia> @which getscore(julia)
getscore(s) in Main at REPL[61]:2
```

Passing an `Article` type will invoke the last definition of `getscore`, the one accepting `Any` type of argument:

```julia
julia> getscore(julia)
ERROR: Article does not have a score property
```

Since the `Article` type does not have a `score` or a `credit_score` property, the `ErrorException` we defined is being thrown.

To find out what methods are defined for a function, use `methods()`:

```julia
julia> methods(getscore)
# 4 methods for generic function "get_score":
getscore(c::Customer) in Main at REPL[59]:2
getscore(p::Player) in Main at REPL[58]:2
getscore(t::Union{Customer, Player}) in Main at REPL[60]:2
getscore(s) in Main at REPL[61]:2
```

Working with relational databases

Our web crawler is quite performant—using CSS selectors is very efficient. But, as it is right now, if we end up with the same Wikipedia article in different game sessions, we'll have to fetch it, parse it, and extract its contents multiple times. This is a time-consuming and resource-expensive operation—and, more importantly, one we can easily eliminate if we just store the article information once we fetch it the first time.

We could use Julia's serialization features, which we've already seen, but since we're building a fairly complex game, we would benefit from adding a database backend. Besides storing articles' data, we could also persist information about players, scores, preferences, and whatnot.

We have already seen how to interact with MongoDB. In this case, though, a relational database is the better choice, as we'll work with a series of related entities: articles, games (referencing articles), players (referencing games), and more.

Julia's package ecosystem provides a good range of options for interacting with relational databases, from generic ODBC and JDBC libraries to dedicated packages for the main backends—MySQL/MariaDB, SQLite, and Postgres, to name just a few. For our game, we'll use MySQL. If you don't already have MySQL installed on your system, please follow the instructions at `https://dev.mysql.com/downloads/mysql/`. Alternatively, if you're using Docker, you can get the official MySQL Docker image from `https://hub.docker.com/r/library/mysql/`.

On Julia's side, `(sixdegrees) pkg>add MySQL` is all we need in order to add support for MySQL. Make sure you're within the `sixdegrees/` project before adding MySQL. You can confirm this by looking at the prefix of the `pkg>` cursor; it should look like this: `(sixdegrees) pkg>`. If that is not the case, just execute `pkg> activate .` while making sure that you're within the `sixdegrees/` folder.

Adding MySQL support

When working with SQL databases, it's a good practice to abstract away the DB-related logic and to avoid littering all the codebase with SQL strings and database-specific commands. It will make our code more predictable and manageable and will provide a safe level of abstraction if we ever need to change or upgrade the database system. I'm a big fan of using ORM systems, but in this case, as a learning device, we'll be adding this functionality ourselves.

Connecting to the database

For starters, let's instruct our application to connect to and disconnect from our MySQL database. Let's extend our game by adding a new `Database` module within its corresponding file:

```
module Database

using MySQL

const HOST = "localhost"
const USER = "root"
const PASS = ""
const DB = "six_degrees"

const CONN = MySQL.connect(HOST, USER, PASS, db = DB)

export CONN

disconnect() = MySQL.disconnect(CONN)

atexit(disconnect)

end
```

Your `Database.jl` file should look like the snippet—with the exception maybe of the actual connection data. Please set up the `HOST`, `USER`, and `PASS` constants with your correct MySQL connection info. Also, please don't forget to create a new, empty database called `six_degrees`—otherwise the connection will fail. I suggest using `utf8` for the encoding and `utf8_general_ci` for the collation, in order to accommodate all the possible characters we might get from Wikipedia.

Calling `MySQL.connect` returns a connection object. We'll need it in order to interact with the database, so we'll reference it via the `CONN` constant:

```
julia> Main.Database.CONN
MySQL Connection
------------
Host: localhost
Port: 3306
User: root
DB:   six_degrees
```

Since various parts of our code will access this connection object in order to perform queries against the database, we `export` it. Equally importantly, we need to set up some cleanup mechanism, to automatically disconnect from the database when we're done. We've defined a `disconnect` function that can be manually called. But, it's safer if we make sure that the cleanup function is automatically invoked. Julia provides an `atexit` function, which registers a zero-argument function `f` to be called at process exit. The `atexit` hooks are called in **last-in-first-out** (**LIFO**) order.

Setting up our Article module

The next step is to add a few more functions to the `Article` module to enable database persistence and retrieval functionality. Since it will need access to our DB connection object, let's give it access to the `Database` module. We'll also want to use `MySQL` functions. So, under the `export Article` line, add `using ..Database, MySQL`.

Next, we'll add a `createtable` method. This will be a one-off function that will create the corresponding database table. We use this instead of just typing `CREATE TABLE` queries in the MySQL client, in order to have a consistent and reproducible way of (re)creating the table. In general, I prefer the use of a fully fledged database migration library, but for now, better to keep things simple (you can read about schema migrations at `https://en.wikipedia.org/wiki/Schema_migration`).

Without further ado, here's our function:

```
function createtable()
  sql = """
    CREATE TABLE `articles` (
      `title` varchar(1000),
      `content` text,
      `links` text,
      `image` varchar(500),
      `url` varchar(500),
      UNIQUE KEY `url` (`url`)
    ) ENGINE=InnoDB DEFAULT CHARSET=utf8
  """

  MySQL.execute!(CONN, sql)
end
```

Here, we define an `sql` variable, which references the MySQL `CREATE TABLE` query, in the form of a `String`. The table will have four columns corresponding to the four fields of our `Article` type. Then, there's a fifth column, `url`, which will store the article's Wikipedia URL. We'll identify articles by URL—and for this reason, we add a unique index on the `url` column.

At the end of the function, we pass the query string to `MySQL.execute!` to be run against the DB connection. Please append the `createtable` definition to the end of the `Articles` module (within the module, above the closing `end`).

Now, let's see it in action. Open a new REPL session in the `sixdegrees/` folder and run the following:

```
julia> using Pkg
julia> pkg"activate ."
julia> include("Database.jl")
julia> include("Articles.jl")
julia> using .Articles
julia> Articles.createtable()
```

That's it, our table is ready!

The workflow should be pretty clear—we made sure we're loading our project's dependencies, we included the `Database.jl` and `Articles.jl` files, we brought `Articles` into scope, and then invoked its `createtable` method.

Adding the persistence and retrieval methods

We said that when an article is fetched and parsed, we want to store its data in the database. Thus, before fetching an article, we'll first want to check our database. If the article was previously persisted, we'll retrieve it. If not, we'll perform the original fetch-and-parse workflow. We use the `url` property to uniquely identify articles.

Let's start by adding the `Articles.save(a::Article)` method for persisting an article object:

```
function save(a::Article)
  sql = "INSERT IGNORE INTO articles (title, content, links, image, url)
VALUES (?, ?, ?, ?, ?)"
  stmt = MySQL.Stmt(CONN, sql)
  result = MySQL.execute!(stmt, [a.title, a.content, JSON.json(a.links),
a.image, a.url])
end
```

Here, we use MySQL.Stmt to create a MySQL prepared statement. The query itself is very simple, using MySQL's INSERT IGNORE statement, which makes sure that the INSERT operation is performed only if there is no article with the same url. If there is already an article with the same url, the query is ignored.

The prepared statement accepts a specially formatted query string, in which the actual values are replaced with placeholders, designated by question marks—?. We can then execute the prepared statement by passing it to MySQL.execute!, together with an array of corresponding values. The values are passed directly from the article object, with the exception of links. Since this represents a more complex data structure, a Vector{String}, we'll first serialize it using JSON and store it in MySQL as a string. To access functions from the JSON package, we'll have to add it to our project, so please execute (sixdegrees) pkg> add JSON in the REPL.

Prepared statements provide a safe way to execute queries because the values are automatically escaped, eliminating a common source of MySQL injection attacks. In our case, MySQL injections are less of a worry since we're not accepting user-generated input. But, the approach is still valuable, avoiding insert errors caused by improper escaping.

Next, we need a retrieval method. We'll call it find. As its only attribute, it will take an article URL in the form of a String. It will return an Array of Article objects. By convention, if no corresponding article is found, the array will be empty:

```
function find(url) :: Vector{Article}
  articles = Article[]

  result = MySQL.query(CONN, "SELECT * FROM `articles` WHERE url = '$url'")

  isempty(result.url) && return articles

  for i in eachindex(result.url)
    push!(articles, Article(result.content[i], JSON.parse(result.links[i]),
result.title[i],
                            result.image[i], result.url[i]))
  end

  articles
end
```

In this function's declaration, we can see another Julia feature: return value types. After the regular function declaration, `function find(url)`, we appended `:: Vector{Article}`. This constrains the return value of `find` to an array of `Article`. If our function won't return that, an error will be thrown.

The rest of the code, although very compact, has quite a lot of functionality. First, we create `articles`, a vector of `Article` objects, which will be the return value of our function. Then, we execute a `SELECT` query against the MySQL database through the `MySQL.query` method, attempting to find rows that match the `url`. The result of the query is stored in the `result` variable, which is a `NamedTuple` (each field in the `result NamedTuple` references an array of values corresponding to the database column of the same name). Next, we peek into our query `result` to see if we got anything—we chose to sample the `result.url` field—if it's empty, it means our query didn't find anything and we can just exit the function, returning an empty `articles` vector.

On the other hand, if `result.url` does contain entries, it means our query brought at least one row; so we iterate over the `result.url` array using `eachindex`, and for each iteration we construct an `Article` object with the corresponding values. Finally, we `push!` this new `Article` object into the `articles` vector which is returned, at the end of the loop.

Putting it all together

The last thing we need to do is update the rest of the code to work with the changes we've made so far.

First of all, we need to update the `Article` type to add the extra `url` field. We need it in the list of fields and in the two constructors. Here is the final version of `Articles.jl`:

```
module Articles

export Article, save, find

using ...Database, MySQL, JSON

struct Article
  content::String
  links::Vector{String}
  title::String
  image::String
  url::String

  Article(; content = "", links = String[], title = "", image = "", url =
"") =
```

```
        new(content, links, title, image, url)
    Article(content, links, title, image, url) = new(content, links, title,
image, url)
end

function find(url) :: Vector{Article}
  articles = Article[]
  result = MySQL.query(CONN, "SELECT * FROM `articles` WHERE url = '$url'")

  isempty(result.url) && return articles

  for i in eachindex(result.url)
    push!(articles, Article(result.content[i], JSON.parse(result.links[i]),
result.title[i],
                            result.image[i], result.url[i]))
  end

  articles
end

function save(a::Article)
  sql = "INSERT IGNORE INTO articles (title, content, links, image, url)
VALUES (?, ?, ?, ?, ?)"
  stmt = MySQL.Stmt(CONN, sql)
  result = MySQL.execute!(stmt, [ a.title, a.content, JSON.json(a.links),
a.image, a.url])
end

function createtable()
  sql = """
    CREATE TABLE `articles` (
      `title` varchar(1000),
      `content` text,
      `links` text,
      `image` varchar(500),
      `url` varchar(500),
      UNIQUE KEY `url` (`url`)
    ) ENGINE=InnoDB DEFAULT CHARSET=utf8
  """

  MySQL.execute!(CONN, sql)
end

end
```

We also need to make a few important changes to `Wikipedia.jl`. First, we'll remove `Article` instantiation from `Wikipedia.articleinfo` since creating `Article` objects should now also take into account database persistence and retrieval. Instead, we'll return a tuple representing the article data:

```
function articleinfo(content)
   dom = articledom(content)
   (content, extractlinks(dom.root), extracttitle(dom.root),
extractimage(dom.root))
end
```

We can now add a new function, `persistedarticle`, which will accept as arguments the article content plus the article URL. It will instantiate a new `Article` object, save it to the database, and return it. In a way, `persistedarticle` can be considered a database-backed constructor, hence the name:

```
function persistedarticle(article_content, url)
   article = Article(articleinfo(article_content)..., url)
   save(article)

   article
end
```

Here, you can see the *splat* operator . . . in action—it decomposes the `articleinfo` result `Tuple` into its corresponding elements so they can be passed into the `Article` constructor as individual arguments.

Also, we have to deal with a minor complication. When we start a new game and call the `/wiki/Special:Random` URL, Wikipedia automatically performs a redirect to a random article. When we fetch the page, we get the redirected page content—but we don't have its URL.

So, we need to do two things. Firstly, we need to check if our request has been redirected and, if so, get the redirection URL. In order to do this, we can check the `request.parent` field of the `response` object. In the case of a redirect, the `response.request.parent` object will be set and will present a `headers` collection. The collection will include a `"Location"` item—and that's what we're after.

Secondly, we also need to return the URL together with the HTML content of the page. This is easy—we'll return a tuple.

Here is the updated `fetchpage` function:

```
function fetchpage(url)
  url = startswith(url, "/") ? buildurl(url) : url
  response = HTTP.get(url)
  content = if response.status == 200 && length(response.body) > 0
              String(response.body)
            else
              ""
            end
  relative_url = collect(eachmatch(r"/wiki/(.*)$",
(response.request.parent == nothing ? url :
Dict(response.request.parent.headers)["Location"])))[1].match

  content, relative_url
end
```

Note that we also use `eachmatch` to extract the part corresponding to the relative URL out of the absolute URL.

Here is the whole `Wikipedia.jl` file:

```
module Wikipedia
using HTTP, Gumbo, Cascadia
import Cascadia: matchFirst

include("Articles.jl")
using .Articles

const PROTOCOL = "https://"
const DOMAIN_NAME = "en.m.wikipedia.org"
const RANDOM_PAGE_URL = PROTOCOL * DOMAIN_NAME * "/wiki/Special:Random"

export fetchrandom, fetchpage, articleinfo, persistedarticle

function fetchpage(url)
  url = startswith(url, "/") ? buildurl(url) : url
  response = HTTP.get(url)
  content = if response.status == 200 && length(response.body) > 0
              String(response.body)
            else
              ""
            end
  relative_url = collect(eachmatch(r"/wiki/(.*)$", (response.request.parent
== nothing ? url :
Dict(response.request.parent.headers)["Location"])))[1].match

  content, relative_url
```

```
  end

  function extractlinks(elem)
    map(eachmatch(Selector("a[href^='/wiki/']:not(a[href*=':'])"), elem)) do
e
      e.attributes["href"]
    end |> unique
  end

  function extracttitle(elem)
    matchFirst(Selector("#section_0"), elem) |> nodeText
  end

  function extractimage(elem)
    e = matchFirst(Selector(".content a.image img"), elem)
    isa(e, Nothing) ? "" : e.attributes["src"]
  end

  function fetchrandom()
    fetchpage(RANDOM_PAGE_URL)
  end

  function articledom(content)
    if ! isempty(content)
      return Gumbo.parsehtml(content)
    end

    error("Article content can not be parsed into DOM")
  end

  function articleinfo(content)
    dom = articledom(content)
    (content, extractlinks(dom.root), extracttitle(dom.root),
extractimage(dom.root))
  end

  function persistedarticle(article_content, url)
    article = Article(articleinfo(article_content)..., url)
    save(article)

    article
  end

  function buildurl(article_url)
    PROTOCOL * DOMAIN_NAME * article_url
  end

end
```

Now, let's focus on `Gameplay.jl`. We need to update the `newgame` function to take advantage of the newly available methods from the `Wikipedia` module:

```
module Gameplay

using ..Wikipedia, ..Wikipedia.Articles

export newgame

const DIFFICULTY_EASY = 2
const DIFFICULTY_MEDIUM = 4
const DIFFICULTY_HARD = 6

function newgame(difficulty = DIFFICULTY_HARD)
  articles = Article[]

  for i in 1:difficulty+1
    article = if i == 1
                article = persistedarticle(fetchrandom()...)
              else
                url = rand(articles[i-1].links)
                existing_articles = Articles.find(url)

                article = isempty(existing_articles) ?
persistedarticle(fetchpage(url)...) : existing_articles[1]
              end

    push!(articles, article)
  end

  articles
end

end
```

If it's the first article, we fetch a random page and persist its data. Otherwise, we pick a random URL from the previously crawled page and check if a corresponding article already exists. If not, we fetch the page, making sure it's also persisted to the DB.

Lastly, our point of entry into the app, the `six_degrees.jl` file, needs to look like this:

```
using Pkg
pkg"activate ."

include("Database.jl")
include("Wikipedia.jl")
include("Gameplay.jl")
```

```
using .Wikipedia, .Gameplay

articles = newgame(Gameplay.DIFFICULTY_EASY)

for article in articles
  println(article.title)
end
```

A final test run should confirm that all is good:

```
$ julia six_degrees.jl
Hillary Maritim
Athletics at the 2000 Summer Olympics - Men's 400 metres hurdles
Zahr-el-Din El-Najem
```

Running the `six_degrees.jl` file with the `julia` binary in a terminal will output three Wikipedia article titles. And we can check the database to confirm that the data has been saved:

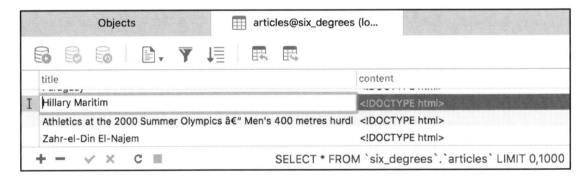

The data for the three previously crawled pages has been safely persisted.

Summary

Congratulations, this was quite a journey! We've learned about three key Julia concepts—modules, types and their constructors, and methods. We've applied all this knowledge to develop the backend of our *Six Degrees of Wikipedia* game, and in the process we've seen how to interact with MySQL databases, persisting and retrieving our `Article` objects.

At the end of the next chapter, we'll get the chance to enjoy the fruits of our hard work: after we add a web UI to our *Six degrees of Wikipedia* backend, we'll relax by playing a few rounds. Let's see if you can beat my best score!

Adding a Web UI for the Wiki Game

5

Developing the backend of our game was quite a learning experience. This strong foundation will serve us well—the modular approach will allow us to easily convert the **read-eval-print loop** (**REPL**) app into a web app, while our understanding of types will prove to be priceless when dealing with Julia's web stack and its rich taxonomy.

We're now entering the last stage of our game development journey—building a web user interface for the *Six Degrees of Wikipedia*. Since building a full-featured web app is no simple feat, this last part will be dedicated to this task alone. In the process, we will learn about the following topics:

- Julia's web stack; namely, the `HTTP` package and its main components—`Server`, `Router`, `HandlerFunction`, and `Response`
- Architecting a web app to take advantage of `HTTP` and integrate it with existing Julia modules
- Exposing features on the web by defining routes that map URLs to Julia functions
- Spawning a web server to handle user requests and send back proper responses to the clients

The end of this chapter comes with a cool reward—our game will be ready and we'll play a few rounds of *Six Degrees of Wikipedia*!

Technical requirements

The Julia package ecosystem is under continuous development and new package versions are released on a daily basis. Most of the times this is great news, as new releases bring new features and bug fixes. However, since many of the packages are still in beta (version 0.x), any new release can introduce breaking changes. As a result, the code presented in the book can stop working. In order to ensure that your code will produce the same results as described in the book, it is recommended to use the same package versions. Here are the external packages used in this chapter and their specific versions:

```
Cascadia@v0.4.0
Gumbo@v0.5.1
HTTP@v0.7.1
IJulia@v1.14.1
```

In order to install a specific version of a package you need to run:

```
pkg> add PackageName@vX.Y.Z
```

For example:

```
pkg> add IJulia@v1.14.1
```

Alternatively you can install all the used packages by downloading the `Project.toml` file provided with the chapter and using `pkg>` instantiate as follows:

```
julia>
download("https://raw.githubusercontent.com/PacktPublishing/Julia-Programmi
ng-Projects/master/Chapter05/Project.toml", "Project.toml")
pkg> activate .
pkg> instantiate
```

The game plan

We're onto the last stage of our project—the web UI. Let's start by discussing the spec; we need to lay out the blueprint before we can proceed with the implementation.

The player will start on the landing page. This will display the rules and will provide options for launching a new game, allowing the user to choose a difficulty level. Following this starting point, the player will be redirected to the new game page. Here, taking into account the selected difficulty level, we'll bootstrap a new game session by fetching the articles with the algorithm we wrote in the previous chapter. Once we pick the articles that represent the *Six Degrees of Wikipedia*, we will display a heading with the game's objective—the titles of the start and end articles. We'll also display the content of the first article, thus kickstarting the game. When the player clicks on a link in this article, we have to respond accordingly by checking if the player has found the end article and won the game. If not, render the new article and increment the number of steps taken.

We'll also need an area to display the progress of the game—the articles that were viewed in the current session, how many steps have been taken in total, and a form of navigation to allow the players to go back and rethink their choices if they find themselves on the wrong track. Therefore, we'll need to store the player's navigation history. Finally, it would be nice to provide an option to solve the puzzle—of course, as a result, the player will lose the game.

A very important piece of the spec is that between the stateless browser requests and the server responses, while navigating through the Wikipedia articles, we need some sort of mechanism to allow us to maintain the state of the game, that is, to retrieve a game with its corresponding data—difficulty, path (articles) and progress, navigation history, number of steps taken, and so on. This will be achieved by creating a unique game identifier at the beginning of each play session and passing it with every request as a part of the URL.

Learning about Julia's web stack

Julia's package ecosystem has long provided a variety of libraries for building web apps. Some of the most mature are `HttpServer`, `Mux`, `WebSockets`, and `JuliaWebAPI` (to name just a few; this list is not exhaustive). But as the ecosystem settled with Julia version 1, a lot of community effort has been put into a newer package, simply known as `HTTP`. It provides a web server, an HTTP client (which we already used in the previous chapters to fetch the web pages from Wikipedia), as well as various utilities for making web development simpler. We'll learn about key `HTTP` modules ,such as `Server`, `Router`, `Request`, `Response`, and `HandlerFunction`, and we'll put them to good use.

Beginning with a simple example – Hello World

Let's take a look at a simple example of employing the HTTP server stack. This will help us understand the foundational building blocks before we dive into the more complex issue of exposing our game on the web.

If you followed the previous chapter, you should already have the HTTP package installed. If not, you know the drill—run pkg> add HTTP in Julia's REPL.

Now, somewhere on your computer, create a new file called hello.jl. Since this will be a simple piece of software contained in just one file, there's no need to define a module. Here is the full code, the whole eight lines, in all their glory. We'll go over them next:

```
using HTTP, Sockets
const HOST = ip"0.0.0.0"
const PORT = 9999
router = HTTP.Router()
server = HTTP.Server(router)
HTTP.register!(router, "/", HTTP.HandlerFunction(req ->
HTTP.Messages.Response(200, "Hello World")))
HTTP.register!(router, "/bye", HTTP.HandlerFunction(req ->
HTTP.Messages.Response(200, "Bye")))
HTTP.register!(router, "*", HTTP.HandlerFunction(req ->
HTTP.Messages.Response(404, "Not found")))
HTTP.serve(server, HOST, PORT)
```

The workflow for handling web requests with HTTP requires four entities—Server, Router, HandlerFunction, and Response.

Beginning our analysis of the code with the simplest part, on the last line, we start our server by calling HTTP.serve. The serve function takes a server, an object of type Server, plus the HOST information (an IP string) and the PORT (an integer) that are used to attach to and listen to requests as arguments. We have defined HOST and PORT at the top of the file as constants. The value of HOST is defined using the non-standard ip"" string literal. We learned about non-standard string literals when we discussed the String type. In this regard, the ip"..." notation is similar to regular expressions (r"..."), version strings (v"..."), or Pkg commands (pkg"...").

Instantiating a new `Server` requires a `Router` object, which we will name `router`. The job of the `Router` is to register a list of mappings (called **routes**) between the links (URIs) that are exposed by our app on the internet and our Julia functions (called `HandlerFunctions`), which provide the response. We have set up the routes using the `register!` function, passing the `router` object, the URI structures (like / or /bye) and the corresponding `HandlerFunction` objects as arguments.

Now, if you look at the body of the `HandlerFunction`, you'll see that the root page / will display the string `"Hello World"`; the /bye URL will display the string `"Bye"`; and finally, every other URI, expressed by the star symbol *, will return a `"Not found"` text, accompanied by the correct `404 Not Found` header.

I'm sure you can now recognize the arrow -> operator, hinting to the use of lambdas. Each `HandlerFunction` constructor takes an anonymous function. This function is responsible for processing the request and generating the appropriate `Response`. As its argument, it accepts the `Request` object (named `req`), and it is expected to return an instance of `Response`.

In our example code, we constructed three `Response` objects using two of the available HTTP status codes (`200` for `OK` and `404` for page not found), plus some strings for the body of the responses (the simple strings `"Hello World"`, `"Bye"`, and `"Not found"`, respectively).

To conclude, when the server receives a request, it delegates it to the router, which matches the URI of the request to the most appropriately mapped URI pattern and invokes the corresponding `HandlerFunction`, passing in the `Request` as the argument. The handler function returns a `Response` object, which is sent by the server back to the client.

Let's see it in action. You can use the Run functionality in your editor or you can execute $ julia hello.jl in the Terminal. Alternatively, you can run the code in this chapter's accompanying IJulia notebook:

The preceding screenshot shows the hello.jl file running in Juno. The REPL pane displays debugging information from the web server as requests are received and handled.

As soon as the server is ready, you'll get a log message saying that the server is listening on the indicated socket. At this point, you can open a web browser and navigate to http://localhost:9999. You'll be greeted by the (in)famous **Hello World** message, as follows:

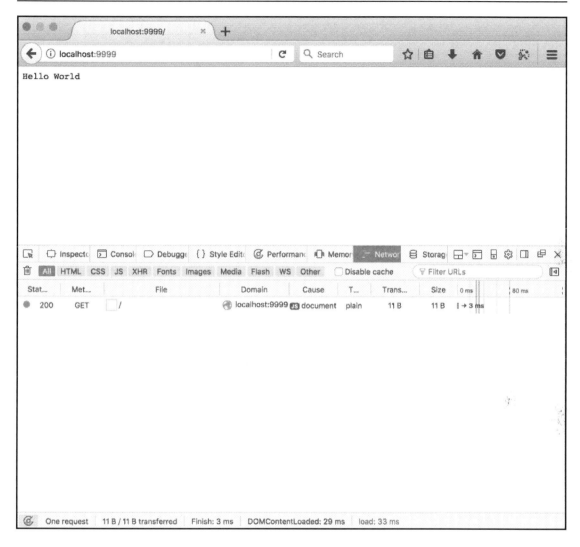

Congratulations—we've just developed our first web app with Julia!

No bonus points for guessing what happens when navigating to
`http://localhost:9999/bye`.

Finally, you can confirm that any other request will result in a `404 Not Found` page by attempting to navigate to any other link under `http://localhost:9999`—for instance, `http://localhost:9999/oh/no`:

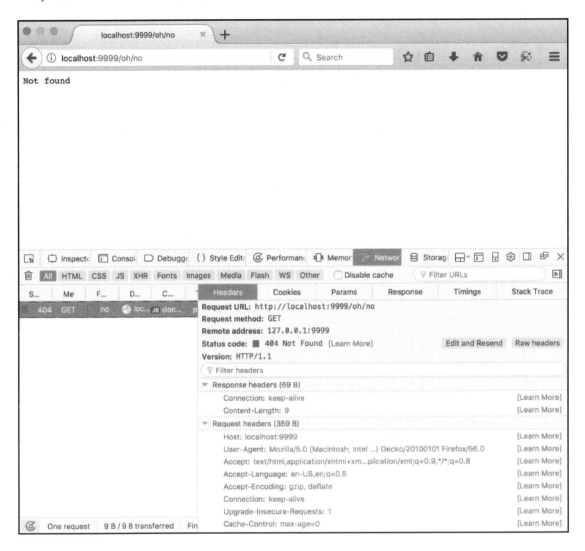

Here is the **Not Found** page, correctly returning the `404` status code.

Developing the game's web UI

Please start your favorite Julia editor and open the `sixdegrees/` folder we used in the previous chapter. It should contain all the files that we've worked on already—`six_degrees.jl`, plus the `Articles`, `Database`, `Gameplay`, and `Wikipedia` modules.

 If you haven't followed through the code up to this point, you can download this chapter's accompanying support files, which are available at `https://github.com/PacktPublishing/Julia-Programming-Projects/tree/master/Chapter05`.

Add a new file for our web app. Since the code will be more complex this time and should integrate with the rest of our modules, let's define a `WebApp` module within a new `WebApp.jl` file. Then, we can add these first few lines of code:

```
module WebApp

using HTTP, Sockets

const HOST = ip"0.0.0.0"
const PORT = 8888
const ROUTER = HTTP.Router()
const SERVER = HTTP.Server(ROUTER)

HTTP.serve(SERVER, HOST, PORT)

end
```

No surprises here—similar to the previous example, we define constants for `HOST` and `PORT`, and then instantiate a `Router` and a `Server` and start listening for requests. The code should work just fine, but it's not worth running it yet as it won't do anything useful. We need to define and register our routes, and then set up the handler functions for generating the game's pages.

Defining our routes

By reviewing the high-level spec that we defined at the beginning of the chapter, we can identify the following pages:

- **Landing page**: The starting place of our web app and the home page, where the player can begin a new game and choose the difficulty.
- **New game page**: Bootstraps a new game, taking into account the difficulty settings.
- **Wiki article page**: This will display the Wikipedia article corresponding to a link in the chain and will update the game's stats. Here, we'll also check if the current article is the goal (the end) article, which is to finish the game as a winner. If not, we'll check if the maximum number of articles has been reached, and if so finish the game as a loser.
- **Back page**: This will allow the player to go back up the chain if the solution wasn't found. We'll display the corresponding Wikipedia article while correctly updating the game's stats.
- **Solution page**: If the player gives up, this page will display the last article in the chain, together with the path to it. The game is ended as a loss.
- Any other page should end up as Not Found.

Taking into account that the route handlers will be fairly complex, it's best if we *don't* define them inline with the route definitions. Instead, we'll use separately defined functions. Our route's definitions will look like this—please add them to the WebApp module, as follows:

```
HTTP.register!(ROUTER, "/", landingpage) # root page
HTTP.register!(ROUTER, "/new/*", newgamepage) # /new/$difficulty_level --
new game
HTTP.register!(ROUTER, "/*/wiki/*", articlepage) #
/$session_id/wiki/$wikipedia_article_url -- article page
HTTP.register!(ROUTER, "/*/back/*", backpage) #
/$session_id/back/$number_of_steps -- go back the navigation history
HTTP.register!(ROUTER, "/*/solution", solutionpage) # /$session_id/solution
-- display the solution
HTTP.register!(ROUTER, "*", notfoundpage) # everything else -- not found
```

You might be wondering what's with the extra * in front of the URI patterns. We stated that we'll need a way to identify a running game session between the otherwise stateless web requests. The `articlepage`, `backpage`, and `solutionpage` functions will all require an existing game session. We'll pass this session ID as the first part of the URL. Effectively, their paths are to be interpreted as /`$session_id`/wiki/*, /`$session_id`/back/*, and /`$session_id`/solution, where the `$session_id` variable represents the unique game identifier. As for the trailing *, it represents different things for different routes—in the case of `new`, it's the difficulty level of the game; for `articlepage`, it's the actual Wikipedia URL, which is also our article identifier; and for the `backpage`, it represents the index in the navigation stack. Similar to regular expressions, for route matching as well, the * will match anything. If this sounds complicated, don't worry—seeing and running the code will make things clear.

Let's add placeholder definitions for each handler function—please add these *before* the list of routes:

```
const landingpage = HTTP.HandlerFunction() do req
end
const newgamepage = HTTP.HandlerFunction() do req
end
const articlepage = HTTP.HandlerFunction() do req
end
const backpage = HTTP.HandlerFunction() do req
end
const solutionpage = HTTP.HandlerFunction() do req
end
const notfoundpage = HTTP.HandlerFunction() do req
end
```

Preparing the landing page

Straight away, we can address the landing page handler. All it needs to do is display some static content describing the game's rules, as well as provide a way to start a new game with various levels of difficulty. Remember that the difficulty of the game determines the length of the article chain, and we need this information when we start a new game. We can pass it to the new game page as part of the URL, under the format /new/`$difficulty_level`. The difficulty levels are already defined in the `Gameplay` module, so don't forget to declare that we're `using Gameplay`.

Taking this into account, we'll end up with the following code for our WebApp module. We're putting everything together and we're also adding the landingpage HandlerFunction. This works in correlation with the first route—HTTP.register!(ROUTER, "/",landingpage). What this means is that when we access the / route in the browser, the landingpage HandlerFunction will be executed and its output will be returned as the response. In this case, we're simply returning a bunch of HTML code. If you're not familiar with HTML, here's what the markup does—we include the Twitter Bootstrap CSS theme to make our page prettier, we display a few paragraphs of text explaining the rules of the game, and we display three buttons for starting a new game—one button for each level of difficulty.

Here is the code:

```
module WebApp

using HTTP, Sockets
using ..Gameplay

# Configuration
const HOST = ip"0.0.0.0"
const PORT = 8888
const ROUTER = HTTP.Router()
const SERVER = HTTP.Server(ROUTER)

# Routes handlers
const landingpage = HTTP.HandlerFunction() do req
  html = """
  <!DOCTYPE html>
  <html>
  <head>
    <meta charset="utf-8" />
    <link rel="stylesheet"
href="https://stackpath.bootstrapcdn.com/bootstrap/4.1.3/css/bootstrap.min.
css" integrity="sha384-
MCw98/SFnGE8fJT3GXwEOngsV7Zt27NXFoaoApmYm81iuXoPkFOJwJ8ERdknLPMO"
crossorigin="anonymous">
    <title>6 Degrees of Wikipedia</title>
  </head>

  <body>
    <div class="jumbotron">
      <h1>Six degrees of Wikipedia</h1>
      <p>
        The goal of the game is to find the shortest path between two
random Wikipedia articles.<br/>
        Depending on the difficulty level you choose, the Wiki pages will
```

be further apart and less related.
        If you can't find the solution, you can always go back up the
articles chain, but you need to find the solution within the maximum number
of steps, otherwise you lose.
        If you get stuck, you can always check the solution, but you'll
lose.
        Good luck and enjoy!
    </p>

    <hr class="my-4">

    <div>
       <h4>New game</h4>
        <a href="/new/$(Gameplay.DIFFICULTY_EASY)" class="btn btn-primary
btn-lg">Easy ($(Gameplay.DIFFICULTY_EASY) links away)</a> |
        <a href="/new/$(Gameplay.DIFFICULTY_MEDIUM)" class="btn btn-
primary btn-lg">Medium ($(Gameplay.DIFFICULTY_MEDIUM) links away)</a> |
        <a href="/new/$(Gameplay.DIFFICULTY_HARD)" class="btn btn-primary
btn-lg">Hard ($(Gameplay.DIFFICULTY_HARD) links away)</a>
    </div>
  </div>
  </body>
  </html>
  """

  HTTP.Messages.Response(200, html)
end

const newgamepage = HTTP.HandlerFunction() do req
end

const articlepage = HTTP.HandlerFunction() do req
end

const backpage = HTTP.HandlerFunction() do req
end

const solutionpage = HTTP.HandlerFunction() do req
end

const notfoundpage = HTTP.HandlerFunction() do req
end

Routes definitions
HTTP.register!(ROUTER, "/", landingpage) # root page
HTTP.register!(ROUTER, "/new/*", newgamepage) # /new/$difficulty_level --
new game
HTTP.register!(ROUTER, "/*/wiki/*", articlepage) #
```
```

```
/$session_id/wiki/$wikipedia_article_url -- article page
HTTP.register!(ROUTER, "/*/back/*", backpage) #
/$session_id/back/$number_of_steps -- go back the navigation history
HTTP.register!(ROUTER, "/*/solution", solutionpage) # /$session_id/solution
-- display the solution
HTTP.register!(ROUTER, "*", notfoundpage) # everything else -- not found

# Start server
HTTP.serve(SERVER, HOST, PORT)

end
```

Let's update the `six_degrees.jl` file to bootstrap our web app. Please make sure that it now reads as follows:

```
using Pkg
pkg"activate ."

include("Database.jl")
include("Wikipedia.jl")
include("Gameplay.jl")
include("WebApp.jl")

using .Wikipedia, .Gameplay, .WebApp
```

Run `six_degrees.jl` using your preferred approach, either in the editor or the Terminal ($ `julia six_degrees.jl`). Look for the message `Info: Listening on:...`, which notifies us that the web server has been started. Visit `http://localhost:8888/` in your browser and feast your eyes on our landing page! I'm sure you'll notice the effect of including the Twitter Bootstrap CSS file—adding just a few CSS classes to our code makes for a great visual impact!

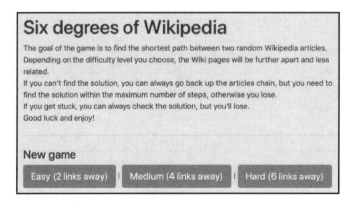

The preceding screenshot is of our game's landing page running on localhost at port 8888.

Starting a new game

Excellent! Now, let's focus on the functionality for starting a new game. Here, we need to implement the following steps:

1. Extract the difficulty settings from the URL.
2. Start a new game. This game should have an ID, which will be our `session id`. Plus, it should keep track of the list of articles, progress, navigation history, the total number of steps taken, and the difficulty.
3. Render the first Wikipedia article.
4. Set up in-article navigation. We need to make sure that the links within the Wikipedia article will properly link back into our app, and not the Wikipedia website itself.
5. Display information about the game session, such as the objective (start and end articles), number of steps taken, and so on.

We'll look at all of these steps next.

Extracting the difficulty settings from the page URL

This is the very first step. Remember that within our `HandlerFunction`, we have access to the `Request` object, `req`. All the `Request` objects expose a field called `target` that references the URL of the request. The `target` does not include the protocol or the domain name, so it will be of the form `/new/$difficulty_level`. A quick way to extract the value of `$difficulty_level` is to simply replace the first part of the URI with an empty string, `""`, effectively removing it. The result will be used in a function, `newgamesession`, to create a new game of the indicated difficulty. Put into code, it will look like this:

```
game = parse(UInt8, (replace(req.target, "/new/"=>""))) |> newgamesession
```

Since we represent difficulty levels as integers (number of articles), we parse the string into an integer (specifically of type `UInt8`) before using it.

Starting a new game session

Starting a new game session is the second step. The game session manager, which should include the preceding `newgamesession` function, is missing entirely, so it's time we added it. We'll represent a game session as an instance of a corresponding type. Let's pack the `type` definition and the methods for manipulating it into a dedicated module. We can name the module `GameSession`, and the type `Game`. Please create the `GameSession.jl` file within the `"sixdegrees/"` folder.

Our `Game` type will need a custom constructor. We'll provide the difficulty level, and the constructor will take care of setting all of the internals—it will fetch the right number of Wikipedia articles using the previously created `Gameplay.newgame` function; it will create a unique game ID (which will be our session ID); and it'll initialize the rest of the fields with default values.

A first attempt will look like this:

```
module GameSession

using ..Gameplay, ..Wikipedia, ..Wikipedia.Articles
using Random

mutable struct Game
  id::String
  articles::Vector{Article}
  history::Vector{Article}
  steps_taken::UInt8
  difficulty::UInt8

  Game(game_difficulty) =
    new(randstring(), newgame(game_difficulty), Article[], 0,
game_difficulty)
end

const GAMES = Dict{String,Game}()

end
```

The `Random.randstring` function creates a random string. This is our game's and our session's ID.

We've also defined a `GAMES` dictionary, which will store all the active games and will allow us to look them up by their `id` field. Remember, our game is exposed on the web, so we'll have multiple game sessions running in parallel.

We can now add the rest of the functions. Add the following definitions before the module's closing end, as follows:

```
export newgamesession, gamesession, destroygamesession

function newgamesession(difficulty)
  game = Game(difficulty)
  GAMES[game.id] = game
  game
end

function gamesession(id)
  GAMES[id]
end

function destroygamesession(id)
  delete!(GAMES, id)
end
```

This is very straightforward. The snippet defines the newgamesession function, which creates a new Game of the indicated difficulty and stores it into the GAMES dict data structure. There's also a getter function, gamesession, which retrieves a Game by id. Finally, we add a destructor function, which removes the corresponding Game from the GAMES dict, effectively making it unavailable on the frontend and leaving it up for garbage collection. All of these functions are exported.

It's worth noting that storing our games in memory is fine for the purpose of this learning project, but in production, with a lot of players, you'd risk running out of memory quickly. For production use, we'd be better off persisting each Game to the database and retrieving it as necessary.

Rendering the first Wikipedia article from the chain

This is the third step. Going back to our WebApp module (in WebApp.jl), let's continue with the logic for the newgamepage handler. The implementation will look like this:

```
using ..GameSession, ..Wikipedia, ..Wikipedia.Articles

const newgamepage = HTTP.HandlerFunction() do req
  game = parse(UInt8, (replace(req.target, "/new/"=>""))) |> newgamesession
  article = game.articles[1]
  push!(game.history, article)
```

```
    HTTP.Messages.Response(200, wikiarticle(article))
end
```

Once we create a new game, we need to reference its first article. We add the starting article to the game's history and then we render it as HTML using the following `wikiarticle` function:

```
function wikiarticle(article)
  html = """
  <!DOCTYPE html>
  <html>
  <head>
    <meta charset="utf-8" />
    <link rel="stylesheet"
href="https://stackpath.bootstrapcdn.com/bootstrap/4.1.3/css/bootstrap.min.
css" integrity="sha384-
MCw98/SFnGE8fJT3GXwEOngsV7Zt27NXFoaoApmYm81iuXoPkFOJwJ8ERdknLPMO"
crossorigin="anonymous">
    <title>6 Degrees of Wikipedia</title>
  </head>

  <body>
    <h1>$(article.title)</h1>
    <div id="wiki-article">
      $(article.content)
    </div>
  </body>
  </html>
  """
end
```

We simply display the title of the Wikipedia article as the main heading, and then the content.

Finally, don't forget to load `GameSession` into our app by adding it to `"six_degrees.jl"`. Beware that it needs to be loaded before `WebApp` to be available for `WebApp`. The full `"six_degrees.jl"` file should now look like this:

```
using Pkg pkg"activate ." include("Database.jl") include("Wikipedia.jl")
include("Gameplay.jl") include("GameSession.jl") include("WebApp.jl") using
.Wikipedia, .Gameplay, .GameSession, .WebApp
```

If you rerun our code and navigate to `http://localhost:8888/new/2`, you'll see our app rendering a random Wikipedia article:

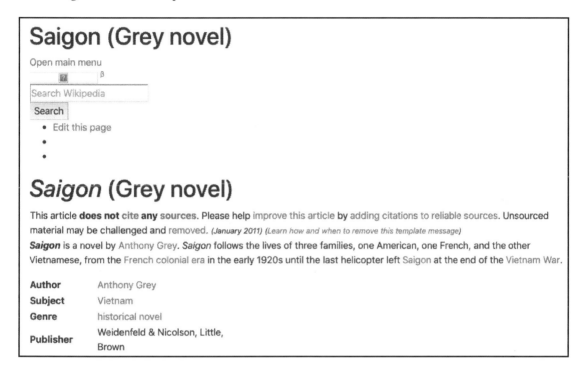

It's a good start, but there are some problems. First, we were a bit too greedy when fetching the content from Wikipedia. It includes the full page HTML, which contains things we don't really need, like the invisible `<head>` section and the all-too visible Wikipedia content from above the article's text (the search form, the menu, and so on). This is easy to fix—all we need to do is be a bit more specific about the content we want by using a better-defined CSS selector. A bit of playing around with the browser's inspector will reveal that the desired selector is `#bodyContent`.

Armed with this knowledge, we need to update the `Wikipedia` module. Please replace the existing `articleinfo` function with this one:

```
function articleinfo(content)
  dom = articledom(content)
  (extractcontent(dom.root), extractlinks(dom.root),
extracttitle(dom.root), extractimage(dom.root))
end
```

Instead of using the whole HTML, we will now extract just the content of the desired CSS selector:

```
function extractcontent(elem)
  matchFirst(Selector("#bodyContent"), elem) |> string
end
```

Please add the definition of `extractcontent` to the `Wikipedia.jl` file, under the `extractimage` function.

By revisiting our page at `http://localhost:8888/new/2`, we will see our efforts rewarded with a much better-looking replacement:

Millwall F.C.–West Ham United F.C. rivalry

The **rivalry between Millwall and West Ham United** is one of the longest-standing and most bitter in English football. The two teams, then known as Millwall Athletic and Thames Ironworks, both originated in the East End of London, and were located under three miles apart. They first played each other in the 1899–1900 FA Cup. The match was historically known as the **Dockers derby**, as both sets of supporters were predominantly dockers at shipyards on either side of the River Thames. Consequently, each set of fans worked for rival firms who were competing for the same business; this intensified the tension between the teams. In 1910, Millwall moved south of the River Thames to New Cross and the teams were no longer East London neighbours. Both sides have relocated since, but remain just under four miles apart. Millwall moved to The Den in Bermondsey in 1993 and West Ham to the London Stadium in Stratford in 2016.

The last derby at Upton Park.

(4 February 2012)

Locale	London (East and South)
Teams	Millwall and West Ham United

Setting up in-article navigation

All right, that wasn't so hard! But the next issue is more difficult. The fourth step is all about the setup. We established that we need to capture all the internal Wikipedia links so that when the player clicks on a link, they are taken to our app instead of going to the original Wikipedia article. Half of this work is done by Wikipedia's content itself because it uses relative URLs. That is, instead of using absolute URLs in the form of `https://en.wikipedia.org/wiki/Wikipedia:Six_degrees_of_Wikipedia`, it uses the relative form `/wiki/Wikipedia:Six_degrees_of_Wikipedia`. This means that when rendered in the browser, these links will inherit the domain name (or the *base URL*) of the current host. That is, when rendering the content of a Wikipedia article at `http://localhost:8888/`, its relative URLs will be interpreted as `http://localhost:8888/wiki/Wikipedia:Six_degrees_of_Wikipedia`. Therefore, they'll automatically point back to our web app. That's great, but one big piece of the puzzle is missing: we said that we want to maintain the state of our game by passing the session ID as part of the URL. Thus, our URLs should be of the form `http://localhost:8888/ABCDEF/wiki/Wikipedia:Six_degrees_of_Wikipedia`, where `ABCDEF` represents the game (or session) ID. The simplest solution is to replace `/wiki/` with `/ABCDEF/wiki/` when rendering the content—of course, using the actual game ID instead of `ABCDEF`.

In the definition of the `WebApp.wikiarticle` function, please look for this:

```
<div id="wiki-article">
    $(article.content)
</div>
```

Replace it with the following:

```
<div id="wiki-article">
    $(replace(article.content, "/wiki/"=>"/$(game.id)/wiki/"))
</div>
```

Because we now need the `game` object, we must make sure that we pass it into the function, so its declaration should become the following:

```
function wikiarticle(game, article)
```

This means that we also need to update the `newgamepage` route handler to correctly invoke the updated `wikiarticle` function. The last line of the `WebApp.newgamepage` function should now be as follows:

```
HTTP.Messages.Response(200, wikiarticle(game, article))
```

If you execute `six_degrees.jl` and take your browser to `http://localhost:8888/new/2`, you should see a nice rendering of a Wikipedia article with all the internal links containing the game ID:

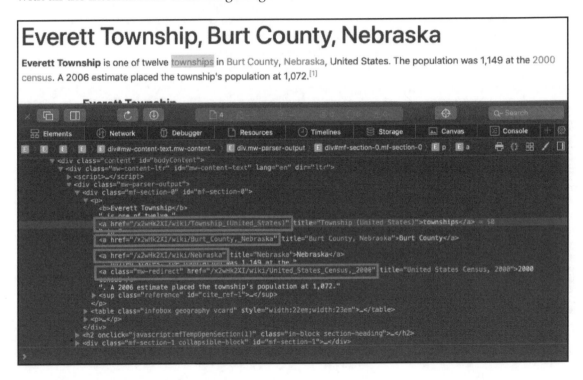

In the preceding screenshot, we can see that all the URLs start with /x2wHk2XI—our game ID.

Displaying information about the game session

For the fifth and very last part of our spec, we need to display information about the game and provide a way to navigate back to the previous articles. We'll define the following functions:

```
function objective(game)
  """
  <h3>
    Go from <i>$(game.articles[1].title)</i>
    to <i>$(game.articles[end].title)</i>
  </h3>
  <h5>
    Progress: $(size(game.history, 1) - 1)
    out of maximum $(size(game.articles, 1) - 1) links
    in $(game.steps_taken) steps
  </h5>
  <h6>
    <a href="/$(game.id)/solution">Solution?</a> |
    <a href="/">New game</a>
  </h6>"""
end
```

The `objective` function informs the player about the start and end articles and about the current progress. It also provides a small menu so that you can view the solution or start a new game.

For navigating back, we need to generate the game history links:

```
function history(game)
  html = "<ol>"
  iter = 0
  for a in game.history
    html *= """
    <li><a href="/$(game.id)/back/$(iter + 1)">$(a.title)</a></li>
    """
    iter += 1
  end
  html * "</ol>"
end
```

Finally, we need a bit of extra logic to check if the game was won or lost:

```
function puzzlesolved(game, article)
  article.url == game.articles[end].url
end
```

We have a winner if the URL of the current article is the same as the URL of the last article in the game.

The game is lost if the player runs out of moves:

```
function losinggame(game)
  game.steps_taken >= Gameplay.MAX_NUMBER_OF_STEPS
end
```

The complete code, so far, should look like this:

```
module WebApp

using HTTP, Sockets
using ..Gameplay, ..GameSession, ..Wikipedia, ..Wikipedia.Articles

# Configuration
const HOST = ip"0.0.0.0"
const PORT = 8888
const ROUTER = HTTP.Router()
const SERVER = HTTP.Server(ROUTER)

# Functions
function wikiarticle(game, article)
  html = """
  <!DOCTYPE html>
  <html>
  $(head())

  <body>
    $(objective(game))
    $(history(game))
    <hr/>
    $(
      if losinggame(game)
        "<h1>You Lost :( </h1>"
      else
        puzzlesolved(game, article) ? "<h1>You Won!</h1>" : ""
      end
    )

    <h1>$(article.title)</h1>
```

```
      <div id="wiki-article">
        $(replace(article.content, "/wiki/"=>"/$(game.id)/wiki/"))
      </div>
    </body>
    </html>
    """
end

function history(game)
  html = "<ol>"
  iter = 0
  for a in game.history
    html *= """
    <li><a href="/$(game.id)/back/$(iter + 1)">$(a.title)</a></li>
    """
    iter += 1
  end

  html * "</ol>"
end

function objective(game)
    """
    <h3>
      Go from <i>$(game.articles[1].title)</i>
      to <i>$(game.articles[end].title)</i>
    </h3>
    <h5>
      Progress: $(size(game.history, 1) - 1)
      out of maximum $(size(game.articles, 1) - 1) links
      in $(game.steps_taken) steps
    </h5>
    <h6>
      <a href="/$(game.id)/solution">Solution?</a> |
      <a href="/">New game</a>
    </h6>"""
end

function head()
    """
    <head>
    <meta charset="utf-8" />
    <link rel="stylesheet"
href="https://stackpath.bootstrapcdn.com/bootstrap/4.1.3/css/bootstrap.min.
css" integrity="sha384-
MCw98/SFnGE8fJT3GXwEOngsV7Zt27NXFoaoApmYm81iuXoPkFOJwJ8ERdknLPMO"
crossorigin="anonymous">
    <title>6 Degrees of Wikipedia</title>
```

```
        </head>
        """
    end

    function puzzlesolved(game, article)
      article.url == game.articles[end].url
    end

    function losinggame(game)
      game.steps_taken >= Gameplay.MAX_NUMBER_OF_STEPS
    end

    # Routes handlers
    const landingpage = HTTP.HandlerFunction() do req
      html = """
      <!DOCTYPE html>
      <html>
      $(head())

      <body>
        <div class="jumbotron">
          <h1>Six degrees of Wikipedia</h1>
          <p>
            The goal of the game is to find the shortest path between two
    random Wikipedia articles.<br/>
            Depending on the difficulty level you choose, the Wiki pages will
    be further apart and less related.<br/>
            If you can't find the solution, you can always go back up the
    articles chain, but you need to find the solution within the maximum number
    of steps, otherwise you lose.<br/>
            If you get stuck, you can always check the solution, but you'll
    lose.<br/>
            Good luck and enjoy!
          </p>

          <hr class="my-4">

          <div>
            <h4>New game</h4>
              <a href="/new/$(Gameplay.DIFFICULTY_EASY)" class="btn btn-primary
    btn-lg">Easy ($(Gameplay.DIFFICULTY_EASY) links away)</a> |
              <a href="/new/$(Gameplay.DIFFICULTY_MEDIUM)" class="btn btn-
    primary btn-lg">Medium ($(Gameplay.DIFFICULTY_MEDIUM) links away)</a> |
              <a href="/new/$(Gameplay.DIFFICULTY_HARD)" class="btn btn-primary
    btn-lg">Hard ($(Gameplay.DIFFICULTY_HARD) links away)</a>
          </div>
        </div>
      </body>
```

```
    </html>
    """

  HTTP.Messages.Response(200, html)
end

const newgamepage = HTTP.HandlerFunction() do req
  game = parse(UInt8, (replace(req.target, "/new/"=>""))) |> newgamesession
  article = game.articles[1]
  push!(game.history, article)

  HTTP.Messages.Response(200, wikiarticle(game, article))
end

const articlepage = HTTP.HandlerFunction() do req
end

const backpage = HTTP.HandlerFunction() do req
end

const solutionpage = HTTP.HandlerFunction() do req
end

const notfoundpage = HTTP.HandlerFunction() do req
end


# Routes definitions
HTTP.register!(ROUTER, "/", landingpage) # root page
HTTP.register!(ROUTER, "/new/*", newgamepage) # /new/$difficulty_level --
new game
HTTP.register!(ROUTER, "/*/wiki/*", articlepage) #
/$session_id/wiki/$wikipedia_article_url -- article page
HTTP.register!(ROUTER, "/*/back/*", backpage) #
/$session_id/back/$number_of_steps -- go back the navigation history
HTTP.register!(ROUTER, "/*/solution", solutionpage) # /$session_id/solution
-- display the solution HTTP.register!(ROUTER, "*", notfoundpage) #
everything else -- not found # Start server HTTP.serve(SERVER, HOST, PORT)

end
```

Please note that we've also refactored the <head> of the pages, abstracting it away into the head function, which is used by both landingpage and wikiarticle. This way, we keep our code DRY, avoiding the repetition of the same <head> HTML element.

Now, let's make sure that we add `Gameplay.MAX_NUMBER_OF_STEPS` to `Gameplay.jl`. Add it at the top, under the difficulty constants:

```
const MAX_NUMBER_OF_STEPS = 10
```

Displaying a Wikipedia article page

The player has read the starting article and clicked on a link within the content. We need to add the logic for rendering the linked article. We'll have to fetch the article (or read it from the database if it was already fetched), display it, and update the game's state.

Here is the code:

```
const articlepage = HTTP.HandlerFunction() do req
  uri_parts = parseuri(req.target)
  game = gamesession(uri_parts[1])
  article_uri = "/wiki/$(uri_parts[end])"
  existing_articles = Articles.find(article_uri)
  article = isempty(existing_articles) ?
    persistedarticle(fetchpage(article_uri)...) :
    existing_articles[1]
  push!(game.history, article)
  game.steps_taken += 1
  puzzlesolved(game, article) && destroygamesession(game.id)
  HTTP.Messages.Response(200, wikiarticle(game, article))
end
```

We start by parsing the `Request` URI to extract all the values sent via GET. It is a string with the format `/$session_id/wiki/$article_name`, for example, `/c701b1b0b1/wiki/Buenos_Aires`. We want to break it into its parts. Since this is an operation that we'll need to perform more than once, we will abstract this functionality into the `parseuri` function:

```
function parseuri(uri)
  map(x -> String(x), split(uri, "/", keepempty = false))
end
```

Here, we use Julia's `split` function to break the URI string into an `Array` of `SubString`, corresponding to the segments between forward slashes `/`. Then, we convert the resulting `Array` of `SubString` to an `Array` of `String`, which is returned and stored in the `uri_parts` variable.

Continuing with the definition of the `articlepage` handler, we use the first element of the `uri_parts` array, which corresponds to the session ID, to retrieve our game object, by invoking `gamesession(uri_parts[1])`. With the last element, we generate the Wikipedia article URL. We then look up the article by URL, and either retrieve it from the database or fetch it from the website.

Once we have the article, we add it to the game's history and increase the `game.steps_taken` counter. Then, we check if we should end the game as a win:

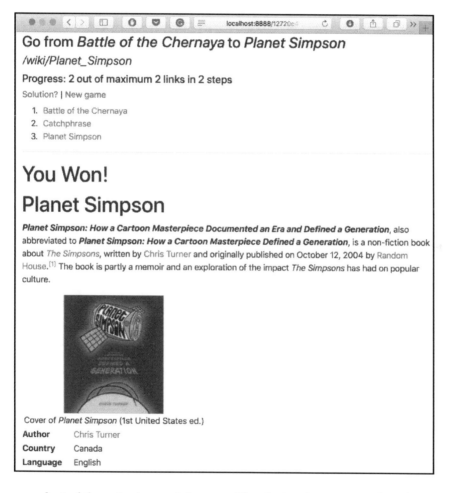

This is a screenshot of the winning article page. The design is not great, but the sweet taste of victory surely is!

Finally, similar to the new game page, we respond by rendering the article and all the game information.

Navigating back up the article chain

Keep in mind that a back navigation URL looks like `/c701b1b0b1/back/1`, where the first part is the session ID and the last part is the index of the item in the history stack. To implement it, the workflow is similar to `articlepage`—we parse the `Request` URI, retrieve the game by session ID, and get the article from the game's history stack. Since we go back in the game's history, everything beyond the current article index is to be removed from the navigation stack. When done, we respond by rendering the corresponding Wikipedia article. The code is short and readable:

```
const backpage = HTTP.HandlerFunction() do req
  uri_parts = parseuri(req.target)
  game = gamesession(uri_parts[1])
  history_index = parse(UInt8, uri_parts[end])

  article = game.history[history_index]
  game.history = game.history[1:history_index]

  HTTP.Messages.Response(200, wikiarticle(game, article))
end
```

Showing the solution

For the solution page, the only thing we need from the `Request` URI is the session ID. Then, we follow the same workflow to get the current `Game` object. Once we have it, we copy the list of articles into the history stack to display the game's solution using the existing rendering logic. We also set the `steps_taken` counter to the maximum because the game is considered a loss. Finally, we display the last article:

```
const solutionpage = HTTP.HandlerFunction() do req
  uri_parts = parseuri(req.target)
  game = gamesession(uri_parts[1])
  game.history = game.articles
  game.steps_taken = Gameplay.MAX_NUMBER_OF_STEPS
  article = game.articles[end]
  HTTP.Messages.Response(200, wikiarticle(game, article))
end
```

The solution page appears as follows, settling the game as a loss:

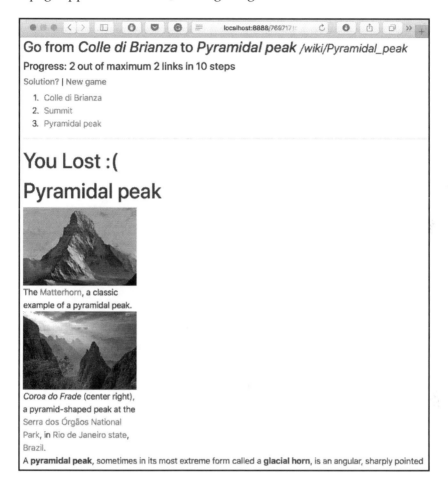

Handling any other requests

Similar to our `Hello World` example, we'll respond to any other requests with a `404 Not Found` response:

```
const notfoundpage = HTTP.HandlerFunction() do req
  HTTP.Messages.Response(404, "Sorry, this can't be found")
end
```

Wrapping it up

I've added a few more UI tweaks to the `WebApp.jl` file to spice things up a bit. Here are the important parts—please download the full file from `https://github.com/PacktPublishing/Julia-Programming-Projects/blob/master/Chapter05/sixdegrees/WebApp.jl`:

```julia
module WebApp

# code truncated #

function history(game)
  html = """<ol class="list-group">"""
  iter = 0
  for a in game.history
    html *= """
      <li class="list-group-item">
        <a href="/$(game.id)/back/$(iter + 1)">$(a.title)</a>
      </li>
    """
    iter += 1
  end

  html * "</ol>"
end

function objective(game)
  """
  <div class="jumbotron">
    <h3>Go from
      <span class="badge badge-info">$(game.articles[1].title)</span>
      to
      <span class="badge badge-info">$(game.articles[end].title)</span>
    </h3>
    <hr/>
    <h5>
      Progress:
      <span class="badge badge-dark">$(size(game.history, 1) - 1)</span>
      out of maximum
      <span class="badge badge-dark">$(size(game.articles, 1) - 1)</span>
      links in
      <span class="badge badge-dark">$(game.steps_taken)</span>
      steps
    </h5>
    $(history(game))
    <hr/>
    <h6>
```

```
      <a href="/$(game.id)/solution" class="btn btn-primary btn-
lg">Solution?</a> |
      <a href="/" class="btn btn-primary btn-lg">New game</a>
    </h6>
  </div>
  """
end

# code truncated #

end
```

You will see that I have reorganized the layout a bit and that I've added a few extra styles to make our UI prettier. Here is our game with its updated look:

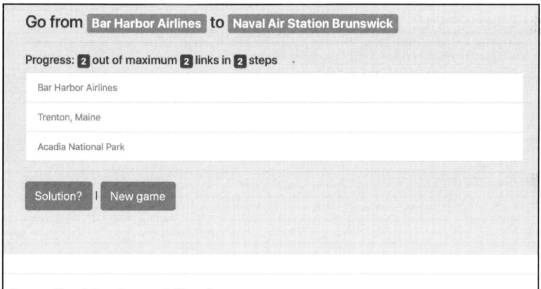

As for the rest of the files, if you need them, they are available for download in this chapter's GitHub repository, which is accessible at `https://github.com/PacktPublishing/Julia-Programming-Projects/tree/master/Chapter05/sixdegrees`.

That is all we need to do to run a full game of *Six Degrees of Wikipedia*. Now, it's time to enjoy it!

Summary

Julia focuses on scientific computing and data science. But thanks to its great qualities as a generic programming language, its native parallel computing features, and its performance, we have an excellent use case for Julia in the area of web development.

The package ecosystem provides access to a powerful set of libraries dedicated to web programming. They are relatively low level, but still abstract away most of the complexities of working directly with the network stack. The `HTTP` package provides a good balance between usability, performance, and flexibility.

The fact that we managed to build a fairly complex (albeit small) web app with so little code is a testimony to the power and expressiveness of the language and to the quality of the third-party libraries. We did a great job with our learning project—it's now time to relax a bit and enjoy a round of *Six Degrees of Wikipedia*, Julia style!

6
Implementing Recommender Systems with Julia

In the previous chapters, we took a deep dive into data mining and web development with Julia. I hope you enjoyed a few relaxing rounds of *Six Degrees of Wikipedia* while discovering some interesting articles. Randomly poking through the millions of Wikipedia articles as part of a game is a really fun way to stumble upon interesting new content. Although I'm sure that, at times, you've noticed that not all the articles are equally good—maybe they're stubs, or subjective, or not so well written, or simply irrelevant to you. If we were able to learn about each player's individual interests, we could filter out certain Wikipedia articles, which would turn each game session into a wonderful journey of discovery.

It turns out that we're not the only ones struggling with this—information discovery is a multibillion-dollar problem, regardless of whether it's articles, news, books, music, movies, hotels, or really any kind of product or service that can be sold over the internet. As consumers, we are exposed to an immense variety of choices, while at the same time, we have less and less time to review them—and our attention span is getting shorter and shorter. Making relevant recommendations instantly is a key feature of all successful online platforms, from Amazon to Booking.com, to Netflix, to Spotify, to Udemy. All of these companies have invested in building powerful recommender systems, literally inventing new business models together with the accompanying data collection and recommendation algorithms.

In this chapter, we'll learn about recommender systems—the most common and successful algorithms that are used in the wild for addressing a wide variety of business needs. We'll look at the following topics:

- What recommender systems are and how are they used
- Content-based versus collaborative filtering recommender systems
- User-based and item-based recommender systems

- More advanced data analysis using `DataFrames` and statistical functions
- How to roll out our own recommender systems using content-based and collaborative filtering algorithms

Technical requirements

The Julia package ecosystem is under continuous development and new package versions are released on a daily basis. Most of the times this is great news, as new releases bring new features and bug fixes. However, since many of the packages are still in beta (version 0.x), any new release can introduce breaking changes. As a result, the code presented in the book can stop working. In order to ensure that your code will produce the same results as described in the book, it is recommended to use the same package versions. Here are the external packages used in this chapter and their specific versions:

```
CSV@v0.4.3
DataFrames@v0.15.2
Distances@v0.7.4
IJulia@v1.14.1
Plots@v0.22.0
StatPlots@v0.8.2
```

In order to install a specific version of a package you need to run:

```
pkg> add PackageName@vX.Y.Z
```

For example:

```
pkg> add IJulia@v1.14.1
```

Alternatively you can install all the used packages by downloading the `Project.toml` file provided with the chapter and using `pkg>` instantiate as follows:

```
julia>
download("https://raw.githubusercontent.com/PacktPublishing/Julia-Programmi
ng-Projects/master/Chapter06/Project.toml", "Project.toml")
pkg> activate .
pkg> instantiate
```

Understanding recommender systems

In its broadest definition, a **recommender system** (**RS**) is a technique that's used for providing suggestions for items that are useful to a person. These suggestions are meant to help in various decision-making processes, usually related to buying or consuming a certain category of products or services. They can be about buying a book, listening to a song, watching a movie, eating out at a certain restaurant, reading a news article, or picking the hotel for your next holiday.

People have relied on recommendations pretty much since the beginning of history. Some RS researchers talk about the first recommendations as being the first orally transmitted information about dangerous plants, animals, or places. Others think that recommendations systems functioned even before language, by simply observing the effects on other humans of consuming plants or unwisely confronting dangerous creatures (that could count as an extreme and possibly violent example of implicit ratings, as we'll see in the following paragraphs).

But we don't have to go that far into human history. In more recent (and less dangerous) times, we can find some great examples of highly successful recommender systems, such as librarians suggesting books based on your tastes and interests, the butcher presenting meat products for your Sunday recipe, your friends' opinion of the latest blockbuster, your neighbor's stories about the kindergarten across the street, and even your MD recommending what treatment to follow to alleviate the symptoms and eliminate the cause of your disease. Other recommender systems are more formal, but equally pervasive and familiar, such as the star category ranking of hotels or the blue flags on top beaches around the world.

For a very long time, the experts in various fields played the part of recommenders, using their expertise in combination with their understanding of our tastes and interests, skillfully probing us for details. However, the rise of the internet and online platforms (e-commerce websites, online radios, movie streaming platforms, and social networks) has replaced the traditional models by making a huge catalog of items (products) available to a potentially very large consumer base (now called **users**). Due to considerations like 24-hour availability, language barriers, and sheer volume, personal recommendations were no longer a feasible option (although in the last couple of years, there was a certain recurrence of human-curated recommendations, from music, to books, to luxury products—but that's a different discussion).

This expansion in the number of choices made finding the right product a very difficult task. At that point, software-based recommender systems entered the stage.

Amazon.com is credited as being the first online business that deployed software recommender systems at scale, with extraordinary business benefits. Later on, Netflix became famous for awarding a one million dollar prize to the team that came up with a recommendation algorithm better than theirs. Nowadays, automated recommender systems power all major platforms, from Spotify's *Discover Weekly* playlists to Udemy's recommended courses.

Classifying recommender systems

Different business needs—from suggesting related products after buying your new laptop, to compiling the perfect driving playlist, to helping you reconnect with long lost schoolmates—led to the development of different recommendation algorithms. A key part of rolling out a recommender system is picking the right approach for the problem at hand to fully take advantage of the data available. We'll take a look at the most common and most successful algorithms.

Learning about non-personalized, stereotyped, and personalized recommendations

The simplest types of recommendations, from a technical and algorithmic perspective, are the non-personalized ones. That is, they are not customized to take into account specific user preferences. Such recommendations can include best-selling products, various top 10 songs, blockbuster movies, or the most downloaded apps of the week.

Non-personalized recommendations are less challenging technically, but also considerably less powerful. They can be good approximations in certain cases, especially when the product catalog is not very large (there are not that many Hollywood releases, for example). But for an e-commerce retailer like Amazon, with millions of products available at any given time, the chances of getting it right using generic recommendations are slim.

An improvement in non-personalized recommendations comes from combining them with a classification strategy. By stereotyping, we can make the recommended items more relevant, especially when we can identify significantly different user demographics. A good example of this is app store recommendations, which are broken down by country. Take, for instance, the following list of recommended new games. This is what it looks like if you are a user accessing the app store from the US:

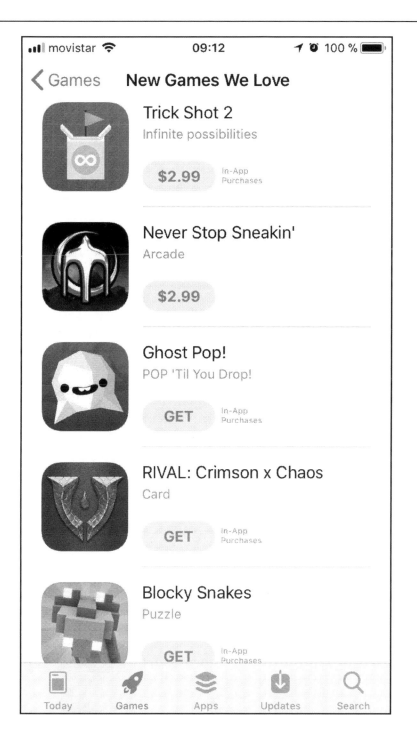

This is what it looks like for a user in Romania, at the exact same time:

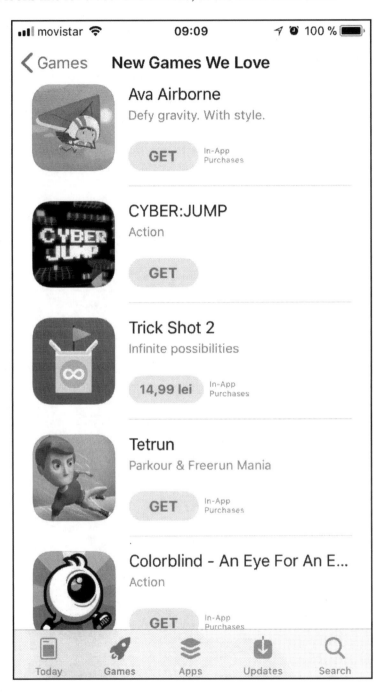

You can easily notice that the top selections vary widely. This is driven by both cultural differences and preferences, but also by availability (copyright and distribution) issues.

We won't focus on non-personalized recommendations in this chapter, since implementing them is quite straightforward. All that is needed for making such recommendations is to identify the relevant metrics and the best performing items, such as the number of downloads for apps, copies sold for a book, volume of streams for a song or movie, and so on. However, non-personalized recommendations, as a business solution, should not be dismissed, as they can be useful when dealing with users that don't present any relevant personal preferences—usually new users.

Understanding personalized recommendations

Both from a business and a technical perspective, the most interesting recommender systems are the ones that take into account the user's preferences (or user's ranking).

Explicit and implicit ratings

When looking for personalization features, we must take into account both explicit data that's willingly provided by the user, as well as relevant information that's generated by their behavior in the app or on the website (or anywhere else where we're tracking user behavior really, since the boundary between the online and physical realms is becoming more blurry, for example, with the introduction of smart cars and autonomous shop checkouts, to name just a few). The explicit rating includes actions such as grading a product or an experience, awarding stars to a movie or purchase, and retweeting or liking a post. On the other hand, not bouncing back to the search results page, sharing a song, or watching a video until the end are all examples of an implicit positive rating, while returning a product, canceling a subscription, or not finishing an online training course or an eBook are instances of negative implicit ranking.

Understanding content-based recommender systems

One of the most common and successful types of recommendations are content-based. The core idea is that if I expressed a preference for a certain set of items, I will most likely be interested in more items that share the same attributes. For example, the fact that I watched `Finding Nemo (2003)` can be used as an indication that I will be interested in other movies from the animation and comedy genres.

Alternatively, watching one of the original *Star Wars* movie can be interpreted as a signal that I like other movies from the franchise, or movies with Harrison Ford, or directed by George Lucas, or science fiction in general. Indeed, Netflix employs such an algorithm, except at a more granular level. Per a recent article, Netflix has a large team that's tasked with watching and tagging movies in detail—later on, matching movie features with users groups. The users themselves are equally carefully classified into thousands of categories.

More advanced content-based recommender systems also take into account the relative weight of the different tags. In the case of the previously mentioned `Finding Nemo (2003)`, the suggestions should be less about movies with fish and sharks and more about the fact that it's a funny, light-hearted family movie, so hopefully, the recommendation will be more `Finding Dory (2016)` and less *Jaws*.

Let's see how we can build a basic movie recommender using a content-based algorithm. To keep things simple, I have set up a table with the top 10 movies of 2016 and their genres. You can find this file in this book's GitHub repository, as `top_10_movies.tsv`, at https://github.com/PacktPublishing/Julia-Programming-Projects/blob/master/Chapter06/top_10_movies.tsv:

	A	B	C	D	E	F	G	H	I
1	Movie title	Action	Animation	Comedy	Drama	Kids	Mistery	Musical	SF
2	Moonlight (2016)	0	0	0	1	0	0	0	0
3	Zootopia (2016)	1	1	1	0	0	0	0	0
4	Arrival (2016)	0	0	0	1	0	1	0	1
5	Hell or High Water (2016)	0	0	0	1	0	1	0	0
6	La La Land (2016)	0	0	1	1	0	0	1	0
7	The Jungle Book (2016)	1	0	0	0	1	0	0	0
8	Manchester by the Sea (2016)	0	0	0	1	0	0	0	0
9	Finding Dory (2016)	0	1	0	0	0	0	0	0
10	Captain America: Civil War (2016)	1	0	0	0	0	0	0	1
11	Moana (2016)	1	1	0	0	0	0	0	0

In the preceding screenshot, you can see how we use a binary system to represent whether a movie belongs to a genre (encoded by a 1) or not (a 0).

We can easily load such a table from a CSV/TSV file into Julia by using the `readdlm` function, which is available in the `DelimitedFiles` module. This module comes with the default Julia installation, so there's no need to add it:

```
julia> using DelimitedFiles
Julia> movies = readdlm("top_10_movies.tsv", '\t', skipstart=1)
```

In the preceding snippet, `skipstart=1` tells Julia to skip the first line when reading the *Tab* separated `top_10_movies.tsv` file—otherwise, Julia would interpret the header row as a data row as well.

There is also the option of letting `readdlm` know that the first row is the header, passing `header = true`. However, this would change the return type of the function invocation to a tuple of (`data_cells`, `header_cells`), which is not pretty-printed in interactive environments. At this exploratory phase, we're better off with a table-like representation of the data. The result is a tabular data structure that contains our movie titles and their genres:

```
10×9 Array{Any,2}:
"Moonlight (2016)"                 0  0  0  1  0  0  0  0
"Zootopia (2016)"                  1  1  1  0  0  0  0  0
"Arrival (2016)"                   0  0  0  1  0  1  0  1
"Hell or High Water (2016)"        0  0  0  1  0  1  0  0
"La La Land (2016)"                0  0  1  1  0  0  1  0
"The Jungle Book (2016)"           1  0  0  0  1  0  0  0
"Manchester by the Sea (2016)"     0  0  0  1  0  0  0  0
"Finding Dory (2016)"              0  1  0  0  0  0  0  0
"Captain America: Civil War (2016)" 1  0  0  0  0  0  0  1
"Moana (2016)"                     1  1  0  0  0  0  0  0
```

Let's see what movie from the top 10 list we could recommend to a user who watched the aforementioned movie, `Finding Nemo (2003)`. Rotten Tomatoes classifies `Finding Nemo (2003)` under the *Animation, Comedy,* and *Kids* genres. We can encode this as follows:

```
julia> nemo = ["Finding Nemo (2003)", 0, 1, 1, 0, 1, 0, 0, 0] 9-element
Array{Any,1}:
  "Finding Nemo (2003)"
 0
 1
 1
 0
 1
 0
 0
 0
```

To make a movie recommendation based on genre, all we have to do is find the ones that are the most similar, that is, the movies that share the most genres with our `Finding Nemo (2003)`.

There is a multitude of algorithms for computing the similarity (or on the contrary, the distance) between items—in our case, as we're dealing with binary values only, the Hamming distance looks like a good choice. The Hamming distance is a number that's used to denote the difference between two binary strings. This distance is calculated by comparing two binary values and taking into account the number of positions at which the corresponding bits are different. We'll compare each bit in succession and record either 1 or 0, depending on whether or not the bits are different or the same. If they are the same, we record a 0. For different bits, we record a 1. Then, we add all the 1s and 0s in the record to obtain the Hamming distance.

A function for calculating the Hamming distance is available in the Distances package. This is a third-party Julia package that provides access to a multitude of functions for evaluating distances between vectors, including Euclidian, Jaccard, Hemming, Cosine, and many others. All we need to do to access this treasure of functionality is run the following:

```julia
julia> using Pkg
pkg> add Distances
julia> using Distances
```

Then, we need to iterate over our movies matrix and compute the Hamming distance between each movie and Finding Nemo (2003):

```julia
julia> distances = Dict{String,Int}()
Dict{String,Int64} with 0 entries

julia> for i in 1:size(movies, 1)
           distances[movies[i,:][1]] = hamming(Int[movies[i,2:end]...],
Int[nemo[2:end]...])
       end
```

In the preceding snippet, we iterated over each movie and calculated the Hamming distance between its genres and the genres of Finding Nemo (2003). To do this, we only extracted the genres (leaving off the name of the movie) and converted the list of values into an array of Int. Finally, we placed the result of the computation into the distances Dict we defined previously, which uses the name of the movie as the key, and the distance as the value.

This is the end result:

```julia
julia> distances
Dict{String,Int64} with 10 entries:
  "The Jungle Book (2016)"        => 3
  "Hell or High Water (2016)"     => 5
  "Arrival (2016)"                => 6
  "La La Land (2016)"             => 4
```

```
"Moana (2016)"                       => 3
"Captain America: Civil War (2016)"  => 5
"Moonlight (2016)"                   => 4
"Finding Dory (2016)"                => 2
"Zootopia (2016)"                    => 2
"Manchester by the Sea (2016)"       => 4
```

Since we're computing distances, the most similar movies are the ones within the shortest distance. So, according to our recommender, a user who watched `Finding Nemo (2003)` should next watch `Finding Dory (2016)` or `Zootopia (2016)` (distance 2) and when done, should move on to `The Jungle Book (2016)` and `Moana (2016)` (both at a distance of 3). If you haven't watched all of these recommended movies already, I can tell you that the suggestions are quite appropriate. Similarly, the least recommended movie is `Arrival (2016)`, which although is an excellent science fiction drama, has nothing in common with cute Nemo and forgetful Dory.

Beginning with association-based recommendations

Although content-based recommender systems can produce great results, they do have limitations. For starters, they can't be used to recommend new items. Based on my initial `Finding Nemo (2003)` ranking alone, I would be stuck getting suggestions for animated movies alone and I'd never get the chance to hear about any new documentaries or car or cooking shows that I sometimes enjoy.

Also, it works best for categories of items that can be purchased repeatedly, like books, apps, songs, or movies, to name a few. But if I'm on Amazon and purchase a new dishwasher from the *Home and kitchen* category, it doesn't make a lot of sense to get recommendations about products within the same group, such as a fridge or a washing machine, as chances are I'm not replacing all of the expensive kitchen appliances at the same time. However, I will most likely need the corresponding joints and taps and pipes and whatever else is needed to install the dishwasher, together with the recommended detergent and maybe other accessories. Since the e-commerce platform is selling all of these products as well, it's beneficial to order them together and receive them at the same time, saving on transport too.

These bundles of products can form the foundation of a RS based on product association. These types of recommendations are quite common, and are usually presented as *frequently bought together* on e-commerce platforms. For physical stores, this type of data analysis—also known as **market basket analysis**—is used to place products that are purchased together in close physical proximity. Think, for example, about pasta being side by side with sauces, or shampoo with conditioners.

One of the most popular algorithms used for association based recommendations is the `Apriori` algorithm. It is used to identify items that frequently occur together in different scenarios (shopping baskets, web browsing, adverse drug reactions, and so on). The `Apriori` algorithm helps us identify correlations through data mining by employing association rules.

Space constraints don't allow us to get into the details of building such as system, but if you would like to dive deeper into this topic, there are many free resources to get you started. I recommend beginning with *Movie Recommendation with Market Basket Analysis* (`https://rpubs.com/vitidN/203264`) as it builds a movie recommender that's very similar to ours.

Learning about collaborative filtering

Collaborative filtering (**CF**) is another very successful and widely used recommendation algorithm. It is based on the idea that people with similar preferences will have similar interests. If two customers, let's call them Annie and Bob, give `Finding Nemo (2003)` a good rating and Annie also highly ranks `Finding Dory (2016)`, then chances are that Bob will also like `Finding Dory (2016)`. Of course, comparing two users and two products may not seem like much, but applied to very large datasets representing both users and products, the recommendations become highly relevant.

If you're confused as to what the difference between CF and content filtering is, since both can be used to infer `Finding Dory (2016)` based on `Finding Nemo (2003)`, the key point is that CF does not care about item attributes. Indeed, when using CF, we don't need the movie genre information, nor any other tags. The algorithm is not concerned with the classification of the items. It pretty much states that if, for whatever reason, the items were ranked highly by a subset of users, then other items that are highly ranked by the same subset of users will be relevant for our target user, hence making for a good recommendation.

Understanding user-item CF

This was the basic idea, and with the advent of big data, the CF technique has become quite powerful. As it's been applied to different business needs and usage scenarios, the algorithm was refined to better address the problems it was attempting to solve. As a consequence, a few other approaches emerged, and the original one became known as **user-item CF**.

It's gotten this name because it takes as its input user data (user preferences, rankings) and outputs item data (item recommendations). It's also known as **user-based CF**.

You can see it illustrated in the following diagram:

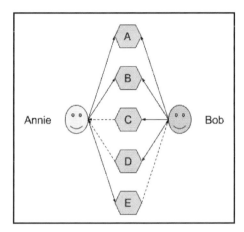

The preceding diagram shows that **Annie** likes **A**, **B**, and **E**, while **Bob** likes **A**, **B**, **C**, and **D**.

The `recommender` algorithm established that, between **Annie** and **Bob**, there's a high degree of similarity because they both like items **A** and **B**. Next, it will assume that **Annie** will also like other items from Bob's list of preferences that she hasn't discovered yet, and the reverse for **Bob**—he'll like items from Annie's list that he hasn't discovered yet. Thus, since Annie also likes item E, we can recommend it to **Bob**, and since Bob's very fond of **C** and **D** and Annie has no knowledge about these yet, we can confidently suggest that she checks them out.

Let's take another very simple example, also from the realm of movie recommendations. Sticking to our previous list of top 10 movies for the year 2016 on Rotten Tomatoes, this time, let's ignore the classification by genre and imagine that we have user ratings data instead:

Movie title	Acton	Annie	Comey	Dean	Kit	Missie	Musk	Sam
Moonlight (2016)		3		10		9	2	
Zootopia (2016)	9	10	7		10		5	
Arrival (2016)	5		6	10		9		10
Hell or High Water (2016)	3		3	10		8		
La La Land (2016)	6		8	9			10	
The Jungle Book (2016)	8	7		2	9		6	
Manchester by the Sea (2016)			2	8				
Finding Dory (2016)	7	8	5	4	10			
Captain America: Civil War (2016)	10		5	6				9
Moana (2016)	8	9			10		7	

The preceding screenshot shows a table of movie titles and users and their corresponding ratings. As it happens in real life, not all of the users have rated all of the moves—the absence of a rating is indicated by an empty cell.

You will notice in the preceding screenshot that by a strange twist of faith, the user's names provide a hint as to what kind of movies they prefer. Acton is very much into action movies, while Annie loves animations. Comey's favorites are the comedies, while Dean enjoys good dramas. Kit's highest rankings went to kids movies, Missie loves mystery movies, while musical's are Musk reasons for binge watching. Finally, Sam is a science fiction fan.

The dataset is provided in this chapter's files under the name `top_10_movies_user_rankings.csv`. Please download it from `https://github.com/PacktPublishing/Julia-Programming-Projects/blob/master/Chapter06/top_10_movies_user_rankings.csv` and place it somewhere on your hard drive where you can easily access it from Julia's REPL.

We can load it into memory using the same `readdlm` Julia function as before:

```
movies = readdlm("/path/to/top_10_movies_user_rankings.csv", ';')
```

This file uses the ; char as the column separator, so we need to pass that into the `readdlm` function call. Remember that in Julia, `";"` is different from `':'`. The first is a `String` of length one, while the second is a `Char`.

This is the result of the `.csv` file being read—a matrix containing movies on rows and people on columns, with each person's rating at the corresponding intersection between rows and columns:

```
11×9 Array{Any,2}:
 "Movie title"                      "Acton"   "Annie"  …   "Dean"   "Kit"    "Missie"   "Musk"    "Sam"
 "Moonlight (2016)"                 ""        3            10       ""       9          2         ""
 "Zootopia (2016)"                  9         10           ""       10       ""         5         ""
 "Arrival (2016)"                   5         ""           10       ""       9          ""        10
 "Hell or High Water (2016)"        3         ""           10       ""       8          ""        ""
 "La La Land (2016)"                6         ""       …   9        ""       ""         10        ""
 "The Jungle Book (2016)"           8         7            2        9        ""         6         ""
 "Manchester by the Sea (2016)"     ""        ""           8        ""       ""         ""        ""
 "Finding Dory (2016)"              7         8            4        10       ""         ""        ""
 "Captain America: Civil War (2016)" 10       ""           6        ""       ""         ""        9
 "Moana (2016)"                     8         9        …   ""       10       ""         7         ""
```

It works, but the data doesn't look too good. As usually happens with data in real life, we don't always have ratings from all the users. The `missing` values were imported as empty strings `""`, and the headers were interpreted as entries in the matrix. Julia's `readdlm` is great for quick data imports, but for more advanced data wrangling, we can benefit considerably from using Julia's powerful `DataFrames` package.

`DataFrames` is a third-party Julia package that exposes a rich set of functions for manipulating tabular data. You should remember it from our introduction in Chapter 1, *Getting Started with Julia Programming*—if not, please take a few minutes to review that part. The rest of our discussion will assume that you have a basic understanding of `DataFrames` so that we can now focus on the more advanced features and use cases.

If, for some reason, you no longer have the `DataFrames` package, `pkg> add DataFrames` is all we need. While we're at it, let's also install the `CSV` package—it's a powerful utility library for handling delimited text files. We can add both in one step:

```
pkg> add DataFrames CSV
```

We'll use `CSV` to load the comma-separated file and produce a `DataFrame`:

```
julia> movies = CSV.read("top_10_movies_user_rankings.csv", delim = ';')
```

The resulting `DataFrame` should look like this:

```
10×9 DataFrame
 Row  Movie title                      Acton    Annie    Comey    Dean     Kit      Missie   Musk     Sam
      Union{Missing, String}           Int64⍰   Int64⍰   Int64⍰   Int64⍰   Int64⍰   Int64⍰   Int64⍰   Int64⍰

 1    Moonlight (2016)                 missing  3        missing  10       missing  9        2        missing
 2    Zootopia (2016)                  9        10       7        missing  10       missing  5        missing
 3    Arrival (2016)                   5        missing  6        10       missing  9        missing  10
 4    Hell or High Water (2016)        3        missing  3        10       missing  8        missing  missing
 5    La La Land (2016)                6        missing  8        9        missing  missing  10       missing
 6    The Jungle Book (2016)           8        7        missing  2        9        missing  6        missing
 7    Manchester by the Sea (2016)     missing  missing  2        8        missing  missing  missing  missing
 8    Finding Dory (2016)              7        8        5        4        10       missing  missing  missing
 9    Captain America: Civil War (2016) 10      missing  5        6        missing  missing  missing  9
 10   Moana (2016)                     8        9        missing  missing  10       missing  7        missing
```

We get a beautifully rendered tabular data structure, with the missing ratings correctly represented as `missing` data.

We can get a quick summary of our data by using the `describe` function:

```julia
julia> describe(movies)
```

The output for this is as follows:

```
9×8 DataFrame
 Row  variable      mean      min              median    max               nunique    nmissing  eltype
      Symbol        Union…    Any              Union…    Any               Union…     Int64     DataType

 1    Movie title             Arrival (2016)             Zootopia (2016)   10         0         String
 2    Acton         7.0       3                7.5       10                           2         Int64
 3    Annie         7.4       3                8.0       10                           5         Int64
 4    Comey         5.14286   2                5.0       8                            3         Int64
 5    Dean          7.375     2                8.5       10                           2         Int64
 6    Kit           9.75      9                10.0      10                           6         Int64
 7    Missie        8.66667   8                9.0       9                            7         Int64
 8    Musk          6.0       2                6.0       10                           5         Int64
 9    Sam           9.5       9                9.5       10                           8         Int64
```

Multiple columns have `missing` values. A `missing` value represents a value that is absent in the dataset. It is defined in the `Missings` package (https://github.com/JuliaData/Missings.jl), and it's the singleton instance of the `Missing` type. If you're familiar with `NULL` in SQL or `NA` in R, `missing` is the same in Julia.

Missing values are problematic when working with real-life datasets as they can affect the accuracy of the computations. For this reason, common operations that involve `missing` values usually propagate `missing`. For example, `1 + missing` and `cos(missing)` will both return `missing`.

We can check if a value is missing by using the `ismissing` function:

```julia
julia> movies[1,2]
missing

julia> ismissing(movies[1, 2])
true
```

In many cases, `missing` values will have to be skipped or replaced with a valid value. What value is appropriate for replacing `missing` will depend from case to case, as dictated by the business logic. In our case, for the missing ratings, we can use the value `0`. By convention, we can agree that valid ratings range from `1` to `10`, and that a rating of `0` corresponds to no rating at all.

One way to do the replacement is to iterate over each column except `Movie title` and then over each cell, and if the corresponding value is missing, replace it with `0`. Here is the code:

```julia
julia> for c in names(movies)[2:end]
           movies[ismissing.(movies[c]), c] = 0
       end
```

We're all done—our data is now clean, with zeroes replacing all the previously missing values:

```
10×9 DataFrame
 Row │ Movie title                          Acton  Annie  Comey  Dean   Kit    Missie  Musk   Sam
     │ Union(Missing, String)               Int64@ Int64@ Int64@ Int64@ Int64@ Int64@  Int64@ Int64@
─────┼──────────────────────────────────────────────────────────────────────────────────────────
   1 │ Moonlight (2016)                     0      3      0      10     0      9       2      0
   2 │ Zootopia (2016)                      9      10     7      0      10     0       5      0
   3 │ Arrival (2016)                       5      0      6      10     0      9       0      10
   4 │ Hell or High Water (2016)            3      0      3      10     0      8       0      0
   5 │ La La Land (2016)                    6      0      8      9      0      0       10     0
   6 │ The Jungle Book (2016)               8      7      0      2      9      0       6      0
   7 │ Manchester by the Sea (2016)         0      0      2      8      0      0       0      0
   8 │ Finding Dory (2016)                  7      8      5      4      10     0       0      0
   9 │ Captain America: Civil War (2016)    10     0      5      6      0      0       0      9
  10 │ Moana (2016)                         8      9      0      0      10     0       7      0
```

It would help if you saved this clean version of our data as a *Tab* separated file, for future reference, with the following code:

```julia
julia> CSV.write("top_10_movies_user_rankings.tsv", movies, delim='\t')
```

Now that we have our ratings loaded into Julia, the next step is to compute the similarity between the various users. The Hamming distance, the formula that we used when computing content based recommendations, would not be a good choice for numerical data. A much better alternative is Pearson's correlation coefficient. This coefficient, also known as ***Pearson's r or bivariate correlation***, is a measure of the linear correlation between two variables. It has a value between +1 and −1. A value of 1 indicates total positive linear correlation (both values increase together), while −1 represents total negative linear correlation (one value decreases while the other increases). The value 0 means that there's no linear correlation.

Here are a few examples of scatter diagrams with different visualizations of the correlation coefficient (By Kiatdd—Own work, CC BY-SA 3.0,
https://commons.wikimedia.org/w/index.php?curid=37108966):

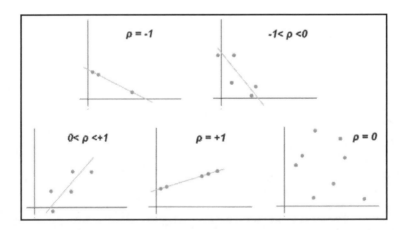

Let's see how we would calculate the similarity between Acton and Annie, based on the movie ratings they provided. Let's make things simpler and focus strictly on their data by extracting the Movie title column, together with the Acton and Annie columns:

```julia
julia> acton_and_annie = movies[:, 1:3]
```

The output is as follows:

```
10x3 DataFrame
 Row │ Movie title                         │ Acton  │ Annie
     │ Union{Missing, String}              │ Int64m │ Int64m
─────┼─────────────────────────────────────┼────────┼───────
  1  │ Moonlight (2016)                    │ 0      │ 3
  2  │ Zootopia (2016)                     │ 9      │ 10
  3  │ Arrival (2016)                      │ 5      │ 0
  4  │ Hell or High Water (2016)           │ 3      │ 0
  5  │ La La Land (2016)                   │ 6      │ 0
  6  │ The Jungle Book (2016)              │ 8      │ 7
  7  │ Manchester by the Sea (2016)        │ 0      │ 0
  8  │ Finding Dory (2016)                 │ 7      │ 8
  9  │ Captain America: Civil War (2016)   │ 10     │ 0
  10 │ Moana (2016)                        │ 8      │ 9
```

This returns another `DataFrame`, referenced as `acton_and_annie`, which corresponds to the columns one to three of the `movies DataFrame`, representing Acton's and Annie's ratings for each of the movies.

This is good, but we're only interested in the movies that were rated by both users. If you remember from our discussion of `DataFrame` in `Chapter 1`, *Getting Started with Julia Programming,* we can select rows (and columns) by passing a Boolean value—`true` to select it, `false` to skip it. We can use this in combination with the dot syntax for element-wise operations to check if the values in the `:Acton` and `:Annie` columns are greater than `0`. The code will look like this:

```
julia> acton_and_annie_in_common = acton_and_annie[(acton_and_annie[:Acton]
.> 0) .& (acton_and_annie[:Annie] .> 0), :]
```

Although it might look a bit intimidating, the snippet should be easy to follow: we use the `(acton_and_annie[:Acton] .> 0) .& (acton_and_annie[:Annie] .> 0)` expression to check element-wise if the values in the `Acton` and `Annie` columns are greater than `0`. Each comparison will return an array of `true`/`false` values—more exactly two `10-element BitArrays`, as follows:

```
julia> acton_and_annie[:Acton] .> 0
10-element BitArray{1}:
 false
  true
  true
  true
  true
  true
 false
```

```
   true
   true
   true

julia> acton_and_annie[:Annie] .> 0
10-element BitArray{1}:
   true
   true
  false
  false
  false
   true
  false
   true
  false
   true
```

Next, we apply the bitwise & operator, which is also element-wise, to the resulting arrays:

```
julia> (acton_and_annie[:Acton] .> 0) .& (acton_and_annie[:Annie] .> 0)
10-element BitArray{1}:
  false
   true
  false
  false
  false
   true
  false
   true
  false
   true
```

Finally, this array of true/false values is passed into the DataFrame to filter the rows. The preceding snippet will produce the following output, a new DataFrame that contains only the movies that have been rated by both Acton and Annie:

The output is as follows:

```
4×3 DataFrame
 Row │ Movie title            Acton   Annie
     │ Union{Missing, String}  Int64⍰  Int64⍰
─────┼─────────────────────────────────────────
   1 │ Zootopia (2016)         9       10
   2 │ The Jungle Book (2016)  8       7
   3 │ Finding Dory (2016)     7       8
   4 │ Moana (2016)            8       9
```

Let's plot the ratings. Julia comes with quite a few options for plotting. We saw some in Chapter 1, *Getting Started with Julia Programming*, and we'll look at plotting in more detail in Chapter 9, *Working with Dates, Time, and Time Series*. For now, we'll use the appropriately named Plots library to quickly visualize our data.

Plots is designed as a higher-level interface to other plotting libraries (named *backends* in Plots language), such as GR or PyPlot. It basically unifies multiple lower-level plotting packages (backends) under a common API.

As always, start with pkg> add Plots and continue with using Plots.

We're now ready to generate the visualization:

```julia
julia> plot(acton_and_annie_in_common[:,2], acton_and_annie_in_common[:,3],
seriestype=:scatter, xticks=0:10, yticks=0:10, lims=(0,11), label="")
```

In the preceding snippet, we invoke the plot function, passing it Acton's and Annie's ratings. As options, we ask it to produce a scatter plot. We also want to make sure that the axes start at **0** and end at 11 (so that value **10** is fully visible), with ticks at each unit. We'll end up with the following plot:

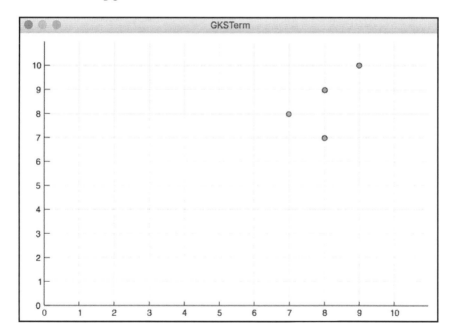

By the looks of it, there is a good correlation between the user's movie preferences. But we can do even better.

Julia's ecosystem provides access to yet another powerful package that combines both plotting and statistical features. It's called `StatPlots` and actually works on top of the `Plots` package, providing statistical plotting recipes for `Plots`. It also supports `DataFrame` visualizations out of the box, so it's a perfect match for our needs.

Let's add it with `pkg> add StatPlots` and bring it into scope (`using StatPlots`). We can now use the `@df` macro that's exposed by `StatPlots` to generate a scatter plot of our data:

```
julia> @df acton_and_annie_in_common scatter([:Acton], [:Annie], smooth =
true, line = :red, linewidth = 2, title = "Acton and Annie", legend =
false, xlimits = (5, 11), ylimits = (5, 11))
```

The preceding code will produce the following visualization:

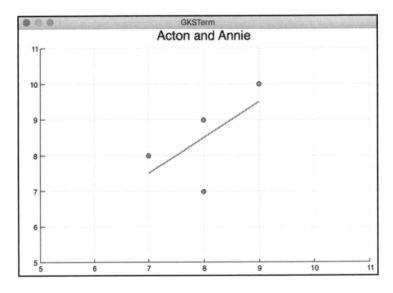

This new plot shows the correlation between the movies, despite the outlier.

Let's compute the Pearson correlation between Acton's and Annie's ratings:

```
julia> using Statistics
julia> cor(acton_and_annie_in_common[:Acton],
acton_and_annie_in_common[:Annie])

0.6324555320336759
```

Pretty much any value over 0.6 indicates a good similarity, so it looks like we're onto something.

Now, we can recommend to Annie some of Acton's favorites that she hasn't seen, as follows:

```julia
julia> annies_recommendations = acton_and_annie[(acton_and_annie[:Annie]
.== 0) .&  (acton_and_annie[:Acton] .> 0), :]
```

This snippet should be easy to understand since it's a slight variation of the common rating formula. From the `acton_and_annie` DataFrame, we only select the rows where Annie's score is 0 (she hasn't rated the movie) and Acton's is greater than 0 (he has rated the movie).

We'll get a DataFrame with four rows:

```
4×3 DataFrame
 Row │ Movie title                       Acton   Annie
     │ Union{Missing, String}            Int64⍰  Int64⍰
─────┼──────────────────────────────────────────────────
   1 │ Arrival (2016)                    5       0
   2 │ Hell or High Water (2016)         3       0
   3 │ La La Land (2016)                 6       0
   4 │ Captain America: Civil War (2016) 10      0
```

However, there's a small glitch. We assumed that all the ratings indicate a strong preference, but in this case, many of Acton's ratings are rather an indication of a dislike. With the exception of Captain America: Civil War (2016), all the possible recommendations have bad ratings. Luckily, that is easy to fix—we just need to recommend movies that have a high rating, let's say, of at least 7:

```julia
julia> annies_recommendations = acton_and_annie[(acton_and_annie[:Annie]
.== 0) .&(acton_and_annie[:Acton] .>= 7 ), :]
```

This leaves us with only one movie, Captain America: Civil War (2016):

```
1×3 DataFrame
 Row │ Movie title                       Acton   Annie
     │ Union{Missing, String}            Int64⍰  Int64⍰
─────┼──────────────────────────────────────────────────
   1 │ Captain America: Civil War (2016) 10      0
```

Now that we understand the logic of user-based recommender systems, let's put all of these steps together to create a simple recommender script.

We'll analyze our users' rating matrix in a script that will take advantage of all the available data to generate recommendations for all of our users.

Here's a possible implementation—please create a `user_based_movie_recommendations.jl` file with the following code. Do make sure that the `top_10_movies_user_rankings.tsv` file is in the same folder (or update the path in the code to match your location). Here's the code:

```julia
using CSV, DataFrames, Statistics

const minimum_similarity = 0.8
const movies = CSV.read("top_10_movies_user_rankings.tsv", delim = '\t')

function user_similarity(target_user)
    similarity = Dict{Symbol,Float64}()
    for user in names(movies[:, 2:end])
        user == target_user && continue
        ratings = movies[:, [user, target_user]]
        common_movies = ratings[(ratings[user] .> 0) .&
(ratings[target_user] .> 0), :]
        correlation = try
            cor(common_movies[user], common_movies[target_user])
        catch
            0.0
        end
        similarity[user] = correlation
    end
    similarity
end

function recommendations(target_user)
    recommended = Dict{String,Float64}()
    for (user,similarity) in user_similarity(target_user)
        similarity > minimum_similarity || continue
        ratings = movies[:, [Symbol("Movie title"), user, target_user]]
        recommended_movies = ratings[(ratings[user] .>= 7) .&
(ratings[target_user] .== 0), :]
        for movie in eachrow(recommended_movies)
            recommended[movie[Symbol("Movie title")]] = movie[user] *
similarity
        end
    end
    recommended
end
```

```
for user in names(movies)[2:end]
    println("Recommendations for $user: $(recommendations(user))")
end
```

In the preceding snippet, we define two functions, `user_similarity` and `recommendations`. They both take, as their single argument, a user's name in the form of a Symbol. This argument matches the column name in our `movies` DataFrame.

The `user_similarity` function computes the similarity of our target user (the one passed into the function as the argument) with all the other users and returns a dictionary of the form:

```
Dict(
    :Comey => 1.0,
    :Dean => 0.907841,
    :Missie => NaN,
    :Kit => 0.774597,
    :Musk => 0.797512,
    :Sam => 0.0,
    :Acton => 0.632456
)
```

The `dict` represents Annie's similarity with all the other users.

We use the similarities in the recommendations function to pick the relevant users and make recommendations based on their favorite movies, which were not already rated by our target user.

I've also added a little twist to make the recommendations more relevant—a weight factor. This is computed by multiplying the user's rating with the user's similarity. If, say, `Comey` gives a movie an 8 and is 100% similar to `Missie` (correlation coefficient equals 1), the weight of the recommendation will also be 8 *(8 * 1)*. But if Comey is only 50% similar to Musk (0.5 correlation coefficient), then the weight of the recommendation (corresponding to the estimated rating) will be just 4 *(8 * 0.5)*.

At the end of the file, we bootstrap the whole process by looping through an array of all the users, and we produce and print the movie recommendations for each of them.

Running this will output movie recommendations, together with their weights for each of our users:

```
Recommendations for Acton: Dict("Moonlight (2016)"=>9.0)
Recommendations for Annie: Dict("La La Land (2016)"=>8.0)
Recommendations for Comey: Dict("The Jungle Book (2016)"=>7.0,"Moana
(2016)"=>7.0,"Moonlight (2016)"=>9.0)
Recommendations for Dean: Dict("Moana (2016)"=>10.0,"Zootopia
```

```
(2016)"=>10.0)
Recommendations for Kit: Dict("Hell or High Water (2016)"=>10.0,"Arrival
(2016)"=>10.0,"La La Land (2016)"=>9.0,"Moonlight (2016)"=>10.0,"Manchester
by the Sea (2016)"=>8.0)
Recommendations for Missie: Dict("The Jungle Book (2016)"=>8.0,
"Moana (2016)"=>8.0, "La La Land (2016)"=>8.0,"Captain America: Civil War
(2016)"=>10.0,"Finding Dory (2016)"=>7.0,"Zootopia (2016)"=>9.0)
Recommendations for Musk: Dict{String,Float64}()
Recommendations for Sam: Dict("Hell or High Water (2016)"=>10.0,
"La La Land (2016)"=>9.0,"Moonlight (2016)"=>10.0,"Zootopia
(2016)"=>7.0,"Manchester by the Sea (2016)"=>8.0)
```

The data looks quite good, considering that this is a toy example. A production quality recommender system should be based on millions of such ratings.

However, if you look closely, you might notice that something's not quite right—the `Recommendations for Kit`. Kit likes kids movies—light-hearted animated comedies. Our system recommends him, with quite a lot of weight, a lot of dramas! What gives? If we look at the similarity data for Kit, we'll see that he's very well correlated with Dean and Dean likes drama. That might sound weird, but it's actually correct if we check the data:

```julia
julia> movies[:, [Symbol("Movie title"), :Dean, :Kit]]
```

The output is as follows:

```
10×3 DataFrame
 Row │ Movie title                         │ Dean  │ Kit
     │ Union{Missing, String}              │ Int64m│ Int64m
─────┼────────────────────────────────────┼───────┼───────
 1   │ Moonlight (2016)                    │ 10    │ 0
 2   │ Zootopia (2016)                     │ 0     │ 10
 3   │ Arrival (2016)                      │ 10    │ 0
 4   │ Hell or High Water (2016)           │ 10    │ 0
 5   │ La La Land (2016)                   │ 9     │ 0
 6   │ The Jungle Book (2016)              │ 2     │ 9
 7   │ Manchester by the Sea (2016)        │ 8     │ 0
 8   │ Finding Dory (2016)                 │ 4     │ 10
 9   │ Captain America: Civil War (2016)   │ 6     │ 0
 10  │ Moana (2016)                        │ 0     │ 10
```

Notice how the only movies they both watched are `The Jungle Book (2016)` and `Finding Dory (2016)`, and how the ratings are correlated since both give higher ratings to `Finding Dory (2016)`. Therefore, there is a strong positive correlation between Dean and Kit. But what our algorithm doesn't take into account is that even if Dean likes `Finding Dory (2016)` more than `The Jungle Book (2016)`, he still doesn't really like either, as indicated by the low ratings of 4 and 2, respectively.

The solution is quite simple, though—we just need to remove ratings that don't indicate a strong positive preference. Again, we can use a rating equal to or larger than 7 to count as a like. So, in the `user_similarity` function, please look for the following line:

```
common_movies = ratings[(ratings[user] .> 0) .& (ratings[target_user] .>
0), :]
```

Replace `ratings[user] .> 0` with `ratings[user] .> 7` so that the whole line now reads as follows:

```
common_movies = ratings[Array(ratings[user] .> 7) .&
Array(ratings[target_user] .> 0), :]
```

What this does is now compute similarity only based on favorites. As a result, `Kit` is no longer similar to `Dean` (the correlation coefficient is 0).

Another consequence of the fact that our recommendations are more targeted is that we no longer have recommendations for all the users—but this is, again, caused by the fact that we're working with a very small example dataset. Here are the final recommendations:

```
Recommendations for Acton: Dict("Moonlight (2016)"=>9.0)
Recommendations for Annie: Dict{String,Float64}()
Recommendations for Comey: Dict(
"Moana (2016)"=>9.0,
"Moonlight (2016)"=>9.0)
Recommendations for Dean: Dict(
"Moana (2016)"=>8.0,
"Zootopia (2016)"=>9.0)
Recommendations for Kit: Dict{String,Float64}()
Recommendations for Missie: Dict{String,Float64}()
Recommendations for Musk: Dict{String,Float64}()
Recommendations for Sam: Dict{String,Float64}()
```

We only have suggestions for Acton, Comey, and Dean, but they are now much more accurate.

Item-item CF

User-based CF works quite well and is widely used in production in the wild, but it does have a few considerable downsides. First, it's difficult to get enough preference information from users, leaving many of them without a solid base for relevant recommendations. Second, as the platform and the underlying business grows, the number of users will grow much faster than the number of items. Netflix, for example, to keep the discussion in the familiar area of movies, grows its user base massively by expanding into new countries, while the production of movies stays pretty much the same on a yearly basis. Finally, the user's data does change quite a lot, so the rating matrix would have to be updated often, which is a resource-intensive and time-consuming process.

These problems became painfully obvious at Amazon, some 10 years ago. They realized that since the number of products grows at a much slower rate than the number of users, instead of computing user similarity, they could compute item similarity and make recommendations stemming from the list of related items.

The following diagram should help you understand the difference between item-based (or item-item) and user-based (or user-item) CF:

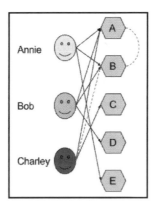

The preceding diagram shows that **Annie** purchased **A**, **B**, and **E**, **Bob** purchased **A**, **B**, and **D**, and **Charley** purchased **A** and **C**. The purchasing behavior of **Annie** and **Bob** will indicate a correlation between **A** and **B**, and since **Charley** already purchased **A** but not **B**, we can recommend **Charley** to take a look at **B**.

From an implementation perspective, there are similarities to user-item CF, but it is more involved as it includes an extra layer of analysis. Let's try this out with our imaginary movie rankings. Let's create a new file called `item_based_recommendations.jl` to host our code.

Here is the complete implementation:

```
using CSV, DataFrames, DelimitedFiles, Statistics

const minimum_similarity = 0.8

function setup_data()
    movies = readdlm("top_10_movies_user_rankings.tsv", '\t')
    movies = permutedims(movies, (2,1))
    movies = convert(DataFrame, movies)
    names = convert(Array, movies[1, :])[1,:]
    names!(movies, [Symbol(name) for name in names])
    deleterows!(movies, 1)
    rename!(movies, [Symbol("Movie title") => :User])
end

function movie_similarity(target_movie)
    similarity = Dict{Symbol,Float64}()
    for movie in names(movies[:, 2:end])
        movie == target_movie && continue
        ratings = movies[:, [movie, target_movie]]
        common_users = ratings[(ratings[movie] .>= 0) .&
(ratings[target_movie] .> 0), :]
        correlation = try
            cor(common_users[movie], common_users[target_movie])
        catch
            0.0
        end

        similarity[movie] = correlation
    end

    # println("The movie $target_movie is similar to $similarity")
    similarity
end

function recommendations(target_movie)
    recommended = Dict{String,Vector{Tuple{String,Float64}}}()
    # @show target_movie
    # @show movie_similarity(target_movie)

    for (movie, similarity) in movie_similarity(target_movie)
        movie == target_movie && continue
        similarity > minimum_similarity || continue
        # println("Checking to which users we can recommend $movie")
        recommended["$movie"] = Vector{Tuple{String,Float64}}()

        for user_row in eachrow(movies)
```

```
            if user_row[target_movie] >= 5
                # println("$(user_row[:User]) has watched $target_movie so
we can recommend similar movies")
                if user_row[movie] == 0
                    # println("$(user_row[:User]) has not watched $movie so
we can recommend it")
                    # println("Recommending $(user_row[:User]) the movie
$movie")
                    push!(recommended["$movie"], (user_row[:User],
user_row[target_movie] * similarity))
                end
            end
        end
    end

    recommended
end

const movies = setup_data()
println("Recommendations for users that watched Finding Dory (2016):
$(recommendations(Symbol("Finding Dory (2016)")))")
```

To keep the code simpler, we're only generating recommendations for a single movie—but it should be relatively simple to extend it to come up with recommendations for each movie in our list (you can try this as an exercise). We'll only suggest similar movies to the users that have watched Finding Dory (2016).

Let's take it apart and see how the script works.

As you can see, I've added some println and @show calls that output extra debug information—they're commented out, but feel free to uncomment them when running the file to help you better understand what each section does and what the workflow of the code is.

Setting up our data matrix is more difficult now. We need to transpose our initial dataset, that is, rotate it. The setup_data function is dedicated to this task alone—loading the data file, transposing the matrix, and setting up the data into a DataFrame. It's a proper **extract, transform, load (ETL)** process in just a few lines of code, which is pretty cool! Let's look at this closely—it's quite a common day-to-day data science task.

In the first line of the function, we load the data into a Julia matrix. The readdlm function is not as powerful as DataFrames, so it has no knowledge of headers, gobbling everything into an Array:

```
julia> movies = readdlm("top_10_movies_user_rankings.tsv", '\t')
```

We'll end up with the following matrix:

```
11×9 Array{Any,2}:
 "Movie title"                        "Acton"   "Annie"   "Comey"   "Dean"   "Kit"   "Missie"   "Musk"   "Sam"
 "Moonlight (2016)"                      0          3        0        10       0        9          2        0
 "Zootopia (2016)"                       9         10        7         0      10        0          5        0
 "Arrival (2016)"                        5          0        6        10       0        9          0       10
 "Hell or High Water (2016)"             3          0        3        10       0        8          0        0
 "La La Land (2016)"                     6          0        8         9       0        0         10        0
 "The Jungle Book (2016)"                8          7        0         2       9        0          6        0
 "Manchester by the Sea (2016)"          0          0        2         8       0        0          0        0
 "Finding Dory (2016)"                   7          8        5         4      10        0          0        0
 "Captain America: Civil War (2016)"    10          0        5         6       0        0          0        9
 "Moana (2016)"                          8          9        0         0      10        0          7        0
```

As we can see, the headings are mixed with the actual data.

Now, we need to transpose the matrix. Unfortunately, transposing doesn't work smoothly for all kinds of matrices in Julia yet, and the recommended way is to do this via `permutedims`:

```julia
julia> movies = permutedims(movies, (2,1))
```

The output is as follows:

```
9×11 Array{Any,2}:
 "Movie title"   "Moonlight (2016)"   "Zootopia (2016)"   "Arrival (2016)"   …   "Moana (2016)"
 "Acton"                0                    9                   5                       8
 "Annie"                3                   10                   0                       9
 "Comey"                0                    7                   6                       0
 "Dean"                10                    0                  10                       0
 "Kit"                  0                   10                   0              …        10
 "Missie"               9                    0                   9                       0
 "Musk"                 2                    5                   0                       7
 "Sam"                  0                    0                  10                       0
```

We're getting closer!

Next, we convert it into a `DataFrame`:

```julia
julia> movies = convert(DataFrame, movies)
```

The output is as follows:

```
9×11 DataFrame
 Row │ x1           x2                x3               x4               x5
     │ Any          Any               Any              Any              Any
─────┼──────────────────────────────────────────────────────────────────────────────────────
   1 │ Movie title  Moonlight (2016)  Zootopia (2016)  Arrival (2016)   Hell or High Water (2016)
   2 │ Acton        0                 9                5                3
   3 │ Annie        3                 10               0                0
   4 │ Comey        0                 7                6                3
   5 │ Dean         10                0                10               10
   6 │ Kit          0                 10               0                0
   7 │ Missie       9                 0                9                8
   8 │ Musk         2                 5                0                0
   9 │ Sam          0                 0                10               0

 Row │ x6                x7                     x8
     │ Any               Any                    Any
─────┼───────────────────────────────────────────────────────────────────
   1 │ La La Land (2016) The Jungle Book (2016) Manchester by the Sea (2016)
   2 │ 6                 8                      0
   3 │ 0                 7                      0
   4 │ 8                 0                      2
   5 │ 9                 2                      8
   6 │ 0                 9                      0
   7 │ 0                 0                      0
   8 │ 10                6                      0
   9 │ 0                 0                      0

 Row │ x9                 x10                            x11
     │ Any                Any                            Any
─────┼──────────────────────────────────────────────────────────────────
   1 │ Finding Dory (2016) Captain America: Civil War (2016) Moana (2016)
   2 │ 7                  10                             8
   3 │ 8                  0                              9
   4 │ 5                  5                              0
   5 │ 4                  6                              0
   6 │ 10                 0                              10
   7 │ 0                  0                              0
   8 │ 0                  0                              7
   9 │ 0                  9                              0
```

> If you run the previous code yourself, you might notice that the REPL will omit some of the `DataFrame` columns, since the output is too wide. To get Julia to display all the columns, like in this snippet, you can use the `showall` function, as in `showall(movies)`.

It looks good, but we need to give the columns proper names, using the data that is now on the first row. Let's extract all the columns names into a `Vector`:

```julia
julia> movie_names = convert(Array, movies[1, :])[1,:]
11-element Array{Any,1}:
 "Movie title"
 "Moonlight (2016)"
```

```
"Zootopia (2016)"
"Arrival (2016)"
"Hell or High Water (2016)"
"La La Land (2016)"
"The Jungle Book (2016)"
"Manchester by the Sea (2016)"
"Finding Dory (2016)"
"Captain America: Civil War (2016)"
"Moana (2016)"
```

Now, we can use it to name the columns:

```
julia> names!(movies, [Symbol(name) for name in movie_names])
```

The output is as follows:

```
9×11 DataFrame
 Row  Movie title  Moonlight (2016)  Zootopia (2016)  Arrival (2016)  Hell or High Water (2016)
      Any          Any               Any              Any             Any

 1    Movie title  Moonlight (2016)  Zootopia (2016)  Arrival (2016)  Hell or High Water (2016)
 2    Acton        0                 9                5               3
 3    Annie        3                 10               0               0
 4    Comey        0                 7                6               3
 5    Dean         10                0                10              10
 6    Kit          0                 10               0               0
 7    Missie       9                 0                9               8
 8    Musk         2                 5                0               0
 9    Sam          0                 0                10              0
```

```
 Row  La La Land (2016)  The Jungle Book (2016)  Manchester by the Sea (2016)
      Any                Any                     Any

 1    La La Land (2016)  The Jungle Book (2016)  Manchester by the Sea (2016)
 2    6                  8                       0
 3    0                  7                       0
 4    8                  0                       2
 5    9                  2                       8
 6    0                  9                       0
 7    0                  0                       0
 8    10                 6                       0
 9    0                  0                       0
```

```
 Row  Finding Dory (2016)  Captain America: Civil War (2016)  Moana (2016)
      Any                  Any                                Any

 1    Finding Dory (2016)  Captain America: Civil War (2016)  Moana (2016)
 2    7                    10                                 8
 3    8                    0                                  9
 4    5                    5                                  0
 5    4                    6                                  0
 6    10                   0                                  10
 7    0                    0                                  0
 8    0                    0                                  7
 9    0                    9                                  0
```

Our `DataFrame` looks better already. The only things left to do are to remove the extra row with the headers and change the `Movie title` header to `User`:

```julia
julia> deleterows!(movies, 1) julia> rename!(movies, Symbol("Movie title")
=> :User)
```

The output is as follows:

```
8×11 DataFrame
 Row │ User     Moonlight (2016)   Zootopia (2016)   Arrival (2016)   Hell or High Water (2016)
     │ Any      Any                Any               Any              Any

 1   │ Acton    0                  9                 5                3
 2   │ Annie    3                  10                0                0
 3   │ Comey    0                  7                 6                3
 4   │ Dean     10                 0                 10               10
 5   │ Kit      0                  10                0                0
 6   │ Missie   9                  0                 9                8
 7   │ Musk     2                  5                 0                0
 8   │ Sam      0                  0                 10               0

 Row │ La La Land (2016)   The Jungle Book (2016)   Manchester by the Sea (2016)
     │ Any                 Any                      Any

 1   │ 6                   8                        0
 2   │ 0                   7                        0
 3   │ 8                   0                        2
 4   │ 9                   2                        8
 5   │ 0                   9                        0
 6   │ 0                   0                        0
 7   │ 10                  6                        0
 8   │ 0                   0                        0

 Row │ Finding Dory (2016)   Captain America: Civil War (2016)   Moana (2016)
     │ Any                   Any                                 Any

 1   │ 7                     10                                  8
 2   │ 8                     0                                   9
 3   │ 5                     5                                   0
 4   │ 4                     6                                   0
 5   │ 10                    0                                   10
 6   │ 0                     0                                   0
 7   │ 0                     0                                   7
 8   │ 0                     9                                   0
```

All done—our ETL process is complete!

We start our recommender by invoking the `recommendations` function, passing in the name of the movie, `Finding Dory (2016)`, as a `Symbol`. The first thing this function does is invoke the `movie_similarity` function, which computes which other movies are similar to `Finding Dory (2016)` based on the users' ratings. For our target movie, we'll get the following results:

```
Dict(
Symbol("La La Land (2016)")=>-0.927374,
Symbol("Captain America: Civil War (2016)")=>-0.584176,
Symbol("The Jungle Book (2016)")=>0.877386,
Symbol("Manchester by the Sea (2016)")=>-0.785933,
Symbol("Arrival (2016)")=>-0.927809,
Symbol("Zootopia (2016)")=>0.826331,
Symbol("Moonlight (2016)")=>-0.589269,
Symbol("Hell or High Water (2016)")=>-0.840462,
Symbol("Moana (2016)")=>0.933598
)
```

We can see here that there's an almost perfect negative correlation with `La La Land (2016)` (so users that like `La La Land (2016)` do not like `Finding Dory (2016)`). There is also a very strong positive correlation with `The Jungle Book (2016)`, `Zootopia (2016)`, and `Moana (2016)`, which makes sense, since they're all animations.

Here is where the logic gets a bit more complicated. Now, we have a list of movies that are similar to `Finding Dory (2016)`. To make recommendations, we want to look at all the users that have watched `Finding Dory (2016)` (and gave it a good enough rating), and suggest similar movies that they haven't watched yet (movies that have a rating of 0). This time, we'll be using a minimum rating of 5 instead of the previous 7, since given our very limited dataset, 7 would be too restrictive and would yield no recommendations. We'll compute the weight of the suggestions as the product between the user's rating of `Finding Dory (2016)` and the correlation coefficient between `Finding Dory (2016)` and the recommended movie. Makes sense? Let's see it in action!

If we run the script, we get the following output:

```
Recommendations for users that watched Finding Dory (2016):
Dict(
    "The Jungle Book (2016)"=> Tuple{String,Float64}[("Comey", 4.38693)],
    "Moana (2016)"=> Tuple{String,Float64}[("Comey", 4.66799)],
    "Zootopia (2016)"=> Tuple{String,Float64}[]
)
```

The only user that would be (kind of) interested in watching movies similar to `Finding Dory (2016)` in our small dataset is `Comey`—but the recommendations won't be great. The algorithm estimates a weight (and thus, a rating) of `4.38693` for `The Jungle Book (2016)` and `4.66799` for `Moana (2016)`.

Summary

This concludes the first part of our journey into recommender systems. They are an extremely important part of today's online business models and their usefulness is ever-growing, in direct relation to the exponential growth of data generated by our connected software and hardware. Recommender systems are a very efficient solution to the information overload problem—or rather, an information filter problem. Recommenders provide a level of filtering that's appropriate for each user, turning information, yet again, into a vector of customer empowerment.

Although it's critical to understand how the various types of recommender systems work, in order to be able to choose the right algorithm for the types of problems you'll solve in your work as a data scientist, implementing production-grade systems by hand is not something most people do. As with almost everything in the realm of software development, it's best to use stable, powerful, and mature existing libraries when they're available.

In the next chapter, we'll learn how to build a more powerful recommender system using existing Julia libraries. We'll generate recommendations for a dating site, taking advantage of publicly available and anonymized dating data. In the process, we'll learn about yet another type of recommender system, called model-based (as a side note, all of the algorithms that were discussed in this chapter were memory-based, but don't worry—I'll explain everything in a minute).

7
Machine Learning for Recommender Systems

I hope that you are now excited about the amazing possibilities offered by the recommender systems that we've built. The techniques we've learned will provide you with a tremendous amount of data-taming prowess and practical abilities that you can already apply in your projects.

However, there is more to recommendation systems than that. Due to their large-scale applications in recent years, as an efficient solution to the information overload caused by the abundance of offerings on online platforms, recommenders have received a lot of attention, with new algorithms being developed at a rapid pace. In fact, all the algorithms that we studied in the previous chapter are part of a single category, called **memory-based recommenders**. Besides these, there's another very important class or recommender, which is known as **model-based**.

In this chapter, we'll learn about them. We will discuss the following topics:

- Memory-based versus model-based recommendation systems
- Data processing for training a model-based recommender
- Building a model-based recommender
- Hybrid recommendation systems

Technical requirements

The Julia package ecosystem is under continuous development and new package versions are released on a daily basis. Most of the times this is great news, as new releases bring new features and bug fixes. However, since many of the packages are still in beta (version 0.x), any new release can introduce breaking changes. As a result, the code presented in the book can stop working. In order to ensure that your code will produce the same results as described in the book, it is recommended to use the same package versions. Here are the external packages used in this chapter and their specific versions:

```
CSV@v.0.4.3
DataFrames@v0.15.2
Gadfly@v1.0.1
IJulia@v1.14.1
Recommendation@v0.1.0+
```

In order to install a specific version of a package you need to run:

```
pkg> add PackageName@vX.Y.Z
```

For example:

```
pkg> add IJulia@v1.14.1
```

Alternatively you can install all the used packages by downloading the `Project.toml` file provided with the chapter and using `pkg>` instantiate as follows:

```
julia>
download("https://raw.githubusercontent.com/PacktPublishing/Julia-Projects/
master/Chapter07/Project.toml", "Project.toml")
pkg> activate .
pkg> instantiate
```

Comparing the memory-based versus model-based recommenders

It is important to understand the strengths and weaknesses of both memory-based and model-based recommenders so that we can make the right choice according to the available data and the business requirements. As we saw in the previous chapter, we can classify recommender systems according to the data they are using and the algorithms that are employed.

First, we can talk about non-personalized versus personalized recommenders. Non-personalized recommenders do not take into account user preferences, but that doesn't make them less useful. They are successfully employed when the relevant data is missing, for example, for a user that is new to the system or just not logged in. Such recommendations can include the best apps of the week on the Apple App Store, trending movies on Netflix, songs of the day on Spotify, NY Times bestsellers, Billboard Top 10, and so on.

Moving on to personalized recommender systems, these can be further split into content-based and collaborative system. A content-based system makes recommendations by matching an item, specifications. A famous example of this category is Pandora and its Music Genome Project. The Music Genome Project, which powers Pandora, is the most comprehensive analysis of music ever undertaken. They worked with trained musicologists who listened to music across all genres and decades, studying and collecting musical details on every track—450 musical attributes altogether. Pandora makes recommendations by picking other songs from its catalog that closely match the features (*features* is data-science language for attributes, properties, or tags) of the tracks that the user previously liked.

As for collaborative filtering, the idea behind it is that we can identify a metric that correctly reflects a user's tastes and then exploit it in combination with a dataset of other users, whose preferences were already collected. The underlying supposition is that if we have a pool of users that enjoy many of the same things, we can recommend to one of them some items from another's user list, which were not yet discovered by the targeted user. Any item in the list of options that is not part of the targeted user's list can readily be offered as a recommendation because similar preferences will lead to other similar choices.

This specific type of collaborative filtering was named user-based since the primary focus of the algorithm is the similarity between the target user and other users.

Another variation of the collaborative algorithm is **item-based filtering**. The main difference between this and user-based filtering is that the focus is on similar items. Which approach is the best depends on the specific use case—item-based recommendations are more efficient when the product catalog is considerably smaller and changes less often than the number of users and their preferences.

The last of the commonly accepted typologies divides the recommender systems into memory-based and model-based. *Memory-based* refers to the fact that the system requires the whole dataset to be loaded into working memory (the RAM). The algorithms rely on mapping to and from memory to consequently calculate the similarity between two users or items, and produce a prediction for the user by taking the weighted average of all the ratings. A few ways of computing the correlation can be used, such as *Pearson's r*. There are certain advantages to this approach, like the simplicity of the implementation, the easy facilitation of new data, or the fact that the results can be easily explained. But, unsurprisingly, it does come with significant performance downsides, creating problems when the data is sparse and the datasets are large.

Because of the limitations of the memory-based recommender systems, alternative solutions were needed, mainly driven by the continuous growth of online businesses and their underlying data. These were characterized by large volumes of users and an increasing number of products. The most famous example is Netflix's one million dollar competition—in 2006, Netflix offered a one million dollar prize to the individual or team that could improve their existing recommendations algorithm, called **Cinematch**, by at least 10%. It took three years for this feat to be achieved, and it was done by a joint team of initial competitors, who ultimately decided to join forces to grab the prize.

Learning about the model-based approach

This innovative approach to recommender systems was named *model-based*, and it made extensive use of matrix factorization techniques. In this approach, models are developed using different machine learning algorithms to predict a user's ratings. In a way, the model-based approach can be seen as a complementary technique to improve memory-based recommendations. They address the matrix sparsity problem by guessing how much a user will like a new item. Machine learning algorithms are used to train on the existing vector of ratings of a specific user, and then build a model that can predict the user's score for an item that the user hasn't tried yet. Popular model-based techniques are Bayesian Networks, **singular value decomposition (SVD)**, and **Probabilistic Latent Semantic Analysis (PLSA)** or **Probabilistic Latent Semantic Indexing (PLSI)**.

There are a number of popular approaches for building the models:

- **Probability**: Making a recommendation is framed as a problem of predicting the probability of a rating being of a particular value. Bayesian networks are often used with this implementation.

- **Enhanced memory-based**: This uses a model to represent the similarities between users or items and then predicts the ratings. The Netflix prize-winning ALS-WR algorithm represents this type of implementation.
- **Linear algebra**: Finally, recommendations can be made by performing linear algebra operations on the matrices of users and ratings. A commonly used algorithm is SVD.

In the following sections, we'll implement a model-based recommender. We'll use a third-party Julia package and code our business logic around it.

Understanding our data

To get conclusive results from our **Machine Learning** (ML) models, we need data—and plenty of it. There are many open source datasets available online. Kaggle, for example, provides a large collection of high quality and anonymized data dumps that can be used for training and experimenting, and is available for download at `https://www.kaggle.com/datasets`. Another famous data repository is provided by FiveThirtyEight, at `https://github.com/fivethirtyeight/data`. Buzzfeed also makes a large treasure of data public at `https://github.com/BuzzFeedNews`.

For our project, we'll create a book recommendation system. We'll use the *Book-Crossing Dataset*, which is available for download at `http://www2.informatik.uni-freiburg.de/~cziegler/BX/`. This data was collected during the months of August and September 2004, under permission, from the Book-Crossing community (`https://www.bookcrossing.com/`). It includes over 1.1 million book ratings, for more than 270,000 books, from 278,000 users. The user data is anonymized, but still includes demographic information (location and age, where available). We'll use this data to train our recommendation system and then ask it for interesting new books for our users.

A first look at the data

The dataset is composed of three tables—one for users, one for books, and one for ratings. The `BX-Users` table contains the users' data. The `User-ID` is a sequential integer value, as the original user ID has been anonymized. The `Location` and `Age` columns contain the corresponding demographic information. This is not available for all the users and in these cases, we'll encounter the `NULL` value (as the `NULL` string).

The `BX-Books` table stores the information about the books. For the unique identifier, we have the standard ISBN book code. Besides this, we are also provided with the book's title (the `Book-Title` column), author (`Book-Author`), publishing year (`Year-of-Publication`), and the publisher (`Publisher`). URLs of thumbnail cover images are also provided, corresponding to three sizes—small (`Image-URL-S`), medium (`Image-URL-M`), and large (`Image-URL-L`).

Finally, the `BX-Book-Ratings` table contains the actual ratings. The table has a simple structure, with three columns—`User-ID`, for the user making the rating; the ISBN of the book; and `Book-Rating`, which is the score. The ratings are expressed on a scale from 1 to 10, where higher is better. The value 0 signifies an implicit rating.

This dataset is available in SQL and CSV formats, packaged as ZIP archives. Please download the CSV version from `http://www2.informatik.uni-freiburg.de/~cziegler/BX/BX-CSV-Dump.zip`.

Unzip the file somewhere on your computer.

Loading the data

Loading this dataset is going to be a bit more challenging, as we have to work with three distinct files, and due to the particularities of the data itself. Here is the head of the `BX-Users.csv` file, in a plain text editor:

```
"User-ID";"Location";"Age"
"1";"nyc, new york, usa";NULL
"2";"stockton, california, usa";"18"
"3";"moscow, yukon territory, russia";NULL
"4";"porto, v.n.gaia, portugal";"17"
"5";"farnborough, hants, united kingdom";NULL
"6";"santa monica, california, usa";"61"
```

We have to explicitly handle the following formatting particularities, which will otherwise cause the import to fail:

- The columns are separated by ; instead of the more customary comma or *Tab*
- Missing values are represented by the string NULL
- The first row is the header, representing the column names
- The data is enclosed in double quotes " ", and double quotes within the data itself are escaped by backslashes, for example, `"1273";"valladolid, \"n/a\", spain";"27"`

Fortunately, the CSV package provides additional options for passing in all of this information when reading in the file:

```
julia> users = CSV.read("BX-Users.csv", header = 1, delim = ';',
missingstring = "NULL", escapechar = '\\')
```

It might take a bit of time to load the table, but eventually, we'll get the sweet taste of success—278858 rows loaded into memory!

```
278858×3 DataFrames.DataFrame
 Row │ User-ID │ Location                         │ Age
     │ Int64◑  │ Union{Missing, String}           │ Int64◑
─────┼─────────┼──────────────────────────────────┼─────────
  1  │ 1       │ nyc, new york, usa               │ missing
  2  │ 2       │ stockton, california, usa        │ 18
  3  │ 3       │ moscow, yukon territory, russia  │ missing
  4  │ 4       │ porto, v.n.gaia, portugal        │ 17
  5  │ 5       │ farnborough, hants, united kingdom │ missing
  6  │ 6       │ santa monica, california, usa    │ 61
```

We'll use the same approach to load the books and rankings tables:

```
julia> books = CSV.read("BX-Books.csv", header = 1, delim = ';',
missingstring = "NULL", escapechar = '\\')
271379×8 DataFrames.DataFrame
# output omitted #

julia> books_ratings = CSV.read("BX-Book-Ratings.csv", header = 1, delim =
';', missingstring = "NULL", escapechar = '\\')
1149780×3 DataFrames.DataFrame
# output omitted #
```

Excellent! We now have all three tables loaded into memory as `DataFrames`.

Handling missing data

In data science, missing values occur when no data value is stored for a field in a record—in other words, when we don't have a value for a column in a row. It is a common scenario, but nonetheless, it can have a significant negative effect on the usefulness of the data, so it needs to be explicitly handled.

The approach in `DataFrames` is to mark the missing value by using the `Missing` type. The default behavior is the propagation of the missing values, thus *poisoning* the data operations that involve `missing`—that is, operations involving valid input, and `missing` will return `missing` or `fail`. Hence, in most cases, the missing values need to be addressed in the data-cleaning phase.

The most common techniques for handling missing values are as follows:

- **Deletion**: The rows containing the missing variables are deleted (also called **listwise deletion**). The downside of this approach is that it leads to loss of information. However, if we have plenty of data and not many incomplete records (say, under 10%), this is the simplest approach and the most commonly used.
- **Imputation**: The `missing` values are inferred using some technique, usually `mean`, `median`, or `mode`. However, you need to be careful, as this artificially reduces the variation of the dataset. As an alternative, a predictive model could be used to infer the missing value by applying statistical methods.

 You can read more about Julia's treatment of missing values in the documentation at `https://docs.julialang.org/en/v1.0/manual/missing/`, while a more advanced discussion of the theoretical aspects of handling missing data can be found at `https://datascience.ibm.com/blog/missing-data-conundrum-exploration-and-imputation-techniques/`.

Data analysis and preparation

Let's get a feel of the data, starting with the users:

```julia
julia> using DataFrames
julia> describe(users, stats = [:min, :max, :nmissing, :nunique, :eltype])
```

The output is as follows:

3×6 DataFrame

Row	variable Symbol	min Any	max Any	nmissing Int64	nunique Union…	eltype DataType
1	User-ID	1	278858	0		Int64
2	Location	"alexandria"., "alexandria"., egypt	\xfdzm\xfdr, n/a, turkey	0	57339	String
3	Age	0	244	110762		Int64

We chose a few key stats—the minimum and maximum values, the number of missing and unique values, and the type of data. Unsurprisingly, the `User-ID` column, which is the table's primary key, starts at `1` and goes all the way up to `278858` with no missing values. However, the `Age` column shows a clear sign of data errors—the maximum age is `244` years! Let's see what we have there by plotting the data with `Gadfly`:

```julia
julia> using Gadfly
julia> plot(users, x = :Age, Geom.histogram(bincount = 15))
```

The output is as follows:

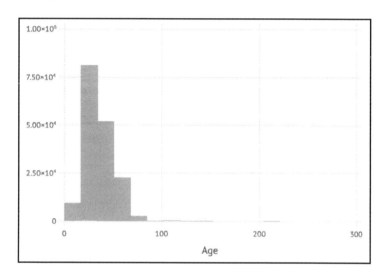

We rendered a histogram of the ages, splitting the data into 15 intervals. We have some outliers indicating incorrect ages, but most of the data is distributed within the expected range, up to 80-90 years old. Since anything after **100** years old is highly unlikely to be correct, let's get rid of it. The simplest way is to filter out all the rows where the age is greater than **100**:

```julia
julia> users = users[users[:Age] .< 100, :]
ERROR: ArgumentError: unable to check bounds for indices of type Missing
```

Oops! Our `Age` column has `missing` values that cannot be compared. We could remove these as well, but in this case, the missing age seems to be more of a symptom of the user not disclosing the information, rather than a data error. Therefore, I'm more inclined to keep the rows while replacing the missing data with valid values. The question is, what values? Imputation using the `mean` seems like a good option. Let's compute it:

```julia
julia> using Statistics
```

```
julia> mean(skipmissing(users[:Age]))
34.75143370454978
```

We used the `skipmissing` function to iterate over all the non-missing `Age` values and compute the `mean`. Now, we can use this in conjunction with `coalesce` to replace the missing values:

```
julia> users[:Age] = coalesce.(users[:Age], mean(skipmissing(users[:Age])))
278858-element Array{Real,1}:
 34.75143370454978
 18
 34.75143370454978
 17
 34.75143370454978
# output omitted #
```

We are effectively replacing the `Age` column of the `users` `DataFrame` with a new array, resulting from the application of `coalesce` to the same `Age` column. Please notice the dot in the invocation of `coalesce`, indicating that it is applied element-wise.

Great—finally, we need to get rid of those erroneous ages:

```
julia> users = users[users[:Age] .< 100, :]
278485×3 DataFrame
 # output omitted #

julia> head(users)
```

The output is as follows:

```
6×3 DataFrame
 Row │ User-ID │ Location                         │ Age
     │ Int64  │ Union{Missing, String}           │ Real
─────┼────────┼──────────────────────────────────┼─────────
 1   │ 1      │ nyc, new york, usa                │ 34.7514
 2   │ 2      │ stockton, california, usa         │ 18
 3   │ 3      │ moscow, yukon territory, russia   │ 34.7514
 4   │ 4      │ porto, v.n.gaia, portugal         │ 17
 5   │ 5      │ farnborough, hants, united kingdom│ 34.7514
 6   │ 6      │ santa monica, california, usa     │ 61
```

Looking good!

We're done with the users, so let's move on to the books data:

```
julia> describe(books, stats = [:nmissing, :nunique, :eltype])
```

The output is as follows:

```
8×4 DataFrame
 Row │ variable               nmissing   nunique   eltype
     │ Symbol                 Int64      Union…    DataType
─────┼──────────────────────────────────────────────────────
   1 │ ISBN                   0          271379    String
   2 │ Book-Title             0          242154    String
   3 │ Book-Author            0          102028    String
   4 │ Year-Of-Publication    0                    Int64
   5 │ Publisher              0          16807     String
   6 │ Image-URL-S            0          271063    String
   7 │ Image-URL-M            0          271063    String
   8 │ Image-URL-L            0          271063    String
```

The data looks much cleaner—first of all, there's no missing values. Then, looking at the counts for nunique, we can tell that some of the books have identical titles and that there's a considerable amount of authors that have published more than one book. Finally, the books come from almost 17,000 publishers.

So far, so good, but let's take a look at the Year-Of-Publication:

```
julia> maximum(skipmissing(books[Symbol("Year-Of-Publication")]))
2050

julia> minimum(skipmissing(books[Symbol("Year-Of-Publication")]))
0
```

Something's not right here—we have some publishing years that don't make sense. Some are too far in the past, while others are way in the future. I wonder what the distribution looks like. Let's render another histogram:

```
julia> plot(books, x = Symbol("Year-Of-Publication"), Geom.histogram)
```

The output is as follows:

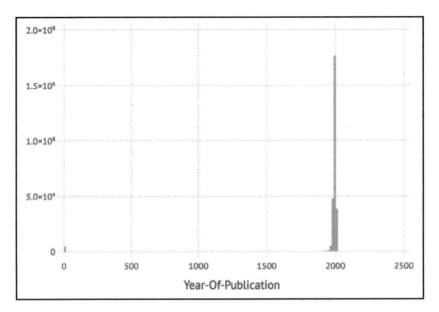

Most of the data seems to be correct, but there are some faulty outliers. We can take a look at the values:

```julia
julia> unique(books[Symbol("Year-Of-Publication")]) |> sort
116-element Array{Union{Missing, Int64},1}:
     0
  1376
  1378
# output omitted #
  2037
  2038
  2050
```

At first sight, we can get rid of the rows that have the publishing year equal to 0. We can also safely assume that all the rows where the publishing date is greater than the year when the data was collected (2004) are also wrong, and so they can be removed. It's difficult to say what to do about the rest, but still, it's hard to believe that people have ranked books that were published in the Middle Ages. Let's just keep the books that were published between 1970 and 2004:

```julia
julia> books = books[books[Symbol("Year-Of-Publication")] .>= 1970, :]
264071x8 DataFrame
# output omitted #
```

```
julia> books = books[books[Symbol("Year-Of-Publication")] .<= 2004, :]
263999×8 DataFrame
# output omitted #

julia> plot(books, x = Symbol("Year-Of-Publication"), Geom.histogram)
```

The output is as follows:

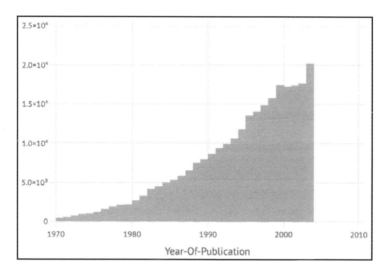

This is much better and entirely plausible.

Finally, let's check the ratings:

```
julia> describe(books_ratings)
```

The output is as follows:

```
3×8 DataFrame
```

Row	variable Symbol	mean Union...	min Any	median Union...	max Any	nunique Union...	nmissing Int64	eltype DataType
1	User-ID	1.40386e5	2	141010.0	278854		0	Int64
2	ISBN		0330299891		Microsoft	340556	0	String
3	Book-Rating	2.86695	0	0.0	10		0	Int64

There's no missing values, which is great. The `Book-Rating` values are between 0 (implicit rating) and 10, where 1 to 10 represent explicit ratings. The median of 0.0 is a bit of a concern though, so let's take a look:

```julia
julia> plot(books_ratings, x = Symbol("Book-Rating"), Geom.histogram)
```

The output is as follows:

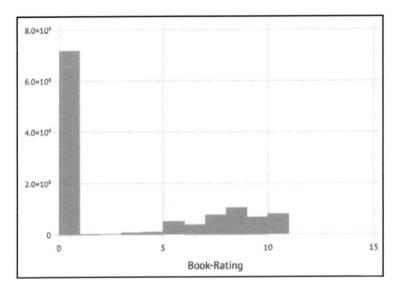

It turns out that most of the ratings are implicit, thus set to 0. These are not relevant to our recommender, so let's get rid of them:

```julia
julia> books_ratings = books_ratings[books_ratings[Symbol("Book-Rating")]
.> 0, :]
433671×3 DataFrame
# output omitted #

julia> plot(books_ratings, x = Symbol("Book-Rating"), Geom.histogram)
```

Here is the output:

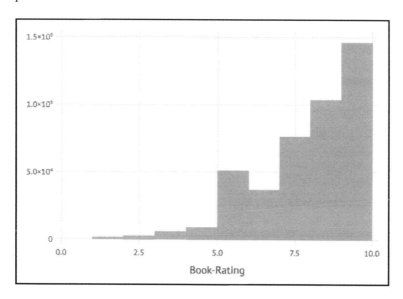

We're doing great! There's one more step in our **extract, transform, load (ETL)** process—let's put the three DataFrames together by joining them on the matching columns, thus removing the various orphan entries (the ones that don't have corresponding rows in all the other tables).

First, we'll join book ratings and books:

```julia
julia> books_ratings_books = join(books_ratings, books, on = :ISBN, kind =
:inner)
374896x10 DataFrame
# output omitted #
```

We're using the join method, indicating the two DataFrames we want to join, plus the join column and the kind of join we want. An inner join requires that the result contains rows for values of the key that exist in both the first and second DataFrame.

Now, let's join with the user's data:

```julia
julia> books_ratings_books_users = join(books_ratings_books, users, on =
Symbol("User-ID"), kind = :inner)
374120x12 DataFrame
# output omitted #
```

Our dataset now contains only the valid data, nicely packed in a single DataFrame.

As our ratings are on a scale between 1 and 10, not all of these ratings can be considered an endorsement for the book. It's true that the vast majority of the rankings are above 5, but a 5 is still not good enough for a useful recommendation. Let's simplify our data a bit to make the computations faster by assuming that any ranking starting with 8 represents a positive review and would make for a strong recommendation. Therefore, we'll keep only these rows and discard the rest:

```julia
julia> top_ratings =
books_ratings_books_users[books_ratings_books_users[Symbol("Book-Rating")]
.>= 8, :]
217991x12 DataFrame
# output omitted #
```

This is looking good, but it will look even better with just a small tweak to make the column names more Julia-friendly:

```julia
julia> for n in names(top_ratings) rename!(top_ratings, n =>
Symbol(replace(string(n), "-"=>""))) end
```

We will iterate over each column name and remove the dashes. This way, we'll be able to use the names without having to explicitly use the `Symbol` constructor every time. We'll end up with the following names:

```julia
julia> names(top_ratings)
12-element Array{Symbol,1}:
 :UserID
 :ISBN
 :BookRating
 :BookTitle
 :BookAuthor
 :YearOfPublication
 :Publisher
 :ImageURLS
 :ImageURLM
 :ImageURLL
 :Location
 :Age
```

We're getting closer—the last step in our data processing workflow is to check the number of reviews per user. The more reviews we have from a user, the better the preference profile we can create, leading to more relevant and better quality recommendations. Basically, we want to get a count of ratings, per user, and then get a count of each count (that is, how many rating of ones, twos, threes, and so on, up to ten ratings we have):

```julia
julia> ratings_count = by(top_ratings, :UserID, df -> size(df[:UserID])[1])
```

Here, we group the `top_ratings` data by `UserID` and use the `size` function as our `aggregation` function, which returns a tuple of dimensions—out of which we retrieve just its first dimension. We'll get the following result, where the `x1` column contains the number of ratings provided by the corresponding user:

The output is as follows:

Row	UserID	x1
	Int64	Int64
1	276747	3
2	276751	1
3	276754	1
4	276762	1
5	276772	2
6	276774	1

46106×2 DataFrame

Wondering what this data will reveal? Let's find out:

```julia
julia> describe(ratings_count)
```

Here is the output:

2×8 DataFrame

Row	variable	mean	min	median	max	nunique	nmissing	eltype
	Symbol	Float64	Int64	Float64	Int64	Nothing	Union...	DataType
1	UserID	1.39098e5	12	1.38387e5	278854		0	Int64
2	x1	4.72804	1	1.0	5491			Int64

The minimum number of ratings is `1`, while the most productive user has provided no less than `5491`, with a mean of around `5` reviews per user. Considering that the recommendations for a user with less than `5` reviews would be pretty weak anyway, we're better off removing the users without enough data:

```julia
julia> ratings_count = ratings_count[ratings_count[:x1] .>= 5, :]
7296×2 DataFrame
# output omitted #
```

We're only keeping the users that have at least `5` ratings. Let's see how the number of ratings is distributed now:

```julia
julia> plot(ratings_count, x = :x1, Geom.histogram(maxbincount = 6))
```

The output is as follows:

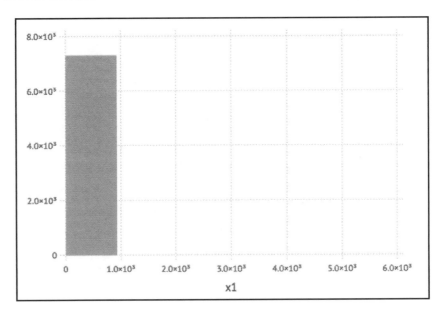

Looks like the vast majority of users have up to 1000 ratings. What about the outliers with lots of reviews?

```julia
julia> ratings_count[ratings_count[:x1] .> 1000, :]
```

The output is as follows:

3×2 DataFrame		
Row	UserID	x1
	Int64▦	Int64
1	11676	3639
2	98391	5491
3	153662	1579

There's only 3 users. We'd better remove them so that they don't skew our results:

```julia
julia> ratings_count = ratings_count[ratings_count[:x1] .<= 1000, :]
7293×2 DataFrame
# output omitted #
```

Now that we have the list of final users, the next step is to remove all the others from the `top_ratings` DataFrame. Again, let's use an inner join—it's pretty straightforward:

```
julia> top_ratings = join(top_ratings, ratings_count, on = :UserID, kind =
:inner)
150888x13 DataFrame
# output omitted #
```

That's it, our data is ready. Great job!

If you want, you can save this data to file by using `CSV.write`:

```
julia> CSV.write("top_ratings.csv", top_ratings)
```

 If you've had problems following along, don't worry. In a few paragraphs, I'll explain how you can load a ready-made dataset, which is provided in this chapter's support files.

Training our data models

Machine learning can be divided into four main types, depending on the methodology and the type of data that is used:

- Supervised
- Unsupervised
- Semi-supervised
- Reinforcement

In supervised learning, we start with a dataset that contains training (or teaching) data, where each record is labeled, representing both input (let's call it X), and output values (named Y). Then, the algorithm's job is to identify a function f from input to output, so that $Y = f(X)$. Once this function is identified, it can be used on new data (that is, new inputs that are not labeled) to predict the output. Depending on the type of output that needs to be computed, if the output has to be assigned to a certain class of entities (as in, it represents categorical data), then a classification algorithm will be used. Alternatively, if the type of output is a numeric value, we'll be dealing with a regression problem.

With unsupervised machine learning, we have the inputs, but not the outputs. In such a scenario, once we use the learning dataset to train our system, the main goal will be data clustering, that is, generating different clusters of inputs and being able to assign new data to the most appropriate cluster.

Semi-supervised, as the name suggests, represents a mixture of the two previously described approaches, both of which are applicable when our data contains both labeled and unlabeled records.

In reinforcement learning, the algorithm is informed about the success of its previous decisions. Based on this, the algorithm modifies its strategy in order to maximize the outcome.

Depending on the learning style and the specific problem that's meant to be solved, there are a multitude of algorithms that can be applied. For supervised learning, we can use regression (linear or logistic), decision trees, or neural networks, to name just a few. With unsupervised learning, we could choose k-means clustering or `Apriori` algorithms.

Since our data is tagged (we have the rating for each user), we are dealing with a supervised machine learning problem. For our test case, since our data is represented as a matrix, we'll employ an algorithm called **Matrix Factorization** (**MF**).

> You can read more about the various types of ML algorithms and how to choose them at the following links:
> `https://docs.microsoft.com/en-us/azure/machine-learning/studio/algorithm-choice`
> `https://blog.statsbot.co/machine-learning-algorithms-183cc73197c`
> `https://elitedatascience.com/machine-learning-algorithms`
> `https://machinelearningmastery.com/a-tour-of-machine-learning-algorithms/`

Scaling down our dataset

Training machine learning models at scale usually requires (lots of) powerful computers and plenty of time. If you have neither of these while reading this book, I have prepared a smaller dataset so that you can go through our project.

Training the recommender on the full `top_ratings` data took over 24 hours on my quad-core, 16 GB RAM laptop. If you're so inclined, feel free to try it. It is also available for download at `https://github.com/PacktPublishing/Julia-Projects/blob/master/Chapter07/data/large/top_ratings.csv.zip`.

However, if you'd like to follow through the code while reading this chapter, please download the `top_ratings.csv` file that's provided with this chapter's support files at `https://github.com/PacktPublishing/Julia-Projects/blob/master/Chapter07/data/top_ratings.csv`. I will be using the data from this smaller file for the remainder of this chapter.

Once you've downloaded the file, you can load its content into the `top_ratings` variable by using the `CSV.read` function:

```
julia> top_ratings = CSV.read("top_ratings.csv")
11061×13 DataFrame
# output omitted #
```

Training versus testing data

A common strategy in machine learning implementations is to split the data into training (some 80-90%) and testing (the remaining 10-20%) datasets. First, we'll initialize two empty `DataFrames` to store this data:

```
julia> training_data = DataFrame(UserID = Int[], ISBN = String[], Rating =
Int[])
0×3 DataFrame

julia> test_data = DataFrame(UserID = Int[], ISBN = String[], Rating =
Int[])
0×3 DataFrame
```

Next, we'll iterate through our `top_ratings` and put the contents into the corresponding `DataFrame`. We'll go with 10% of data for testing—so with each iteration, we'll generate a random integer between 1 and 10. The chances of getting a 10 are, obviously, one in ten, so when we get it, we put the corresponding row into the test dataset. Otherwise, it goes into the training one, as follows:

```
julia> for row in eachrow(top_ratings)
  rand(1:10) == 10 ?
  push!(test_data, convert(Array, row[[:UserID, :ISBN, :BookRating]])) :
  push!(training_data, convert(Array, row[[:UserID, :ISBN, :BookRating]]))
  end
```

There's no canonical way for pushing a `DataFrameRow` onto another `DataFrame`, so we're using one of the recommended approaches, which is to convert the row into an `Array` and `push!` it to the `DataFrame`. Our training and testing datasets are now ready.

For me, they look like this, but since the data was generated randomly, it will be different for you:

```
julia> test_data
1056×3 DataFrame
 # output omitted #

julia> training_data
```

```
10005×3 DataFrame
# output omitted #
```

If you prefer for us to work with the same datasets, you can download the data dump from this chapter's support files (available at `https://github.com/PacktPublishing/Julia-Projects/blob/master/Chapter07/data/training_data.csv` and `https://github.com/PacktPublishing/Julia-Projects/blob/master/Chapter07/data/test_data.csv`, respectively) and read them in as follows:

```
julia> test_data = CSV.read("data/test_data.csv")
julia> training_data = CSV.read("data/training_data.csv")
```

Machine learning-based recommendations

Julia's ecosystem provides access to `Recommendation.jl`, a package that implements a multitude of algorithms for both personalized and non-personalized recommendations. For model-based recommenders, it has support for SVD, MF, and content-based recommendations using TF-IDF scoring algorithms.

There's also another very good alternative—the `ScikitLearn.jl` package (`https://github.com/cstjean/ScikitLearn.jl`). This implements Python's very popular scikit-learn interface and algorithms in Julia, supporting both models from the Julia ecosystem and those of the scikit-learn library (via `PyCall.jl`). The Scikit website and documentation can be found at `http://scikit-learn.org/stable/`. It is very powerful and definitely worth keeping in mind, especially for building highly efficient recommenders for production usage. For learning purposes, we'll stick to `Recommendation`, as it provides for a simpler implementation.

Making recommendations with Recommendation

For our learning example, we'll use `Recommendation`. It is the simplest of the available options, and it's a good teaching device, as it will allow us to further experiment with its plug-and-play algorithms and configurable model generators.

Before we can do anything interesting, though, we need to make sure that we have the package installed:

```
pkg> add Recommendation#master
julia> using Recommendation
```

Please note that I'm using the `#master` version, because the tagged version, at the time of writing this book, was not yet fully updated for Julia 1.0.

The workflow for setting up a recommender with `Recommendation` involves three steps:

1. Setting up the training data

2. Instantiating and training a recommender using one of the available algorithms

3. Once the training is complete, asking for recommendations

Let's implement these steps.

Setting up the training data

`Recommendation` uses a `DataAccessor` object to set up the training data. This can be instantiated with a set of `Event` objects. A `Recommendation.Event` is an object that represents a user-item interaction. It is defined like this:

```
struct Event
    user::Int
    item::Int
    value::Float64
end
```

In our case, the `user` field will represent the `UserID`, the `item` field will map to the ISBN, and the `value` field will store the `Rating`. However, a bit more work is needed to bring our data in the format required by `Recommendation`:

1. First of all, our ISBN data is stored as a string and not as an integer.
2. Second, internally, `Recommendation` builds a sparse matrix of `user * item` and stores the corresponding values, setting up the matrix using sequential IDs. However, our actual user IDs are large numbers, and `Recommendation` will set up a very large, sparse matrix, going all the way from the minimum to the maximum user IDs.

What this means is that, for example, we only have 69 users in our dataset (as confirmed by `unique(training_data[:UserID]) |> size`), with the largest ID being 277,427, while for books we have 9,055 unique ISBNs. If we go with this, `Recommendation` will create a 277,427 x 9,055 matrix instead of a 69 x 9,055 matrix. This matrix would be very large, sparse, and inefficient.

Therefore, we'll need to do a bit more data processing to map the original user IDs and the ISBNs to sequential integer IDs, starting from 1.

We'll use two `Dict` objects that will store the mappings from the `UserID` and `ISBN` columns to the recommender's sequential user and book IDs. Each entry will be of the form `dict[original_id] = sequential_id`:

```
julia> user_mappings, book_mappings = Dict{Int,Int}(), Dict{String,Int}()
```

We'll also need two counters to keep track of, and increment, the sequential IDs:

```
julia> user_counter, book_counter = 0, 0
```

We can now prepare the `Event` objects for our training data:

```
julia> events = Event[]
julia> for row in eachrow(training_data)
 global user_counter, book_counter user_id, book_id, rating = row[:UserID],
 row[:ISBN], row[:Rating] haskey(user_mappings, user_id) ||
 (user_mappings[user_id] = (user_counter += 1)) haskey(book_mappings,
 book_id) || (book_mappings[book_id] = (book_counter += 1)) push!(events,
 Event(user_mappings[user_id], book_mappings[book_id], rating)) end
```

This will fill up the events array with instances of `Recommendation.Event`, which represent a unique `UserID`, `ISBN`, and `Rating` combination. To give you an idea, it will look like this:

```
julia> events
10005-element Array{Event,1}:
 Event(1, 1, 10.0)
 Event(1, 2, 8.0)
 Event(1, 3, 9.0)
 Event(1, 4, 8.0)
 Event(1, 5, 8.0)
 # output omitted #
```

Please remember this very important aspect—in Julia, the `for` loop defines a new scope. This means that variables defined outside the `for` loop are not accessible inside it. To make them visible within the loop's body, we need to declare them as `global`.

Now, we are ready to set up our `DataAccessor`:

```
julia> da = DataAccessor(events, user_counter, book_counter)
```

Building and training the recommender

At this point, we have all that we need to instantiate our recommender. A very efficient and common implementation uses MF—unsurprisingly, this is one of the options provided by the `Recommendation` package, so we'll use it.

Matrix Factorization

The idea behind MF is that, if we're starting with a large sparse matrix like the one used to represent *user x profile* ratings, then we can represent it as the product of multiple smaller and denser matrices. The challenge is to find these smaller matrices so that their product is as close to our original matrix as possible. Once we have these, we can fill in the blanks in the original matrix so that the predicted values will be consistent with the existing ratings in the matrix:

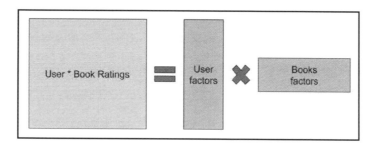

Our *user x books* rating matrix can be represented as the product between smaller and denser users and books matrices.

To perform the matrix factorization, we can use a couple of algorithms, among which the most popular are SVD and **Stochastic Gradient Descent (SGD)**. `Recommendation` uses SGD to perform matrix factorization.

The code for this looks as follows:

```
julia> recommender = MF(da)
julia> build(recommender)
```

We instantiate a new MF recommender and then we build it—that is, train it. The build step might take a while (a few minutes on a high-end computer using the small dataset that's provided in this chapter's support files).

If we want to tweak the training process, since SGD implements an iterative approach for matrix factorization, we can pass a `max_iter` argument to the build function, asking it for a maximum number of iterations. The more iterations we do, in theory, the better the recommendations—but the longer it will take to train the model. If you want to speed things up, you can invoke the build function with a `max_iter` of 30 or less—`build(recommender, max_iter = 30)`.

We can pass another optional argument for the learning rate, for example, `build (recommender, learning_rate=15e-4, max_iter=100)`. The learning rate specifies how aggressively the optimization technique should vary between each iteration. If the learning rate is too small, the optimization will need to be run a lot of times. If it's too big, then the optimization might fail, generating worse results than the previous iterations.

Making recommendations

Now that we have successfully built and trained our model, we can ask it for recommendations. These are provided by the `recommend` function, which takes an instance of a recommender, a user ID (from the ones available in the training matrix), the number of recommendations, and an array of books ID from which to make recommendations as its arguments:

```
julia> recommend(recommender, 1, 20, [1:book_counter...])
```

With this line of code, we retrieve the recommendations for the user with the recommender ID 1, which corresponds to the `UserID 277427` in the original dataset. We're asking for up to 20 recommendations that have been picked from all the available books.

We get back an array of a `Pair` of book IDs and recommendation scores:

```
20-element Array{Pair{Int64,Float64},1}:
 5081 => 19.1974
 5079 => 19.1948
 5078 => 19.1946
 5077 => 17.1253
 5080 => 17.1246
 # output omitted #
```

Testing the recommendations

Finally, our machine learning-based recommender system is ready. It will provide a significant boost in user experience for any bookshop, for sure. But before we start advertising it, we should make sure that it's reliable. Remember that we put aside 10% of our dataset for testing purposes. The idea is to compare the recommendations with actual ratings from the test data to see what degree of similarity exists between the two; that is, how many of the actual ratings from the dataset were in fact recommended. Depending on the data that's used for the training, you may want to test that both correct recommendations are made, but also that bad recommendations are not included (that is, the recommender does not suggest items that got low ratings, indicating a dislike). Since we only used ratings of 8, 9, and 10, we won't check if low-ranked recommendations were provided. We'll just focus on checking how many of the recommendations are actually part of the user's data.

Because the test data uses the original user and profile IDs, and our recommender uses the normalized, sequential IDs, we'll need a way to convert the data between the two. We already have the `user_mappings` and `book_mappings` dictionaries, which map from the original IDs to recommender IDs. However, we'll also need the reverse. So, let's start by defining a helper function for reversing a dictionary:

```
julia> function reverse_dict(d) Dict(value => key for (key, value) in d)
end
```

This is simple, but very useful—we can now use this function to look up the original IDs based on the recommender IDs. For instance, if we want to test the recommendations for user 1, we'll need to retrieve this user's actual ratings, so we'll need the original ID. We can easily get it with the following code:

```
julia> reverse_dict(user_mappings)[1]
277427
```

The same applies to the books mappings—for instance, the recommendation with ID 5081 corresponds to ISBN 981013004X from the original dataset:

```julia
julia> reverse_dict(book_mappings)[5081]
"981013004X"
```

All right, let's check the test data that we put aside for UserID 277427 (recommender user 1):

```julia
julia> user_testing_data = test_data[test_data[:UserID] .==
reverse_dict(user_mappings)[1], :]
8×3 DataFrame
```

The output is as follows:

Row	UserID	ISBN	Rating
	Int64	String	Int64
1	277427	0060006641	10
2	277427	0441627404	10
3	277427	0446600415	10
4	277427	0671727079	9
5	277427	0671740504	8
6	277427	0671749897	8
7	277427	0836218817	10
8	277427	0842370668	10

The snippet filters the testing_data DataFrame by doing an element-wise comparison—for each row, it checks if the UserID column equals 277427 (which is the ID returned by reverse_dict(user_mappings)[1], remember?). If yes, then the whole row is added to user_testing_data.

To check for recommended versus actually rated profiles, the easiest approach is to intersect the vector of recommendations with the vector of ratings. So, the first thing to do is put the test ratings into a vector, out of the DataFrame:

```julia
julia> test_profile_ids = user_testing_data[:, :ISBN]
8-element Array{Union{Missing, String},1}:
 "0060006641"
 "0441627404"
 "0446600415"
 "0671727079"
 "0671740504"
 "0671749897"
 "0836218817"
 "0842370668"
```

We just select the ISBN column data, for all the rows, as an `Array`.

Doing the same for the recommendations is a bit more involved. Also, since I expect we'll want to test with various recommender settings and with different numbers of recommendations, it's best to define a function that converts the recommendations to a vector of ISBNs, so that we can easily reuse the code:

```julia
julia> function recommendations_to_books(recommendations)
           [reverse_dict(book_mappings)[r[1]] for r in recommendations]
       end
```

The `recommendations_to_books` function takes the vector of `id => score` pairs generated by the recommender as its only argument and converts it into a vector of original ISBNs:

```julia
julia> recommendations_to_books(recommend(recommender, 1, 20,
[1:book_counter...]))
20-element Array{String,1}:
 "981013004X"
 "1856972097"
 "1853263656"
 "1853263133"
 "1857231791"
 # output omitted #
```

The `recommendations_to_books` function outputs the ISBNs for the 20 recommended books.

Now, we have all of the pieces to check recommendations versus ratings:

```julia
julia> intersect(test_profile_ids,
recommendations_to_books(recommend(recommender, 1, 500,
[1:book_counter...])))
1-element Array{Union{Missing, String},1}:
 "0441627404"
```

We use the intersect function to check what elements from the first vector—the list of books we put away for testing—also show up in the second vector, that is, the recommendations. We had to ask for 500 recommendations as the chances of hitting one of the eight test books in a pool of 9,055 books were very slim. This is due to the fact that we worked with very little data, but in a production environment and potentially billions of rows, we would get a lot more overlapping data.

Let's see what the top five recommendations were:

```julia
julia> for i in recommendations_to_books(recommend(recommender, 1, 20,
[1:book_counter...])) top_ratings[top_ratings.ISBN .== i, :BookTitle] |>
println end

Union{Missing, String}["Fun With Chinese Characters Volume 1"]
Union{Missing, String}["Fantasy Stories (Story Library)"]
Union{Missing, String}["The Wordsworth Complete Guide to Heraldry
(Wordsworth Reference)"]
Union{Missing, String}["The Savoy Operas (Wordsworth Collection)"]
Union{Missing, String}["Against a Dark Background"]
```

In an IJulia Notebook, we can even look at the covers, thus rendering a small piece of HTML using the cover's URLs:

```julia
thumbs = DataFrame(Thumb = String[])

for i in recommendations_to_profiles(recommend(recommender, 1, 20,
[1:book_counter...]))
    push!(thumbs, top_ratings[top_ratings.ISBN .== i, :ImageURLL])
end

for img in thumbs[:, :Thumb]
    HTML("""<img src="$(img)">""") |> display
end
```

The output will be as follows:

Excellent! We did a great job. We tamed a very complex dataset, performed advanced analysis, and then we optimized it for usage in our recommender. We then successfully trained our recommender and used it to generate book recommendations for our users.

Deploying and working with the `Recommendation` package is very straightforward, as I'm sure you've come to appreciate. Again, as in most data science projects, the ETL step was the most involved.

Learning about hybrid recommender systems

There are some clear advantages when using model-based recommenders. As mentioned already, scalability is one of the most important. Usually, the models are much smaller than the initial dataset, so that even for very large data samples, the models are small enough to allow efficient usage. Another benefit is the speed. The time required to query the model, as opposed to querying the whole dataset, is usually considerably smaller.

These advantages stem from the fact that the models are generally prepared offline, allowing for almost instantaneous recommendations. But since there's no such thing as free performance, this approach also comes with a few significant negatives—on one hand, it is less flexible, because building the models takes considerable time and resources, making the updates difficult and costly; on the other hand, because it does not use the whole dataset, the predictions can be less accurate.

As with everything, there's no silver bullet, and the best approach depends on the data you have at hand and the problem you need to solve. However, it doesn't always have to be memory-based versus model-based. Even more, it doesn't have to be just one recommender system. It turns out that multiple algorithms and approaches can be efficiently combined to compensate for the limitations of one type of recommender. Such architectures are called **hybrid**. Due to space limitations, we won't cover any implementations of hybrid recommender systems, but I want to give you an idea of the possible approaches. I'm just going to refer you to Robin Burke's classification from *Chapter 12* of *The Adaptive Web*, entitled *Hybrid Web Recommender Systems*. The whole chapter is available online for free at `https://www.researchgate.net/publication/200121024_Hybrid_Web_Recommender_Sy stems`. If you're interested in this topic, I highly recommended it.

Summary

Recommender systems represent a very active and dynamic field of study. They started initially as a marginal application of machine learning algorithms and techniques, but due to their practical business value, they have become mainstream in recent years. These days, almost all major programming languages provide powerful recommendations systems libraries—and all major online businesses employ recommenders in one form or another.

Julia is a great language for building recommenders due to its excellent performance. Despite the fact that the language is still young, we already have a couple of interesting packages to choose from.

Now, you have a solid understanding of the model-based recommendation systems and of their implementation workflow—both on a theoretical and practical level. Plus, throughout our journey, we've also been exposed to more advanced data wrangling using `DataFrames`, an invaluable tool in Julia's data science arsenal.

In the next chapter, we'll further improve our mastery of `DataFrames`, as we'll learn the secrets of metaprogramming in Julia, while developing an unsupervised machine learning system.

8
Leveraging Unsupervised Learning Techniques

Our supervised machine learning project was a success and we're well on our way to becoming experts in recommender systems. It's now time to leave behind the safety of our neatly tagged data and venture into the unknown. Yes, I'm talking about unsupervised machine learning. In this chapter, we'll train a model that will help us find hidden patterns in a mountain of data. And since we've come so far on our journey of learning Julia, it's time to take off the training wheels and take on our first client.

Just kidding—for now, we'll play pretend, but we'll indeed tackle a machine learning problem that could very well be one of the first tasks of a junior data scientist. We'll help our imaginary customer discover key insights for supporting their advertising strategy, a very important component of beginning their operations in San Francisco.

In the process, we'll learn about the following:

- What unsupervised machine learning is and when and how to use it
- The basics of clustering, one of the most important unsupervised learning tasks
- How to perform efficient data munging with the help of query
- Metaprogramming in Julia
- Training and running unsupervised machine learning models with clustering

Technical requirements

The Julia package ecosystem is under continuous development and new package versions are released on a daily basis. Most of the times this is great news, as new releases bring new features and bug fixes. However, since many of the packages are still in beta (version 0.x), any new release can introduce breaking changes. As a result, the code presented in the book can stop working. In order to ensure that your code will produce the same results as described in the book, it is recommended to use the same package versions. Here are the external packages used in this chapter and their specific versions:

```
CSV@v.0.4.3
DataFrames@v0.15.2
DataValues@v0.4.5
Gadfly@v1.0.1
IJulia@v1.14.1
Query@v0.10.1
```

In order to install a specific version of a package you need to run:

```
pkg> add PackageName@vX.Y.Z
```

For example:

```
pkg> add IJulia@v1.14.1
```

Alternatively you can install all the used packages by downloading the `Project.toml` file provided with the chapter and using `pkg>` instantiate as follows:

```
julia>
download("https://raw.githubusercontent.com/PacktPublishing/Julia-Programmi
ng-Projects/master/Chapter08/Project.toml", "Project.toml")
pkg> activate .
pkg> instantiate
```

Unsupervised machine learning

In `Chapter 7`, *Machine Learning For Recommender Systems*, we learned about supervised machine learning. We used various features in the data (such as the user's ratings) to perform classification tasks. In supervised machine learning, we act a bit like a teacher—we provide a multitude of examples to our algorithm, which, once it gets enough data (and so its training is complete), is able to make generalizations about new items and infer their category or class.

But not all of the data lends itself to these kinds of tasks. Sometimes our data isn't labeled in any way. Imagine items as diverse as a website's traffic logs or the appointments made by customers at a dental clinic. These are just raw observations that aren't categorized in any way and don't contain any meaning. In such cases, data analysts employ unsupervised machine learning algorithms.

Unsupervised machine learning is used to discover hidden structures and patterns in otherwise unlabeled data. It is a very powerful machine learning task, successfully employed in a variety of fields, such as marketing (to identify groups of customers who share similar purchase preferences), medicine (used to spot tumours), IT security (by flagging abnormal user behaviour or web traffic), tax collection (alerting of possible tax evasion), and many, many more.

Any supervised machine learning task can be treated as unsupervised if we simply ignore the features that provide data classification. For example, we could use the famous Iris flower dataset to perform unsupervised learning if we didn't want to take into account the Species column. This would leave us with unlabeled sepal and petal lengths and widths, which could form interesting clusters.

As we've seen in `Chapter 1`, *Getting Started with Julia Programming*, **setosa** can be reliably identified, as it consistently has lower petal length and width. But **versicolor** and **virginica**? Not so much. You can view this in the following diagram:

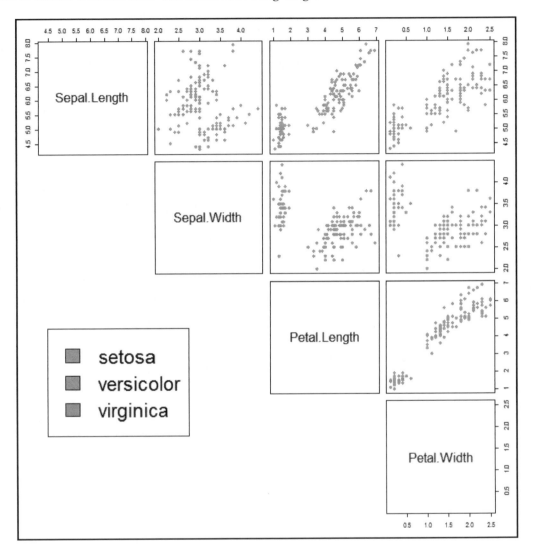

The diagram shows how **setosa** forms distinct clusters in almost all of the plots—but **versicolor** and **virginica** don't. This is unsupervised learning. Easy, right?

Not quite—it gets trickier than that. In our Iris flowers example, we cheat a bit as we color code the plots by species. So, the data is not really unlabeled. In a real unsupervised learning scenario, the plots would look like this, with all of the species information removed:

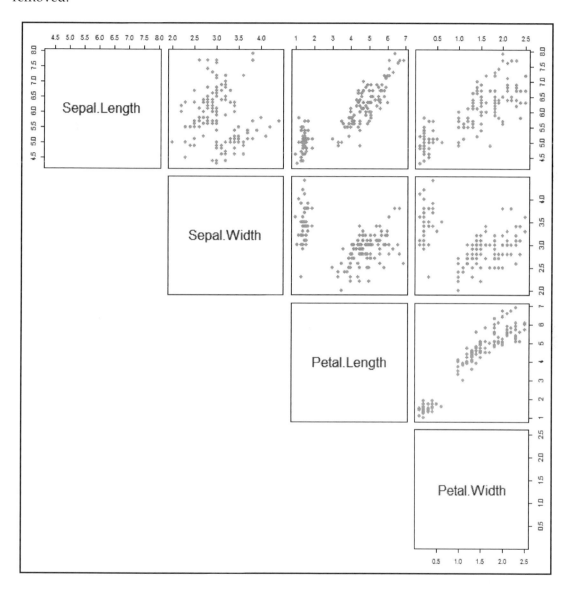

Even without the colors and the labels, since the distribution of the points is the same, we can still easily identify the **setosa** cluster. Except that, obviously, without the species labels we'd have absolutely no idea what it represents. And this is a very important point—*the algorithm cannot label the clusters by itself*. It can identify a degree of similarity between the various data points, but it can't tell what that *means* (it won't know it's **setosa**). A corollary of this is that there isn't a correct way of defining the clusters. They're the result of exploratory data mining techniques—and just like the exploration of an unknown territory, taking slightly different paths (looking at data from a different perspective) will lead to different results. To paraphrase the famous saying, the clusters are in the eye of the beholder.

The most common tasks of unsupervised machine learning are defined as follows:

- **Clustering (or cluster analysis)**: Clustering is used to identify and group objects that are more similar to each other when compared to items in other potential groups or clusters. The comparison is done by using some metric present in the features of the data.
- **Anomaly detection**: It is used to flag entities that do not fall within an expected pattern, as defined by the other items in the dataset. They are important as, in general, anomalies represent some kind of a problem, such as bank or tax fraud, a software bug, or a medical condition.

In the remainder of this chapter, we'll focus exclusively on clustering—a very useful and valuable unsupervised machine learning task. We'll take a closer look at the theory behind clustering and then we'll implement an unsupervised machine learning project using the San Francisco business data.

Clustering

As you've probably come to realize by now, when it comes to data science, there are almost always multiple avenues to attack a problem. At the algorithmic level, depending on the particularities of the data and the specific problem we're trying to solve, we'll usually have more than one option. A wealth of choices is usually good news as some algorithms can produce better results than others, depending on the specifics. Clustering is no exception—a few well-known algorithms are available, but we must understand their strengths and their limitations in order to avoid ending up with irrelevant clusters.

Scikit-learn, the famous Python machine learning library, drives the point home by using a few toy datasets. The datasets produce easily recognizable plots, making it easy for a human to identify the clusters. However, applying unsupervised learning algorithms will lead to strikingly different results—some of them in clear contradiction of what our human pattern recognition abilities would tell us:

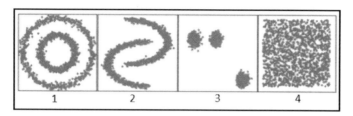

The preceding four plots illustrate the following:

1. Two concentrical circular clusters
2. Two curves
3. Three blobs
4. A square made of uniformly distributed values resulting in a single cluster

Color coding the clusters would result in the following diagram:

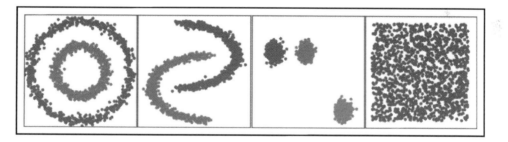

Using our innate pattern recognition abilities, we can easily see the well-defined clusters.

If the clusters are obvious enough for you, you might be surprised to discover that, when it comes to machine learning, things are not that clear-cut. Here is how some of the most common algorithms interpret the data (the following diagram and all of the details of the tests are available on the Scikit-learn website at `http://scikit-learn.org`):

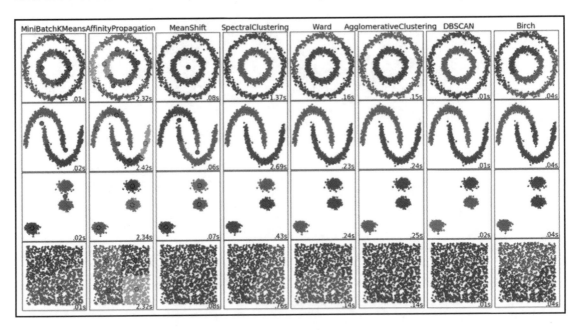

The diagram shows the color-coded clusters together with the computing times for eight well-known algorithms—MiniBatchKMeans, Affinity Propagation, Mean Shift, Spectral Clustering, Ward, Agglomerative Clustering, DBSCAN, and Birch.

Data analysis of the San Francisco business

As our learning project for this chapter, let's imagine that we have been hired by a new client, the famous ACME Recruiting. They are a major HR company and want to open a new office in San Francisco. They are working on a very ambitious marketing strategy to accompany their launch. ACME wants to run outdoor campaigns via billboards; employ transit advertising with posters on buses, taxis, and bikes; and use direct mail by sending leaflets via snail mail.

They're targeting business clients and came to us to help them with two things:

- They want to know the best areas to run their campaign where to place the billboards, on what bus lines to place the ads and to what mail addresses to send the leaflets.
- They would like to understand the market's recruiting needs so that they can get in touch with professionals with the required qualifications.

Our plan is to use a database with information about the companies registered in San Francisco and employ unsupervised learning, in the form of clustering, to detect the areas with the highest density of companies. That's where ACME should spend their advertising dollars. Once we identify the companies they'll target, we'll be able to see what domain of activity they have. Our client will use this information to assess their recruiting needs.

Data-wise, we're off to a good start, as the city of San Francisco makes a lot of interesting data openly available at `https://data.sfgov.org`. Browsing through the website, we can find a database of registered tax-paying businesses. It provides a wealth of information including the name, address, opening and closing dates (if the business is closed), location geo-coordinates (and sometimes the name of the neighborhood), and more.

You can download the file at `https://data.sfgov.org/Economy-and-Community/Map-of-Registered-Business-Locations/ednt-jx6u` by clicking the **Export** button in the toolbar, or use the direct download URL: `https://data.sfgov.org/api/views/ednt-jx6u/rows.csv?accessType=DOWNLOAD`.

However, I strongly suggest using the file provided in this chapter's support files, just to make sure that we use exactly the same data and get the same results if you follow through. Please download it from `https://github.com/PacktPublishing/Julia-Programming-Projects/blob/master/Chapter08/data/Map_of_Registered_Business_Locations.csv.zip`.

For each entry, we also get the **North American Industry Classification System** (**NAICS**) Code, which is (the standard used by Federal statistical agencies in classifying business establishments for the purpose of collecting, analyzing, and publishing statistical data related to the U.S. business economy). This is important as we'll use it to identify the top most common types of businesses, which will help our client attract relevant candidates.

In our dataset, the NAICS code is indicated as a range, for example, 4400–4599. Fortunately, we also get the name of the corresponding sector of activity. In this example, 4400–4599 stands for *retail trade*.

It's time to load the data and slice and dice! By now, I'm sure you know the drill:

```julia
julia> using CSV, DataFrames
julia> df = CSV.read("Map_of_Registered_Business_Locations.csv")
```

Using `describe(df)` gives us a treasure trove of information about each column. I'm including just `nunique` and `nmissing` in the next screenshot, for the sake of brevity, but feel free to check the data in more detail as an exercise:

Row	variable Symbol	nunique Union…	nmissing Int64
1	Location Id	222871	0
2	Business Account Number		0
3	Ownership Name	164934	0
4	DBA Name	190345	0
5	Street Address	156657	4
6	City	2373	266
7	State	61	678
8	Source Zipcode		103
9	Business Start Date	11597	0
10	Business End Date	2958	173184
11	Location Start Date	11480	0
12	Location End Date	3207	154644
13	Mail Address	104156	49688
14	Mail City	2328	47521
15	Mail Zipcode	4105	47570
16	Mail State	71	49751
17	NAICS Code	661	89763
18	NAICS Code Description	18	89763
19	Parking Tax		0
20	Transient Occupancy Tax		0
21	LIC Code	747	212545
22	LIC Code Description	104	212545
23	Supervisor District		86899
24	Neighborhoods - Analysis Boundaries	41	86904
25	Business Corridor	10	222597
26	Business Location	104904	50638

Check the number and percentage of missing values (under the `nmissing` column) and the number of unique values (as `nunique`). We can see that, for the `Location Id` column, we get 222871 unique values and zero missing entries. The number of unique location IDs is equal to the number of rows in the dataset:

```julia
julia> size(df, 1)
222871
```

Moving on, `Ownership Name` stands for the entity that registered the business (either a person or another company) while `DBA Name` represents the name of the business itself. For both of these, we can see that `Number Unique` is smaller than `Location Id`, meaning that some companies are owned by the same entities—and that some companies will have the same name. Looking further at `Street Address`, it turns out that a large number of companies share the location with other businesses (156,658 unique addresses for `222871` companies). Finally, we can see that we have `City`, `State`, and `Zipcode` information for almost all of our records.

The dataset also provides information about the date when a business was registered (`Business Start Date`), closed (`Business End Date`), and when it started and finished operating at that location (`Location Start Date` and `Location End Date` respectively). There are more details, but they are mostly irrelevant for our analysis, such as `Parking Tax`, `Transient Occupancy Tax`, and `LIC Code` data (missing for over 95% of the records) and the `Supervisor District`, `Neighborhoods Analysis Boundaries`, and `Business Corridor` information (the business corridor data is missing in 99.87% of cases though).

It's time to clean up our data and get it ready for analysis!

Data wrangling with query

So far, we've seen how to manipulate `DataFrame` instances using the `DataFrames` API. I'm sure that you're by now aware that we can remove uninteresting columns by using `delete!(df::DataFrame, column_name::Symbol)`, for instance. You may remember from the previous chapter that you can filter a `DataFrame` instance using the square brackets notation in combination with the *dot* element-wise operations, such as in the following example:

```
julia> df[df[Symbol("Parking Tax")] .== true, :][1:10, [Symbol("DBA Name"),
Symbol("Parking Tax")]]
```

The previous snippet will return the top 10 rows (the `DBA Name` and `Parking Tax` columns only) where the business pays parking tax:

```
10×2 DataFrame
 Row │ DBA Name                            │ Parking Tax
     │ Union{Missing, String}              │ Bool
─────┼─────────────────────────────────────┼─────────────
   1 │ Test 12/28/2017 Location 1 / Parking│ true
   2 │ Douglas Parking                     │ true
   3 │ Douglas Parking                     │ true
   4 │ Douglas Parking                     │ true
   5 │ Volume Parking Services             │ true
   6 │ Douglas Parking                     │ true
   7 │ Douglas Parking                     │ true
   8 │ Hyde Park Management Llc            │ true
   9 │ Chestnut Street Lot                 │ true
  10 │ Fillmore Heritage Garage            │ true
```

Now, if you're thinking that Julia spoils us with beautiful syntax and great readability and that the preceding has neither—well, you'd be right! The previous syntax, although usable, can definitely be improved. And I bet you won't be too surprised to hear that Julia's package ecosystem already provides better ways of wrangling `DataFrames`. Enter `Query`!

Query is a package for querying Julia data. It works with a multitude of data sources, including Array, DataFrame, CSV, SQLite, ODBC, and others. It provides filter, project, join, and group functionality, and it's heavily inspired by Microsoft's **Language Integrated Query (LINQ)**. If this doesn't mean a lot to you, don't worry; you'll see it in action right away.

Here is how the preceding operation would be refactored to use query in order to filter out the businesses that pay parking tax:

```
julia> @from i in df begin
          @where i[Symbol("Parking Tax")] == true
          @select i
          @collect DataFrame
       end
```

If you're familiar with SQL, you can easily recognize the familiar language query constructs, `from`, `where`, and `select`. That's powerful!

However, having to use this verbose syntax to convert column names such as `Parking Tax` into symbols in order to access our data is inconvenient. Before we begin, we'd be better off renaming the columns to be more symbol-friendly and replacing the spaces with underscores. We'll use the `DataFrames.rename!` function in combination with a comprehension:

```
julia> rename!(df, [n => replace(string(n), " "=>"_") |> Symbol for n in
names(df)])
```

The `rename!` function accepts a `DataFrame` and an `Array{Pair}` in the form `:current_column_name => :new_current_name`. We use the comprehension to build the array, and we do this by iterating over each current column name (returned by `names(df)`), converting the resulting symbol into a string, replacing " " with "_" and then converting the string back to a symbol.

Now we can use the more succinct dot notation with query, so the preceding snippet will look like this:

```
@from i in df begin
    @where i.Parking_Tax == true
    @select i
    @collect DataFrame
end
```

Metaprogramming in Julia

If you noticed the @ sign prefixing the various query parts in the preceding snippet, don't worry, it's not a typo. The @ prefix represents a macro—which introduces a very powerful programming technique called **metaprogramming**.

If you haven't heard about it before, it basically means that a program has the ability to read, analyse, and transform, and even modify itself while running. Some languages, called **homoiconic**, come with very powerful metaprogramming facilities. In homoiconic languages, the program itself is internally represented as a data structure that's available to the program and can be manipulated. Lisp is the prototypical homoiconic programming language, and for this reason, this kind of metaprogramming is done through Lisp-style macros. They work with the code's representation and are different from preprocessor macros of C and C++ fame, where the text files containing the code are manipulated before parsing and evaluation.

Julia, inspired to a certain degree by Lisp, is also a homoiconic language. Hence, for metaprogramming in Julia, we need to understand two key aspects—the representation of the code by means of expressions and symbols and the manipulation of the code using macros. If we see the execution of a Julia program as a sequence of steps, metaprogramming kicks in and modifies the code after the parsing step, but before the code is evaluated by the compiler.

Learning about symbols and expressions in metaprogramming

Understanding metaprogramming is not easy, so don't panic if it doesn't come naturally from the start. One of the reasons for this, I think, is that it takes place at a level of abstraction higher than what we're used to with regular programming. I'm hoping that opening the discussion with symbols will make the introduction less abstract. We've used symbols extensively throughout this book, especially as arguments for the various functions. They look like this—`:x` or `:scientific` or `:Celsius`. As you may have noticed, a symbol represents an identifier and we use it very much like a constant. However, it's more than that. It represents a piece of code that, instead of being evaluated as the variable, is used to refer to a variable itself.

A good analogy for understanding the relationship between a symbol and a variable has to do with the words in a phrase. Take for example the sentence: *Richard is tall*. Here, we understand that *Richard* is the name of a person, most likely a man. And Richard, the person, is tall. However, in the sentence: *Richard has seven letters*, it is obvious that now we aren't talking about Richard the person. It wouldn't make too much sense to assume that Richard the person has seven letters. We are talking about the word *Richard* itself.

The equivalent, in Julia, of the first sentence (*Richard is tall*) would be `julia> x`. Here, x is immediately evaluated in order to produce its value. If it hasn't been defined, it will result in an error, shown as follows:

```
julia> x
ERROR: UndefVarError: x not defined
```

Julia's symbols mimic the second sentence, where we talk about the word itself. In English, we wrap the word in single quotes, 'Richard', to indicate that we're not referring to a person but to the word itself. In the same way, in Julia, we prefix the variable name with a column, `:x`:

```
julia> :x
:x
```

```
julia> typeof(:x)
Symbol
```

Hence, the column : prefix is an operator that stops the evaluation. An unevaluated expression can be evaluated on demand by using the `eval()` function or the `@eval` macro, as follows:

```
julia> eval(:x)
ERROR: UndefVarError: x not defined
```

But we can go beyond symbols. We can write more complex symbol-like statements, for example, `:(x = 2)`. This works a lot like a symbol but it is, in fact, an `Expr` type, which stands for expression. The expression, like any other type, can be referenced through variable names and, like symbols, they can be evaluated:

```
julia> assign = :(x = 2)
:(x = 2)
julia> eval(assign)
2
julia> x
2
```

The preceding snippet demonstrates that we can reference an `Expr` type with the `assign` variable and then `eval` it. Evaluation produces side effects, the actual value of the variable x now being 2.

Even more powerful, since `Expr` is a type, it has properties that expose its internal structure:

```
julia> fieldnames(typeof(assign))
(:head, :args)
```

Every `Expr` object has two fields—head representing its kind and args standing for the arguments. We can view the internals of `Expr` by using the `dump()` function:

```
julia> dump(assign)
Expr
head: Symbol =
args: Array{Any}((2,))
1: Symbol x
2: Int64 2
```

This leads us to even more important discoveries. First, it means that we can programmatically manipulate `Expr` through its properties:

```
julia> assign.args[2] = 3
3
julia> eval(assign)
3
julia> x
3
```

Our expression is no longer : (x = 2); it's now : (x = 3). By manipulating the `args` of the `assign` expression, the value of x is now 3.

Second, we can programmatically create new instances of `Expr` using the type's constructor:

```
julia> assign4 = Expr(:(=), :x, 4) :(x = 4)
julia> eval(assign4) 4
  julia> x 4
```

Please notice here that we wrapped the equals sign (=) in parenthesis to designate an expression, as Julia gets confused otherwise, thinking we want to perform an assignment right there.

Quoting expressions

The previous procedure, in which we wrap an expression within : (...) in order to create `Expr` objects, is called **quoting**. It can also be done using quote blocks. Quote blocks make quoting easier as we can pass *regular-looking* code into them (as opposed to translating everything in to symbols), and supports quoting multiple lines of code in order to build randomly complex expressions:

```
julia> quote
            y = 42
            x = 10
        end

julia> eval(ans)
10

julia> y
42

julia> x
10
```

Interpolating strings

Just like with string interpolation, we can reference variables within the expressions:

```julia
julia> name = "Dan"
"Dan"

julia> greet = :("Hello " * $name)
:("Hello " * "Dan")

julia> eval(greet)
"Hello Dan"
```

Macros

Now, we finally have the knowledge to understand macros. They are language constructs, which are executed after the code is parsed, but before it is evaluated. It can optionally accept a tuple of arguments and must return an `Expr`. The resulting `Expression` is directly compiled, so we don't need to call `eval()` on it.

For example, we can implement a configurable version of the previous `greet` expression as a macro:

```julia
julia> macro greet(name)
           :("Hello " * $name)
       end
@greet (macro with 1 method)
julia> @greet("Adrian")
"Hello Adrian"
```

As per the snippet, macros are defined using the `macro` keyword and are invoked using the `@...` syntax. The brackets are optional when invoking macros, so we could also use `@greet "Adrian"`.

Macros are very powerful language constructs that allow parts of the code to be customized before the full program is run. The official Julia documentation has a great example to illustrate this behavior:

```julia
julia> macro twostep(arg)
           println("I execute at parse time. The argument is: ", arg)
           return :(println("I execute at runtime. The argument is: ", $arg))
       end
@twostep (macro with 1 method)
```

We define a macro called `twostep`, which has a body that calls the `println` function to output text to the console. It returns an expression which, when evaluated, will also output a piece of text via the same `println` function.

Now we can see it in action:

```
julia> ex = macroexpand(@__MODULE__, :(@twostep :(1, 2, 3)));
I execute at parse time. The argument is: $(Expr(:quote, :((1, 2, 3))))
```

The snippet shows a call to `macroexpand`, which takes as an argument the module in which to expand the expression (in our case, `@__MODULE__` stands for the current module) and an expression that represents a macro invocation. The call to `macroexpand` converts (expands) the macro into its resulting expressions. The output of the `macroexpand` call is suppressed by appending `;` at the end of the line, but the resulting expression is still safely stored in `ex`. Then, we can see that the expanding of the macro (its parsing) takes place because the `I execute at parse time` message is output. Now look what happens when we evaluate the expression, `ex`:

```
julia> eval(ex)
I execute at runtime. The argument is: (1, 2, 3)
```

The `I execute at runtime` message is outputted, but not the `I execute at parse time` message. This is a very powerful thing. Imagine that output instead of a simple text output if we'd had some very computationally intensive or time-consuming operations. In a simple function, we'd have to run this code every time, but with a macro, this is done only once, at parse time.

Closing words about macros

Besides they're very powerful, macros are also very convenient. They can provide a lot of functionality with minimal overhead and can simplify the invocation of functions that take expressions as arguments. For example, `@time` is a very useful macro that executes an `Expression` while measuring the execution time. And the great thing is that we can pass the argument expression as *regular* code, instead of building the `Expr` by hand:

```
julia> @time rand(1000);
  0.000007 seconds (5 allocations: 8.094 KiB)
```

Macros—and metaprogramming in general—are powerful concepts that require whole books to discuss at length. We must stop here in order to get back to our machine learning project. ACME Recruiting is eagerly waiting for our findings. I recommend going over the official documentation at https://docs.julialang.org/en/stable/manual/metaprogramming/.

Beginning with Query.jl basics

The Query package can be added in the standard way—pkg> add Query. Once you bring it into scope using Query, it makes a rich API available for querying Julia data sources, DataFrames being the most common source. A query is initiated using the @from macro.

@from

The general structure of a query is as follows:

```
@from var in data_source begin
    # query statements here
end
```

Within the begin...end block, var represents a row in the data_source. The query statements are given one per line and can include any combination of available query commands, such as @select, @orderby, @join, @group, and @collect. Let's take a closer look at the most important ones.

@select

The @select query command, similar to its SQL SELECT counterpart, indicates which values are to be returned. Its general syntax is @select condition, where condition can be any Julia expression. Most commonly, we'll want to return the whole row and, in this case, we'll just pass var itself. For instance, let's create a new DataFrame to hold a shopping list:

```
julia> shopping_list = DataFrame(produce=["Apples", "Milk", "Bread"],
qty=[5, 2, 1])
```

The output is as follows:

```
3×2 DataFrame
 Row │ produce │ qty
     │ String  │ Int64
─────┼─────────┼──────
   1 │ Apples  │ 5
   2 │ Milk    │ 2
   3 │ Bread   │ 1
```

A cool (geeky!) and handy shopping list.

We can `@select` the whole row with the following:

```
@from p in shopping_list begin
    @select p
end
```

It's not very useful, as this basically returns the whole `DataFrame`, but we can also reference a column using `dot` notation, for example, `p.produce`:

```
julia> @from p in shopping_list begin
           @select p.produce
       end
3-element query result
 "Apples"
 "Milk"
 "Bread"
```

Given that `@select` accepts any random `Julia` expression, we're free to manipulate the data as we see fit:

```
julia> @from p in shopping_list begin
           @select uppercase(p.produce), 2p.qty
       end
3-element query result
 ("APPLES", 10)
 ("MILK", 4)
 ("BREAD", 2)
```

In the preceding snippet, we select the uppercase `produce` and two times the `qty`.

However, a better approach is to return `NamedTuple`, using the special query curly brackets syntax:

```julia
julia> @from p in shopping_list begin
           @select { produce = uppercase(p.produce), qty = 2p.qty }
       end
```

The output is as follows:

```
3x2 query result
produce | qty

APPLES  | 10
MILK    | 4
BREAD   | 2
```

Here, we pass both the keys and the values for `NamedTuple`, but they're not mandatory. They are, however, useful if we want properly named columns (and who doesn't, right?):

```julia
julia> @from p in shopping_list begin
           @select { uppercase(p.produce), 2p.qty }
       end
```

The output is as follows:

```
3-element query result
("APPLES", 10)
("MILK", 4)
("BREAD", 2)
```

Without the explicit labels, `query` will assign column names such as __1__, __2__, and so on. It's not very readable!

@collect

You might've noticed in the previous screenshots that the type of the returned value was `query result`. A query will return an iterator that can be further used to loop over the individual elements of the result set. But we can use the `@collect` statement to materialize the result into a specific data structure, most commonly `Array` or `DataFrame`. This is shown as follows:

```julia
julia> @from p in shopping_list begin
           @select { PRODUCE = uppercase(p.produce), double_qty = 2p.qty }
           @collect
       end
```

We get the following:

```
3-element Array{NamedTuple{(:PRODUCE, :double_qty),Tuple{String,Int64}},1}:
 (PRODUCE = "APPLES", double_qty = 10)
 (PRODUCE = "MILK", double_qty = 4)
 (PRODUCE = "BREAD", double_qty = 2)
```

By default, `@collect` will produce an `Array` of `NamedTuple` elements. But we can pass it an extra argument for the data type we desire:

```
julia> @from p in shopping_list begin
           @select {PRODUCE = uppercase(p.produce), double_qty = 2p.qty}
           @collect DataFrame
       end
```

The output looks like this:

```
3×2 DataFrame
 Row │ PRODUCE   double_qty
     │ String    Int64

   1 │ APPLES    10
   2 │ MILK      4
   3 │ BREAD     2
```

Our result is now a `DataFrame`.

@where

One of the most useful commands is `@where`, which allows us to filter a data source so that only the elements that satisfy the condition are returned. Similar to `@select`, the condition can be any arbitrary `Julia` expression:

```
julia> @from p in shopping_list begin
           @where p.qty < 2
           @select p
           @collect DataFrame
       end
```

We get the following output:

```
1×2 DataFrame
 Row │ produce  qty
     │ String   Int64
─────┼──────────────
   1 │ Bread    1
```

Only bread has a `qty` smaller than `2`.

Filtering can be made even more powerful by means of range variables. These act like new variables belonging to the `query` expression and can be introduced using the `@let` macro:

```julia
julia> @from p in shopping_list begin
           @let weekly_qty = 7p.qty
           @where weekly_qty > 10
           @select { p.produce, week_qty=weekly_qty }
           @collect DataFrame
       end
```

The output is as follows:

```
2×2 DataFrame
 Row │ produce  week_qty
     │ String   Int64
─────┼──────────────────
   1 │ Apples   35
   2 │ Milk     14
```

Here, you can see how, within the `begin...end` block, we defined a local variable called `weekly_qty` with a value equal to `7 * p.qty`. We used the `@let` macro to introduce new variables. In the next line, we used it to filter out the rows that have a `weekly_qty` smaller than `10`. And then finally, we selected it and collected it into a `DataFrame`.

@join

Let's make things even more interesting:

```julia
julia> products_info = DataFrame(produce = ["Apples", "Milk", "Bread"],
       price = [2.20, 0.45, 0.79], allergenic = [false, true, true])
```

The output is as follows:

```
3×3 DataFrame
 Row │ produce │ price   │ allergenic
     │ String  │ Float64 │ Bool
─────┼─────────┼─────────┼───────────
  1  │ Apples  │ 2.2     │ false
  2  │ Milk    │ 0.45    │ true
  3  │ Bread   │ 0.79    │ true
```

We instantiate a new `DataFrame`, called `products_info`, which contains important information about items in our shopping list—their prices and whether or not they can be considered allergenic. We could use `DataFrames.hcat!` to append some columns from `products_info` to `shopping_list`, but again, the syntax is not so nice and the approach is not that flexible. We've been spoiled by Julia and we like it that way! Fortunately, Query provides a `@join` macro:

```
shopping_info = @from p in shopping_list begin
    @join pinfo in products_info on p.produce equals pinfo.produce
    @select { p.produce, p.qty, pinfo.price, pinfo.allergenic }
    @collect DataFrame
end
```

If you're familiar with SQL, the preceding snippet should be crystal clear. We execute a query from `shopping_list` as `p`, adding an inner join, `@join`, with `products_info` as `pinfo`, on the condition that `p.produce` equals `pinfo.produce`. We basically put together the `produce` and `qty` columns from `shopping_list` `DataFrame` with the `price` and `allergenic` columns from `products_info`. The resulting `DataFrame` can now be referenced as `shopping_info`:

```
3×4 DataFrame
 Row │ produce │ qty   │ price   │ allergenic
     │ String  │ Int64 │ Float64 │ Bool
─────┼─────────┼───────┼─────────┼───────────
  1  │ Apples  │ 5     │ 2.2     │ false
  2  │ Milk    │ 2     │ 0.45    │ true
  3  │ Bread   │ 1     │ 0.79    │ true
```

The general syntax of a `@join` command is as follow:

```
@from var1 in datasource1 begin
    @join var2 in datasource2 on var1.column equals var2.column
end
```

Query provides two other variants of @join: group join and left outer join. If you would like to read about them, please check the official documentation at
http://www.queryverse.org/Query.jl/stable/querycommands.html#Joining-1.

@group

The @group statement groups elements by some attribute:

```
julia> @from p in shopping_info begin
           @group p.produce by p.allergenic
           @collect
       end
2-element Array{Grouping{Bool,String},1}:
 ["Apples"]
 ["Milk", "Bread"]
```

Not bad, but what we'd really like is to summarize the data. Query provides this under the name split-apply-combine (also known as, dplyr). This requires an aggregation function that will be used to collapse the dataset based on the Grouping variable. If that's too abstract, an example will surely clear things up.

Say we want to get a count of allergenic items together with a comma-separated list of their names, so we know what to stay away from:

```
@from p in shopping_info begin
    @group p by p.allergenic into q
    @select { allergenic = key(q),
    count = length(q.allergenic),
    produce = join(q.produce, ", ") }
    @collect DataFrame
end
```

We can see in this snippet how we do the grouping into the q variable and then pass the aggregation function, length, to get a count of the values of the allergenic column. We then use the join function to concatenate the values in the produce column.

The result will be a two-row `DataFrame`:

```
2×3 DataFrame
 Row │ allergenic │ count │ produce
     │ Bool       │ Int64 │ String
─────┼────────────┼───────┼─────────────
   1 │ false      │ 1     │ Apples
   2 │ true       │ 2     │ Milk, Bread
```

@orderby

Query also provides a sorting macro named `@orderby`. It takes a list of attributes upon which to apply the sorting. Similar to SQL, the order is ascending by default, but we can change that by using the `descending` function.

Given our previously defined `products_info DataFrame`, we can easily sort it as needed, for example, with the most expensive products first and then by product name:

```julia
julia> @from p in products_info begin
          @orderby descending(p.price), p.produce
          @select p
          @collect DataFrame
       end
```

The snippet shows how to employ `@orderby` to sort the values in the source. Unsurprisingly, the resulting `DataFrame` will be properly sorted with the most expensive products on top:

```
3×3 DataFrame
 Row │ produce │ price   │ allergenic
     │ String  │ Float64 │ Bool
─────┼─────────┼─────────┼────────────
   1 │ Apples  │ 2.2     │ false
   2 │ Bread   │ 0.79    │ true
   3 │ Milk    │ 0.45    │ true
```

All right, that was quite a detour! But now that we have knowledge of the great `Query` package, we're ready to efficiently slice and dice our data. Let's go!

Preparing our data

Our data cleaning plan is to only keep the businesses registered in San Francisco, CA, for which we have the address, zip code, NAICS code, and business location and which have not been closed (so they don't have a business end date) and have not moved away (don't have a location end date).

Using the `DataFrame` API to apply the filters would be tedious. But with Query, it's a walk in the park:

```
pkg> add DataValues
julia> using DataValues
julia> clean_df = @from b in df begin
    @where lowercase(b.City) == "san francisco" && b.State == "CA" &&
        ! isna(b.Street_Address) && ! isna(b.Source_Zipcode) &&
        ! isna(b.NAICS_Code) && ! isna(b.NAICS_Code_Description) &&
        ! isna(b.Business_Location) &&
        occursin(r"\((.*), (.*)\)", get(b.Business_Location)) &&
        isna(b.Business_End_Date) && isna(b.Location_End_Date)
    @select { b.DBA_Name, b.Source_Zipcode, b.NAICS_Code,
        b.NAICS_Code_Description, b.Business_Location }
    @collect DataFrame
end
```

We can see how `@where` filters are applied, requiring that `lowercase(b.City)` equals `"san francisco"` and that `b.State` equals `"CA"`. Then, we use `!  isna` to make sure we only keep the rows where `b.Street_Address`, `b.Source_Zipcode`, `b.NAICS_Code`, `b.NAICS_Code_Description`, and `b.Business_Location` are not missing. The `isna` function is provided by the `DataValues` package (which is used by Query itself) and that's why we're adding and using it.

We also make sure that `b.Business_Location` matches a certain format that corresponds to geolocation coordinates. Finally, we make sure that, on the contrary, `b.Business_End_Date` and `b.Location_End_Date` are in fact missing.

Executing the query produces a new `DataFrame` with almost 57,000 rows.

The next step is to take our `clean_df` data and extract the geo-coordinates out of the `Business_Location` column. Again, Query comes to the rescue:

```
clean_df_geo = @from b in clean_df begin
    @let geo = split(match(r"(\-?\d+(\.\d+)?),\s*(\-?\d+(\.\d+)?)",
                    get(b.Business_Location)).match, ", ")
    @select {b.DBA_Name, b.Source_Zipcode, b.NAICS_Code,
                b.NAICS_Code_Description,
                lat = parse(Float64, geo[1]), long = parse(Float64,
geo[2])}
    @collect DataFrame
end
```

We make good use of the range variables feature (defined by `@let`) to introduce a `geo` variable, which uses `match` to extract the latitude and longitude pairs from the `Business_Location` data. Next, inside the `@select` block, the two values in the geo array are converted in to proper float values and added to the resulting `DataFrame`:

```
56549×6 DataFrame
Row   DBA_Name                       Source_Zipcode  NAICS_Code  NAICS_Code_Description                            lat       long
      Union{Missing, String}         Int64⍰          String⍰     Union{Missing, String}                            Float64   Float64

1     Zaalouk Market & Deli Grocery  94109           4400-4599   Retail Trade                                      37.7877   -122.42
2     1-11 Lilac St Apts             94110           5300-5399   Real Estate and Rental and Leasing Services       37.7519   -122.418
3     Global-Exchange.org            94117           5100-5199   Information                                       37.7725   -122.45
4     3101 Laguna Apts               94123           5300-5399   Real Estate and Rental and Leasing Services       37.7998   -122.431
5     Gosha Do Co                    94118           4400-4599   Retail Trade                                      37.7829   -122.451
6     Sunflower Restaurant           94103           7220-7229   Food Services                                     37.7649   -122.422
7     Academy Of Art University      94105           6100-6299   Private Education and Health Services             37.7877   -122.401
8     Burma Super Star Restaurant    94118           7220-7229   Food Services                                     37.783    -122.463
9     Jug Shop Inc                   94108           4400-4599   Retail Trade                                      37.795    -122.421
10    Miller Fleming & Assocs        94104           5210-5239   Financial Services                                37.7912   -122.402
```

We're done! Our data is now neatly represented in our `clean_df_geo DataFrame`, containing the name of the business, zip code, NAICS code, NAICS code description, latitude, and longitude.

If we run `describe(clean_df_geo)`, we'll see that we have 56,549 businesses with 53,285 unique names with only 18 NAICS code descriptions. We don't know how many zip codes the companies are spread across, but it's easy to find out:

```
julia> unique(clean_df_geo[:, :Source_Zipcode]) |> length
79
```

Our businesses are registered within `79` zip codes in the city of San Francisco.

Unsupervised machine learning with clustering

Julia's package ecosystem provides a dedicated library for clustering. Unsurprisingly, it's called **Clustering**. We can simply execute `pkg> add Clustering` to install it. The `Clustering` package implements a few common clustering algorithms—k-means, affinity propagation, DBSCAN, and kmedoids.

The k-means algorithm

The k-means algorithm is one of the most popular ones, providing a balanced combination of good results and good performance in a wide range of applications. However, one complication is that we're required to give it the number of clusters beforehand. More exactly, this number, called **k** (hence the first letter of the name of the algorithm), represents the number of centroids. A **centroid** is a point that is representative of each cluster.

The k-means algorithm applies an iterative approach—it places the centroids using the algorithm defined by the seeding procedure, then it assigns each point to its corresponding centroid, the mean to which is closest. The algorithm stops on convergence, that is, when the point assignment doesn't change with a new iteration.

Algorithm seeding

There are a few ways to pick the centroids. Clustering provides three, one of which is random (labeled as the `:rand` option in clustering), which randomly selects a subset of points as seeds (so all centroids are random). This is the default seeding strategy in classical k-means. There's also k-means++, a better variation proposed in 2007 by David Arthur and Sergei Vassilvitskii (labeled as `:kmpp`), which picks one cluster center randomly, but then searches for the other centers in relation to the first one. The last available approach is centrality seeding (`:kmcen`), which picks the samples with the highest centrality.

Finding the areas with the most businesses

In the previous section, we successfully cleaned our data, now neatly accessible in `clean_df_geo` DataFrame. If you run into any problems with the data cleaning process, you can just go ahead and load the dataset from scratch by using the `clean_df_geo.tsv` file provided in this chapter's support files (https://github.com/PacktPublishing/Julia-Programming-Projects/blob/master/Chapter08/data/clean_df_geo.tsv.zip). In order to load it, all you have to do is run the following:

```
julia> using CSV
julia> clean_df_geo = CSV.read("clean_df_geo.tsv", delim = '\t', nullable =
false)
```

So we want to identify the areas with the highest density of businesses. One approach is to use unsupervised machine learning to identify the areas by zip code and the number of businesses registered.

We'll train our model using the data in the `:zipcode` column plus the number of businesses registered in the area. We'll need the number of businesses per zip code:

```
julia> model_data = @from b in clean_df_geo begin
    @group b by b.Source_Zipcode into g
    @let bcount = Float64(length(g))
    @orderby descending(bcount)
    @select { zipcode = Float64(get(key(g))), businesses_count = bcount }
    @collect DataFrame
end
```

We execute a query against `clean_df_geo` DataFrame, grouping it by `:Source_Zipcode` into g. We store the number of businesses from the current zip code in the `bcount` range variable, as returned by `length(g)`, but not before converting the number into a `Float64`. The reason we're doing this is that, as we'll see right away, clustering expects the input to be `Float64`, so this will save us another processing step later. Back to our query. We also apply sorting by `bcount` to allow us, the humans, to better understand the data (not needed for training the model). Finally, we instantiate a new `DataFrame`, with two columns, a zip code, and `businesses_count`, without forgetting to convert the zip code into `Float64` too, for the same reason as before. When converting `key(g)`, please also note that we're first calling the `get` function. This is because, within a query block, the computed values are represented as `DataValues` and to access the wrapped value we need to invoke `get`:

```
79×2 DataFrame
 Row │ zipcode   businesses_count
     │ Float64   Float64

   1 │ 94110.0   4528.0
   2 │ 94103.0   3862.0
   3 │ 94109.0   3575.0
   4 │ 94118.0   2974.0
   5 │ 94107.0   2960.0
   6 │ 94122.0   2829.0
   7 │ 94102.0   2767.0
   8 │ 94117.0   2559.0
   9 │ 94114.0   2541.0
  10 │ 94133.0   2516.0
```

Our training data is made of `79` zip codes and their corresponding businesses count. The top 22 areas have over 1,000 businesses each, and the number drops sharply for the rest:

```julia
julia> last(model_data)
```

The output is as follows:

```
6×2 DataFrame
 Row │ zipcode   businesses_count
     │ Float64   Float64

   1 │ 98104.0   1.0
   2 │ 95202.0   1.0
   3 │ 94546.0   1.0
   4 │ 96150.0   1.0
   5 │ 94966.0   1.0
   6 │ 94028.0   1.0
```

You probably remember Gadfly, the Julia plotting library we used in Chapter 1, *Getting Started with Julia Programming,* to visualize the Iris flowers dataset. Let's use it to quickly get a glimpse of our data:

```julia
julia> using Gadfly
julia> plot(model_data, x=:businesses_count, Geom.histogram)
```

This will render the following histogram:

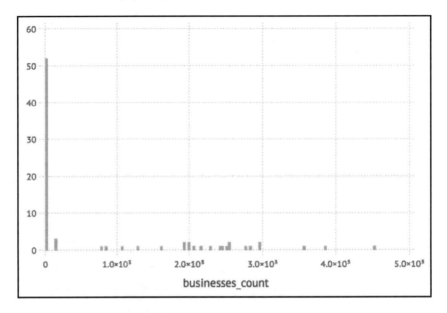

We can easily see that most of the areas only have one registered business, followed by a few others, which only have a few. We can safely remove these from our training dataset as they won't be useful to our client. The only thing we need to do is to add the `@where bcount > 10` filter in the query for computing `model_data`, between the `@let` and the `@orderby` statements:

```
model_data = @from b in clean_df_geo begin
    @group b by b.Source_Zipcode into g
    @let bcount = Float64(length(g))
    @where bcount > 10
    @orderby descending(bcount)
    @select { zipcode = Float64(get(key(g))), businesses_count = bcount }
    @collect DataFrame
end
```

Once we remove all of the areas that host less than 10 companies, we're left with only 28 zip codes.

Training our model

Only one small step and we're ready to train our model. We need to convert the `DataFrame` into an array and to permute the dimensions of the array so that the `DataFrame` columns become rows. In the new structure, each column (zip code and count pair) is considered a training sample. Let's do it:

```julia
julia> training_data = permutedims(convert(Array, model_data), [2, 1])
```

Our training data is ready! It's time to put it to good use:

```julia
julia> using Clustering
julia> result = kmeans(training_data, 3, init=:kmpp, display=:iter)
```

```
    Iters               objv        objv-change | affected
---------------------------------------------------------------
       0         6.726516e+06
       1         4.730363e+06       -1.996153e+06 |        0
       2         4.730363e+06        0.000000e+00 |        0
K-means converged with 2 iterations (objv = 4.73036279655838e6)
```

We're using the k-means algorithm by invoking the function with the same name. As arguments, we provide the `training_data` array and give it three clusters. We want to split the areas into three tiers—low, medium, and high density. The training shouldn't take more than a few seconds. And since we gave it the `display=:iter` argument, we get progressive debug info at each iteration. For the seeding algorithm, we have used k-means++ (`:kmpp`).

Interpreting the results

Now we can take a look at how the points were assigned:

```julia
julia> result.assignments
28-element Array{Int64,1}:
 3
 3
 3
 1
 1
# some 1 values omitted from the output for brevity
 1
 1
 2
 2
```

```
# some 2 values omitted from the output for brevity
2
2
```

Each element in the array corresponds to the element at the same index in the `model_data`. Let's combine the data so it's easier to follow:

```
julia> model_data[:cluster_id] = result.assignments
28-element Array{Int64,1}:
# output truncated #
```

Now let's see what we end up with:

```
julia> model_data
```

The output is as follows:

```
28×3 DataFrame
 Row │ zipcode   businesses_count   cluster_id
     │ Float64   Float64            Int64
─────┼──────────────────────────────────────────
 1   │ 94110.0   4528.0             3
 2   │ 94103.0   3862.0             3
 3   │ 94109.0   3575.0             3
 4   │ 94118.0   2974.0             1
 5   │ 94107.0   2960.0             1
 6   │ 94122.0   2829.0             1
 7   │ 94102.0   2767.0             1
 8   │ 94117.0   2559.0             1
 9   │ 94114.0   2541.0             1
 10  │ 94133.0   2516.0             1
 11  │ 94123.0   2453.0             1
 12  │ 94115.0   2416.0             1
 13  │ 94108.0   2287.0             1
 14  │ 94111.0   2157.0             1
 15  │ 94121.0   2071.0             1
 16  │ 94105.0   1999.0             1
 17  │ 94112.0   1996.0             1
 18  │ 94104.0   1943.0             1
 19  │ 94124.0   1929.0             1
 20  │ 94116.0   1631.0             1
 21  │ 94131.0   1289.0             2
 22  │ 94127.0   1062.0             2
 23  │ 94134.0   848.0              2
 24  │ 94132.0   782.0              2
 25  │ 94158.0   145.0              2
 26  │ 94130.0   142.0              2
 27  │ 94129.0   141.0              2
 28  │ 94143.0   14.0               2
```

We can see that the first three zip codes have been assigned to cluster 3, the last eight to cluster 2, and the rest to cluster 1. You've probably noticed that the IDs of the clusters don't follow the actual count values, which is normal since the data is unlabeled. It is us who must interpret the meaning of the clusters. And our algorithm has decided that the areas with the highest density of businesses will stay in cluster 3, the low densities in cluster 2, and the average ones in cluster 1. Plotting the data with `Gadfly` will confirm our findings:

```
julia> plot(model_data, y = :zipcode, x = :businesses_count, color =
result.assignments, Geom.point, Scale.x_continuous(minvalue=0,
maxvalue=5000), Scale.y_continuous(minvalue=94050, maxvalue=94200),
Scale.x_continuous(format=:plain))
```

It produces this plot:

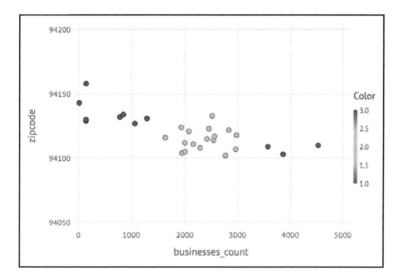

Excellent! We can now inform our client that the best areas to target are in the zip codes 94110, 94103, and 94109, allowing them to reach 11,965 businesses in these dense parts of the city. They would also like to know which are these companies, so let's prepare a list:

```
companies_in_top_areas = @from c in clean_df_geo begin
      @where in(c.Source_Zipcode, [94110, 94103, 94109])
      @select c
      @collect DataFrame
end
```

We use the zip codes we extracted in the clustering step to filter the `clean_df_geo` dataset:

```
11965×6 DataFrame
 Row   DBA_Name                        Source_Zipcode  NAICS_Code   NAICS_Code_Description                              lat      long
       Union{Missing, String}          Int64s          Strings      Union{Missing, String}                             Float64s Float64s

 1     Zaalouk Market & Deli Grocery   94109           4400-4599    Retail Trade                                       37.7877  -122.42
 2     1-11 Lilac St Apts              94110           5300-5399    Real Estate and Rental and Leasing Services        37.7519  -122.418
 3     Sunflower Restaurant            94103           7220-7229    Food Services                                      37.7649  -122.422
 4     Bay Music & Entertainment Inc   94109           7100-7199    Arts, Entertainment, and Recreation                37.7957  -122.423
 5     Impark 0376                     94109           4400-4599    Retail Trade                                       37.7891  -122.417
 6     Geologica Inc                   94103           5400-5499    Professional, Scientific, and Technical Services   37.7875  -122.403
 7     Impark 0315                     94109           4400-4599    Retail Trade                                       37.7894  -122.422
 8     Impark 0324                     94103           4400-4599    Retail Trade                                       37.7867  -122.405
 9     Impark 0370                     94103           4400-4599    Retail Trade                                       37.7818  -122.405
 10    Impark 0377                     94103           4400-4599    Retail Trade                                       37.787   -122.403
```

We end up with 11,965 companies concentrated in three area codes. Let's plot the points using the `geo` coordinates:

```julia
julia> plot(companies_in_top_areas, y = :long, x = :lat, Geom.point,
Scale.x_continuous(minvalue=36, maxvalue=40),
Scale.y_continuous(minvalue=-125, maxvalue=-120), color=:Source_Zipcode)
```

The output is as follows:

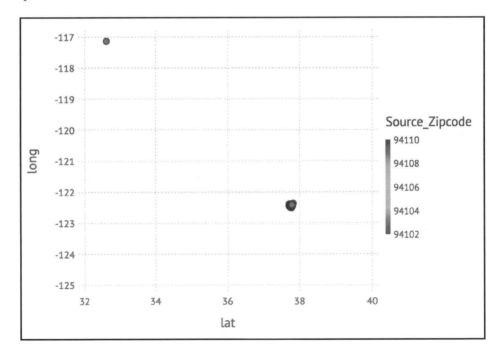

As expected, the locations are in close proximity, but there is one outlier whose coordinates are way off. Maybe there's an error in our data. Using Query, we can easily remove the culprit:

```
julia> companies_in_top_areas = @from c in companies_in_top_areas begin
           @where c.lat != minimum(companies_in_top_areas[:lat])
           @select c
           @collect DataFrame
       end
```

With our cleaned-up list, we can now explore the domain of activity for these companies. This will help our client reach out to candidates that fit the market's demand, as follows:

```
julia> activities = @from c in companies_in_top_areas begin
           @group c by c.NAICS_Code_Description into g
           @orderby descending(length(g))
           @select { activity = key(g), number_of_companies = length(g) }
           @collect DataFrame
       end
```

That was easy:

| 18×2 DataFrame | | |
Row	activity Union{Missing, String}	number_of_companies Int64
1	Real Estate and Rental and Leasing Services	3198
2	Professional, Scientific, and Technical Services	1596
3	Retail Trade	1467
4	Food Services	1154
5	Arts, Entertainment, and Recreation	894
6	Private Education and Health Services	568
7	Accommodations	537
8	Construction	496
9	Multiple	343
10	Wholesale Trade	343
11	Certain Services	341
12	Information	235
13	Transportation and Warehousing	194
14	Manufacturing	187
15	Financial Services	184
16	Administrative and Support Services	176
17	Insurance	39
18	Utilities	12

All the companies in the targeted area are active in just 18 domains, out of which real estate is the most common one. Surely, our client's executives would appreciate a chart:

```julia
julia> plot(activities, y=:number_of_companies, Geom.bar, color=:activity,
Scale.y_continuous(format=:plain), Guide.XLabel("Activities"),
Guide.YLabel("Number of companies"))
```

This is what we get:

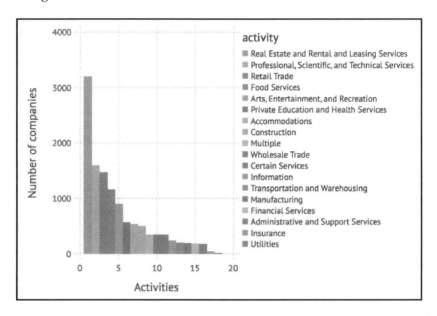

Yes, the chart clearly shows that real estate is the activity in which most of the businesses are involved, with tech and retail coming in next.

Refining our findings

Great progress so far, but a list of almost 12,000 companies is still hard to handle. We can help our client by breaking it down into clusters of businesses located in close proximity. It's the same workflow as before. First, we extract our training data:

```julia
julia> model_data = @from c in companies_in_top_areas begin
         @select { latitude = c.lat, longitude = c.long }
         @collect DataFrame
       end
```

The output is as follows:

```
11964×2 DataFrame
 Row  │ latitude │ longitude
      │ Float64  │ Float64

   1  │ 37.7877  │ -122.42
   2  │ 37.7519  │ -122.418
   3  │ 37.7649  │ -122.422
   4  │ 37.7957  │ -122.423
   5  │ 37.7891  │ -122.417
   6  │ 37.7875  │ -122.403
   7  │ 37.7894  │ -122.422
   8  │ 37.7867  │ -122.405
   9  │ 37.7818  │ -122.405
  10  │ 37.787   │ -122.403
```

Now we permute the dimensions to set the data in the format expected by clustering (just like we did before):

```
julia> training_data = permutedims(convert(Array{Float64}, model_data), [2,
1])
```

Our training array is ready!

We'll use the same k-means algorithm with k-means++ seeding.

Please be aware that k-means is generally not the best choice for clustering geolocation data. DBSCAN is usually better suited and I recommend that you look into it for production applications. The k-means algorithm will fail, for example, when dealing with close points that wrap over 180 degrees. For our example project and for the data we're handling, k-means works fine, but keep this limitation in mind.

Training works in the same way. We'll go with 12 clusters, in order to get roughly 1,000 companies per group:

```
julia> result = kmeans(training_data, 12, init=:kmpp, display=:iter)
  # output truncated
K-means converged with 24 iterations (objv = 0.28192820139520336)
```

This time it takes 24 iterations to reach convergence. Let's see what we've got:

```
julia> result.counts
12-element Array{Int64,1}:
 1076
 1247
  569
```

```
1180
1711
1191
 695
   1
1188
  29
1928
1149
```

Most of the data is evenly spread, but we can spot a few clusters which don't get that many businesses. Plotting the numbers gives us a clear picture:

```
julia> plot(result.counts, Geom.bar, y=result.counts, Guide.YLabel("Number
of businesses"), Guide.XLabel("Cluster ID"), color=result.counts)
```

Here is the plot:

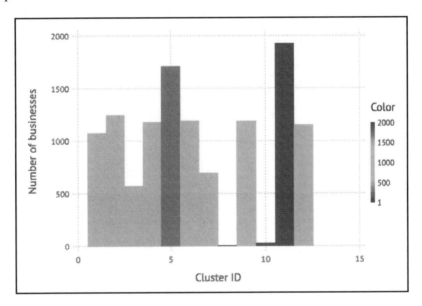

Now we can *paste* the cluster assignments onto the `companies_in_top_areas`
`DataFrame`:

```
julia> companies_in_top_areas[:cluster_id] = result.assignments
```

Visualizing our clusters on the map

To get a better understanding of our data, in terms of points density and location proximity, we can render a plot with `Gadfly`:

```julia
julia> plot(companies_in_top_areas, color=:cluster_id, x=:lat, y=:long)
```

The output is as follows:

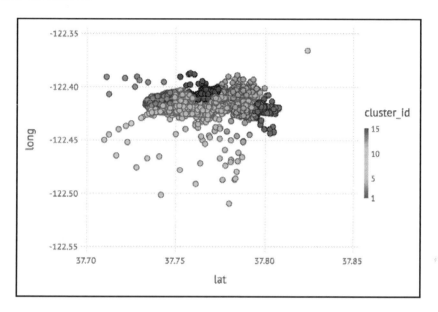

We can see a pretty good cluster distribution, so our approach worked!

However, it would be even better if we could display the clusters on a map. Unfortunately, at the moment, there's no easy way to do this in Julia, so we'll use a third-party tool.

> PlotlyJS (`https://github.com/sglyon/PlotlyJS.jl`) provides related functionality, but my tests didn't produce good results given that the coordinates are tightly packed in the San Francisco area.

Using BatchGeo to quickly build maps of our data

BatchGeo (`https://batchgeo.com`) is a popular web app for creating map-based data visualizations. It uses high-definition maps from Google and it provides a no-login, albeit limited, free version, which we can try out right away.

BatchGeo expects a CSV file with a series of columns, so our first job is to set that up. It couldn't be any simpler with Query:

```
julia> export_data = @from c in companies_in_top_areas begin
                        @select { Name = c.DBA_Name,
                                   Zip = c.Source_Zipcode,
                                   Group = string("Cluster
$(c.cluster_id)"),

                                   Latitude = c.lat, Longitude = c.long,
                                   City = "San Francisco", State = "CA" }
                        @collect DataFrame
                 end
```

The output is as follows:

```
11964×7 DataFrame
 Row  Name                          Zip     Group      Latitude  Longitude  City           State
      Union{Missing, String}        Int64m  String     Float64m  Float64m   String         String

 1    Zaalouk Market & Deli Grocery 94109   Cluster 2  37.7877   -122.42    San Francisco  CA
 2    1-11 Lilac St Apts            94110   Cluster 9  37.7519   -122.418   San Francisco  CA
 3    Sunflower Restaurant          94103   Cluster 5  37.7649   -122.422   San Francisco  CA
 4    Bay Music & Entertainment Inc 94109   Cluster 4  37.7957   -122.423   San Francisco  CA
 5    Impark 0376                   94109   Cluster 8  37.7891   -122.417   San Francisco  CA
 6    Geologica Inc                 94103   Cluster 6  37.7875   -122.403   San Francisco  CA
 7    Impark 0315                   94109   Cluster 2  37.7894   -122.422   San Francisco  CA
 8    Impark 0324                   94103   Cluster 6  37.7867   -122.405   San Francisco  CA
 9    Impark 0370                   94103   Cluster 6  37.7818   -122.405   San Francisco  CA
 10   Impark 0377                   94103   Cluster 6  37.787    -122.403   San Francisco  CA
```

The structured data is available in a new `DataFrame` called `export_data`. Unfortunately, BatchGeo has added a 250-row limit for free accounts, so we'll have to limit our export to just the top 250 rows.

Here's how we can export it:

```julia
julia> CSV.write("businesses.csv", head(export_data, 250))
```

Success! The only thing left to do is to open `https://batchgeo.com` in your favorite web browser and drag and drop the `business.csv` file to the designated place:

1. This is done by performing the steps, as shown in the following screenshot:

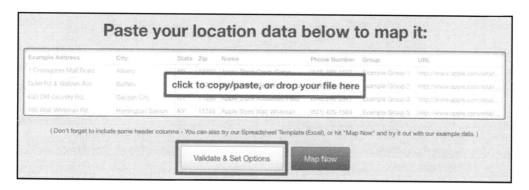

2. Click **Validate & Set Options**. You'll see that the columns were picked correctly and the defaults are good:

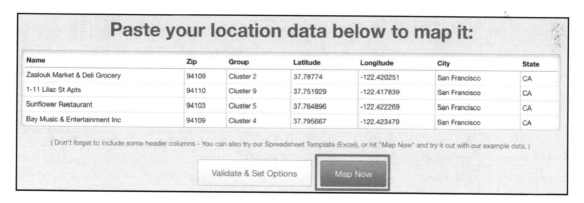

3. Clicking on **Make Map** will render our clusters on top of the map of San Francisco:

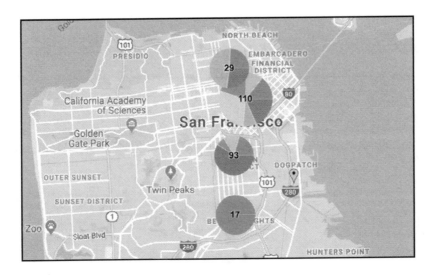

Victory—a beautiful rendering of our data!

We can also disable the clustering so that each individual business will be plotted:

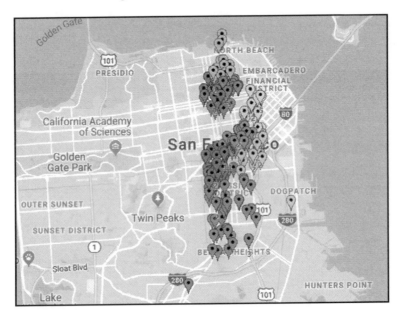

Finally, we can save our map, follow the instructions, and get a unique URL for our visualization. Mine can be found at `https://batchgeo.com/map/7475bf3c362eb66f37ab8ddbbb718b87` .

Excellent, just in time for the meeting with our client!

Choosing the optimal number of clusters for k-means (and other algorithms)

Depending on the nature of the data and the problem you'll be looking to solve, the number of clusters can come as a business requirement, or it may be an obvious choice (as in our case, where we wanted to identify low, middle, and high business density zones and so ended up with three clusters). However, in some cases, the answer might not be that obvious. In such situations, we'll need to apply a different algorithm to evaluate the optimal number of clusters.

One of the most common is the Elbow method. It is an iterative approach where we run the clustering algorithm with different values for k, for example between 1 and 10. The goal is to compare the total intra-cluster variation by plotting the sum of squared errors between each point and the mean of its cluster as a function of k. Using the visualization, we identify the *elbow-like* point of inflection, like this:

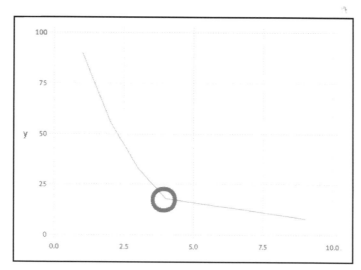

This is the elbow.

You can read more about this at `http://www.sthda.com/english/`
`articles/29-cluster-validation-essentials/96-determining-the-`
`optimal-number-of-clusters-3-must-know-methods/` (with examples in
R).

Clustering validation

Besides picking the optimum number of clusters, another aspect is cluster validation, that
is, to determine how well the items fit the assigned clusters. This can be used to confirm
that patterns do indeed exist and to compare competing clustering algorithms.

Clustering provides a small API for clustering validation with three techniques, including
Silhouettes, one of the most common. You can find the documentation at `http://`
`clusteringjl.readthedocs.io/en/latest/validate.html` and you can read more about
validation theory at `http://www.sthda.com/english/articles/29-cluster-validation-`
`essentials/97-cluster-validation-statistics-must-know-methods/`.

Summary

In this chapter, we looked into unsupervised machine learning techniques with Julia. We
focused on clustering, one of the most widely used applications of unsupervised learning.
Starting with a dataset about businesses registered in San Francisco, we performed
complex—but not complicated, thanks to Query—data cleansing. In the process, we also
learned about metaprogramming, a very powerful coding technique and one of Julia's most
powerful and defining features.

Once our data was in top shape and after mastering the basics of clustering theory, using
the k-means algorithm, we got down to business. We performed clustering to identify the
areas with the highest density of companies to help our imaginary customer, ACME
Recruiting, to target the best areas for advertising. After identifying the parts of the city that
would give ACME the best reach, we performed data analysis to get the top domains of
activity required by our customer so they could build a database of relevant candidates.

Finally, we performed clustering on the geolocation data of the businesses in the targeted areas and then we rendered these on top of a map. Our client was thrilled with our findings and their marketers now having all the necessary information to start planning their campaigns. Congratulations!

In the next chapter, we'll leave the fascinating world of machine learning in order to discover yet another key concept in data science—time series. We'll learn how to handle dates and time in Julia, how to work with time series data, and how to make forecasts. Exciting, isn't it?

9
Working with Dates, Times, and Time Series

We've had quite an amazing and rewarding journey through the realm of machine learning. We have learned how to use algorithms to classify labeled data and apply our findings to make recommendations. We have seen how to extract business value from raw, unlabeled information by using unsupervised machine learning and clustering algorithms. However, one key component has been missing from our analysis so far—the temporal dimension.

Time is money, the saying goes—and as such, organisations of all sizes, from small businesses to large corporations, to governments, to complex multinational institutions such as the European Union, continuously measure and monitor a multitude of economic indicators over time. To be meaningful, the data is collected at regular intervals, allowing analysts to identify hidden structures and patterns, and predict future developments based on past and present conditions. These values, measured regularly on a time scale, represent a time series. Time series analysis and forecasting can provide extremely valuable insight, allowing market actors to understand trends and make informed decisions based on accurate historical data.

We will dedicate two chapters, this one and the next one, to learning about time series and performing analysis and forecasting. In this chapter, we'll lay the foundations by learning about:

- Working with dates and times in Julia
- Handling time zone information
- Processing time series data with `TimeSeries`
- Plotting time series data with the powerful `Plots` package
- The `TimeArray` data structure

Technical requirements

The Julia package ecosystem is under continuous development and new package versions are released on a daily basis. Most of the times this is great news, as new releases bring new features and bug fixes. However, since many of the packages are still in beta (version 0.x), any new release can introduce breaking changes. As a result, the code presented in the book can stop working. In order to ensure that your code will produce the same results as described in the book, it is recommended to use the same package versions. Here are the external packages used in this chapter and their specific versions:

```
IJulia@v1.14.1
MarketData@v0.11.0
Plots@v0.22.0
TimeZones@v0.8.2
```

In order to install a specific version of a package you need to run:

```
pkg> add PackageName@vX.Y.Z
```

For example:

```
pkg> add IJulia@v1.14.1
```

Alternatively you can install all the used packages by downloading the `Project.toml` file provided with the chapter and using `pkg>` instantiate as follows:

```
julia>
download("https://raw.githubusercontent.com/PacktPublishing/Julia-Programmi
ng-Projects/master/Chapter09/Project.toml", "Project.toml")
pkg> activate .
pkg> instantiate
```

Working with dates and times

Julia provides a very rich API for handling date and time information. All the functionality is packed into the `Dates` module. The module is built in to the language so there's no need for additional package installs. In order to access its functionality, all we have to do is declare that we'll be `using Dates`.

The dates module exposes three main types—`Date`, `DateTime`, and `Time`. They are all subtypes of the abstract `TimeType` type and represent day, millisecond, and nanosecond precision, respectively.

Julia tries to make working with dates and times as simple as possible. This is the reason why, on the one hand, it provides three distinct types, each with its own temporal representation:

- A `Date` object maps to a date—a time entity defined by a day, a month, and a year
- An instance of `Time` is a moment in time—the hour, the minute, the second, and the milliseconds, but with absolutely no information about the date itself
- The `DateTime`, as you may have guessed from the name, is an object which puts together a `Date` and a `Time`, specifying an exact moment in time

On the other hand, all these types have, by default and by design, a naive approach to representing dates and times—that is, they do not take into consideration things like time zones, daylight savings, or leap seconds. It's a portrayal of your computer's local date and time, without any extra information.

Constructing dates and times

In order to construct new date/time objects representing the current date or time, Julia provides two helper functions, `now` and `today`. Let's look at some examples in the **read-eval-print loop (REPL)**:

```
julia> using Dates

julia> d = today()
2018-11-08

julia> typeof(d)
Date

julia> dt = now()
2018-11-08T16:33:34.868

julia> dt |> typeof
DateTime

julia> t = Dates.Time(now())
16:34:13.065

julia> typeof(t)
Time
```

The `now` function can also accept an additional argument to return the UTC time (without local adjustments for daylight savings):

```julia
julia> now(UTC)
2018-11-08T15:35:08.776
```

Internally, all the types wrap an `Int64` value that can be accessed through the `instant` field:

```julia
julia> dt.instant
Dates.UTInstant{Millisecond}(63677378014868 milliseconds)

julia> t.instant
75147529000000 nanoseconds

julia> d.instant
Dates.UTInstant{Day}(737006 days)
```

The `instant` property of the objects reflects the precision level of each type.

Of course, we can also instantiate objects that represent any random moment in time using the dedicated constructors:

```julia
julia> DateTime(2018) # we can pass just the year as a single argument
2018-01-01T00:00:00

julia> DateTime(2018, 6) # passing the year and the month
2018-06-01T00:00:00

julia> DateTime(2018, 6, 15) # year, month and day
2018-06-15T00:00:00

julia> DateTime(2018, 6, 15, 10) # year, month, day and hour (10 AM)
2018-06-15T10:00:00

julia> DateTime(2018, 6, 15, 10, 30) # 15th of June 2018, 10:30 AM
2018-06-15T10:30:00

julia> DateTime(2018, 6, 15, 10, 30, 45) # ...and 45 seconds
2018-06-15T10:30:45

julia> DateTime(2018, 06, 15, 10, 30, 45, 123) # ... and finally,
milliseconds
2018-06-15T10:30:45.123
```

The constructors work in similar ways for `Date` and `Time`—here are a few examples:

```
julia> Date(2019) # January 1st 2019
2019-01-01

julia> Date(2018, 12, 31) # December 31st 2018
2018-12-31

julia> Time(22, 05) # 5 past 10 PM
22:05:00

julia> Time(22, 05, 25, 456) # 5 past 10 PM, 25s and 456 milliseconds
22:05:25.456
```

The constructors will prevent us from passing the wrong values, resulting in an error. This can be different from other languages that automatically perform date-time arithmetic where, for instance, December 22, 2018 would be automatically converted into January 1, 2019. That won't happen in Julia:

```
julia> Date(2018, 12, 32)
ERROR: ArgumentError: Day: 32 out of range (1:31)
Stacktrace:
 [1] Date(::Int64, ::Int64, ::Int64) at ./dates/types.jl:204
```

There are also constructors for the individual date and time components—years, months, days, hours, minutes, seconds, and milliseconds. They return instances of the corresponding `Period` type (we'll take a look at periods in detail a bit later). Periods can be used to create date/time objects:

```
julia> eleven_hours = Hour(11)
11 hours

julia> half_hour = Minute(30)
30 minutes

julia> brunch_time = Time(eleven_hours, half_hour)
11:30:00

julia> this_year = "2018"
julia> xmas_month = "12"
julia> xmas_day = "25"
julia> Date(Year(this_year), Month(xmas_month), Day(xmas_day))
2018-12-25
```

Parsing strings into dates and times

A common requirement is parsing properly formatted strings coming from an external input (databases, files, user input, and so on) into corresponding date and time objects:

```
julia> Date("25/12/2019", "dd/mm/yyyy") # Christmas day in 2019
2019-12-25

julia> DateTime("25/12/2019 14,30", "dd/mm/yyyy HH,MM") # xmas day in 2019,
at 2:30 PM
2019-12-25T14:30:00
```

These are the special date-time characters recognised by Julia, together with their significations:

- y: Year digit, example yyyy for 2015, yy for 15
- m: Month digit, example m => 3 or 03
- u: Short month name, example Jan
- U: long month name, example January
- e: Short day of week, example Tue
- E: Long day of week, example Tuesday
- d: Day, example 3 or 03
- H: Hour digit, example HH = 00
- M: Minute digit, example MM = 00
- S: Second digit, example s = 00
- s: Millisecond digit, example .000

With these, we can parse any date/time string into the correct object:

```
julia> DateTime("Thursday, 1 of February 2018 at 12.35", "E, d of U yyyy at
HH.MM")
2018-02-01T12:35:00
```

We can also parse multiple strings at once, as elements of an array. First, we create an array of strings that represents valid dates, formatted as yyyy-mm-dd. We use a comprehension to create the array and name it d:

```
julia> d = ["$(rand(2000:2020))-$(rand(1:12))-$(rand(1:28))" for _ in
1:100]
100-element Array{String,1}:
 "2001-7-1"
 "2005-9-4"
```

```
  "2018-3-3"
# output truncated
```

Next, we can use dot notation to process the array element-wise using the `Date` constructor:

```
julia> Date.(d, "yyyy-mm-dd")
100-element Array{Date,1}:
 2001-07-01
 2005-09-04
 2018-03-03
# output truncated
```

Alternatively, instead of using a string to represent the format of the date, we can use a specialized `DateFormat` type:

```
julia> date_format = DateFormat("yyyy-mm-dd")
dateformat"yyyy-mm-dd"

julia> Date.(d, date_format)
100-element Array{Date,1}:
2001-07-01
2005-09-04
2018-03-03
# output truncated
```

Using a `DateFormat` is recommended when parsing a large number of strings for better performance. Julia provides a few formats as part of the standard library, for instance, `ISODateTimeFormat` and `RFC1123Format`:

```
julia> DateTime("2018-12-25", ISODateTimeFormat)
2018-12-25T00:00:00
```

Formatting dates

If we can parse date-formatted strings into date/time objects, we can also do the reverse. We can output our dates and times as strings using various formats. See the following, for instance:

```
julia> Dates.format(now(), RFC1123Format)
"Thu, 08 Nov 2018 20:04:35"
```

Defining other locales

By default, Julia will use the `english` locale, meaning that the names of the days and months will be in English. However, we can internationalize our dates by defining additional locales:

```julia
julia> spanish_months = ["enero", "febrero", "marzo", "abril", "mayo",
"junio", "julio", "agosto", "septiembre", "octubre", "noviembre",
"diciembre"]
12-element Array{String,1} # output truncated

julia> spanish_days = ["lunes", "martes", "miércoles", "jueves", "viernes",
"sábado", "domingo"]
7-element Array{String,1} # output truncated

julia> Dates.LOCALES["es"] = Dates.DateLocale(spanish_months, String[],
spanish_days, String[])
Dates.DateLocale # output truncated
```

The `Dates.DateLocale` function expects four arrays, corresponding to each of the month names, abbreviated month names, day names, and abbreviated day names. As you can see, we haven't provided the abbreviated versions of the names. As long as we don't try to use them, we'll be fine:

```julia
julia> Dates.format(now(), "E, d U yyyy", locale = "es")
"jueves, 8 noviembre 2018"
```

However, attempting to use the abbreviated day name will result in an error:

```julia
julia> Dates.format(now(), "e, d U yyyy", locale = "es")
ERROR: BoundsError: attempt to access 0-element Array{String,1} at index
[4]
```

Working with date and time accessors

If we want to access the individual parts of a date (year, month, day), we can retrieve the various components through the available accessor functions:

```julia
julia> earth_day = Date(2018, 4, 22)
2018-04-22

julia>year(earth_day) # the year
2018

julia> month(earth_day) # the month
```

4

The API also exposes compound methods, for brevity:

```
julia> monthday(earth_day) # month and day
(4, 22)

julia> yearmonthday(earth_day) # year month and day
(2018, 4, 22)
```

Similar accessors are available for `DateTime`—but no compound methods are provided:

```
julia> earth_hour = DateTime(2018, 4, 22, 22, 00)
2018-04-22T22:00:00

julia> hour(earth_hour) # the hour
22

julia> minute(earth_hour) # the minute
0
```

Alternative accessors that return `Period` objects are also defined—they have uppercase names:

```
julia> Hour(earth_hour) # a period of 22 hours
22 hours

julia> Month(earth_hour) # a period of 4 months
4 months

julia> Month(earth_hour) |> typeof |> supertype
 DatePeriod

julia> supertype(DatePeriod)
Period
```

Querying dates

Once we have a date object, we can get a wealth of extra information about it, such as the day of the week, leap year, day of the year, and so on. We can use the `Dates` API to extract this kind of information about our date/time object.

Consider this:

```
julia> yoga_day = Date(2019, 6, 21) # Really, the International Yoga Day
does exist!
2019-06-21
```

Are you curious when Yoga day falls in 2019? Let's use our Julia skills to figure that out:

```
julia> dayname(yoga_day)
"Friday"
```

If you need the numerical value of the day (within the week), there's also `dayofweek(yoga_day)`, that obviously returns 5, since Friday is the fifth day of the week.

Of course, we can use localized names here too:

```
julia> dayname(yoga_day, locale="es")
"viernes"
```

Another useful function we can call is `dayofweekofmonth(yoga_day)`, which will tell us which Friday of the month it is—it's the third Friday of the month of June, in 2019.

If you're not sure how this can be useful, take for example, events that always take place with regularity on a certain day of the month. A good example is a meetup I attend that always takes place on the third Thursday of each month.

We can also get a wealth of information about the month and the year:

```
julia> monthname(yoga_day, locale="es") # June, with the Spanish locale
"junio"

julia> isleapyear(yoga_day) # 2019 is not a leap year
false

julia> dayofyear(yoga_day) # It's the 172nd day of 2019
172

julia> quarterofyear(yoga_day) # 2nd quarter of 2019
2
```

The Dates API is very rich, including a lot more methods than it would make sense to present here. Please visit the documentation page at https://docs.julialang.org/en/v1/stdlib/Dates/index.html#stdlib-dates-api-1.

Defining the date ranges

Julia allows us to define ranges of dates to express continuous periods of time. For example, we could represent the whole year as the range of days between January 1 and December 31:

```
julia> year_2019 = Date(2019, 1, 1):Day(1):Date(2019,12,31)
2019-01-01:1 day:2019-12-31
```

We have created a date range with a step of one day—so `365` items, since 2019 is not a leap year:

```
julia> typeof(year_2019)
StepRange{Date,Day}

julia> size(year_2019)
(365,)
```

We can instantiate the actual `Date` objects using the aptly named `collect` function:

```
julia> collect(year_2019)
365-element Array{Date,1}:
 2019-01-01
 2019-01-02
 2019-01-03
# output truncated
```

Also, of course, we can access the elements by index as follows:

```
julia> year_2019[100] # day 100
2019-04-10
```

It's also possible to define ranges with other steps, such as monthly intervals:

```
julia> year_2019 = Date(2019, 1, 1):Month(1):Date(2019,12,31)
2019-01-01:1 month:2019-12-01

julia> collect(year_2019) # First day of each of the 12 months
12-element Array{Date,1}:
 2019-01-01
 2019-02-01
 2019-03-01
# output truncated
```

We can pass any `Period` object for the step, for instance:

```
julia> year_2019 = Date(2019, 1, 1):Month(3):Date(2019,12,31) # Quarterly
2019-01-01:3 months:2019-10-01

julia> collect(year_2019) # The first of each of the 4 quarters
4-element Array{Date,1}:
 2019-01-01
 2019-04-01
 2019-07-01
 2019-10-01

julia> year_2019 = Date(2019, 1, 1):Week(2):Date(2019,12,31) # Bi weekly
2019-01-01:2 weeks:2019-12-31

julia> collect(year_2019)
27-element Array{Date,1}:
 2019-01-01
 2019-01-15
 2019-01-29
# output truncated
```

Period types and period arithmetic

We have already seen some of the `Period` constructors. These are all the available ones—Day, Week, Month, Year, Hour, Minute, Second, Millisecond, Microsecond, and Nanosecond. The `Period` type is an abstract type with two concrete subtypes, `DatePeriod` and `TimePeriod`:

```
julia> subtypes(Period)
2-element Array{Any,1}:
 DatePeriod
 TimePeriod
```

`Period` in Julia represents a duration of time. It is a very useful abstraction representing vague time concepts that people use routinely. Think about a month—how many days does a month have—30 or 31? What about 28? Or 29?

Many times, it can be useful to work with vague abstractions without switching to actual dates until more information is provided. Take, for instance, the hypothetical case of a trip to Mars. According to https://image.gsfc.nasa.gov/poetry/venus/q2811.html, a return trip to Mars will take 21 months—9 to get there, 3 to stay there, and 9 more to get back:

```julia
julia> duration_of_trip_to_mars = Month(9) * 2 + Month(3)
21 months
```

Exactly how long these 21 months will take is undetermined until we actually decide when we start the trip:

```julia
julia> take_off_day = Date(2020, 1, 15)
2020-01-15
```

Now we can compute how long the astronauts will be gone for:

```julia
julia> return_day = take_off_day + duration_of_trip_to_mars
2021-10-15

julia> time_diff = return_day - take_off_day
639 days
```

However, if, for technical reasons, the launch date will be postponed by five months, the result will be different:

```julia
julia> take_off_day += Month(5)
2020-06-15

julia> return_day = take_off_day + duration_of_trip_to_mars
2022-03-15

julia> time_diff = return_day - take_off_day
638 days
```

It is important to keep in mind that unlike other programming languages, which make assumptions about the default length of a month—such as 31 days in JavaScript or 30 days in PHP—Julia takes a different approach. For a detailed explanation of `Period` arithmetic, you can read the official documentation at https://docs.julialang.org/en/v1/stdlib/Dates/index.html#TimeType-Period-Arithmetic-1.

A period doesn't necessarily need to be a complete amount of time. Julia allows us to express irregular intervals like 1 month and 2 weeks. However, an irregular amount of time (which combines different types of periods) will be internally represented by a different type—not the `Period`, but the `CompoundPeriod`. Here's how this works:

```julia
julia> isa(Month(3), Period)
true

julia> isa(Month(3) + Month(1), Period)
true

julia> isa(Month(1) + Week(2), Period)
false

julia> isa(Month(1) + Week(2), Dates.CompoundPeriod)
true
```

Date adjustments

`Period` arithmetic is very powerful, but sometimes we need to express more flexible rules that are dependent on other dates. I'm thinking about *last day of the next month*, *next Tuesday*, or *the third Monday of each month*.

For such cases, the `Dates` module exposes the adjuster API. For starters, we have the `firstdayof*` and the `lastdayof*` family of functions—`firstdayofweek`, `firstdayofmonth`, `firstdayofquarter`, and `firstdayofyear`; plus `lastdayofweek`, `lastdayofmonth`, `lastdayofquarter`, and `lastdayofyear`, respectively. They take as input a date/time object and *adjust* it to the indicated point in time:

```julia
julia> firstdayofweek(Date(2019, 1, 31))
2019-01-28
```

In 2019, the first day of the week includes January 31 is Monday, 28.

The `lastdayof*` family of functions works in a similar manner. But useful as they are, they don't provide enough flexibility. Luckily, we're covered. If we need other dates apart from the first or the last day, we have to reach for the `tonext` and `toprev` pair of functions. They come in two flavors. The first method takes a subtype of `TimeType` (that is, any `Time`, `Date`, `DateTime`) and a day of the week:

```julia
julia> tonext(Date(2019, 4, 1), Saturday)
2019-04-06
```

The next Saturday after April Fool's Day falls on April 7 2019.

The other method of `tonext` is even more powerful—it accepts a similar `TimeType` and a function. It will adjust the date until the function returns `true`. To understand how useful this is, let's get back to our previous meetup example, the meeting I attend every third Thursday of each month. To find out when the next meeting will take place, all I have to do is ask Julia:

```julia
julia> tonext(today()) do d  # today is Thu 8th of November, 2019
           dayofweek(d) == Thursday && dayofweekofmonth(d) == 3
       end
2018-11-15
```

The `toprev` function works in a similar way.

Another function, `filter`, allows us to obtain all the matching dates as an `Iterator`. Following up on our meetups schedule, let's try to find out the dates of all the meetings in 2019. But we must also take into account that in the second half of May, the organizer will attend a business trip, and that August is a holiday month. So, there won't be meetings during these intervals. How would we express this? It turns out that with Julia, it's quite simple (and very readable):

```julia
julia> filter(Date(2019):Day(1):Date(2020)) do d
           ! in(d, Date(2019, 5, 15):Day(1):Date(2019, 5, 31)) &&
           month(d) != August &&
           dayofweek(d) == Thursday &&
           dayofweekofmonth(d) == 3
    end |> collect
10-element Array{Date,1}:
 2019-01-17
 2019-02-21
 2019-03-21
 2019-04-18
 2019-06-20
 2019-07-18
 2019-09-19
 2019-10-17
 2019-11-21
 2019-12-19
```

Rounding of dates

There might be situations where we have a date/time and a need to compute the previous, or next complete time interval, for example, the next hour, or the previous day. The `Dates` API exposes a few methods for rounding `Date` and `DateTime` objects—`floor`, `ceil`, and `time`. They are quite intuitive and very powerful:

```
julia> now()
2018-11-08T21:13:20.605

# round down to the nearest hour
julia> floor(now(), Hour)
2018-11-08T21:00:00

# or to the nearest 30 minutes increment
julia> floor(now(), Minute(30))
2018-11-08T21:00:00

# it also works with dates
julia> floor(today(), Month) # today() is the 8th of Nov 2018
2018-11-01
```

The `ceil` function works similarly, but instead of rounding down, it rounds up. As for the `round` function, it will round up or down, depending on whichever is the closest value:

```
julia> round(today(), Month)
2018-11-01 # today is the 11th so beginning of month is closer

julia> round(today() + Day(10), Month)
2018-12-01 # end of month is closer
```

 Rounding can behave unexpectedly in a few edge cases—for more details please check the official documentation at `https://docs.julialang.org/en/v1/stdlib/Dates/index.html#Rounding-1`.

Adding support for time zones

As previously mentioned, by default, Julia's date/time objects operate in local time, completely ignoring time zones. However, we can easily extend them to become time-zone aware using the `TimeZones` package. Please install it in the usual way:

```
julia> using Pkg
pkg> add TimeZones
```

Once we inform the compiler that we'll be using `TimeZones`, a wealth of timezone-related functionalities become available at our fingertips.

We can start by exploring the available time zones:

```
julia> timezone_names()
439-element Array{AbstractString,1}:
 "Africa/Abidjan"
 "Africa/Accra"
# output truncated
```

Let's create a time zone object for `Amsterdam`:

```
julia> amstz = TimeZone("Europe/Amsterdam")
Europe/Amsterdam (UTC+1/UTC+2)
```

In Julia, a `TimeZone` is an abstract type that represents information regarding a specific time zone, which means that it can't be instantiated—we can't create objects of this type. Instead, one of its two subtypes will be automatically used—`VariableTimeZone` or `FixedTimeZone`. `VariableTimeZone` represents a time zone whose offset changes depending on the time of the year—to take into account summertime/daylight savings time. `FixedTimeZone` has an invariable offset.

The `Europe/Amsterdam (UTC+1/UTC+2)` is such a `VariableTimeZone`. This is indicated by the information within the round brackets, signaling the two offsets of this time zone. Checking the type will confirm it:

```
julia> typeof(amstz)
TimeZones.VariableTimeZone
```

The time zones that don't change their offsets are instances of `FixedTimeZone`. Such examples are `UTC` and `GMT`:

```
julia> typeof(TimeZone("GMT"))
TimeZones.FixedTimeZone
```

The `TimeZones` package also provides a special string literal, `tz"..."`. It exposes the same functionality as `TimeZone(...)` with a bit less typing:

```
julia> tz"Europe/Bucharest"
Europe/Bucharest (UTC+2/UTC+3)
```

Armed with this knowledge, we can now create time zone-aware date/time values. These come in the form of `ZonedDateTime` objects, and, as the name suggests, represent a mixture of `DateTime` and `TimeZone`:

```
# 8 PM, Christmas Day in Vienna, 2018
julia> ZonedDateTime(DateTime(2018, 12, 25, 20), tz"Europe/Vienna")
2018-12-25T20:00:00+01:00
```

This can be written a bit more succinctly by skipping the explicit invocation of `DateTime`:

```
julia> ZonedDateTime(2018, 12, 25, 20, tz"Europe/Vienna")
2018-12-25T20:00:00+01:00
```

The `TimeZones` module also provides a series of utility methods. First of all, we can retrieve the local time zone by using the aptly named `localzone`:

```
julia> localzone()
Europe/Madrid (UTC+1/UTC+2)
```

I live in Barcelona, so this is my current time zone—your output will correspond to your actual time zone.

Two extension methods are provided for `now` and `today`—in the form of `now(::TimeZone)` and `today(::TimeZone)`, respectively:

```
julia> now()
2018-11-08T22:32:59.336

julia> now(tz"Europe/Moscow")
2018-11-09T00:33:23.138+03:00

julia> today()
2018-11-08

julia> today(tz"Europe/Moscow")
2018-11-09
```

Instead of `today(::TimeZone)`, another function, `todayat`, can be used with two arguments—the time of the day as a `Time` object and a `TimeZone`:

```
julia> todayat(Time(22, 30), tz"Europe/Moscow")
2018-11-09T22:30:00+03:00
```

This time we get 10:30 P.M., `Moscow` time.

Converting time zones

One of the most basic things we'll want to do is to convert a `DateTime` from one time zone to another. That's straightforward with the `astimezone` function:

```
julia> xmas_day = ZonedDateTime(2018, 12, 25, 20, tz"Europe/Vienna")
2018-12-25T20:00:00+01:00

julia> astimezone(xmas_day, tz"Australia/Sydney")
2018-12-26T06:00:00+11:00
```

While you're celebrating Christmas in Vienna at 8 P.M., in Sydney, Australia, it will already be 6 A.M. the next day.

Parsing date strings

We have already seen how to parse date and date/time strings using Julia's `Dates` API. The `TimeZones` package takes this functionality one step further, allowing us to parse date/time strings that include time zones:

```
julia> ZonedDateTime("2018-12-25T20:00:00+01:00", "yyyy-mm-
ddTHH:MM:SSzzzz")
2018-12-25T20:00:00+01:00
```

ZonedDateTime period arithmetic

You will be happy to hear that arithmetic with time zone-aware objects works just like its regular `TimeType` counterpart. However, you have to take extra care when dealing with periods of time that start in an offset (as in wintertime) and finish in another offset (say, summertime). For instance, let's see what happens when we play with times around the moment when Europe switches to daylight savings time.

The clock changes during the last Sunday of March. Take a minute and try to find out the date of the last Sunday of March in 2019.

Here's my solution:

```
julia> last_day_of_winter = tonext(today()) do d
           dayofweek(d) == Sunday &&
           month(d) == March &&
           dayofmonth(d) > dayofmonth(lastdayofmonth(d) - Day(7))
       end
2019-03-31
```

Now, let's give it a time zone—let's say, London's:

```
london_time = ZonedDateTime(DateTime(last_day_of_winter),
tz"Europe/London")
2019-03-31T00:00:00+00:00
```

Adding a day to this will cause the time zone to change:

```
julia> next_day = london_time + Day(1)
2019-04-01T00:00:00+01:00
```

But what if we now remove the equivalent of one day, but in hours? We should get the value of london_time again, right? Take a look:

```
julia> next_day - Hour(24)
2019-03-30T23:00:00+00:00
```

Oops, not quite! Subtracting 24 hours actually pushed us one hour earlier than london_time. The reason for this is that the change of offset (switching to summertime) effectively caused a whole hour at 2 A.M. to be skipped on the 25th, making that day only 23 hours long.

Time zone-aware date ranges

Another important thing to keep in mind when dealing with time zones involves date ranges. If the start item of your range is in a time zone, but the end item is in a different time zone, the resulting value corresponding to the end item will be silently converted to the time zone of the start item. An example will make this clear:

```
julia> interval = ZonedDateTime(2019, 8, 1,
tz"Europe/London"):Hour(1):ZonedDateTime(2019, 8, 2, tz"Australia/Sydney")
2019-08-01T00:00:00+01:00:1 hour:2019-08-02T00:00:00+10:00

julia> collect(interval)
16-element Array{TimeZones.ZonedDateTime,1}:
2019-08-01T00:00:00+01:00
# output truncated
2019-08-01T15:00:00+01:00
```

The last item in the array, `2018-08-01T15:00:00+01:00`, represents the same time as the end item in the interval, `2018-08-02T00:00:00+10:00`—but it's using the London time zone, not Sydney's:

```
julia> astimezone(ZonedDateTime("2019-08-01T00:00:00+01:00", "yyyy-mm-
ddTHH:MM:SSzzzz"), tz"Australia/Sydney" )
2019-08-01T09:00:00+10:00
```

It's the same time, but a different time zone.

Time series data in Julia

A time series is a collection of observations of well-defined data items obtained via repeated measurements over time. This collection of quantitative observations is ordered, allowing us to understand the underlying structure. Examples of such data include the daily closing price of a company's stock, quarterly sales figures for a retailer, continuous monitoring of a person's blood glucose levels, or hourly air temperatures.

Julia's package ecosystem provides a powerful functionality for working with time series through the `TimeSeries` package. The package provides an extensive API that covers the full range of tasks, from reading and writing CSV files with temporal data, to filtering and segmenting time series, to mathematical and logical operators, and plotting. Let's add it to our toolbox:

```
julia> using Pkg
pkg> add TimeSeries
```

Now, let's get some time series data. The easiest thing we can do is to reach for the `MarketData` package, it provides open source financial data for research and testing and works flawlessly with `TimeSeries`. Once you install it in the usual way (`pkg> add MarketData`), the module will expose a series of variables corresponding to different datasets. Some of them are small test databases, called `cl`, `ohcl`, `ohlcv`, and so on. For example, the `ohcl` dataset contains 500 rows of market data, from January 3, 2000 to December 31, 2001—each row contains a `Date`, plus the `Open`, `High`, `Low`, and `Close` values. Here's what it looks like:

```
julia> using MarketData
julia> MarketData.ohlc
500x4 TimeSeries.TimeArray{Float64,2,Date,Array{Float64,2}} 2000-01-03 to
2001-12-31
```

You can see that it's of the type `TimeArray` and it spans the time interval I just mentioned:

```
500×4 TimeArray{Float64,2,Date,Array{Float64,2}} 2000-01-03 to 2001-12-31
            Open    High    Low     Close
2000-01-03  104.88  112.5   101.69  111.94
2000-01-04  108.25  110.62  101.19  102.5
2000-01-05  103.75  110.56  103.0   104.0
2000-01-06  106.12  107.0   95.0    95.0
2000-01-07  96.5    101.0   95.5    99.5
2000-01-10  102.0   102.25  94.75   97.75
2000-01-11  95.94   99.38   90.5    92.75
2000-01-12  95.0    95.5    86.5    87.19
```

The `MarketData` module also exposes larger historical prices and volume data for three major companies—Apple (`AAPL`), Boeing (`BA`), and Caterpillar (`CAT`).

A quick look at our data with Plots and PyPlot

As the old saying goes, A *picture is worth a thousand words*, so let's get a quick feel for our data by plotting it. It's a great opportunity to introduce one of the best Julia data visualization packages—`Plots`. Unlike `Gadfly`, which we've previously used, `Plots` takes a different approach—it's an interface over many different plotting libraries. Basically, it's like middleware, providing a common, unifying API for other plotting packages (called **backends**). In Julia, different plotting packages have different features and strengths—and depending on the user's specific needs, they may be forced to learn yet another library, change the code, and so on, in order to interchangeably use different plotting packages. `Plots` addresses this problem through a unifying API coupled with a simple mechanism that allows for swapping backends on the fly.

The `Plots` package supports the following backends—`PyPlot`, `Plotly` or `PlotlyJS`, `GR`, `UnicodePlots`, `PGFPlots`, `InspectDR`, and `HDFS5`. Which one should you use? It depends on the actual use case, but as a general rule, in the words of `Plots` author—*GR for speed, Plotly(JS) for interactivity, PyPlot otherwise.*

 Please read the official documentation at `http://docs.juliaplots.org/latest/backends/` to understand the pros and cons of each backend.

We'll use `PyPlot`, a Julia wrapper for the popular Python package with the same name. Let's install both `Plots` and `PyPlot`. Running `pkg> add Plots` should be straightforward. Next, `pkg> add PyPlot` will be more involved. As `PyPlot` uses `PyCall.jl` to invoke Python code, depending on your current Julia installation, `Pkg` might also have to install the `miniconda` Python distribution. So it might take a few minutes.

To start using `Plots` with `PyPlot`, please make sure you run the following:

```
julia> using Plots
julia> pyplot()
Plots.PyPlotBackend()
```

The `pyplot` function configures the `PyPlot` backend to be used by `Plots`.

> Right after installing `PyPlot`, when attempting to run `pyplot()`, you might get an error. Please follow the instructions provided by the package and restart the Julia REPL if so advised.

We're now ready to go! The module exposes the `plot` function, which at its simplest can be invoked with two collections of values, corresponding to the x and y coordinates:

```
julia> plot(1:10, rand(10))
```

You should see a plot being rendered in a new window—mine looks like this, but since we're visualising random values, yours will be different:

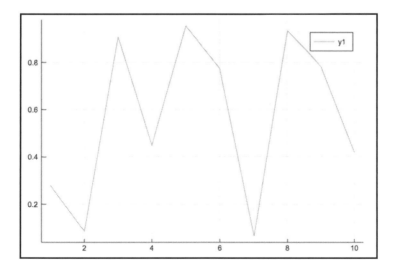

It's a plot of ten random values, rendered by `PyPlot`.

One cool thing about these plots is that they can be mutated using the `plot!` function. For instance, we can add two lines to it by plotting a matrix:

```julia
julia> plot!(rand(10, 2))
```

The resulting output is as follows:

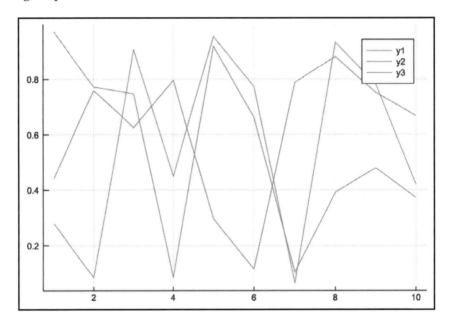

Plots can be enhanced using attributes. They allow us to add labels, titles, and to style the visualizations and so on. For instance, here's how we'd render our previous plot with extra attributes:

```julia
julia> plot(1:10, rand(10,3), title="Three Lines",label=["First" "2nd"
"Third Line"],lw=3) # lw stands for line width
```

The output is as follows:

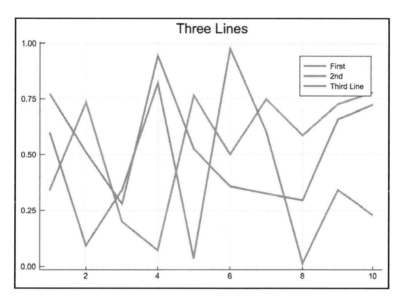

The API also exposes functions for modifying the plot after it has been rendered:

```julia
julia> xlabel!("Beautiful lines")
julia> ylabel!("Small lines")
```

The output is as follows:

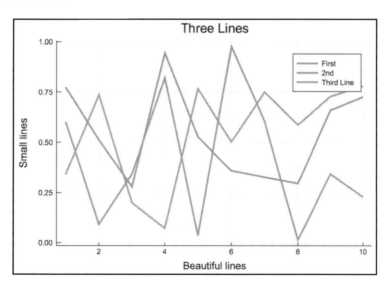

Going back to our market data, you'll be happy to hear that `TimeSeries` provides out-of-the-box integration with `Plots`. All we have to do is run the following:

```julia
julia> plot(MarketData.ohlc)
```

This is what we get:

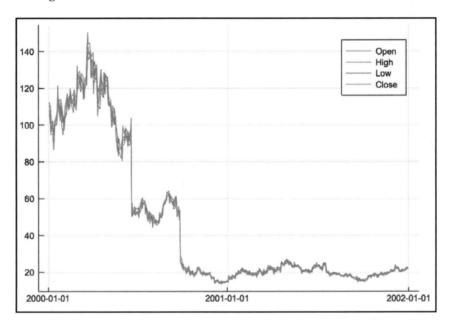

We can see that the market had been growing, reaching a peak in March 2000, then dropping suddenly to around 50–60. It stayed there for a few months, and then it dropped again at the end of September and stayed under 30 all the way through to the end of 2001. The four values, `Open`, `Close`, `High`, and `Low` seem to be highly correlated. We can plot them individually:

```julia
julia> plot(MarketData.ohlc[:High])
```

We get the following result:

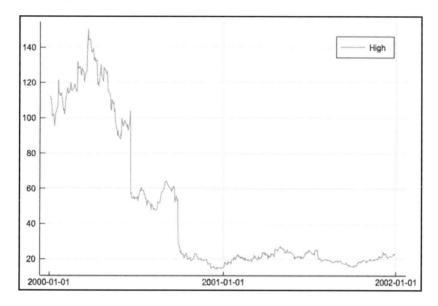

We can append extra values like this:

```julia
julia> plot!(MarketData.ohlc[:Low])
```

The output is as follows:

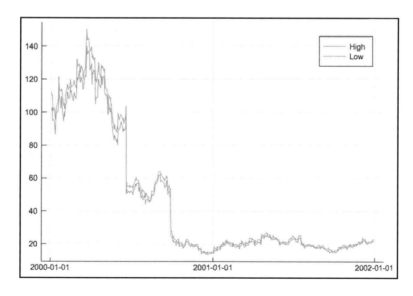

Visualizing the high versus low values, we can see higher variations in the periods before the market crash.

The TimeArray type

So what's with this `TimeArray` then, you may be wondering? It does look like an interesting beast, in that we can index into it using square brackets and the names of columns. We can use the `fieldnames` function to see what properties it exposes:

```
julia> fieldnames(typeof(MarketData.ohlc))
(:timestamp, :values, :colnames, :meta)
```

Indeed, a `TimeArray` is a composite type—a `struct`, in Julia parlance—with four fields.

The `timestamp` field represents a vector of time values—the ones that hold the temporal coordinates of our time series. So if we look at our `TimeArray` object, we'll see this in the first row:

```
julia> MarketData.ohlc |> head
6x4 TimeArray{Float64,2,Date,Array{Float64,2}} 2000-01-03 to 2000-01-10
```

It looks like this:

	Open	High	Low	Close
2000-01-03	104.88	112.5	101.69	111.94
2000-01-04	108.25	110.62	101.19	102.5
2000-01-05	103.75	110.56	103.0	104.0
2000-01-06	106.12	107.0	95.0	95.0
2000-01-07	96.5	101.0	95.5	99.5
2000-01-10	102.0	102.25	94.75	97.75

In this output, `2000-01-03` is the first value in the `timestamp` array. We can access the array using the `timestamp` getter:

```
julia> timestamp(MarketData.ohlc)
500-element Array{Date,1}:
 2000-01-03
 2000-01-04
 2000-01-05
# output truncated

julia> timestamp(MarketData.ohlc)[1]
2000-01-03
```

Depending on the actual information in the dataset, its type can be `Date` (as in our case), `Time`, or `DateTime`—any subtype of `TimeType`.

When constructing a `TimeArray`, you must be careful because the `timestamp` data has to be sorted—otherwise, the constructor will error out.

By analogy, with the `timestamp` field, you can probably guess what the `values` property is all about. It holds the numerical data of the time series:

```julia
julia> values(MarketData.ohlc)
500×4 Array{Float64,2}
```

The output is as follows:

```
500×4 Array{Float64,2}:
 104.88  112.5   101.69  111.94
 108.25  110.62  101.19  102.5
 103.75  110.56  103.0   104.0
 106.12  107.0    95.0    95.0
  96.5   101.0    95.5    99.5
```

Obviously, the row count of the `values` array must match the length of the `timestamp` collection. Less obviously, all the values inside the `values` array must be of the same type.

Thus, each row in a `TimeArray` is composed of an item from the `timestamp` collection and the corresponding row from the `values` array:

```
6×4 TimeArray{Float64,2,Date,Array{Float64,2}} 2000-01-03 to 2000-01-10
             │ Open    │ High    │ Low     │ Close
─────────────┼─────────┼─────────┼─────────┼────────
 2000-01-03  │ 104.88  │ 112.5   │ 101.69  │ 111.94
 2000-01-04  │ 108.25  │ 110.62  │ 101.19  │ 102.5
 2000-01-05  │ 103.75  │ 110.56  │ 103.0   │ 104.0
 2000-01-06  │ 106.12  │ 107.0   │ 95.0    │ 95.0
 2000-01-07  │ 96.5    │ 101.0   │ 95.5    │ 99.5
 2000-01-10  │ 102.0   │ 102.25  │ 94.75   │ 97.75
```

The `colnames` function returns the array of column names for each column in the values field. They are returned as symbols:

```julia
julia> colnames(MarketData.ohlc)
4-element Array{Symbol,1}:
 :Open
 :High
 :Low
 :Close
```

The only hard constraint here is that the number of items in the `colnames` vector must match the number of columns in the `values` collection. Due to the fact that `TimeArrays` are indexable by column name, duplicate strings in the `colnames` vector will be modified automatically by the constructor. Each subsequent duplicate name will be appended with *n*, where *n* starts from 1.

If you are not happy with the columns names, they can be changed using the `rename` method, passing in the `TimeArray` object and an array of column names as symbols:

```julia
julia> rename(MarketData.ohlc, [:Opening, :Maximum, :Minimum, :Closing])
```

Finally, the `meta` field is supposed to be used for attaching meta-information to the object. By default, it is empty and can be set by the programmer, as needed.

Indexing the TimeArray objects

The `TimeSeries` library exposes a powerful API for accessing information structured as `TimeArray` data. We have already seen that we can access individual columns by indexing by column name:

```julia
julia> MarketData.ohlc[:High]
500x1 TimeArray{Float64,1,Date,Array{Float64,1}} 2000-01-03 to 2001-12-31
```

It results in this:

	High
2000-01-03	112.5
2000-01-04	110.62
2000-01-05	110.56
2000-01-06	107.0

We can even use a combination of columns:

```julia
julia> MarketData.ohlc[:High, :Low]
```

The output is as follows:

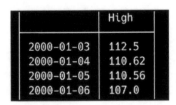

	High	Low
2000-01-03	112.5	101.69
2000-01-04	110.62	101.19
2000-01-05	110.56	103.0
2000-01-06	107.0	95.0

We can also index into the array using row IDs and dates/times (corresponding to the `timestamp` values). Let's try to pick up the row with the highest `Close` value. First, let's find it:

```julia
julia> maximum(values(MarketData.ohlc[:Close]))
144.19
```

The highest closing value was `144.19`. Please note that indexing by column name returns another instance of `TimeArray`, so to get its underlying numerical values, we need to use the `values` function.

Now we can find its corresponding index. We can quickly get an array of the indices of all the values that are equal to `144.19` by using `findall`:

```julia
julia> findall(values(MarketData.ohlc[:Close]) .== 144.19)
1-element Array{Int64,1}:
 56
```

That would be row `56`. We can use this information to index into the time series:

```julia
julia> MarketData.ohlc[56]
1×4 TimeArray{Float64,2,Date,Array{Float64,2}} 2000-03-22 to 2000-03-22
```

The output is as follows:

	Open	High	Low	Close
2000-03-22	132.78	144.38	131.56	144.19

This is March 22, 2000. If we'd like to see the rows before and after, we can do it easily:

```julia
julia> MarketData.ohlc[50:60]
11×4 TimeArray{Float64,2,Date,Array{Float64,2}} 2000-03-14 to 2000-03-28
```

This is the resulting `TimeArray`:

	Open	High	Low	Close
2000-03-14	121.22	124.25	114.0	114.25
2000-03-15	115.62	120.25	114.12	116.25
2000-03-16	117.31	122.0	114.5	121.56
2000-03-17	120.12	125.0	119.62	125.0
2000-03-20	123.5	126.25	122.38	123.0
2000-03-21	122.56	136.75	121.62	134.94
2000-03-22	132.78	144.38	131.56	144.19
2000-03-23	142.0	150.38	140.0	141.31
2000-03-24	142.44	143.94	135.5	138.69
2000-03-27	137.62	144.75	136.88	139.56
2000-03-28	137.25	142.0	137.12	139.12

If we want to check the values for the same day of the week, before and after our date, indexing by range supports a step parameter. We can use it as follows:

```
julia> MarketData.ohlc[7:7:70]
```

We filter every seventh day, starting with the seventh row, all the way to the seventieth row; that is, every `Wednesday`, as indicated by `Dates.dayname`:

```
julia> dayname(timestamp(MarketData.ohlc)[56])
"Wednesday"
```

If we want to retrieve all the Wednesdays, we can, of course, use the `end` keyword, as in `MarketData.ohlc[7:7:end]`.

Let's say we're happy with this, but we'd like to get more context on our date. So, we want all the Wednesdays plus the day before and the day after our date. We can do this too by indexing with an array of indices:

```
julia> MarketData.ohlc[[7:7:49; 54;55;56;57; 63:7:70]]
13x4 TimeArray{Float64,2,Date,Array{Float64,2}} 2000-01-11 to 2000-04-11
```

The output is as follows:

	Open	High	Low	Close
2000-01-11	95.94	99.38	90.5	92.75
2000-01-21	114.25	114.25	110.19	111.31
2000-02-01	104.0	105.0	100.0	100.25
2000-02-10	112.88	113.88	110.0	113.5
2000-02-22	110.12	116.94	106.69	113.81
2000-03-02	127.0	127.94	120.69	122.0
2000-03-13	122.12	126.5	119.5	121.31
2000-03-20	123.5	126.25	122.38	123.0
2000-03-21	122.56	136.75	121.62	134.94
2000-03-22	132.78	144.38	131.56	144.19
2000-03-23	142.0	150.38	140.0	141.31
2000-03-31	127.44	137.25	126.0	135.81
2000-04-11	123.5	124.88	118.06	119.44

Here, we pull each seventh row between 7 and 49, then the rows 54, 55, 56, and 57, and then each seventh row between 63 and 70.

> `TimeArray` indexing is very flexible, but keep in mind that the rows must always be ordered by date. This is the reason why we can't say, for instance, `[7:7:70; 54;55;56;57]`—the elements would be out of order. And speaking of errors, including duplicate rows will also result in an error.

We can also index using date/time objects:

```
julia> MarketData.ohlc[Date(2000, 03, 22)]
1×4 TimeArray{Float64,2,Date,Array{Float64,2}} 2000-03-22 to 2000-03-22
```

This produces the following:

	Open	High	Low	Close
2000-03-22	132.78	144.38	131.56	144.19

And yes, we can use date/time ranges too:

```
julia> MarketData.ohlc[Date(2000, 03, 20):Day(1):Date(2000, 04,30)]
29×4 TimeArray{Float64,2,Date,Array{Float64,2}} 2000-03-20 to 2000-04-28
```

The output is as follows:

	Open	High	Low	Close
2000-03-20	123.5	126.25	122.38	123.0
2000-03-21	122.56	136.75	121.62	134.94
2000-03-22	132.78	144.38	131.56	144.19
2000-03-23	142.0	150.38	140.0	141.31

Using other date range steps will work equally well:

```
julia> MarketData.ohlc[Date(2000, 03, 20):Dates.Week(1):Date(2000, 04,30)]
6×4 TimeArray{Float64,2,Date,Array{Float64,2}} 2000-03-20 to 2000-04-24
# output truncated
```

Combining multiple indices works too:

```
julia> MarketData.ohlc[[Date(2000, 03, 20):Day(1):Date(2000, 04,30);
Date(2000, 05, 01)]]
30×4 TimeArray{Float64,2,Date,Array{Float64,2}} 2000-03-20 to 2000-05-01
```

Finally, we can come up with any combination of columns and rows we can imagine:

```
julia> MarketData.ohlc[:High, :Low][Date(2000, 03, 20):Day(1):Date(2000,
03,25)]
5×2 TimeArray{Float64,2,Date,Array{Float64,2}} 2000-03-20 to 2000-03-24
```

This is the result:

	High	Low
2000-03-20	126.25	122.38
2000-03-21	136.75	121.62
2000-03-22	144.38	131.56
2000-03-23	150.38	140.0
2000-03-24	143.94	135.5

Querying TimeArray objects

The `TimeSeries` module exposes a powerful, query-like API for filtering time series data. Let's take a look at each of them.

The when() method

The `when` method allows for aggregating elements from a `TimeArray` into specific time periods. For instance, we can use this function to pick the Wednesdays in our dataset in a more concise fashion:

```
julia> when(MarketData.ohlc[1:70], Dates.dayname, "Wednesday")
14x4 TimeArray{Float64,2,Date,Array{Float64,2}} 2000-01-05 to 2000-04-05
# output truncated
```

We are not limited to just `Dates.dayname`; we can use many of the `Dates` functions we covered in the previous section—day, dayname, week, month, monthname, year, dayofweek, dayofweekofmonth, dayofyear, quarterofyear, and dayofquarter:

```
julia> when(MarketData.ohlc, Dates.monthname, "August")
46x4 TimeArray{Float64,2,Date,Array{Float64,2}} 2000-08-01 to 2001-08-31
# output truncated
```

The from() method

This function truncates a `TimeArray` starting with the date passed to the method. The row corresponding to the passed date is included in the result:

```
julia> from(MarketData.ohlc, Date(2000, 3, 22))
445x4 TimeArray{Float64,2,Date,Array{Float64,2}} 2000-03-22 to 2001-12-31
```

The output is as follows:

	Open	High	Low	Close
2000-03-22	132.78	144.38	131.56	144.19
2000-03-23	142.0	150.38	140.0	141.31
2000-03-24	142.44	143.94	135.5	138.69
2000-03-27	137.62	144.75	136.88	139.56
2000-03-28	137.25	142.0	137.12	139.12

The to() method

The `to()` method returns the rows up to and including the date passed as an argument:

```
julia> to(MarketData.ohlc, Date(2000, 3, 22))
56x4 TimeArray{Float64,2,Date,Array{Float64,2}} 2000-01-03 to 2000-03-22
# output truncated
```

The findall() and findwhen() methods

This family of functions tests a condition and returns the results for which the condition is true. The only difference is that `findall()` returns an array containing the numbers of the rows, while `findwhen()` returns a vector of date/time objects. For example, if we want to find all the rows where the closing value was at least 10% higher than the opening value, we can run the following:

```
julia> findall(MarketData.ohlc[:Close] .>= MarketData.ohlc[:Open] .+
MarketData.ohlc[:Open] .* 0.1)
7-element Array{Int64,1}:
   55
   74
  119
  254
  260
  271
  302
```

`findwhen` will produce a similar output, but for the dates:

```
julia> findwhen(MarketData.ohlc[:Close] .>= MarketData.ohlc[:Open] .+
MarketData.ohlc[:Open] .* 0.1)
7-element Array{Date,1}:
 2000-03-21
 2000-04-17
 2000-06-21
 2001-01-03
```

```
2001-01-11
2001-01-29
2001-03-14
```

Manipulating time series objects

`TimeSeries` exposes a minimalist, yet productive set of methods for modifying `TimeArray` objects.

merge()

For starters, we can combine the data from two `TimeArrays`. The `merge` method uses the timestamps as the join columns—and by default, it performs an inner join. But it's also possible to perform left, right, and outer joins. Let's generate some random data to experiment with. We'll start by creating a time series with random values, spread over a week, starting today:

```julia
julia> d1 = today():Day(1):today() + Week(1) |> collect
8-element Array{Date,1}:
 2018-11-08
 2018-11-09
 2018-11-10
 2018-11-11
 2018-11-12
 2018-11-13
 2018-11-14
 2018-11-15

julia> t1 = TimeArray(d1, rand(length(d1)), [:V1])
8x1 TimeArray{Float64,1,Date,Array{Float64,1}} 2018-11-08 to 2018-11-15
```

The output is as follows:

	V1
2018-11-08	0.9199
2018-11-09	0.2914
2018-11-10	0.3226
2018-11-11	0.7523
2018-11-12	0.1259
2018-11-13	0.4498
2018-11-14	0.9366
2018-11-15	0.1943

Next, we'll create another time series object spread over ten days:

```julia
julia> d2 = today():Day(1):today() + Day(10) |> collect
11-element Array{Date,1}:
 2018-11-08
 2018-11-09
 2018-11-10
 2018-11-11
 2018-11-12
 2018-11-13
 2018-11-14
 2018-11-15
 2018-11-16
 2018-11-17
 2018-11-18

julia> t2 = TimeArray(d2, rand(length(d2)), [:V2])
11x1 TimeArray{Float64,1,Date,Array{Float64,1}} 2018-11-08 to 2018-11-18
```

This results in the following:

	V2
2018-11-08	0.8039
2018-11-09	0.0753
2018-11-10	0.3964
2018-11-11	0.4068
2018-11-12	0.9322
2018-11-13	0.9196
2018-11-14	0.6745
2018-11-15	0.5368
2018-11-16	0.8061
2018-11-17	0.8796
2018-11-18	0.5846

So now we have two `TimeArray` instances, t1 and t2. The t2 object has values for all the days in t1 plus three more days. A regular (inner join) `merge` will only use the rows with timestamps that are present in both t1 and t2:

```julia
julia> merge(t1, t2)
8x2 TimeArray{Float64,2,Date,Array{Float64,2}} 2018-11-08 to 2018-11-15
```

This is the output:

	V1	V2
2018-11-08	0.9199	0.8039
2018-11-09	0.2914	0.0753
2018-11-10	0.3226	0.3964
2018-11-11	0.7523	0.4068
2018-11-12	0.1259	0.9322
2018-11-13	0.4498	0.9196
2018-11-14	0.9366	0.6745
2018-11-15	0.1943	0.5368

Right, left, and outer joins will introduce NaN values for the rows that don't correspond:

```
julia> merge(t1, t2, :right)
11x2 TimeArray{Float64,2,Date,Array{Float64,2}} 2018-11-08 to 2018-11-18
```

The output is as follows:

	V1	V2
2018-11-08	0.9199	0.8039
2018-11-09	0.2914	0.0753
2018-11-10	0.3226	0.3964
2018-11-11	0.7523	0.4068
2018-11-12	0.1259	0.9322
2018-11-13	0.4498	0.9196
2018-11-14	0.9366	0.6745
2018-11-15	0.1943	0.5368
2018-11-16	NaN	0.8061
2018-11-17	NaN	0.8796
2018-11-18	NaN	0.5846

The vcat() method

The vcat() method can be considered the counterpart of merge. If merge joins the columns of two time series, vcat combines their rows. Its most obvious use case is for putting together data from a dataset that is split into multiple files. Let's see it in action:

```
julia> d3 = today() + Week(2):Day(1):today() + Week(3) |> collect
8-element Array{Date,1}:
 2018-11-22
 2018-11-23
 2018-11-24
 2018-11-25
 2018-11-26
 2018-11-27
```

```
    2018-11-28
    2018-11-29
julia> t3 = TimeArray(d3, rand(length(d3)), [:V1])
8×1 TimeArray{Float64,1,Date,Array{Float64,1}} 2018-11-22 to 2018-11-29
```

The output is as follows:

	V1
2018-11-22	0.9044
2018-11-23	0.7665
2018-11-24	0.3149
2018-11-25	0.2854
2018-11-26	0.109
2018-11-27	0.324
2018-11-28	0.7132
2018-11-29	0.7046

We have created a new `TimeArray` which covers the time period between two weeks and three weeks from today:

```
julia> vcat(t1, t3)
16×1 TimeArray{Float64,1,Date,Array{Float64,1}} 2018-11-08 to 2018-11-29
```

This is the resulting `TimeArray`:

	V1
2018-11-08	0.9199
2018-11-09	0.2914
2018-11-10	0.3226
2018-11-11	0.7523
2018-11-12	0.1259
2018-11-13	0.4498
2018-11-14	0.9366
2018-11-15	0.1943
2018-11-22	0.9044
2018-11-23	0.7665
2018-11-24	0.3149
2018-11-25	0.2854
2018-11-26	0.109
2018-11-27	0.324
2018-11-28	0.7132
2018-11-29	0.7046

The resulting time series combines data from both `t1` and `t3`.

The collapse() method

This method allows for compressing data into a larger time frame, for instance converting daily data into weekly data:

```
julia> january = TimeArray(Date(2018, 1, 1):Day(1):Date(2018, 1, 31) |>
collect, rand(31), [:values])
31x1 TimeArray{Float64,1,Date,Array{Float64,1}} 2018-01-01 to 2018-01-31
```

It produces the following output:

	values
2018-01-01	0.2241
2018-01-02	0.0431
2018-01-03	0.6478
2018-01-04	0.5862
2018-01-05	0.3729
2018-01-06	0.2994
2018-01-07	0.8512
2018-01-08	0.8587
2018-01-09	0.4847
2018-01-10	0.9509
2018-01-11	0.5016
2018-01-12	0.7146
2018-01-13	0.5238
2018-01-14	0.2815
2018-01-15	0.6264
2018-01-16	0.002
2018-01-17	0.895
2018-01-18	0.9428
2018-01-19	0.8887
2018-01-20	0.1303
2018-01-21	0.9959
2018-01-22	0.6023
2018-01-23	0.8203
2018-01-24	0.1072
2018-01-25	0.6632
2018-01-26	0.1004
2018-01-27	0.9838
2018-01-28	0.4962
2018-01-29	0.0499
2018-01-30	0.6711
2018-01-31	0.7284

If we want to `collapse` the `january` time series, we need to decide what to do about the data that's being collapsed. This is achieved by passing function arguments. The general form of the method is the following:

```
collapse(<time series>, <time function>, <time filtering function>, <value
collapsing function>)
```

For instance, we can `collapse` the data for January into a weekly period (the `<time function>`) by keeping the last day of the period (the `<time filtering function>`) and by computing the mean of the values (the `<value collapsing function>`):

```
julia> using Statistics
julia> collapse(january, week, last, mean)
5×1 TimeArray{Float64,1,Date,Array{Float64,1}} 2018-01-07 to 2018-01-31
```

The output is as follows:

	values
2018-01-07	0.4321
2018-01-14	0.6165
2018-01-21	0.6401
2018-01-28	0.5391
2018-01-31	0.4831

The `<value collapsing function>` is optional and if not provided, the values that correspond to the timestamp will be used:

```
julia> collapse(january, week, first)
5×1 TimeArray{Float64,1,Date,Array{Float64,1}} 2018-01-01 to 2018-01-29
```

This is what we get:

	values
2018-01-01	0.2241
2018-01-08	0.8587
2018-01-15	0.6264
2018-01-22	0.6023
2018-01-29	0.0499

The map() method

Finally, the `map()` function allows us to iterate over each row in the time series and apply a function to both the timestamps and the values. We could easily postpone the first week in the `january` time series by one year, as follows:

```
julia> map(january[1:7]) do ts, values
           ts += Year(1)
           (ts, values)
       end
7×1 TimeArray{Float64,1,Date,Array{Float64,1}} 2019-01-01 to 2019-01-07
```

The output is as follows:

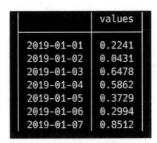

	values
2019-01-01	0.2241
2019-01-02	0.0431
2019-01-03	0.6478
2019-01-04	0.5862
2019-01-05	0.3729
2019-01-06	0.2994
2019-01-07	0.8512

There is more to say about `TimeSeries`. But for now, we'll stop here. We'll get back to `TimeArray` in the next chapter, where we will use it to perform time series analysis and forecasting on the European Union's unemployment numbers.

Summary

In this chapter, we have learned about working with dates and times in Julia. The language provides a powerful, yet accessible API that follows Julia's overall philosophy—you can start simple and augment your code as you become more knowledgeable. Thus, by default, the date/time objects use local time, ignoring complex details like time zones. However, time zone support is only one package away. We have seen how to extend Julia's `Dates` API by using the functionality provided by `TimeZones`.

Using our understanding of temporal data, we were able to take yet another step towards becoming proficient Julia programmers and learned about time series and the powerful `TimeArray`. We've seen how to plot time series with `Plots`, an extremely versatile plotting library for Julia—in fact, it's middleware providing a common API for a series of visualization packages, allowing us to swap backends as needed.

In the next chapter, we will continue our discussion of time series by performing analytics and forecasting on unemployment levels in the European Union. In the process, we'll learn about the most important patterns of time series analysis—trends, seasonality, and irregularity, and we will expand our knowledge of `TimeSeries` by performing various time series transformations.

10
Time Series Forecasting

In the previous chapter, we learned how to handle date and time with Julia. This allowed us to understand the very important concept of time series data. Now, we are ready to discuss yet another highly important data science topic—time series analysis.

Time series analysis and forecasting represents a key strategic and decisive component of any organization, from understanding top sales periods to end of season intervals and discounts, scheduling employees' time off, budgets, fiscal years, product release cycles, increased demand in raw materials, and many, many other aspects. Understanding and predicting the evolution of various business indicators over time is a necessary part of doing business, whether we're talking about a school, a billion dollar corporation, a hotel, a supermarket, or a government.

However, time series data analysis is one of the most fairly complex tasks of data science. The nature and particularities of chronological events led to the development of specialized algorithms and methodologies.

In this chapter, we'll study the basics of time series analysis and forecasting using Julia. Although a fairly young language, Julia already has good support for handling time-related data. In the previous chapter, we've learned about the Dates module and about the `TimeSeries` package. In this chapter, we'll dive deeper and apply what we have previously studied. We'll also learn about more advanced `TimeSeries` methods and about a few other packages for working with temporal data. We will be covering the following topics:

- Exploratory data analysis of the unemployment figures of the **European Union (EU)**
- Trends, cycles, seasonality, and errors—components of a time series
- Time series decomposition
- Stationarity, differencing, and autocorrelation of time series data
- Learning to apply simple forecasting techniques

Technical requirements

The Julia package ecosystem is under continuous development and new package versions are released on a daily basis. Most of the times this is great news, as new releases bring new features and bug fixes. However, since many of the packages are still in beta (version 0.x), any new release can introduce breaking changes. As a result, the code presented in the book can stop working. In order to ensure that your code will produce the same results as described in the book, it is recommended to use the same package versions. Here are the external packages used in this chapter and their specific versions:

```
CSV@v0.4.3
DataFrames@v0.15.2
IJulia@v1.14.1
Plots@v0.22.0
TimeSeries@v0.14.0
```

In order to install a specific version of a package you need to run:

```
pkg> add PackageName@vX.Y.Z
```

For example:

```
pkg> add IJulia@v1.14.1
```

Alternatively you can install all the used packages by downloading the `Project.toml` file provided with the chapter and using `pkg>` instantiate as follows:

```
julia>
download("https://raw.githubusercontent.com/PacktPublishing/Julia-Programmi
ng-Projects/master/Chapter10/Project.toml", "Project.toml")
pkg> activate .
pkg> instantiate
```

A quick look at our data

In this chapter, we will use some real-life data provided by Eurostat, the official EU office for statistics. Eurostat has a wealth of databases available on its website. For our learning project, we'll take a look at the unemployment numbers—with the EU's economy growing after a long recession, these stats should be quite interesting. Various EU employment and unemployment figures can be downloaded from `http://ec.europa.eu/eurostat/web/lfs/data/database`. We'll be using the **Unemployment by sex and age – monthly average** dataset.

You don't need to download this because a better structured dataset is provided in this chapter's support files. However, if you're curious and want to take a look, you can get the raw data from under the **Employment and unemployment (Labour force survey)** category | **LFS main indicators** subcategory | **Unemployment - LFS adjusted series** folder.

I've also customized the data by using *thousand persons* for the unit of measure (the default is *percentage of active population*), and unadjusted data (neither seasonally, nor calendar). I've also kept the numbers for the EU only (no individual countries). Finally, I've included all the data from January 2005 to December 2017. You can make all of these adjustments in the data explorer and then download the table as TSV file. As for the TSV formatting, I went with these options:

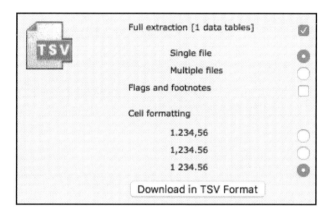

Visualized in the Eurostat data explorer tool, the data looks like this:

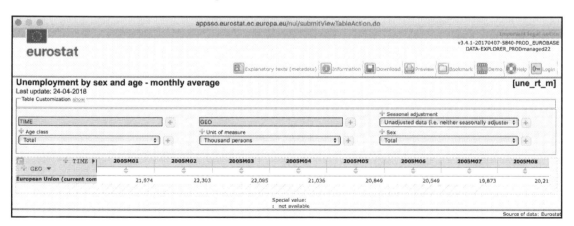

We can see a list of geographical areas in the first column and unemployment numbers on a monthly basis in the rest of the columns. This dataset is structured in a different way than what we require. For starters, `TimeSeries` requires the matrix to be transposed (as in, the dates should become rows instead of columns). Additionally, dates are formatted in a non-standard way, for example, `2017M01` designates January 2017. Finally, the numbers are formatted as strings, with spaces for thousand separators. You can download this raw data file from this chapter's support files, which are hosted at `https://github.com/PacktPublishing/Julia-Programming-Projects/blob/master/Chapter10/data/une_rt_m_1.tsv`.

Such issues are a common occurrence when working with real-life data—differences in standards regarding structure and formatting make data sanitization and transformation a key first step, and usually also a time-consuming one, in any data science project. For the sake of brevity, I have prepared a simplified dataset that's already been transformed for seamless usage with `TimeSeries`, which you can download from this chapter's support files.

Data processing

If you would like to follow along, here is how I processed the raw data using Julia:

```
# load the raw data file as a DataFrame
julia> using CSV, DataFrames
julia> df = CSV.read("une_rt_m_1.tsv", header = true, delim = '\t')
1×157 DataFrames.DataFrame. Omitted printing of 148 columns
```

This is what it looks like in a Jupyter Notebook:

GEO,S_ADJ,AGE,UNIT,SEX\TIME	2005M01	2005M02	2005M03	2005M04	2005M05	2005M06	2005M07	2005M08	2005M09	2005M10	2005M11	2005M12
	String	String	String	String	String	String	String	String	String	String	String	String
1	European Union (current composition),Unadjusted data (i.e. neither seasonally adjusted nor calendar adjusted data),Total,Thousand persons,Total	21 974	22 303	22 085	21 036	20 849	20 549	19 873	20 210	20 554	20 919	20 599	20 470

In the next step, we will extract the values by selecting a `DataFrame` composed of 1 row and 2 columns to `end` and converting it into an `Array`:

```
julia> values = convert(Array, df[1, 2:end]) 1×156 Array{Union{Missing,
String},2}: "21 974" "22 303" "22 085" "21 036" "20 849" ... # output
omitted
```

Now, we can parse the previously extracted string values and convert them into integers. The new integer values are stored in a vector as well:

```
julia> values = map(x -> parse(Int, replace(x, " "=>"")), values)[:]
156-element Array{Int64,1}:
 21974
 22303
 22085
 21036
# output omitted
```

Great—our values are ready! We can now focus on the headers. Our goal is to extract the date information contained in the labels. As a first step, we pull the names of the columns into a vector, as follows:

```
julia> dates = names(df)[2:end]
156-element Array{Symbol,1}:
 Symbol("2005M01")
 Symbol("2005M02")
 Symbol("2005M03")
 Symbol("2005M04")
 Symbol("2005M05")
# output omitted
```

Now, let's transform the symbols to bring them closer to what we need—that is, something resembling a standard date format. We'll replace the "M" with a dash, and in the process, we'll convert the symbol into a String, as replacing does not work on symbols:

```
julia> dates = map(x -> replace(string(x), "M"=>"-"), dates)
156-element Array{String,1}:
 "2005-01"
 "2005-02"
 "2005-03"
 "2005-04"
 "2005-05"
# output omitted
```

Excellent! Now, we can define a DateFormat matching our strings—year plus dash plus month, with the month as a numeric value with a leading zero. We'll use this to convert the strings to proper date objects:

```
julia> using Dates
julia> dateformat = DateFormat("y-m")
dateformat"y-m"

julia> dates = map(x -> Date(x, dateformat), dates)
156-element Array{Date,1}:
```

```
2005-01-01
2005-02-01
2005-03-01
2005-04-01
2005-05-01
# output omitted
```

We're getting closer! To safely persist the data to a file, I created a new `DataFrame`, this time using the proper dates and the original values, as follows:

```
# store the extracted data in a new DataFrame
julia> df2 = DataFrame(Dates = dates, Values = values)
156×2 DataFrames.DataFrame
 | Row | Dates      | Values |
 | 1   | 2005-01-01 | 21974  |
 | 2   | 2005-02-01 | 22303  |
 | 3   | 2005-03-01 | 22085  |
 | 4   | 2005-04-01 | 21036  |
 | 5   | 2005-05-01 | 20849  |
# output omitted
```

We can use `CSV.write` to store the snapshot of our data to file by using the following code:

```
# write DataFrame to file
julia> CSV.write("UE-unemployment.tsv", df2)
```

We can now load the data as a `TimeArray` from the TSV file:

```
julia> using TimeSeries
julia> unemployment_data = readtimearray("UE-unemployment.tsv")
156x1 TimeArray{Float64,2,Date,Array{Float64,2}} 2005-01-01 to 2017-12-01
```

 If you would like to directly convert from `DataFrame` to `TimeSeries` data, without resorting to loading a TSV file, you can use the `IterableTables` package. `IterableTables` provides a wealth of converter methods between different table types in Julia. You can read more in the package's README at https://github.com/davidanthoff/IterableTables.jl.

Our time series data was correctly loaded—there are 156 entries between January 2005 and December 2017. It will look like this:

```
julia> TimeSeries.head(unemployment_data, 10)
10x1 TimeArray{Float64,2,Date,Array{Float64,2}} 2005-01-01 to 2005-10-01
```

The output is as follows:

	Values
2005-01-01	21974.0
2005-02-01	22303.0
2005-03-01	22085.0
2005-04-01	21036.0
2005-05-01	20849.0
2005-06-01	20549.0
2005-07-01	19873.0
2005-08-01	20210.0
2005-09-01	20554.0
2005-10-01	20919.0

We had to use the fully qualified name of the head function, `TimeSeries.head`, because both `TimeSeries` and `DataFrames` export a head method, and both packages are loaded into the current scope.

Attempting to call the head function without the module's name would result in an error:

```
julia> head(unemployment_data, 10)
WARNING: both TimeSeries and DataFrames export "head"; uses of it in module
Main must be qualified
ERROR: UndefVarError: head not defined
```

The best way to get a quick insight into our data is to render a plot. We'll use the `Plots` package with the `PyPlot` backend—we installed them both in `Chapter 9`, *Working with Dates, Time, and Time Series*:

```
julia> using Plots
julia> pyplot()
```

The `PyPlot` backend has complex dependencies, so if you run into problems executing the indicated code, please follow the instructions provided by the warnings and errors.

For instance, at some point, I had to install two extra packages by hand:

```
julia> using Pkg
julia> pkg"add PyCall LaTeXStrings"
```

Now, we can plot the unemployment numbers:

```
julia> plot(unemployment_data)
```

Julia will render the following plot:

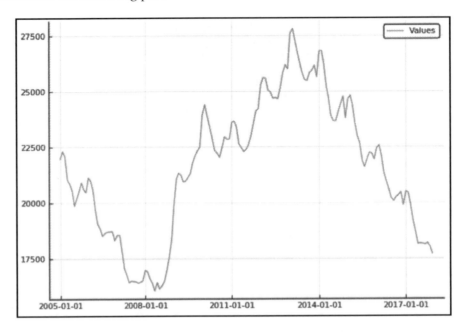

We can easily see that the number of unemployed people had been steadily decreasing since 2005, reaching a historical minimum in the second half of 2008. From there, over a couple of months, it skyrocketed to levels unknown since 2005. This was the moment when the recession hit the EU's economy. From that point on, unemployment numbers continued to grow, until they finally reached a peak at the beginning of 2013. The maximum number of people without a job was reached in February 2013, after which the European economy began to recover, with the unemployment numbers rapidly declining and approaching pre-recession levels.

Understanding time series components

There are three components of time series that are key to understanding time-related data. They are *trend*, *seasonality*, and *noise*. Let's look at each of them in the context of our EU unemployment data.

Trend

The trend can be defined as the long-term tendency of the time series data—the fact that, on average, the values tend to increase or decrease over a period of time. Looking at our plot, we can identify three distinct trends:

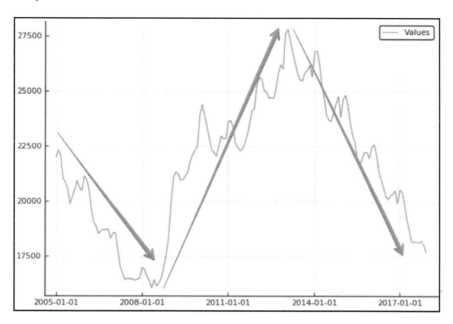

A downward trend from 2005 until 2008 (less people unemployed on a year-on-year basis); an upward trend starting in 2008 and manifesting until 2013 (unemployment rose on average); and again, a downward trend between 2013, all the way until the end of 2017 (the number of people without work constantly decreased).

Seasonality

Seasonality is a regularly repeating pattern of highs and lows that is related to calendar time; that is, it's directly influenced by seasons, quarters, months, and so on. Think, for instance, about the electricity usage in a city—we'll probably see increases in consumption during the summer due to air conditioning, and in wintertime due to needing to heat the houses instead. In a similar manner, by looking at a hotel at the seaside, we'll see a significant increase in bookings during the summer, followed by a decrease in the winter.

Thus, seasonality generates effects that are reasonably stable with respect to timing, direction, and magnitude. The most common calendar-related influences are natural conditions (the weather), business and administrative procedures (fiscal year), and social and cultural behaviors (bank holidays due to national and religious holidays, key dates like Christmas, Valentine's Day, and so on). It also includes effects that are caused by calendar events, which are recurrent but not fixed in terms of date (such as Easter, whose date falls on a certain Sunday each year, but the actual date varies).

Unemployment data suffers a strong seasonal influence—during the summer months, more people are employed. These seem to be temporary jobs, probably in tourism, to help hotels and restaurants cope with the influx of holiday goers—but maybe also in the office and retail sectors to cover for the regular employees' time off. We can clearly identify this on our plot—the summer months bring the lowest unemployment figures for the year, with the values beginning to go up again in autumn:

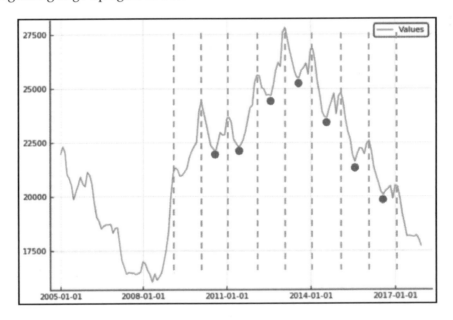

During the three summer months in the middle of the year, unemployment reaches the lowest levels. Once the peak of the season passes, unemployment steeply rises once more.

Random noise

The default assumption when analyzing time series data is that we can identify an underlying pattern (as defined by its trend and seasonality components). However, when there is such a systematic pattern in the data (some time series data is completely random, for example, earthquake incidence), it will also be accompanied by variances—fluctuations in the data that are categorized as random noise, errors, or irregularities. They make the task of identifying the patterns more difficult, and for this reason, data scientists will use some form of noise filtering.

In other words, this irregular component is what remains after the seasonal and trend components have been computed and removed. They are short-term fluctuations, and are neither systematic nor predictable.

Cyclicity

Cyclicity is similar to seasonality in a way, and for this reason, the two are often confused. However, they are two different things, and the distinction is important. Cyclical periods represent larger swathes of time where we can identify recurring patterns in the data (periods of growth or decline) and which can't be explained away by calendar patterns. They are usually larger, spanning a few years, and do not overlap with calendar events. Such cyclical elements can be introduced by product release cycles (the release of a car model, or a new version of an operating system, or an upgrade to a line of laptops), election cycles (for government budgeting or companies working with government contracts), and so on.

Time series decomposition

We can thus say that any value in a time series can be represented through a function of the four components we discussed earlier—trend, seasonality, error, and cycle. The relationship between the four components can be either *additive* or *multiplicative*.

The additive model is used when the seasonal variation stays about the same across time. The trend may be upward or downward, but the seasonality stays more or less the same. A plot of such data will look very similar to this:

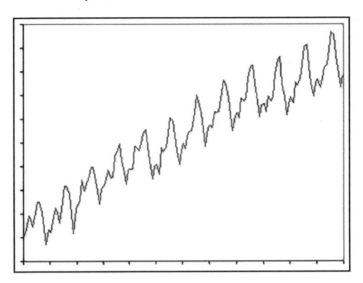

If we draw two imaginary lines between the yearly maximums and the yearly minimums, the lines will be pretty much parallel.

For an additive time series model, the four components are summed up to produce the values in the series. Thus, a time series Y can be decomposed into $Y = Trend + Cycle + Seasonality + Noise$.

A multiplicative model should be used with a time series where the seasonal variability increases over time. For example, a typical multiplicative time series is represented by the international airline passenger data between January 1949 and January 1960:

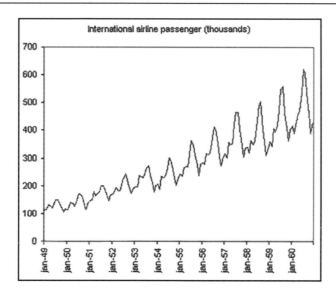

We can see how the variation in the seasonal pattern is correlated with the level of the time series: the more passengers we have, the higher the variation. A multiplicative time series Y can be represented as $Y = Trend * Cycle * Seasonality * Noise$.

As a side note, we can convert a multiplicative model into an additive model by transforming the data until it becomes stable over time, for example, by means of log transformations—$Y = Trend * Cycle * Seasonality * Noise$ is equivalent to $log\ Y = log\ Trend + log\ Cycle + log\ Seasonality + log\ Noise$.

Splitting a time series into its components is a widely employed technique for time data analysis. This is known as **time series decomposition**, and it also represents the foundation of time series forecasting.

Explaining data – an additive approach or multiplicative approach?

This is the question—which of the two approaches does a better job of explaining our data? One way to answer this question is to look at the cycle-by-cycle values and see if there is significant variation. As we're dealing with yearly cycles, let's extract and plot the year on year values as follows:

```julia
julia> plot()
julia> for y in 2005:2017
```

```
TimeSeries.values(when(unemployment_data, year, y))[:] |> plot!
gui()
end
```

First, we render an empty plot. Then, we iterate over a range corresponding to our years, between 2005 and 2017, and then we use the `TimeSeries.when` method to filter our data by year. We extract the resulting `TimeArray` values and append them to the plot by using the `plot!` function. However, this is not enough—we also have to call the `Plots.gui` method to actually render the updated plot. This is a very important point, per the official documentation:

> *"A plot is only displayed when returned (a semicolon will suppress the return), or if explicitly displayed with* `display(plt)`, `gui()`, *or by adding* `show = true` *to your plot command."*

You can read more about outputting plots at
`http://docs.juliaplots.org/latest/output/`.

Here's what we get:

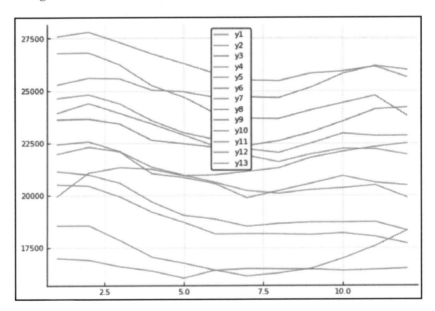

We can see that there is consistent year-after-year variation, which means that we should use the multiplicative model.

Eyeballing the components using `plots` is a common way of recognizing patterns in a time series. In our case, it is pretty easy to tell that there's both trend and seasonality. Also, we can deduce that the data does not exhibit any cyclical pattern.

Remember that the multiplicative model holds that *Y = Trend * Cyclicity * Seasonality * Noise*. We can write this shorter as *Y = TCSN*. Since we just established that our data does not present any cycles, we're going to leave out the cyclicity component, and so *Y = TSN*.

Extracting the trend

The first step in decomposing a time series is to extract the trend component. A widely used technique for computing the trend is called **smoothing**. As the name suggests, it *smooths out* the values by removing the noise and blurring the seasonality so that we can identify the trend.

One way of performing smoothing is through moving averages. In financial applications, the simple moving average is the unweighted mean of the previous *n* points of data. It's like applying a moving window on top of our time series and performing the calculation using the visible data. Then, we slide the window by one position and repeat the calculation. To smooth out seasonal data, the window should be the size of the seasonal period—in our case, 12 months. So, to apply simple moving average smoothing to our data, we'll start by taking the first 12 month period (the year 2005), sum up the values, and then divide them by 12 to get their average. Then, we'll slide our window by one month and repeat the computation. As a result, we eliminate the effect of the seasonal component and cancel out the impact of the noise.

The `TimeSeries` package provides a series of *apply methods* that implement common transformations of time series data. One of them is the `moving` method, which can be used to compute the moving average of a series. Let's compute the moving average for a 12 month interval in order to smooth out the seasonality component:

```
julia> using Statistics
julia> moving_avg = moving(mean, unemployment_data, 12)
145×1 TimeArray{Float64,2,Date,Array{Float64,2}} 2005-12-01 to 2017-12-01
```

The result is as follows:

	Values
2005-12-01	20951.75
2006-01-01	20882.25
2006-02-01	20772.0
2006-03-01	20646.4167
2006-04-01	20534.0

As we can see, the result is a new time series that contains the mean of 12-month periods in our original time series. The first 12 values of the original series are consumed by this operation so that our new series starts with December 2005. If you wish to keep the initial values, the `moving` function takes an additional keyword argument, `padding`. By default, `padding` is `false`, but if set to `true`, the consumed timestamps will be kept and their values will be set to `NaN`:

```
julia> moving(mean, unemployment_data, 12, padding = true)
156x1 TimeArray{Float64,2,Date,Array{Float64,2}} 2005-01-01 to 2017-12-01
```

This will produce the following output:

	Values
2005-01-01	NaN
2005-02-01	NaN
2005-03-01	NaN
2005-04-01	NaN
2005-05-01	NaN
2005-06-01	NaN
2005-07-01	NaN
2005-08-01	NaN
2005-09-01	NaN
2005-10-01	NaN
2005-11-01	NaN
2005-12-01	20951.75
2006-01-01	20882.25
2006-02-01	20772.0
2006-03-01	20646.4167
2006-04-01	20534.0

Plotting the smoothed values on top of the original data indicates the trend:

```
julia> plot(unemployment_data)
julia> plot!(moving_avg)
```

Here is our plot:

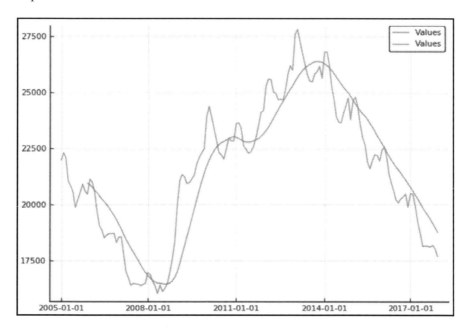

The first call to the `plot` method renders the raw EU unemployment figures, while the subsequent call of the `plot!` method mutates the plot, overlaying the moving average that corresponds to the trend.

Computing the seasonality

Now that we have extracted the trend, we can remove it from the initial time series. This is done by division. We will be left with the product of the seasonal and noise components. Thus, $SN = Y/T$.

To calculate the fraction between `TimeArray` objects, we'll use the element-wise division operator, `./`:

```
julia> sn = unemployment_data ./ moving_avg
145×1 TimeArray{Float64,2,Date,Array{Float64,2}} 2005-12-01 to 2017-12-01
```

We will get the following result:

	Values_Values
2005-12-01	0.977
2006-01-01	1.0123
2006-02-01	1.01
2006-03-01	0.9967
2006-04-01	0.9588
2006-05-01	0.9344

Plotting the resulting `TimeArray` will give us a clearer image of the product of the seasonality and noise components:

```julia
julia> plot(sn)
```

This results in the following plot:

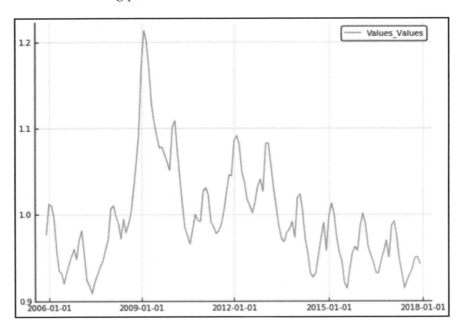

The next step is calculating the sum over years of these values for the same month. That is, we'll sum the value for all of the months of January throughout all the years; then, we will do the same for February, March, and so on. We'll get the average over all the years, for each calendar month. This will lead to the minimization of the noise:

```julia
julia> month_avg = Float64[]
0-element Array{Float64,1}
```

```
julia> for m in 1:12
           md = when(sn, month, m)
           push!(month_avg, mean(TimeSeries.values(md)[:]))
       end
```

First, we instantiate a `Vector` of `Float64` values. Then, we iterate over a range between `1` and `12`, which represents the months. Within the loop, we apply the `when` method to filter the values for the currently iterated month (all the January values for all the years, then all the February values for all the years, then March, and so on), and then we push the mean of these values into the `month_avg` array. At the end of the loop, we collect these values in `month_avg`, where the first is the average value for the month of January across all the years, the second for February, then March, and so on. It will look like this:

```
julia> month_avg
12-element Array{Float64,1}:
 1.0376512639850295
 1.0466377033754193
 1.0301198608484736
 1.0014842494206564
 0.9830320492870818
 0.9705256323692862
 0.9630153389575429
 0.9634443756458616
 0.9763782494700372
 0.9893785521401298
 0.9987100016253194
 0.9913489915307253
```

Theoretically, these values should add up to `12`. In practice, that doesn't happen (although we're pretty close). We can easily sum up all of the elements of an array using the `sum` function:

```
julia> s = sum(month_avg)
11.951726268655563
```

As a consequence, we need to normalize the averages so that they *do* sum up to `12`. This is achieved by multiplying each seasonal factor by `12` and then dividing each factor by their sum:

```
julia> norm_month_avg = map(m -> 12m/s, month_avg)
```

We used the `map` function to iterate over each item in `month_avg` as `m` and applied an anonymous function so that `m = 12m/s`:

```
12-element Array{Float64,1}:
 1.0418423989910408
```

```
1.0508651351431808
1.0342805760704734
1.0055293037095092
0.9870025740450584
0.9744456429674838
0.9669050150351592
0.9673357846281114
0.9803218991358666
0.993374710799588
1.0027438505627655
0.9953531089117633
```

Let's check the sum again:

```
julia> sum(norm_month_avg)
12.0
```

Perfection!

Now that we have calculated the monthly seasonal factor, we can perform the seasonal adjustment on our original time series by dividing it by the seasonal factor. This way, we'll get the reminder, which represents the product of trend and noise—$Y/S = TN$. To compute this in Julia, we have to divide each value of unemployment_data by the corresponding monthly seasonal factor.

To keep things clean and tidy, let's copy our original time series into a different object:

```
julia> adj_unemployment_data = deepcopy(unemployment_data)
156x1 TimeArray{Float64,2,Date,Array{Float64,2}} 2005-01-01 to 2017-12-01
```

The deepcopy function creates a deep copy of the object, given as an argument. A deep copy means that everything is copied recursively, resulting in a fully independent object.

Next, we can use the map function to modify the TimeArray in place by recursively applying a function that divides the original value by the seasonality:

```
julia> map(adj_unemployment_data) do d,v
           v[1] /= norm_month_avg[month(d)]
           d,v
       end
156x1 TimeArray{Float64,2,Date,Array{Float64,2}} 2005-01-01 to 2017-12-01
```

The result is as follows:

	Values
2005-01-01	21091.4818
2005-02-01	21223.4656
2005-03-01	21353.0066
2005-04-01	20920.3252
2005-05-01	21123.5518

The `adj_unemployment_data` variable represents the seasonally adjusted time series.

TimeSeries operators

Performing operations between `TimeArray` objects—or rather between the elements contained in them—is a common occurrence in time series analysis. The `TimeSeries` package exposes a complete set of element-wise operators for mathematical, comparison, and logical operations.

As we have already seen when doing division between two `TimeArray` objects, the mathematical operators create a new `TimeArray` instance by using the values with common timestamps. Operations between a single `TimeArray` and `Int` or `Float` are also supported. The following operators are available:

- `.+`: Arithmetic element-wise addition
- `.-`: Arithmetic element-wise subtraction
- `.*`: Arithmetic element-wise multiplication
- `./`: Arithmetic element-wise division
- `.^`: Arithmetic element-wise exponentiation
- `.%`: Arithmetic element-wise remainder

Similar to mathematical operators, in the case of comparison ones, when two `TimeArray` instances are provided, the values are compared on shared timestamps too. However, the difference, in this case, is that the result will be a time array of type `Bool`.

These are the available comparison operators:

- `.>`: Element-wise greater-than comparison
- `.<`: Element-wise less-than comparison
- `.==`: Element-wise equivalent comparison

- .>=: Element-wise greater-than or equal comparison
- .<=: Element-wise less-than or equal comparison
- .!=: Element-wise not-equivalent comparison

Let's look at an example. First, let's create a `TimeArray` spreading between a week ago and today and fill it with random values. Your timestamps will be different as you'll run the code sometime in the future, and so the output will be different compared to mine, but the logic will be the same. Don't forget to execute `using Dates` if the module is not already in scope:

```julia
julia> using Dates
julia> ts1 = TimeArray(Date(today()) - Week(1):Day(1):Date(today()) |>
collect, rand(8))
8x1 TimeArray{Float64,1,Date,Array{Float64,1}} 2018-11-06 to 2018-11-13
```

This is what we get:

	A
2018-11-06	0.3903
2018-11-07	0.5231
2018-11-08	0.104
2018-11-09	0.5523
2018-11-10	0.5699
2018-11-11	0.4076
2018-11-12	0.4027
2018-11-13	0.4274

Now, we'll do the same for the second array:

```julia
julia> ts2 = TimeArray(Date(today()) - Week(1):Day(1):Date(today()) |>
collect, rand(8))
8x1 TimeSeries.TimeArray{Float64,1,Date,Array{Float64,1}} 2018-01-31 to
2018-02-07
```

This is what we get:

	A
2018-11-06	0.2467
2018-11-07	0.3953
2018-11-08	0.018
2018-11-09	0.7987
2018-11-10	0.729
2018-11-11	0.2403
2018-11-12	0.465
2018-11-13	0.7496

Now, we can compare the two objects, for instance:

```
julia> tsc = ts1 .> ts2
8×1 TimeArray{Bool,1,Date,BitArray{1}} 2018-11-06 to 2018-11-13
```

The output is as follows:

Comparisons between a single `TimeArray` and `Int`, `Float`, or `Bool` values are supported too:

```
julia> tsc .== false
8×1 TimeArray{Bool,1,Date,BitArray{1}} 2018-11-06 to 2018-11-13
```

Now, the output is as follows:

	A_A
2018-11-06	false
2018-11-07	false
2018-11-08	false
2018-11-09	true
2018-11-10	true
2018-11-11	false
2018-11-12	true
2018-11-13	true

Finally, we can use the following logic operators:

- `.&` element-wise logical AND
- `.|` element-wise logical OR
- `.!`, `.~` element-wise logical NOT
- `.∨` element-wise logical XOR

They are defined for `TimeArrays` of type `Bool` and return a `TimeArray` of type `Bool`. Values are computed on common timestamps when two `TimeArray` objects are the operands and operations between a single `TimeArray` and a `Bool` are supported.

Time series stationarity

A time series is considered stationary if its statistical properties such as mean, variance, autocorrelation, and so on, are constant over time. **Stationarity** is important because most forecasting models run on the assumption that the time series is stationary or can be rendered (approximately) stationary using transformations. The reason for this approach is that values in a stationary time series are much easier to predict—if its properties are constant, we can simply state that they will be in the future as they were in the past. Once we forecast future values based on stationary time series, we can then reverse the process and the transformations to compute the values that would match the original series.

Thus, the properties of a stationary time series do not depend on the time when the series is observed. Implicitly, this means that time series that present seasonality or trends are not stationary. In this context, again, we must be careful of the difference between seasonality and cyclicity—cyclic time series that do not expose seasonal or trending patterns *are* stationary.

Differencing a time series

One way to make a time series stationary is by *differencing*. This means computing the difference between consecutive values. In this technique, we calculate the difference between a value at a certain point in time and the one at the previous instant.

This can be easily computed by using the `diff` method that's provided by `TimeSeries`. Differentiating a time series calculates the finite difference between two consecutive points in the time series. By default, the difference is by one day. Consider the following, for instance:

```julia
julia> diffts = diff(unemployment_data)
155x1 TimeArray{Float64,2,Date,Array{Float64,2}} 2005-02-01 to 2017-12-01
```

One day from the original series is lost as part of the operation, with the resulting `TimeArray` beginning on January 2, 2005, resulting in the following:

	Values
2005-02-01	329.0
2005-03-01	-218.0
2005-04-01	-1049.0
2005-05-01	-187.0
2005-06-01	-300.0
2005-07-01	-676.0

We can render the result as a bar plot:

```julia
julia> bar(diffts)
```

We get the following result:

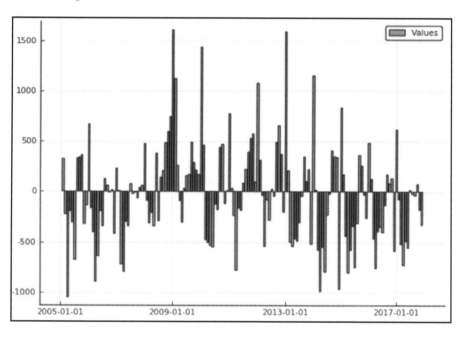

Changes in the values are clearly visible throughout the entire dataset, meaning that the variance is relatively constant.

Autocorrelation

Autocorrelation represents the degree of similarity of a time series and a lagged version of itself over successive time intervals. It is a very important concept as it measures the relationship between a current value and a corresponding past value. Thus, it has many valuable applications in time series forecasting; for example, to match trends and relationships in prices, stocks, returns, and so on.

We want to use autocorrelation to determine if we can reliably identify causality and trend – or if, on the contrary, we're dealing with a random walk model. A random walk would imply that the values in the time series are randomly defined, and this would imply that there's no relationship between past and present values. The random walk model is common, especially for financial and economic data. For a random walk model, forecasting the next value is done by taking the last value in the series. This is due to the fact that future movements are unpredictable—they are equally likely to be increasing or decreasing. Thus, the random walk model underpins naïve forecasts.

We can compute autocorrelation by using a combination of two functions—`TimeSeries.lag` and `xcorr`. The `lag` method works by shifting the values of the time series. For instance, let's use our previously defined `ts1`:

```julia
julia> ts1
8x1 TimeArray{Float64,1,Date,Array{Float64,1}} 2018-11-06 to 2018-11-13
```

We get the following result:

	A
2018-11-06	0.3903
2018-11-07	0.5231
2018-11-08	0.104
2018-11-09	0.5523
2018-11-10	0.5699
2018-11-11	0.4076
2018-11-12	0.4027
2018-11-13	0.4274

We can apply the `lag` function as follows:

```julia
julia> lag(ts1)
7x1 TimeArray{Float64,1,Date,Array{Float64,1}} 2018-11-07 to 2018-11-13
```

This will cause the first value to be assigned to the next timestamp. In my case, the value `0.3903`, which was initially corresponding to `2018-11-06`, now corresponds to `2018-11-07`:

	A
2018-11-07	0.3903
2018-11-08	0.5231
2018-11-09	0.104
2018-11-10	0.5523
2018-11-11	0.5699
2018-11-12	0.4076
2018-11-13	0.4027

Remember that if you run the code in parallel, your data will be different (the actual dates and values are different since we're using random values), but the behavior will be the same.

We can experiment with lagging the unemployment data by 12 intervals (12 months) to account for the yearly seasonality:

```
julia> lagged = lag(unemployment_data, 12)
144×1 TimeArray{Float64,2,Date,Array{Float64,2}} 2006-01-01 to 2017-12-01
```

The output is as follows:

	Values
2006-01-01	21974.0
2006-02-01	22303.0
2006-03-01	22085.0
2006-04-01	21036.0
2006-05-01	20849.0

The values have been shifted and the resulting `TimeArray` starts on the January 1, 2006. We can now use `TimeSeries.merge` to join the two series on the common timestamps:

```
julia> common = merge(unemployment_data, lagged)
144×2 TimeArray{Float64,2,Date,Array{Float64,2}} 2006-01-01 to 2017-12-01
```

This results in the following output:

	Values	Values_1
2006-01-01	21140.0	21974.0
2006-02-01	20980.0	22303.0
2006-03-01	20578.0	22085.0
2006-04-01	19687.0	21036.0
2006-05-01	19047.0	20849.0
2006-06-01	18859.0	20549.0

If we plot the original unemployment data together with the one year lagged series, we can see that the data is positively correlated, indicating strong yearly seasonality:

```
julia> plot(unemployment_data) julia> plot!(lagged)
```

The output is as follows:

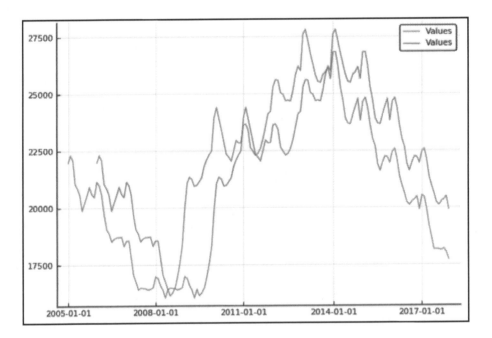

Time series forecasting

Forecasting implies identifying models that fit the historical data and using them to predict future values. When forecasting time series data, decomposition plays a very important part, helping to make predictions more accurate. The underlying assumption is that we can be more precise if we forecast each component individually, using the best-suited method, and then sum or multiply the parts (depending on whether the model is additive or multiplicative) to compute the final value.

Naïve

This is the simplest method, stating that the forecasted value is equal to the last value in the series. As mentioned previously, this is used with random walk models, where future movements are unpredictable. For example, to predict the value for the first unknown month, January 2018, using the naïve model, we can take the seasonally adjusted value from December 2017 and add (multiply) the seasonal component of the month of January:

```julia
julia> update(unemployment_data, Date(2018, 1, 1),
            TimeSeries.values(adj_unemployment_data[end])[:][end] *
norm_month_avg[1] |> round)
157x1 TimeArray{Float64,2,Date,Array{Float64,2}} 2005-01-01 to 2018-01-01
```

We use the `TimeSeries.update` method to append a new item for January 2018. Its value is the seasonality adjusted value of December 2017, multiplied by the normalized seasonality of the month of January:

2017-07-01	18172.0
2017-08-01	18155.0
2017-09-01	18121.0
2017-10-01	18199.0
2017-11-01	18027.0
2017-12-01	17705.0
2018-01-01	18446.0

Notice that we also assume that the seasonal component is unchanged, which means that we're using the seasonal naïve method for the seasonal component.

Simple average

A method that is slightly more advanced involves computing the mean of the previous data points to forecast the next value. It's a basic approach but in some situations, it can be a good fit. To compute it, we can apply the `mean` function to the underlying array of values:

```
julia> mean(TimeSeries.values(adj_unemployment_data)[:])
21589.641025641027
```

Moving average

We covered the moving average in detail when we extracted the trend component of our time series. It can also be employed for forecasting, using the result of the computation to fill up the next value. It is important to pick the right window size by understanding the series' seasonality, for example, by using autocorrelation plots.

Linear regression

We can use linear regression on the seasonally adjusted time series to forecast the next value. Let's take a closer look at this since it presents some good opportunities to dive into interesting Julia code. Since our data presents three trends (down, up, and down again), let's focus only on the last segment, where the current downward trend can be observed:

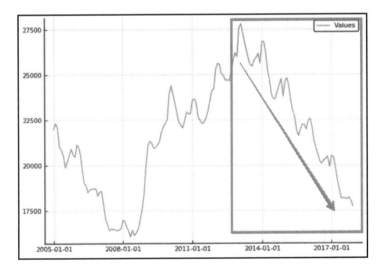

We can see that the current trend had started with an unemployment peak, so all we have to do is look for the maximum value in the series:

```
julia> findall(adj_unemployment_data[:Values] .==
            maximum(TimeSeries.values(adj_unemployment_data)[:]))
1-element Array{Int64,1}:
 98

julia> adj_unemployment_data[98]
1×1 TimeArray{Float64,2,Date,Array{Float64,2}} 2013-02-01 to 2013-02-01
```

We get the following value:

	Values
2013-02-01	27790.0

The downward trend started in February 2013. Let's extract all the data from that moment onward, all the way until the end of the series:

```
julia> last_trend = from(adj_unemployment_data, Date(2013, 2, 1))
59×1 TimeArray{Float64,2,Date,Array{Float64,2}} 2013-02-01 to 2017-12-01
```

The result is as follows:

	Values
2013-02-01	27790.0
2013-03-01	27292.0
2013-04-01	26755.0
2013-05-01	26292.0
2013-06-01	25805.0
2013-07-01	25501.0

We can now compute the linear regression—it will summarize the relationship between the unemployment numbers and the passing of time, allowing us to forecast the next value in the series. We have our unemployment numbers on the y-axis of the plot and the time on the x-axis. In this case, we can express y with the formula `y = a+b*x`, where a and b correspond to the linear regression. We'll compute the linear regression for the trend series to get a and b, and we'll calculate the next value of y (the unemployment forecast), corresponding to the next value of x (January 2018). Let's go through this, step by step.

The first thing we need to do is convert the timestamps in the time series into a simple integer series that we can use in our equation:

```julia
julia> x = 1:length(last_trend)
1:59

julia> y = values(last_trend)[:]
59-element Array{Float64,1}:
 27790.0
 27292.0
# output truncated

julia> linreg(x, y) = reverse([x ones(length(x))]\y)

julia> a, b = linreg(x, y)
2-element Array{Float64,1}:
 27522.02805376972
  -161.58229105786072
```

On the *x*-axis, we use integer values from 1 to 59, instead of the actual dates. In this line of thought, the next value, the one we want to forecast, will be x = 60, which means that our next y (the forecasted unemployment value) will be *27,608.61 + (-167.13 * 60)*:

```julia
julia> y = a+b*60
17827.09059029808
```

Like we did previously, we need to add the seasonality for the month of January:

```julia
julia> y = y * norm_month_avg[1] |> round
18573.0
```

Now, we can append it to our unemployment data and plot it:

```julia
julia> update(unemployment_data, Date(2018, 1, 1), y) |> plot
julia> plot!(unemployment_data)
```

The result is the following plot:

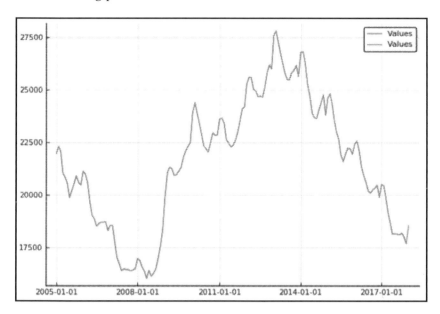

Our forecasted value has shown up on the plot.

Closing thoughts

It should be mentioned that the preceding sections represent only a few of the simplest forecasting methods available. We focused on gaining a good understanding of time series decomposition, which is a key tool for both analysis and forecasting. However, more powerful and more complex forecasting algorithms are available, for example, **autoregressive integrated moving average (ARIMA)**, **artificial neural networks (ANN)**, and Holt-Winters. These are recommended for business-critical predictions. We have now set the foundation for understanding them, but their implementations are more involved and would go beyond the technical expertise assumed by this chapter—especially as Julia's package ecosystem, at the time of writing, does not provide any libraries that implement these algorithms, and we'd have to write them from scratch.

For instance, one commonly-used time series forecasting technique is the Holt-Winters method, also called **Triple exponential smoothing**. It is based on weighted moving averages and exponential smoothing, both of which have been covered already. You can read more about these at `https://www.otexts.org/fpp/7/2` and `https://www.otexts.org/fpp/7/5`.

ARIMA models are yet another very popular forecasting algorithm. They don't use the trend and seasonality components, instead focusing on autocorrelations in the data. If you're curious, a good starting point to learn about ARIMA models is `https://www.otexts.org/fpp/8`.

Summary

Time series are a very common type of data—they can be used to represent key business metrics such as financial prices, resource usage (energy, water, raw materials, and so on), weather patterns, or macroeconomic trends—and the list could go on and on. The particularity of time series is that the data has to be collected at regular intervals, and the key aspect of time series analysis is exploring ways that allow us to understand past values so that we can predict future ones.

One powerful approach is to decompose a time series into a combination of trend, cycle, seasonality, and irregular (also called **error** or **noise**). We learned how to do this in this chapter while we analysed the EU's unemployment data. We started by learning to compute the trend component by means of moving averages. Then, we applied multiplicative series decomposition formulas to calculate seasonality and error, and we also applied basic forecasting methods to predict future values. In the process, we learned about more advanced `TimeSeries` methods and we experimented further with `Plots`. That was quite a ride—congratulations!

In the next chapter, we will look at a few more advanced topics, including package development, benchmarking techniques for measuring and improving performance, generating documentation, and registering packages. How exciting—see you in the next chapter!

11
Creating Julia Packages

We've come a long way since the beginning of our journey toward learning Julia. I hope you enjoyed this process of discovery as much as I did! We've covered a lot of ground, learning about many key topics while developing quite a suite of fully functional applications. Yet, there's one thing left in order to fully earn our Julia developer badge. The signature of every proficient Julia programmer—(drumroll, please!)—creating, publishing, and registering our own *official* Julia package!

In this chapter, we'll build a REPL app and we'll wrap it into a package. Our product will help Julia developers to easily report bugs they encounter in other Julia packages. Once the users install and configure our package, they will be able to open GitHub issues into the corresponding repo, without having to leave their REPL or IDE. In the process, we'll learn about many other very important aspects of programming with Julia, such as the following:

- Using Pkg to scaffold packages
- Package versioning and dependencies
- Test-driven development in Julia and how to unit test our code
- Benchmarking and performance optimization
- Interacting with the GitHub API
- Documenting the code base and generating documentation
- Publishing packages (with a little help from Julia's bots!)

Ready? I sure hope so. Let's go!

Technical requirements

The Julia package ecosystem is under continuous development and new package versions are released on a daily basis. Most of the times this is great news, as new releases bring new features and bug fixes. However, since many of the packages are still in beta (version 0.x), any new release can introduce breaking changes. As a result, the code presented in the book can stop working. In order to ensure that your code will produce the same results as described in the book, it is recommended to use the same package versions. Here are the external packages used in this chapter and their specific versions:

```
BenchmarkTools@v0.4.1
DocStringExtensions@v0.6.0
Documenter@v0.21.0
GitHub@v5.0.2
IJulia@v1.14.1
Traceur@v0.2.0
URIParser@v0.4.0
```

In order to install a specific version of a package you need to run:

```
pkg> add PackageName@vX.Y.Z
```

For example:

```
pkg> add IJulia@v1.14.1
```

Alternatively you can install all the used packages by downloading the `Project.toml` file provided with the chapter and using `pkg>` instantiate as follows:

```
julia>
download("https://raw.githubusercontent.com/PacktPublishing/Julia-Programmi
ng-Projects/master/Chapter11/Project.toml", "Project.toml")
pkg> activate .
pkg> instantiate
```

Creating a new Julia package

In order to create a new package, we must first satisfy a few prerequisites. To start with, we need `git` installed and configured on the development machine. The obvious reason for this is that, by default, Julia uses `git` and GitHub (https://github.com/) to host packages (although third-party, including private package, registries can also be used). If your current choice of operating system does not come with `git` preinstalled, please visit https://git-scm.com/downloads for the official download page. Pick the right version for your OS and follow the installation instructions.

Second, if you don't already have a GitHub account, you'll need one. Please visit https://github.com and set up a free account.

Now that we have `git` installed and a GitHub account, let's set up some global configuration options, as they'll come in handy. Open a new Terminal window and execute the following—please make sure to replace the placeholder text within < . . . > with your actual information:

```
$ git config --global user.name "<FULL_NAME>"
$ git config --global user.email "<EMAIL>"
$ git config --global github.user "<GITHUB_USERNAME>"
```

So for example, in my case, the first command will be as follows:

```
$ git config --global user.name "Adrian Salceanu"
```

Please check that all went well by running `git config -1`. You should get an output similar to mine:

```
$ git config -1
user.name=Adrian Salceanu
user.email=**@**
github.user=essenciary
```

Excellent! We're now ready to get down to the business of setting up our package.

Generating packages

Julia's package manager, `Pkg`, expects a certain file structure in order to manage dependencies, run tests, build binaries, generate documentation, and so on. Thankfully, we don't have to create all these manually: we will use `Pkg` itself, namely the `generate` command. All we need to do is pass it the name of our package. Let's call it `IssueReporter`:

```
julia> ] # enter Pkg mode pkg> generate IssueReporter Generating project
IssueReporter: IssueReporter/Project.toml
IssueReporter/src/IssueReporter.jl
```

A new folder was created for us, named `IssueReporter/`. Within it, we can find a `Project.toml` file and a subfolder, `src/`, which includes an `IssueReporter.jl` file.

The Project.toml file

The `Project.toml` file is very special for `Pkg`, as it's used for managing packages and their dependencies. It is meant to include meta-information, such as the name of the package, its unique identifier (called the **UUID**), the version number, the author's name, and the list of dependencies. `Pkg` has already prepopulated it, to get us started:

```
authors = ["Adrian Salceanu <*@*.com>"] # actual email truncated
name = "IssueReporter"
uuid = "7b29c13e-f3eb-11e8-2be5-fb20b77ad364"
version = "0.1.0"

[deps]
```

As you can see, `Pkg` has picked up the correct author information based on my Git settings; it has filled up the package's name and generated a new UUID, and assigned the version number `0.1.0`.

The src folder and the main module

The `src/` folder also plays a special role. A path of the form `<Package Name>/src/<Package Name>.jl` is used by Julia to identify the entry point into a package—that is, its main module. This path will be searched when we invoke `using IssueReporter`. To get us to a good start, the `IssueReporter.jl` file has already been filled up with a few lines of code, just enough to bootstrap the corresponding module:

```
module IssueReporter

greet() = print("Hello World!")

end # module
```

Using our new package

We can now activate the project and load our package:

```
julia> ; # enter shell mode
shell> cd IssueReporter
julia> ] # enter pkg mode
pkg> activate .
(IssueReporter) pkg>
```

At this point, our package's environment has been activated and the included modules are available:

```
julia> using IssueReporter
[ Info: Precompiling IssueReporter [7b29c13e-f3eb-11e8-2be5-fb20b77ad364]

julia> IssueReporter.greet()
Hello World!
```

Excellent—everything is set up and ready for us to add logic, tests, and documentation.

Defining the requirements for our package

The goal of our project is to create a Julia package that will make it very easy to report bugs in other Julia packages. We want to allow the users of our library to access a simple API for programmatic reporting of issues, without the need to go to GitHub (https://github.com/) to manually create a new issue.

In order to do this, we need to implement the following two features—a way to find out the GitHub URL of a registered package; and the means to access the GitHub API to register a new issue on the found repo. Given that Pkg is capable of cloning a package from GitHub using only the name of the package, we can safely assume that the information is available with our Julia install, and that somehow we'll be able to access that information ourselves. Then, the aptly named GitHub package will help us to interface with GitHub's API. We can start by adding it. Please make sure that the currently active project is IssueReporter. This should be indicated by the (IssuerReporter) prefix, placed in front of the pkg> cursor. If that is not the case, as previously explained, you need to cd into our package's directory and then run pkg> activate . as follows:

```
(IssueReporter) pkg> add GitHub
```

While we're at it, let's also add the URIParser package—we'll work a lot with repo URLs and this functionality will come in handy:

```
(IssueReporter) pkg> add URIParser
```

And, one more thing—we'll use **test-driven development** (**TDD**) in order to build our project, so we'll also need Julia's Test module:

```
(IssueReporter) pkg> add Test
```

At this point, all the packages have been added to the list of dependencies. You can confirm this by checking the Project.toml file, which is under the [deps] section and should now show the following:

```
[deps]
GitHub = "bc5e4493-9b4d-5f90-b8aa-2b2bcaad7a26"
Test = "8dfed614-e22c-5e08-85e1-65c5234f0b40"
URIParser = "30578b45-9adc-5946-b283-645ec420af67"
```

Now we have all the prerequisites for adding our logic, the TDD way.

Beginning with test-driven Julia development

Test-driven development is a software development practice based on a simple workflow that puts automated testing center stage. The basic idea is that the requirements are turned into very specific, well-defined, and targeted test cases. Each test should address only one piece of functionality. Once the test is ready, we run the whole test suite. Obviously, as we first write the test, it will initially fail. Next, we add the minimal implementation to make the test pass. That's it—all we need to do is repeat the same process until all the requirements are implemented. This approach ensures that our code base is thoroughly tested and that we focus on delivering just the requirements, avoiding feature creep.

Julia provides built-in unit testing capabilities under the `Test` module. It is very straightforward and easy to use, providing enough methods to cover all the basic testing scenarios: value and exception checking, approximate values, types, and so on.

The most important ones are the `@test`, `@test_throws`, and `@testset` macros. The `@test` macro checks that the `expression` passed as argument evaluates to true, returning a `PassResult`. If the test does not pass, it will return either a `FailResult` when the expression evaluates to `false`—or an `ErrorResult` if the expression can't be evaluated at all. The `@test_throws` macro checks that the evaluated expression throws an exception. Finally, `@testset` is used to group tests into sets. All the tests in a test set will run, and at the end of the test set, a summary of the results will be displayed. If any of the tests failed, or could not be evaluated due to an error, the test set will throw a `TestSetException`.

For example, consider the following:

```julia
julia> using Test

julia> @test 1 == 1
Test Passed

julia> @test 'A' == 'a'
Test Failed
  Expression: 'A' == 'a'
   Evaluated: 'A' == 'a'
ERROR: There was an error during testing
# output omitted #
```

The previous snippet shows the output from both a passing and a failing test. The following one illustrates the use of test sets, with one passing and one failing test:

```
julia> @testset "Example" begin
           @test :a == :a
           @test 'x' == 'y'
       end
Example: Test Failed
  Expression: 'x' == 'y'
  Evaluated: 'x' == 'y'

Test Summary: | Pass  Fail  Total
Example       |   1     1      2
ERROR: Some tests did not pass: 1 passed, 1 failed, 0 errored, 0 broken.
# output omitted #
```

Finally, this is how exceptions are handled:

```
julia> @testset "Example" begin
           error("Oh no!")
       end
Example: Error During Test
  Got an exception of type ErrorException outside of a @test
  Oh no!

Test Summary: | Error  Total
Example       |   1      1
ERROR: Some tests did not pass: 0 passed, 0 failed, 1 errored, 0 broken.
# output omitted #
```

Now that we have the testing theory covered, let's continue by writing our first test. We will need a method that will take a package name and return the corresponding GitHub repo URL. This URL will be used in order to later interact with the GitHub API and open the issue into the corresponding repo. For now, we'll just check that the return value is a valid URL. We'll use the URIParser package to check the validity.

Julia makes it easy to add and run tests for our package, again, through the functionality provided by Pkg under the test command. When we run (IssueReporter) pkg> test, the Pkg library will look for a file called runtests.jl in the test/ folder.

Time to add them—from within the Julia REPL:

```
julia> mkdir("test")
"test"

julia> touch("test/runtests.jl")
"test/runtests.jl"
```

Now, open the newly created `runtests.jl` file in the editor, for example, by running the following:

```
julia> edit("test/runtests.jl")
```

Please make sure your `runtests.jl` file looks like this:

```
using IssueReporter
using Test, URIParser, GitHub

@testset "Basic features" begin
  @testset "Looking up an existing package returns a proper repo URI" begin
    @test IssueReporter.packageuri("DataFrames") |> URIParser.isvalid
  end
end
```

In this snippet, we define a test set called `"Basic features"`. Within it, we have yet another test set, which contains the actual test. Finally, the test invokes a function called `packageuri` from the `IssueReporter` module, passing it the `DataFrames` string as its argument. What we're trying to do here is get the GitHub URI for a package that we know exists and is registered, namely `DataFrames`. Then, we make sure that the URI is valid by passing it into the `URIParser.isvalid` method.

A test set block, defined by the `@testset` macro, groups multiple tests and/or other tests sets. The reason for using test sets is that when a test fails, an exception is thrown, causing the execution of the script to stop. However, when we have a large batch of tests, we usually prefer to allow all the tests to run and get a full report of what failed and what worked. With a test set, all the tests within the set will be run and a summary will be displayed at the end of the set. If any of the tests fail, or cannot be evaluated due to an error, the test set will then throw a `TestSetException`.

Test sets should have self-explanatory names relevant to the batch of tests they represent, as these labels are outputted when the tests are run.

We can run the test as follows:

```
(IssueReporter) pkg> test
```

It will fail with an informative message:

```
(IssueReporter) pkg> test
   Testing IssueReporter
 Resolving package versions...
Looking up an existing package returns a proper repo URI: Error During Test
at IssueReporter/test/runtests.jl:7
  Test threw exception
```

```
     Expression: IssueReporter.packageuri("DataFrames") |> URIParser.isvalid
     UndefVarError: packageuri not defined
   Test Summary:                                            | Error   Total
   Basic features                                           |   1       1
     Looking up an existing package returns a proper repo URI |   1       1
   ERROR: LoadError: Some tests did not pass: 0 passed, 0 failed, 1 errored, 0
   broken.
   ERROR: Package IssueReporter errored during testing
   # output omitted #
```

The important bit is UndefVarError: packageuri not defined. This is unsurprising, as we have not yet defined the IssueReporter.packageuri function.

Peeking into Julia's registry

As we were saying, we need a way to retrieve the GitHub URI of a package, based on the package's name. Now, given that we're able to successfully execute operations such as add and develop with Pkg, without having to provide the GitHub URI, we can assume that there is a way to convert a package name to a package URL.

Indeed, Julia manages a repository of all the packages that are known to Pkg. These packages are grouped into multiple registries that are copied to your computer. By default, Julia comes with the so-called General registry, which can be found in the .julia/ folder in your home directory. The General registry itself is nothing but a folder that contains subfolders named after each letter in the English alphabet (thus, from A to Z). Within each of these folders, we can find all the packages whose names start with that letter:

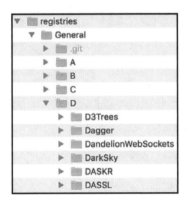

This screenshot shows a part of the General registry, with some of its folders (from A to D) and some of the packages starting with the letter D.

In order to make package retrieval more efficient, a special index file, called `Registry.toml`, is also placed inside the `General` folder. This file defines a hash-based index that maps package UUIDs to a dictionary of `name` and `path` values—the path being relative and pointing to a folder within the `General` registry. For example, this is the entry corresponding to the `D3Trees` package, the first one under the letter `D`:

```
e3df1716-f71e-5df9-9e2d-98e193103c45 = { name = "D3Trees", path =
"D/D3Trees" }
```

Moving on, if we peek into the `D3Trees/` folder itself, we'll see that it contains four files, each of them containing important metadata:

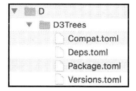

The screenshot shows the four `Pkg` metadata files belonging to the `D3Trees` package.

The `Deps.toml` file includes the list of dependencies (those packages required by `D3Trees` itself). The `Compat.toml` file stores compatibility requirements for the dependencies and for the Julia versions. `Package.toml` defines information such as name, UUID, and repo URL, and finally, `Versions.toml` shows all the known versions of `D3Trees` together with their corresponding Git references. It looks like we need the information within the `Package.toml` file.

The workflow, then, is the following:

1. Get the path to Julia's `General` registry
2. Read the `Registry.toml` file
3. Look for a package with the name that we're searching for
4. If the package exists, get its path in the `General` registry
5. Read the corresponding `Package.toml` file
6. Extract the package's GitHub URL

Working with TOML files

Tom's Obvious, Minimal Language (TOML) is a minimal configuration file format created by Tom Preston-Werner. TOML files serve the same purpose as other configuration formats, for example, the famous INI—although TOML's goal is to be easier to read and easier to parse. YAML and JSON are other very popular configuration formats that you may have encountered. `Pkg` makes extensive usage of TOML for storing package metadata.

> You can read more about TOML, including the full specification, at
> `https://github.com/toml-lang/toml`.

A TOML parser for Julia is available at `https://github.com/wildart/TOML.jl`, but we don't need to explicitly add it as `Pkg` comes bundled with a TOML parser that we will use instead. But, this means that we do have to declare `Pkg` as a dependency of `IssueReporter`:

```
(IssueReporter) pkg> add Pkg
```

Now, to implement the preceding workflow. First, the path to the `General` registry.

Julia keeps track of a list of locations where important information is stored. This info includes configuration files, environments, installed packages, and registries. In Julia's lingo, these are called **depots** and are stored in the `DEPOT_PATH` global variable:

```
julia> DEPOT_PATH 3-element Array{String,1}: "/Users/adrian/.julia"
"/Applications/Julia-1.0.app/Contents/Resources/julia/local/share/julia"
"/Applications/Julia-1.0.app/Contents/Resources/julia/share/julia"
```

The contents of the `DEPOT_PATH` array on my computer are shown here. Your output will be different, but similar.

The first entry is the user depot where registries are cloned, new package versions are installed, package repos are cloned, log files are written, development packages are checked out by default, and global configuration data is saved. Later entries in the depot path are read-only and are used for operations performed by system administrators.

Let's add a new (failing) test for getting the `General` registry path:

```
@testset "Interacting with the registry" begin
  @testset "The General registry is accessible" begin
    IssueReporter.generalregistrypath() |> Base.Filesystem.isdir
  end
end
```

As for the implementation, we will want to loop over each entry in the `DEPOT_PATH` and check if it contains a `registries/General` path of directories. These should be in the user depot, but a more extensive lookup will make our code more robust:

```
function generalregistrypath()
  for i in DEPOT_PATH
    if isdir(joinpath(i, "registries", "General"))
      return joinpath(i, "registries", "General")
    end
  end
end
```

Once we have the path to the `General` registry, we'll want to parse the `Registry.toml` file and extract the information corresponding to the package we'll be searching for. Once parsed, the `Registry.toml` file produces in a dictionary with five entries:

```
Dict{String,Any} with 5 entries:
  "name"        => "General"
  "repo"        => "https://github.com/JuliaRegistries/General.git"
  "packages"    => Dict{String,Any}("c786d6c3-4fbc-59fc-968c-
e848efb65d2d"=>Dict{String,Any}("name"=>"ScHoLP","path"=>"S/ScHoLP"),"88634
af6-177f-5301-88b8-7819386cfa38"=>Dict{String,Any}("name"=>"SaferIntegers",
"path"=>"S/SaferIntegers")...
  "uuid"        => "23338594-aafe-5451-b93e-139f81909106"
  "description" => "Official general Julia package registry where people
# output omitted #
```

We're only interested in the *packages* data, which looks like this:

```
Dict{String,Any} with 2358 entries:
  "c786d6c3-4fbc-59fc-968c-e848efb65d2d" =>
Dict{String,Any}("name"=>"ScHoLP","path"=>"S/ScHoLP")
  "88634af6-177f-5301-88b8-7819386cfa38" =>
Dict{String,Any}("name"=>"SaferIntegers","path"=>"S/SaferIntegers")
  "aa65fe97-06da-5843-b5b1-d5d13cad87d2" =>
Dict{String,Any}("name"=>"SnoopCompile","path"=>"S/SnoopCompile")
# output truncated #
```

And actually, we don't want all that, since we don't care about the UUID; only the name and the path. Let's add a new function to the `IssueReporter` module, to reflect this spec:

```
function generalregistry()
    TOML.parsefile(joinpath(generalregistrypath(),
"Registry.toml"))["packages"] |> values |> collect
end
```

The output of the function is similar to this, an array of `Dict` elements:

```
2358-element Array{Any,1}:
 Dict{String,Any}("name"=>"ScHoLP","path"=>"S/ScHoLP")
 Dict{String,Any}("name"=>"SaferIntegers","path"=>"S/SaferIntegers")
 Dict{String,Any}("name"=>"SnoopCompile","path"=>"S/SnoopCompile")
# output truncated #
```

Once we have this, it is very easy to perform a package lookup by name. We simply iterate over each item and compare the `"name"` value against the search string:

```
function searchregistry(pkgname::String)
  for item in generalregistry()
    item["name"] == pkgname && return item
  end
end
```

After we identify a package by name, we can use the path value to build the path to the folder that contains the package's metadata information. Remember that we're after the `Package.toml` file, as this contains the repo URI.

Putting it all together, we can finally write our `IssueReporter.packageuri` function:

```
function packageuri(pkgname::String)
  TOML.parsefile(joinpath(generalregistrypath(),
searchregistry(pkgname)["path"], "Package.toml"))["repo"]
end
```

Your `IssueReporter.jl` file should look like this:

```
module IssueReporter

using Pkg, Pkg.TOML

function generalregistrypath()
  for i in DEPOT_PATH
    if isdir(joinpath(i, "registries", "General"))
      return joinpath(i, "registries", "General")
    end
  end
```

```
end

function generalregistry()
    TOML.parsefile(joinpath(generalregistrypath(),
"Registry.toml"))["packages"] |> values |> collect
end

function searchregistry(pkgname::String)
  for item in generalregistry()
    item["name"] == pkgname && return item
  end
end

function packageuri(pkgname::String)
  TOML.parsefile(joinpath(generalregistrypath(),
searchregistry(pkgname)["path"], "Package.toml"))["repo"]
end

end # module
```

The IssueReporter.jl package

Running the tests again will be successful:

```
(IssueReporter) pkg> test
```

The output is as follows:

```
          Testing IssueReporter
       Resolving package versions...
Test Summary:                       |
Interacting with the registry | No tests
Test Summary:   | Pass   Total
Basic features  |    1       1
       Testing IssueReporter tests passed
```

If you're curious, the GitHub repo URI for `DataFrames`, according to `IssueReporter`, is as follows:

```
julia> IssueReporter.packageuri("DataFrames")
https://github.com/JuliaData/DataFrames.jl.git
```

If you want, you can check for yourself in the web browser to confirm that it is indeed, the correct URI.

Performance testing

Our code works correctly so far, but what about it's performance? Besides its readable syntax, liberal license, rich package ecosystem, and welcoming community, performance is one of the top reasons why data scientists and software developers choose Julia. The compiler does a great job of providing excellent performance out of the box, but there are certain best practices that we as developers must keep in mind to ensure that we basically don't hinder the compiler. We'll go over the most important ones by looking at a few examples while running some benchmarks.

Benchmarking tools

Given its focus on performance, it should come as no surprise that both core Julia and the ecosystem provide a variety of tools for inspecting our code, looking for bottlenecks and measuring runtime and memory usage. One of the simplest is the @time macro. It takes an expression and then prints its execution time, number of allocations, and the total number of bytes the execution caused to be allocated, before returning the result of the expression. For example, note the following:

```
julia> @time [x for x in 1:1_000_000];
  0.031727 seconds (55.85 k allocations: 10.387 MiB)
```

Generating an array of one million integers by iterating from one to one million takes 0.03 seconds. Not bad, but what if I told you that we can do better—much better? We just committed one of the cardinal sins of Julia—code should not be run (nor benchmarked) in the global scope. So, rule one—always wrap your code into functions.

The previous snippet can easily be refactored as follows:

```
julia> function onetomil()
           [x for x in 1:1_000_000]
       end
onetomil (generic function with 1 method)
```

Now, the benchmark is as follows:

```
julia> @time onetomil();
  0.027002 seconds (65.04 k allocations: 10.914 MiB)
```

All right, that's clearly faster—but not much faster. However, what if we run the benchmark one more time?

```
julia> @time onetomil();
  0.002413 seconds (6 allocations: 7.630 MiB)
```

Wow, that's an order of magnitude faster! So, what gives?

If you remember from our coverage of functions and methods, Julia uses a **just-in-time (JIT)** compiler; that is, a function is compiled in real time when it is invoked for the first time. So, our initial benchmark also included the compilation time. This brings us to the second rule—don't benchmark the first run.

The best way to accurately measure the performance of a piece of code, thus, would be to execute it multiple times and then compute the mean. There is a great tool, specially designed for this use case, called BenchmarkTools. Let's add it and give it a try:

```
(IssueReporter) pkg> add BenchmarkTools
julia> using BenchmarkTools
julia> @benchmark onetomil()
BenchmarkTools.Trial:
  memory estimate:  7.63 MiB
  allocs estimate:  2
  --------------
  minimum time:     1.373 ms  (0.00% GC)
  median time:      1.972 ms  (0.00% GC)
  mean time:        2.788 ms  (34.06% GC)
  maximum time:     55.129 ms  (96.23% GC)
  --------------
  samples:          1788
  evals/sample:     1
```

BenchmarkTools took 1788 samples, with an evals to sample ratio of 1. Here, a sample represents a measurement, while an evaluation is an execution of the benchmark expression. We got a maximum time of 55 milliseconds, driven by the garbage collection, with a minimum of 1.3 milliseconds, and a mean of 2.7 milliseconds. That is in line with what the second @time execution revealed, at 2.4 milliseconds—but this benchmark is far more accurate. We can also use the more compact @btime macro, which has an output similar to @time, but executes an equally comprehensive benchmark:

```
julia> @btime onetomil();
  1.363 ms (2 allocations: 7.63 MiB)
```

> BenchmarkTools exposes a very rich API and it's worth getting to know it well. You can read more about it at
> `https://github.com/JuliaCI/BenchmarkTools.jl/blob/master/doc/man ual.md`.

Type stability is key

If there is one thing that has a direct and massive impact on the performance of Julia code, it's the type system. And the most important thing about it is to write code that is type-stable. Type stability means that the type of a variable (including the return value of a function) must not vary with time or under different inputs. Understanding how to leverage type stability is key to writing fast software. Now that we know how to measure our code's execution time, we can see the effect of type instability with a few examples.

Let's take this innocent-looking function, for example:

```julia
julia> function f1()
           x = 0

           for i in 1:10
               x += sin(i)
           end
           x
       end
f1 (generic function with 1 method)
```

There's nothing fancy about it. We have a variable, x, which is initialized to 0—and then a loop from 1 to 10, where we add the sin of a number to x. And then we return x. Nothing to see, right? Well, actually, quite the contrary—a few bad things, performance-wise, are happening here. And they all have to do with type instability.

Julia provides a great tool for inspecting and diagnosing code for type-related issues—the @code_warntype macro. Here's what we get when we use it with our f1 function:

```julia
julia> @code_warntype f1()
```

The output is as follows:

```
Body::Union{Float64, Int64}
3 1 ──       (Base.ifelse)(true, 10, 0)
        %2  = (Base.slt_int)(10, 1)::Bool
              goto #3 if not %2
  2 ──        goto #4
  3 ──        goto #4
  4 ── %6  = φ (#2 => true, #3 => false)::Bool
        %7  = φ (#3 => 1)::Int64
        %8  = φ (#3 => 1)::Int64
        %9  = (Base.not_int)(%6)::Bool
              goto #15 if not %9
  5 ── %11 = φ (#4 => 0, #14 => %29)::Union{Float64, Int64}
        %12 = φ (#4 => %7, #14 => %35)::Int64
        %13 = φ (#4 => %8, #14 => %36)::Int64
        %14 = (Base.sitofp)(Float64, %12)::Float64
        %15 = invoke Base.Math.sin(%14::Float64)::Float64
        %16 = (isa)(%11, Float64)::Bool
              goto #7 if not %16
  6 ── %18 = π (%11, Float64)
        %19 = (Base.add_float)(%18, %15)::Float64
              goto #10
  7 ── %21 = (isa)(%11, Int64)::Bool
              goto #9 if not %21
  8 ── %23 = π (%11, Int64)
        %24 = (Base.sitofp)(Float64, %23)::Float64
        %25 = (Base.add_float)(%24, %15)::Float64
              goto #10
  9 ──        (Core.throw)(ErrorException("fatal error in type inference (type bound)"))
              $(Expr(:unreachable))
 10 ── %29 = φ (#6 => %19, #8 => %25)::Float64
        %30 = (%13 === 10)::Bool
              goto #12 if not %30
 11 ──        goto #13
 12 ── %33 = (Base.add_int)(%13, 1)::Int64
              goto #13
 13 ── %35 = φ (#12 => %33)::Int64
        %36 = φ (#12 => %33)::Int64
        %37 = φ (#11 => true, #12 => false)::Bool
        %38 = (Base.not_int)(%37)::Bool
              goto #15 if not %38
 14 ──        goto #5
6 15 ── %41 = φ (#13 => %29, #4 => 0)::Union{Float64, Int64}
              return %41
```

This time, I'm using a screenshot for the output, in order to illustrate the color coding. As you might expect, green is good and red is bad. I am also marking the red flags with a rectangle. The problems are with `Body::Union{Float64, Int64}` on the first line, `(#4 => 0, #14 => %29)::Union{Float64, Int64}` on line 12, and `(#13 => %29, #4 => 0)::Union{Float64, Int64}` on the penultimate line.

On the first line, the `Body::Union{Float64, Int64}`, as well as on the penultimate line, `::Union{Float64, Int64}`, tell us the same thing—the function returns a `Union{Float64, Int64}`, meaning that the function can return either a `Float` or an `Integer`. This is textbook type instability and bad news for performance. Next, on line 12, *something* has a type of `Union{Float64, Int64}` and this value is then returned as the result of the function. In case you're wondering, that *something* is x.

The problem is that we unsuspectingly initialized x to 0, an `Integer`. However, the `sin` function will return a `Float`. Adding a `Float` to an `Integer` will result in a `Float`, causing the type of x to change accordingly. Thus, x has two types during the execution of the function, and since we return x, our function is also type-unstable.

Granted, understanding the output of `@code_warntype` is not easy, although it does get easier with time. However, we can make our job easier by using the super-useful `Traceur` package. It provides a `@trace` macro, which generates human-friendly information. Let's add it and try it out; you'll appreciate it, I'm sure:

```
(IssueReporter) pkg> add Traceur
julia> using Traceur
julia> @trace f1()
 ┌ Warning: x is assigned as Int64
 └ @ REPL[94]:2
 ┌ Warning: x is assigned as Float64
 └ @ REPL[94]:4
 ┌ Warning: f1 returns Union{Float64, Int64}
 └ @ REPL[94]:2
1.4111883712180104
```

How cool is that? Crystal clear!

With this feedback in mind, we can refactor our code into a new f2 function:

```
julia> function f2()
           x = 0.0

           for i in 1:10
                   x += sin(i)
           end

           x
       end
f2 (generic function with 1 method)

julia> @trace f2()
1.4111883712180104
```

Awesome, nothing to report! No news is good news!

Now, we can benchmark `f1` and `f2` to see the result of our refactoring:

```julia
julia> @btime f1()
  129.413 ns (0 allocations: 0 bytes)
1.4111883712180104

julia> @btime f2()
  79.241 ns (0 allocations: 0 bytes)
1.4111883712180104
```

That's nice—79 versus 129 nanoseconds! If you're thinking that *It's just 50 nanoseconds, what's all the fuss about?*, you need to look at it this way—`f2`, the type-stable variant, is almost twice as fast as `f1`! And that's a really big deal!

Benchmarking our code

It's time to apply what we've learned to our own code base. Heads up, I have intentionally sneaked in a few problems, to spice things up a bit. Let's fix them together:

```julia
julia> @code_warntype IssueReporter.packageuri("DataFrames")
```

The output is as follows:

```
Body::Any
35 1 ─ %1  = invoke IssueReporter.generalregistrypath()::Union{Nothing, String}
      │ %2  = invoke IssueReporter.searchregistry(_2::String)::Any
      │ %3  = (Base.getindex)(%2, "path")::Any
      │ %4  = (IssueReporter.joinpath)(%1, %3, "Package.toml")::String
      │ %5  = invoke Base.:(#open#294)($(QuoteNode(Base.Iterators.Pairs{Union{},Union{},
OML.parse), %4::String, "r"::Vararg{String,N} where N)::Dict{String,Any}
      │ %6  = invoke Base.ht_keyindex(%5::Dict{String,Any}, "repo"::String)::Int64
      │ %7  = (Base.slt_int)(%6, 0)::Bool
      └──       goto #3 if not %7
   2 ─ %9  = %new(Base.KeyError, "repo")::KeyError
      │         (Base.throw)(%9)
      └──       $(Expr(:unreachable))
   3 ─ %12 = (Base.getfield)(%5, :vals)::Array{Any,1}
      │ %13 = (Base.arrayref)(false, %12, %6)::Any
      └──       goto #5
   4 ─        $(Expr(:unreachable))
   5 ─        return %13
```

This is all very interesting—let's see what we can learn from it.

Starting with line 1, the `IssueReporter.generalregistrypath` function returns a `Union{Nothing, String}`. The reason is that our function does not handle the case when the `for` loop is not entered, or when the `if` statement is not executed. We should make sure that our function always returns a value and that the type of this return value does not change. To be extra sure, we can also add a type assertion to the function definition itself. If we accidentally return the wrong type, Julia will try to convert it to the declared type—if that doesn't work, an error is thrown.

We need to redefine the function as follows:

```
function generalregistrypath() :: String
  for i in DEPOT_PATH
    if isdir(joinpath(i, "registries", "General"))
      return joinpath(i, "registries", "General")
    end
  end
  ""
end
```

Now, on to the line starting with %2 (the third line)—the `searchregistry` function returns a value of type `Any`. The issue here is that we return an item coming from the invocation of `generalregistry`, so we need to look at that first. We'll add a check for the return value of `generalregistrypath`, and we add a default return value, an empty `Vector{Dict{String,Any}}`. Then, for `searchregistry`, we'll also add a default return value—since it returns an item from this `Vector`, it will be of type `Dict{String,Any}`.

Next, in regards to the `packageuri` function, in the line starting with %9 (on line 11), we can see something about a `KeyError` and `repo`. Julia is warning us that it's possible that we won't have a key named `repo`, thus leading to a `KeyError`. Also, the function returns an object of type `Any`.

Here are the three functions, refactored:

```
function generalregistry() :: Vector{Dict{String,Any}}
  if ! isempty(generalregistrypath())
    TOML.parsefile(joinpath(generalregistrypath(),
"Registry.toml"))["packages"] |> values |> collect
  else
    Dict{String,Any}[]
  end
end

function searchregistry(pkgname::String) :: Dict{String,Any}
  for item in generalregistry()
    item["name"] == pkgname && return item
```

```
    end

    Dict{String,Any}()
end

function packageuri(pkgname::String) :: String
    pkg = searchregistry(pkgname)
    isempty(pkg) && return ""
    get!(TOML.parsefile(joinpath(generalregistrypath(), pkg["path"],
"Package.toml")), "repo", "")
end
```

We can now recheck our code:

```
julia> @code_warntype IssueReporter.packageuri("DataFrames")
```

The output is as follows:

Excellent, almost everything is green! There's just one red `Any`, coming from the `TOML.parsefile` function itself, but it's just not worth optimizing that away; the extra work would cancel the benefit.

It's definitely worth spending some time going over the official performance recommendations, available online at `https://docs.julialang.org/en/v1/manual/performance-tips/`.

Interacting with the GitHub API

Now that we can retrieve the GitHub URI for any package in the `General` registry, we can use it to interact with the GitHub API. Julia developers have access to a powerful GitHub library provided by the GitHub package. It's what we'll use in order to create new issues on the packages' GitHub repos.

Authenticating with the GitHub API

In order to be allowed to interact with the GitHub API, we have to authenticate. This will permit our package to execute actions on GitHub under the user's account as if done directly through the website. Please access `https://github.com/settings/tokens/new` to set up a new GitHub access token. If you're not familiar with the concept and would like to learn more about this, please read on and follow the official instructions at `https://help.github.com/articles/creating-a-personal-access-token-for-the-command-line/`. Give the token a good description and, very importantly, make sure that you check the **repo** scope, just as you can see in this screenshot:

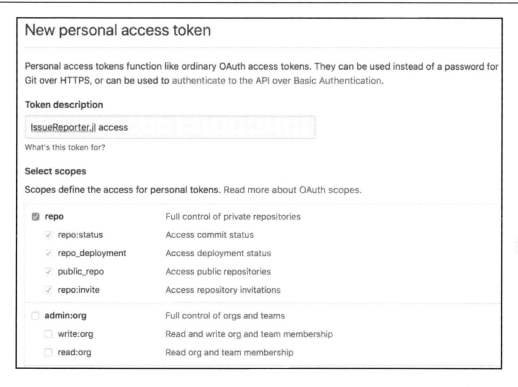

New personal access token

Personal access tokens function like ordinary OAuth access tokens. They can be used instead of a password for Git over HTTPS, or can be used to authenticate to the API over Basic Authentication.

Token description

IssueReporter.jl access

What's this token for?

Select scopes

Scopes define the access for personal tokens. Read more about OAuth scopes.

☑ **repo**		Full control of private repositories
	☑ repo:status	Access commit status
	☑ repo_deployment	Access deployment status
	☑ public_repo	Access public repositories
	☑ repo:invite	Access repository invitations
☐ **admin:org**		Full control of orgs and teams
	☐ write:org	Read and write org and team membership
	☐ read:org	Read org and team membership

Once generated, write down the token—once you leave that page, you won't see it again.

The access tokens must be manipulated with care—and must not be committed to git or other source control systems where they can be accessed by other users. Anybody that gets your access token can use it to impersonate you on GitHub. To be on the safe side, please make sure that for this project, you only check the **repo** scope.

Let's add a bit of logic to make the access token available to our package without compromising security. It should work as follows—first, we check if the access token is provided as a command line parameter to the Julia process—meaning that it will be available in the ENV collection. If it's not, we'll look for a file called secrets.jl in the root folder of the package and include it. The file will contain the access token so we'll add it to .gitignore, to make sure it's not accidentally committed to git.

So, let's write the tests. Append the following at the end of `runtests.jl`:

```julia
@testset "GitHub integration" begin
  delete!(ENV, "GITHUB_ACCESS_TOKEN")

  @testset "An undefined token should return false" begin
    @test ! IssueReporter.tokenisdefined()
  end
  @testset "Attempting to access a token that is not set will error" begin
    @test_throws ErrorException IssueReporter.token()
  end
  # setup a mock token
  ENV["GITHUB_ACCESS_TOKEN"] = "1234"
  @testset "Token is defined" begin
    @test IssueReporter.tokenisdefined()
  end
  @testset "A valid token is a non empty string and has the set value" begin
    token = IssueReporter.token()
    @test isa(token, String) && ! isempty(token)
    @test token == "1234"
  end
end
```

The tests will fail, of course, so let's make them pass.

Add these function definitions to `IssueReporter.jl`:

```julia
function tokenisdefined() :: Bool
    if ! haskey(ENV, "GITHUB_ACCESS_TOKEN")
        secrets_path = joinpath(@__DIR__, "secrets.jl")
        isfile(secrets_path) && include(secrets_path)
        haskey(ENV, "GITHUB_ACCESS_TOKEN") || return false
    end
    true
end

function token() :: String
    tokenisdefined() && return ENV["GITHUB_ACCESS_TOKEN"]
    error("""ENV["GITHUB_ACCESS_TOKEN"] is not set -- please make sure it's
passed as a command line argument or defined in the `secrets.jl` file.""")
end
```

In the `tokenisdefined` function, we check if the `GITHUB_ACCESS_TOKEN` environment variable is already defined—if not, we check for the `secrets.jl` file and, if it exists, we include it. Once included, the `secrets.jl` file should define the variable, so finally, we check again for the existence of `GITHUB_ACCESS_TOKEN`. If the token is still not defined, the function returns `false`—otherwise, `true`. We've also added a token function that invokes `tokenisdefined`, giving the module the chance to set up `GITHUB_ACCESS_TOKEN`. If the token is available, it returns it—if not, this time an error is thrown. Our tests should now pass:

```
pkg> test
```

This is it, as shown here:

```
        Testing IssueReporter
        Resolving package versions...
Test Summary:                      | Pass   Total
Interacting with the registry |      1       1
Test Summary:   | Pass   Total
Basic features  |    1       1
Test Summary:           | Pass   Total
GitHub integration |      5        5
```

Success!

Before moving on, we need to add the `secrets.jl` file to `.gitignore`—committing this to a public GitHub repo would be a huge security error. From the Julia REPL, note the following:

```
julia> write(".gitignore", "secrets.jl")
```

Now, you need to create the `secrets.jl` file itself and make sure that it contains something similar to the next snippet, but adding your own GitHub access token:

```
ENV["GITHUB_ACCESS_TOKEN"] = "0cdf8672e66***" # token truncated
```

Excellent, we're ready to report issues!

Reporting GitHub issues

We're now down to the last step—using the GitHub API to report problems. In order to register an issue, we need two pieces of information—the title and the body. As such, we'll have to define a new function, called `report`, which will accept *three* string arguments—the name of the package, plus two more for the title and the body of the issue. Internally, the function will make an authenticated call to the corresponding GitHub API via the GitHub package.

According to the documentation, a call to the `GitHub.create_issue` method looks like this:

```
GitHub.create_issue("<username>/<repo>", auth = <GitHub.OAuth2>, params...)
```

This means that we need to do the following:

1. Use the GitHub token to authenticate and generate the required `GitHub.OAuth2` authentication object
2. Starting from the Julia package name, compute the GitHub username and repo info—for this, we'll use the already implemented `IssueReporter.packageurl`, plus some extra processing to remove the unwanted parts from the URL
3. Make the call to `GitHub.create_issue`, passing in all the required arguments

Since we're doing TDD, let's begin by converting these specifications into tests. Add the following at the very bottom of the `runtests.jl` file:

```
@testset "Adding GitHub issues" begin
  delete!(ENV, "GITHUB_ACCESS_TOKEN")

  @testset "Successful authentication should return a GitHub.OAuth2
instance" begin
    @test isa(IssueReporter.githubauth(), GitHub.OAuth2)
  end
  @testset "Converting package name to GitHub id" begin
    @test IssueReporter.repoid("IssueReporter") ==
"essenciary/IssueReporter.jl"
  end
  @testset "Submitting an issue should result in a GitHub.Issue object"
begin
    @test isa(IssueReporter.report("IssueReporter", "I found a bug", "Here
is how you can reproduce the problem: ..."), GitHub.Issue)
  end
end
```

The tests mirror, in the exact same order, the requirements we previously expressed in plain English. The first one invokes a function that we'll have to write, called `IssueReporter.githubauth`, which will perform the GitHub authentication and will return a `GitHub.OAuth2` object if successful. Next, we'll need a new `repoid` function, which will take the name of a package and will return the GitHub username and repo name. Notice that we're using my repo of the `IssueReporter` package as the guinea pig for our testing. Finally, we test the issue creation, which will be done by the `IssueReporter.report` method—on success, we expect a `GitHub.Issue` object.

 Don't use Julia for anything evil! The code we're writing will actually register new issues on live GitHub repos. Please be respectful of the hard work of the open source contributors and don't overload them with fake issues.

Time to make the tests pass by writing the implementations. Make sure that the `using` directive of the `IssueReporter` module reads as follows:

```
using Pkg, Pkg.TOML, GitHub, URIParser  # we've added URIParser and GitHub
```

And then, add the following functions to the bottom of the `IssueReporter` module:

```
function githubauth()
  token() |> GitHub.authenticate
end

function repoid(package_name::String)
  pkg_url = packageuri(package_name) |> URIParser.parse_url
  repo_info = endswith(pkg_url.path, ".git") ?
                 replace(pkg_url.path, r".git$"=>"") :
                 pkg_url.path
  repo_info[2:end]
end

function report(package_name::String, title::String, body::String)
  GitHub.create_issue(repoid(package_name), auth = githubauth(),
                      params = Dict(:title => title, :body => body))
end
```

Pretty straightforward. The `githubauth` function invokes the `GitHub.authenticate` method, passing it the auth token provided by a call to the token function.

The `repoid` method accepts a string parameter for the name of the repo, then invokes the `packageuri` and the `URIParse.parse_url` to generate a URI object corresponding to the GitHub repo. We then extract the path component of the URI and process it to keep only the GitHub username and the repo name. In other words, starting with the package named `IssueReporter`, we retrieve the GitHub repo URL, which is `git://github.com/essenciary/IssueReporter.jl.git`. The path component is `/essenciary/IssueReporter.jl.git`. We use replace with the `r".git$"` regex to remove the `.git` ending before returning the substring starting from the second letter. At the end, we have what we need—`essenciary/IssueReporter.jl`.

Lastly, the report function puts it all together by invoking the `GitHub.create_issue` method and passing it the `repoid`, the authentication object, and the title and body of the issue within a `Dict`. All the tests should pass now and the issues are successfully created on Github.com (`https://github.com/`):

Please note that the sample code provided with the chapter has the `create issue` functionality commented out—and instead it has hard-coded a dummy repository. Again, out of respect for the contributors and followers of the real repos, the actual issues will be created on a dummy repository that I created especially for this purpose.

Documenting our package

Our package is now complete! Let's make it easy for our users to take advantage of the amazing convenience provided by `IssueReporter`—we'll supply them an informative documentation. We already know how to document our code by using `DocStrings` - which can be used by ourselves and other developers to understand our source code. It's also used by the REPL's help system (remember from Chapter 1, *Getting Started with Julia Programming* that you can type `?` at the beginning of the line to switch the REPL to help mode). You'll be happy to hear that we can also generate package documentation using the same `DocStrings`, with the help of a package called `Documenter`. Please add it with `(IssueReporter) pkg> add Documenter`.

So, the first thing to do is add some `DocStrings` to our functions. Keep in mind that the *official* recommendation is to include the function's signature together with a small description and a few examples. For instance, the documentation for the `IssueReporter.packageuri` function could look like this:

```
""" packageuri(pkgname::String) :: String
Takes the name of a registered Julia package and returns the associated
repo git URL.
Examples ``` jldoctest julia> IssueReporter.packageuri("IssueReporter")
"git://github.com/essenciary/IssueReporter.jl.git" ``` """ function
packageuri(pkgname::String) :: String # output truncated # end
```

Advanced documentation tips

You may have noticed in the previous snippet that we have to repeat the signature of the `packageuri` function in the `DocString`. The problem here is that the documentation can get out of sync if we change the function declaration, but omit to update the documentation. Julia's package ecosystem provides a library that extends the default documentation functionality, named `DocStringExtensions`. It's a registered package, so it can be added with `(IssueReporter) pkg> add DocStringExtensions`. It provides a series of methods that can be used to automatically generate some of the repetitive parts of the documentation process. For example, once we add `using DocStringExtensions` to the `IssueReporter` module, we can replace the function declaration from the docstring with the `$(SIGNATURES)` *abbreviation*. We'll see how to do that right away.

Another valuable feature of `DocStrings` is that the examples can also serve as tests. This kind of testing is called a **doctest**. Basically, when we provide a REPL example together with the corresponding output, if we tag this as a *jldoctest*, the `Documenter` package used to generate the documentation will also run the examples and compare the result against the provided output, thus testing the examples and, implicitly, our code. Check the next snippet to see what the previous example looks like after we apply these optimizations.

I have added comments to all the functions that represent the *public* API of `IssueReporter`. Here are the updated function definitions (you can get the full file from this chapter's repo at `https://github.com/PacktPublishing/Julia-Programming-Projects/blob/master/Chapter11/IssueReporter/src/IssueReporter.jl`):

```
module IssueReporter

using Pkg, Pkg.TOML, GitHub, URIParser, Documenter, DocStringExtensions

# ... some functions omitted ... #
```

```
"""
$(SIGNATURES)

Takes the name of a registered Julia package and returns the associated
repo git URL.

#Examples
```julia-repl
julia> IssueReporter.packageuri("IssueReporter")
"git://github.com/essenciary/IssueReporter.jl.git"
```
"""
function packageuri(pkgname::String) :: String
    # ... function body omitted ... #
end

"""
$(SIGNATURES)

Checks if the required GitHub authentication token is defined.
"""
function tokenisdefined() :: Bool
  # ... function body omitted ... #
end

... some functions omitted ...

"""
$(SIGNATURES)

Converts a registered Julia package name to the corresponding GitHub
"username/repo_name" string.

#Examples
```jldoctest
julia> IssueReporter.repo_id("IssueReporter")
"essenciary/IssueReporter.jl"
```
"""
function repoid(package_name::String)
    # ... function body omitted ... #
end

... some functions omitted ...

end # module
```

Generating the documentation

In order to create our documentation, we'll need to first create a `docs/` folder inside our `IssueReporter` root directory.

Within the `docs/` folder, we need two more things—first, a `src/` folder, which will contain the markdown template that will be used to build the documentation, the `index.md` file; second, a `make.jl` file that will control the documentation building process. Here is the full file structure of our package, for reference:

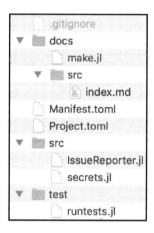

Now, open the `docs/make.jl` file in the editor and add the following:

```
using Pkg
pkg"activate .."
push!(LOAD_PATH, "../src/")
using Documenter, IssueReporter

makedocs(sitename = "IssueReporter Documentation")
```

Next, open the `index.md` file in the editor and add the following:

```
# IssueReporter.jl Documentation
```@meta
CurrentModule = IssueReporter
```

```@contents
```

## Functions
```@docs
packageuri(pkgname::String)
tokenisdefined()
```
```

```
token()
githubauth()
repoid(package_name::String)
report(package_name::String, title::String, body::String)
```
Index
```@index
```

This is the markdown template of our documentation. At the top, we have the title of the page. Then, the @meta block contains information for Documenter, passing in the name of the module. The @contents block will be replaced with the table of contents. The @docs block will contain the documentation for each of the functions included. At the bottom, the @index block will be replaced by a list of links to each of the documented functions.

That's all. In order to generate the documentation, we need to run $ julia --color make.jl from an OS Terminal, from within the docs/ folder.

The output of the command will show the progress of building the docs:

```
Documenter: setting up build directory.
Documenter: expanding markdown templates.
Documenter: building cross-references.
Documenter: running document checks.
 > checking for missing docstrings.
 > running doctests.
 > checking footnote links.
Documenter: populating indices.
Documenter: rendering document.
```

The generated documentation can be found at `docs/build/index.html`, and looks like this:

Registering our package

Now, for the last step—making our package available to the world! For starters, we need to create the remote GitHub repository and push our code to it. The easiest way to do this is with the `hub` binary, provided by GitHub. Please follow the installation instructions for your platform, as described at `https://github.com/github/hub`. Once ready, we'll need to run `hub create` in the root of the `IssueReporter` folder. We can do it in Julia's REPL:

```
julia> cd(Pkg.dir("IssueReporter"))
julia> run(`hub create IssueReporter.jl`)
```

You'll be prompted for your GitHub username and password—and if all goes well, you'll see the output confirming that the repo was created.

Finishing touches

Next, we need to commit and push our changes—but before doing that, let's make a final change to `.gitignore` to also add `docs/build` to the list of ignored files. It is a bad practice to include the built docs into the GitHub commits—for more information about hosting documentation on GitHub, please read the official `Documenter` info at `https://juliadocs.github.io/Documenter.jl/latest/man/guide/#Usage-1` and `https://juliadocs.github.io/Documenter.jl/latest/man/hosting/#Hosting-Documentation-1`.

While we're at it, let's also add a `README.md` file to the root folder of `IssueReporter`, to include a bit of info:

```
# IssueReporter.jl
`IssueReporter.jl` is a Julia package which makes it easy to report a new
issue with a registered package.
In order to use it, it needs to be configured with a valid GitHub
authentication token. Follow the instructions at
https://help.github.com/articles/creating-a-personal-access-token-for-the-c
ommand-line/ to generate a new token -- make sure
that it has the `repo` access.
Once you have the token, add it to the secrets.jl file.
You can now open issues by invoking:
`IssueReporter.report("Julia package name", "issue title", "issue body")`
```

Setting up the repository

Using your favorite git client, `add`, `commit`, and `push` the code base. I'm going to use the Terminal:

```
$ git add . $ git commit -m "initial commit" $ git push origin master
```

Unleashing Julia's army of bots

Our package is looking great—it's now time to tag a release and register it.

Julia contributors have developed a series of very useful GitHub integrations, namely, *bots*. These bots help us, humans, to automate a series of boring tasks so that we can focus on the really important things (mmm, pizza!).

One of them is Attobot, a package release bot for Julia. It creates pull requests to Julia's `General` registry when releases are tagged in GitHub. Try the following:

1. To set up Attobot, open your `IssueReporter` GitHub repo and go to `https://github.com/integration/attobot`. Please make sure that you're logged into your GitHub account.
2. Then, click **Configure** to select the repositories you wish to add.
3. Choose **Only select repositories**, and then select `IssueReporter` and click **Save**. Now, Attobot is configured to monitor packages with the standard `.jl` extension—and publish them on the `Global` registry when new releases are tagged.

> For more details about Attobot, please visit `https://github.com/attobot/attobot`.

4. Now, we need to go to our repo's GitHub page and click on the **releases** link:

5. Next, we are given the option to **Create a new release**:

6. On the next screen, we'll be able to tag our release. Julia uses semantic versioning (which looks like vX.Y.Z) and recommends starting with v0.0.1. Let's do just that:

7. Then, click **Publish release**.

If there are any problems, Attobot will open issues in the repo—make sure you address them. Once done, the package will be registered! Victory!

Summary

It is exciting to see our package finally ready!

While developing it, we've also learned about Julia's powerful toolbox, and about some of the most important best practices of software development in general—TDD, unit testing, benchmarking, and documenting our code base and publishing the resulting documentation.

This also concludes our journey into learning the Julia language. We've come a long way since opening the REPL for the first time—and you have achieved some impressive feats! Data analysis, plotting, web scraping, recommenders, supervised and unsupervised machine learning, and time series analysis and forecasting! You are now able to do all these things using Julia. Wow! That's quite an amazing track record indeed! And, if doing all this seemed easy, it's all due to Julia's incredible features. The productive REPL, the simple package installation, the handy plotting packages, or the readable syntax; they all make programming easy and fun.

Julia really is a new breed of programming language. As it is new, it is able to learn from the most successful programming languages by borrowing from their strengths, and avoid their mistakes. Julia was specifically designed to efficiently address the needs of our generation—machine learning, artificial intelligence, high performance, parallel, GPU, and distributed cloud computing—these are all areas where the language excels.

But, not only does Julia provide efficient language constructs for writing highly performant code—it also makes for a productive development experience. The powerful REPL (one of the best REPLs in all existing programming languages, period!) and the JIT compilation make it easy to quickly prototype solutions, slice and dice large amounts of data, or experiment with data models on the fly. The integrated help mode and the powerful shell mode empower developers, boosting productivity.

Then there's the seamless integration with Jupyter Notebooks via IJulia—and the incredible cross-language integration with established programming languages such as Python and R. If you've used with these technologies, switching to Julia should be straightforward.

But the fact that Julia is new, just reaching version 1, does not mean that Julia is not a mature language. It's been crafted with care and attention for over six years—with contributions from thousands of developers. So, I encourage you to start using Julia for solving real problems. You'd be joining tens of thousands of other developers using the language professionally, for scientific computing, data science, AI, fintech, web development, teaching, and much more. Household names such as Apple, Amazon, Facebook, and Oracle—to name just a few—were all looking to hire Julia programmers in 2017.

I hope you enjoyed reading this book as much as I enjoyed writing it. You are now prepared—and I hope eager—to use Julia in your projects. So, instead of *Goodbye*, I'd like to say—*Welcome to the wonderful world of Julia programming!*

Other Books You May Enjoy

If you enjoyed this book, you may be interested in these other books by Packt:

Julia 1.0 Programming Cookbook
Bogumił Kamiński, Przemysław Szufel

ISBN: 9781788998369

- Boost your code's performance using Julia's unique features
- Organize data in to fundamental types of collections: arrays and dictionaries
- Organize data science processes within Julia and solve related problems
- Scale Julia computations with cloud computing
- Write data to IO streams with Julia and handle web transfer
- Define your own immutable and mutable types
- Speed up the development process using metaprogramming

Julia 1.0 Programming - Second Edition
Ivo Balbaert

ISBN: 9781788999090

- Set up your Julia environment to achieve high productivity
- Create your own types to extend the built-in type system
- Visualize your data in Julia with plotting packages
- Explore the use of built-in macros for testing and debugging, among other uses
- Apply Julia to tackle problems concurrently
- Integrate Julia with other languages such as C, Python, and MATLAB

Leave a review - let other readers know what you think

Please share your thoughts on this book with others by leaving a review on the site that you bought it from. If you purchased the book from Amazon, please leave us an honest review on this book's Amazon page. This is vital so that other potential readers can see and use your unbiased opinion to make purchasing decisions, we can understand what our customers think about our products, and our authors can see your feedback on the title that they have worked with Packt to create. It will only take a few minutes of your time, but is valuable to other potential customers, our authors, and Packt. Thank you!

Index

constants
  about 48, 49
  significance 49
content-based algorithm
  used, for building basic movie recommender
  246, 248
content-based recommender systems 245
CSS selectors
  reference 106
cyclicity 407

D

data analysis, San Francisco businesses 314, 315
data harvesting
  through web scraping 101
data wrangling
  with query 317, 318
data
  preparing 333
date accessors
  working with 362
date adjustments 368, 369
date ranges
  defining 365, 366
date strings
  parsing 373
Dates API
  reference 364
dates
  constructing 357
  converting 359
  formatting 361
  querying 363, 364
  rounding of 370
  strings, parsing into 360, 361
  working with 356
defensive coding 126
dictionaries
  about 115
  constructing 115, 116, 117, 118
  ordered dictionaries 119
  working with 119, 120, 121
Docker 17
docset 461
docstring 135

Document Object Model (DOM) 122
documentation
  generating 463, 464

E

else statement 141
elseif statement 140
Emacs
  reference 22
errors
  exceptions, throwing on 130
  handling 127
Eurostat data
  about 398, 399
  processing 400, 401, 402
exceptions
  rethrowing 131
  throwing, on errors 130
expressions
  in metaprogramming 320
extract, transform, load (ETL) 289

F

finally clause 129, 130
FiveThirtyEight
  reference 279
functions
  about 132
  documenting 135
  multiple values, returning 133

G

generic Linux binaries, Julia
  reference 17
GitHub API
  authenticating with 454, 455, 457
  interacting with 454
GitHub issues
  reporting 458, 459, 460
Gumbo
  HTML, parsing 123

H

higher-order functions 168

Made in the USA
Middletown, DE
22 May 2019